W9-AZE-873

Air University Press
Reader Survey
Help us to improve! Tell us how well we're doing.

5	**4**	**3**	**2**	**1**
Excellent	Good	Fair	Poor	Fail

Book Title(s) _____

_____

Product Rating	**Service Rating**	**Book Design Rating**
_____ Subject Matter	_____ Courtesy	_____ Cover
_____ Readability	_____ Promptness	_____ Format
_____ Condition Upon Receipt	_____ Accuracy	_____ Illustrations

What would you like to see Air University Press publish? _____

_____

_____

_____

Other comments: _____

_____

_____

☐ ☐   **May we use your comments for our marketing/advertising program?**
Yes No   **How did you learn about Air University Press?**

Friend/Acquaintance _____

Display/Exhibit _____

Professional Journal Ad _____

Internet _____

AU Press Home Page _____

Other _____

Name: _____ Date: _____

Organization: _____

Rank/Title: _____

Please fold so our address is on front and tape loose sides before mailing.

Thank You!

Responsibility of Command
How UN and NATO Commanders Influenced Airpower over Bosnia

MARK A. BUCKNAM

Air University Press
Maxwell Air Force Base, Alabama

March 2003

Air University Library Cataloging Data

Bucknam, Mark A.
    Responsibility of command : how UN and NATO commanders influenced airpower over Bosnia / Mark A. Bucknam.
        p. ; cm.
    Includes bibliographical references and index.
    ISBN 1-58566-115-5
    1. Yugoslav War, 1991-1995 -- Aerial operations. 2. Command of troops. 3. Air power -- Political aspects. 4. Military planning. 5. Combined operations (Military science) I. Title.

    949.7103dc21

Disclaimer

Air University Press
131 West Shumacher Avenue
Maxwell AFB AL 36112–6615
http://aupress.maxwell.af.mil

*To all who serve or have served in our armed forces,
and especially to the spouses, children, and other supporting
family members, whose unheralded sacrifices make possible the
service of our soldiers, sailors, airmen, marines, and coasties.*

Contents

About the Author

Col Mark A. Bucknam is chief of the organizational policy branch within the Policy Division, under the director for strategic plans and policy (J-5) of the Joint Staff at the Pentagon. Colonel Bucknam was born 25 September 1959 in Philadelphia, Pennsylvania. He earned a Bachelor of Science degree in physics and a Master of Science degree in materials science and engineering from Virginia Tech in June 1981 and April 1982, respectively. He was a distinguished graduate from Squadron Officer School in 1985 and from Air Command and Staff College in 1995. In 1996 Colonel Bucknam graduated from the School of Advanced Airpower Studies, and in 1999 he was awarded a PhD in war studies from the University of London. He is a distinguished graduate of the National War College.

Colonel Bucknam earned his wings in May 1983 at Sheppard Air Force Base, Texas. His first operational tour was to Royal Air Force Bentwaters, United Kingdom, where he flew the A-10 and served as an instructor pilot, air show demonstration pilot, and the wing's chief functional check-flight pilot. From October 1987 until October 1988, Colonel Bucknam worked in the Pentagon as an air staff training (ASTRA) officer in the Inspector General and Programming Directorates.

Colonel Bucknam's next assignment was as an instructor pilot in the fighter lead-in training program at Holloman Air Force Base, New Mexico, where he served as a flight commander and later as chief of wing training. In 1990 he was the Tactical Air Command instructor pilot of the year for the AT-38 aircraft, and in 1991 he was named by the Big Brothers/Big Sisters of America organization as the national big brother of the year for the entire United States.

After completing F-16 qualification training in September 1991, Colonel Bucknam flew the F-16 at Homestead Air Force Base until August 1992, when Hurricane Andrew forced his unit to move to Shaw Air Force Base, South Carolina. At Shaw, he spent a year as an assistant operations officer, during which his squadron transitioned to the newest variant of the F-16, the Block-50. Colonel Bucknam then moved up to head the current operations flight of the 20th Operations Support Squadron for a year.

He moved to Maxwell Air Force Base, Alabama, where he attended Air Command and Staff College and the School of Advanced Airpower Studies. In 1996 Colonel Bucknam was assigned to King's College, University of London, where, in 1999, he earned a doctoral degree in war studies. His dissertation focused on the use of airpower over Bosnia during Operations Deny Flight and Deliberate Force. Colonel Bucknam next commanded the 8th Operations Support Squadron, Kunsan Air Base, Korea, flying F-16s with the Wolf Pack.

Colonel Bucknam is a command pilot with nearly 2,400 hours in the A-10, AT-38, and F-16 aircraft. He is married to the former Barbara Ann Russell of Norfolk, Virginia. They have two children: eight-year-old Elaine and six-year-old John.

Preface

This book examines the role that theater-level commanders in the UN and NATO played in influencing the use of airpower over Bosnia between the spring of 1993 and the end of 1995. It also uncovers factors explaining why top UN and NATO commanders in the region acted as they did. The central thesis of this study is that the commanders' needs to balance the various responsibilities inherent in command powerfully affected their actions when they tried to influence the use of airpower. Stress on these commanders was greatest when they felt forced to make trade-offs that put their forces at risk without a corresponding payoff in terms of mission accomplishment. In attempting to strike the proper balance between mission accomplishment, acceptable risk, and obedience to civilian political control, commanders drew on their own expertise and that of their staffs. Not surprisingly then the traditional division between soldiers and airmen over the utility of airpower manifested itself in a split dividing UN army generals from senior NATO airmen. That split also helps to explain the commanders' actions.

Because this case is presented in a chronological fashion, it offers a coherent account of Operation Deny Flight—the NATO air operations over Bosnia from April 1993 until December 1995. From start to finish, theater-level commanders acted as more than mere executors of policy. They helped to define their own missions, strove to control the use of airpower, and generally struggled to maintain operational autonomy so they could fulfill their responsibilities for mission accomplishment at acceptable levels of risk to their forces.

When people are killed in military service, there is a powerful need to justify their deaths and to understand why they died. Even in World War II, where the cause was manifestly just and where the stakes were high, good commanders agonized over the rectitude of decisions that led to the deaths of their troops. The Academy Award-winning film *Saving Private Ryan* illustrated this point well. Actor Tom Hanks played Capt John Miller, an Army officer who survived the D day landings of World War II. While the Allies were attempting to secure their foothold on Europe, Miller was tapped to lead a squad of soldiers on a seemingly impossible mission to find and retrieve a private whose three brothers had been killed in combat. In one poignant scene, at the end of a long, grueling day Captain Miller sits with a sergeant in a dark, shattered building. The two laughingly reminisce about a particularly amusing young soldier who had served with them months earlier during combat in Italy. Suddenly, Miller turns somber. Reflecting on a soldier who died in the Italian campaign, Miller explains to the sergeant: "Ya see, when you end up killing one of your men, you tell yourself it happened so you could save the lives of two or three or 10 others. Maybe a hundred. . . . And that's how simple it is. That's how you rationalize making the choice between mission and men." The audience is left knowing that the captain is not entirely satisfied with his rationale, but it worked. It justified the deaths of the captain's forces.

Imagine, then, the difficulty of rationalizing the loss of one's forces in military actions where nothing is accomplished, where no vital interest is at stake, or where the cause is ambiguous. To many observers, that was the situation in Bosnia in the mid-1990s. It was difficult to explain how events in the Balkans related to the national interests of the United States, Britain, France, Canada, or any of the other nations involved in the effort to remedy the humanitarian disaster that accompanied the breakup of Yugoslavia. The use of force seemed to serve little purpose, and outside observers who spent time in Bosnia reported atrocities by all three warring factions: Bosnian Muslims, Bosnian Croats, and Bosnian Serbs. That moral ambiguity and the lack of a compelling national interest translated into an intolerance for costs, a mental attitude that characterized the policies of Western nations as they intervened in Bosnia. Of course, commanders sent to the region were informed by political leaders back home that costs, such as collateral damage, spent resources, and most importantly, friendly casualties, were to be avoided.

And so the situation festered unhappily through 1992, 1993, and 1994. An inadequate force of peacekeepers led by European nations did what they could to dampen the fighting. Meanwhile, to protect the Bosnian Muslims, the United States threatened to bomb the Bosnian Serbs, who were widely seen as the instigators of the war in Bosnia. The Bosnian Serbs could easily retaliate against the UN peacekeepers in Bosnia, so governments of nations providing those peacekeepers strongly opposed bombing. Before long NATO's airpower was checked by Bosnian Serb threats against UN peacekeepers.

In the summer of 1994, things were going badly for the UN, and the Bosnian Serbs became more aggressive in threatening NATO aircraft enforcing the UN-declared no-fly zone over Bosnia. Washington grew increasingly frustrated as leaders there struggled unsuccessfully to forge an effective policy for Bosnia that would be politically acceptable at home and compatible with the approach of America's friends and allies in NATO and the UN. Throughout that autumn, the prospects for successful intervention appeared to grow ever dimmer, and by December, it seemed likely that the UN peacekeepers would have to be pulled out of Bosnia. That was expected to be a messy operation that would precipitate an even bloodier civil war than Bosnia had experienced up to that point. Yet, 10 months later, a NATO bombing campaign played an important part in helping Amb. Richard C. Holbrooke achieve a negotiated end to the war in Bosnia. While much has been written about the war in Bosnia and the efforts to end it through diplomacy and peacekeeping, this book is the first to analyze the significant role of military commanders in influencing the use of airpower during Operations Deny Flight and Deliberate Force, which lasted from April 1993 until September 1995.

For some policy makers and editorialists, airpower—so aptly employed in the 1991 Gulf War—had always promised a quick, clean, and cheap solution to the problem in Bosnia. To this day some of them believe airpower could have ended the war in Bosnia had it been used properly early on. However, for the vast majority of professional military officers, Bosnia seemed the least propitious environment for using airpower. For this latter group, airpower was just one of several necessary elements in a confluence of events leading to an end to the war in Bosnia.

One reason Bosnia presented a difficult environment for employing airpower is that the intervening nations could not come to consensus on an appropriate approach to the war in Bosnia. Should they try peacekeeping? Should they try a more muscular form of intervention, such as peace enforcement? Or should they coerce the warring factions through aerial bombing? Intervening powers could not agree, and the questions of whether, when, and how to employ airpower became inextricably intertwined with debates over policy for Bosnia.

Because of the disagreement in the international political arena, military commanders were dragged deeper into political struggles than they, or some observers, believed appropriate. According to the precepts of democracy, especially the concept of civilian control of the military, political leaders set policy and, where appropriate, military leaders carry it out. That tidy model did not pertain to Western intervention in Bosnia. To be sure, military commanders tried to be responsive to their civilian bosses. However, when those bosses disagreed—that is, when political leaders in the UN, NATO, and within individual nations delivered conflicting guidance—military commanders in the field were left to decide what to do. Time and again, as commanders tried to reconcile their conflicting policy guidance, they confronted the choice between taking action and avoiding unnecessary risks to their troops. When the mission was unclear, the objectives ill defined, or chances for success seemed dubious, the imperative to avoid casualties weighed heavily in the balance. How could risks be justified when the consequences of military action were so much in doubt? The following account challenges some popular assumptions about military leaders, their motivations, and the state of civil-military relations during the conflict in Bosnia. For instance, the supposed American sensitivity to casualties—purportedly born of experience in Vietnam—could be seen in the behavior of Belgian, French, and British commanders as well.

Acknowledgments

This research would not have been possible had senior leaders in the US Air Force not believed in the value of higher education for serving officers. It has been my great fortune to be part of an organization that invests so generously in its people. My special thanks go to the faculty at the School of Advanced Air and Space Studies for selecting me to pursue my work at King's College, especially Col Phillip Meilinger, who steered me toward London, Col Robert Owen, who supported my use of the valuable information his team compiled for the Balkans Air Campaign Study (BACS), and Prof. Hal Winton, for his constant support and stellar example of scholarship. The men and women at the US Air Force's Historical Research Agency were a great help during my research with the BACS archival material, and, in particular, I owe Lt Col Rick Sargent a big thanks for making my time with the BACS Collection so profitable.

My deep, sincere, and personal thanks go to Phil Sabin, my advisor. His patience, high standards, thought-provoking views, and occasional gentle prodding helped to guide me through the travails of research. Though I am solely responsible for any defects or limitations of this study, its merits owe much to Phil's mentoring. I would also like to acknowledge the superb faculty of the War Studies Department. My main regret is that the demands on both their time and mine kept me from spending more hours with them than I did. The chief of the Air Staff's Airpower Workshop acted as an adjunct faculty for my learning, and I would particularly like to thank Group Captains Andy Lambert and Stuart Peach for including me in their intellectually stimulating work. In addition, I want to express my appreciation to Chris Hobson, senior librarian at the Joint Services Command and Staff College, Bracknell, for his friendly assistance.

A glance through the footnotes and bibliography would reveal the enormous debt I owe to the many military officers I interviewed for this study—too many to recognize individually here. Often their candor was startling, and their enthusiasm for my research was an encouraging sign to me of the worth of my chosen topic.

My deepest affection and gratitude go to my wife Barbara for her friendship and support throughout this unique and challenging endeavor.

Chapter 1

Introduction

*This thin edge between what is appropriate for the military
to decide and what the civilians decide is a constantly shifting kaleidoscope in history, depending on the circumstances
and political factors. It is the core of the decision on when
you use airpower.*

—Amb. Richard C. Holbrooke
Interview, 24 May 1996

This study focuses on the influence theater-level commanders had on the use of airpower in Bosnia during Deny Flight—
the North Atlantic Treaty Organization (NATO) air operation
over Bosnia between April 1993 and December 1995. In particular, the aim here is to examine how theater-level commanders in the United Nations (UN) and NATO affected the use of
airpower and, to the extent possible, to explain why they acted
as they did. This is the first in-depth, academic study of Deny
Flight as a whole.

Military influence on the use of force has often been assumed
but not researched, according to Richard Betts, in his study of
post-1945 interventions: *Soldiers, Statesmen, and Cold War
Crises.*[1] Betts broke new ground and found that senior US military officers have generally been less influential than widely
believed in decisions over whether to use force. But, when it
came to the question of how to intervene, Betts concluded that
military leaders jealously protected what they saw as their prerogative for control over operational matters.[2] A decade after
Betts's pioneering work, further research by author David H.
Petraeus into military influence on the use of force showed
that the military has been far more influential in decisions
over how force is used than whether it is used.[3] Moreover,
Petraeus found that theater commanders had the greatest
impact when they "submitted plans that satisfied the objectives of the decision makers in Washington."[4] Petraeus's work
considered intervention decision making prior to 1987, just

when congressionally legislated defense reorganization gave theater commanders a stronger role in controlling decisions over the use of force.[5]

A hypothesis tested in this study is that theater-level commanders were influential in affecting decisions over the use of airpower in Bosnia, rather than being mere executors of policy. Theater-level commanders are defined here as military commanders responsible for a given theater of operations and their principal subordinate commanders.[6] A theater commander's job is to help plan military options to obtain policy objectives and, when directed, to translate military actions into political objectives.[7] If theater-level commanders sometimes played a leading role in shaping policy, rather than just planning for and executing policies on the use of force, it would be interesting to know why they did so. Some observers have cited the apparent risk-averse nature of the American military, largely ascribed to experiences of the Vietnam War, as the root cause for military transgressions into policy decisions.[8] Indeed, former chairman of the Joint Chiefs of Staff, Gen Colin Powell, was a prime example of the Vietnam generation of officers, and his opposition to US intervention in Bosnia has been scrutinized by commentators interested in civil-military relations.[9] However, Petraeus noted that the US military's increased reluctance to intervene abroad after Vietnam was an intensification of existing attitudes rather than a newfound cautiousness.[10] This suggested the basis for risk aversion lay in more enduring elements of the military profession. Another hypothesis tested here, then, is that the role UN and NATO theater-level commanders chose to play, when acting as more than just executors of policy in Bosnia, was rooted in military professionalism and can be explained, in part, in terms of commanders' special expertise and responsibility as managers of violence.

The central question of this study is how did theater-level commanders in the UN and NATO influence the use of airpower in Bosnia? To analyze this military influence, first consider several subsidiary questions. First, what patterns were there to the military positions on using airpower in Bosnia? Were American commanders more apt to push for forceful measures than officers from other nations? Were Army generals consistently more or less willing than Air Force generals to support the use of airpower? Second, what were the primary factors that shaped the various military attitudes toward using airpower? Specifically, how well do expertise and responsibility—two elements of military professionalism—explain the decisions and actions of the theater-level commanders? Third, how were the demands for impartiality and proportionality reconciled with traditional military principles of the objective, offense, mass, and surprise? Fourth, what methods did military leaders use to exert their influence? To what extent were military attempts to influence the use of force confined to traditional or prescribed military roles, and when, if ever, did military leaders seek unconventional means of influencing policy? Did commanders work strictly through the chains of command? Did subordinate commanders follow policy decisions and orders from above so as to implement policy, or did they try to affect the shape of policy? Finally, what happened? In what ways did military advisors and commanders succeed or fail in influencing the use of airpower? How was airpower used?

Existing Literature

Of the books, articles, and other studies on the war in Bosnia, few focus on Deny Flight, and none takes military influence on the use of airpower as its central theme. However, other works touch upon the topic studied here and are divided here into three categories according to the primary focus taken by their authors: political and diplomatic, UN military, and airpower. Lord David Owen recorded important elements of the debates about using airpower in Bosnia in *Balkan Odyssey*, the detailed accounting of his role as the European Union's (EU) principal negotiator to the International Conference on the Former Yugoslavia (ICFY).[11] Despite his numerous references to airpower, though, Lord Owen was primarily concerned with providing an accurate and detailed account of the attempts by the ICFY to produce a negotiated settlement in the former Yugoslavia. Therefore, in his book he understandably gave pride of place to the role of political leaders rather than to operational commanders. However, Owen

3

Left to right (foreground): Lt Gen Bertrand de Lapresle, UN Secretary-General Boutros Boutros-Ghali, Mr. Yasushi Akashi, and Lt Gen Sir Michael Rose

provided sporadic glimpses of theater commanders serving the United Nations Protection Force (UNPROFOR). Of particular interest here, he noted the political-military friction in early 1994 between Gen Jean Cot, the overall force commander, and senior civilian officials with the UN, including Secretary-General Boutros Boutros-Ghali, over the control of airpower.[12] Lord Owen also delivered a snapshot of the tension between Lt Gen Sir Michael Rose, the UN commander in Bosnia during 1994, and US officials over the need for suppressing the Bosnian Serb surface-to-air missile threat in November 1994.[13] Owen captured the issue well in the brief coverage he gave to it, but his anonymous references to NATO missed the important role played by the alliance's two theater-level commanders in the

Photo by Tim Ripley

Lt Gen Sir Michael Rose, British army, commander of Bosnia-Herzegovina Command, 1994 *(right),* shown with US military official Lt Gen Joseph Ashy, USAF, commander AIRSOUTH, 1992–94

region, Lt Gen Michael Ryan and Adm Leighton Smith. Overall, *Balkan Odyssey* is a valuable reference book that details international diplomacy in the region, thus establishing part of the broader context for viewing theater-level commanders' struggles to control airpower.

Dick Leurdijk's *The United Nations and NATO in Former Yugoslavia, 1991–1996: Limits to Diplomacy and Force* focused more on international efforts to use force in Bosnia than *Balkan Odyssey*.[14] Leurdijk's book also presented the UN perspective of the conflict, thus complementing the European viewpoint offered by Lord Owen.[15] Leurdijk reconstructed events and important decisions related to the UN's "safe area" policy in Bosnia and NATO's use of airpower. Though full of insights into the give-and-take amongst the various nations in NATO, Leurdijk diplomatically sidestepped or downplayed major points of friction that lay at the heart of debates over NATO's use of airpower in Bosnia.[16] This masked some of the tension that existed within NATO and glossed over significant strains in civil-military relations within the UN. Still, Leurdijk's work served as a ready reference for documentation on NATO decisions to use airpower in Bosnia.

Amb. Richard Holbrooke's memoir, *To End a War,* told one side of the story about disputes he had with Adm Leighton Smith, the theater commander of forces in NATO's southern region, while Holbrooke was serving as assistant secretary of state for European and Canadian affairs. Holbrooke wanted more control over NATO bombing during his coercive diplomacy with the Serbs in September 1995, but Smith resisted interference in operational matters from outside the chain of command. Holbrooke recognized the admiral's responsibility for the lives of NATO airmen, but he interpreted Smith's claim that NATO was running out of targets during the Deliberate Force bombing campaign to mean: "Smith did not wish to let the bombing be 'used' by the negotiators, and would decide when to stop based on his own judgment."[17] The thrust of Holbrooke's account was that for his important negotiations he needed some control over the coercive "sticks" being used, and Admiral Smith was overly cautious in resisting Holbrooke's inputs into bombing decisions.

James Gow, research officer in the Centre for Defence Studies at the University of London, proposes as his central thesis in *Triumph of the Lack of Will* that the international community could have intervened before the summer of 1995 to stop the war in the former Yugoslavia.[18] Echoing a note sounded by Lord Owen, Gow argued that had there been sufficient international political will to use force to impose the Vance-Owen Peace Plan in the spring of 1993—or to impose successive settlement plans thereafter—then much of the violence over the next two and one-half years probably could have been avoided. Gow went further than Leurdijk in detailing the problems of "dual key" command and control over NATO airpower, and the friction generated between UN military commanders and their civilian superiors over the latter's reluctance to use force.[19] He also gave a fuller account of the

Photo by Tim Ripley

Lt Gen Rupert Smith, British army, UN commander in Bosnia, 1995

divisions within NATO over air strikes, though, for the most part, he focused on differences between the nations rather than on the tensions between civilian and military leaders, or the divisions within the various military organizations involved.[20] Of significance to this study, Gow analyzed the change of heart by Gen Sir Michael Rose after the failed attempt to use airpower effectively at Gorazde in April 1994.[21] Of General Rose, Gow noted, "Like any good commander, his loyalty was with his troops: if the UN could not be relied on to back him and the force in critical moments, then for the sake of the soldiers' morale and credibility it was simply better not to move to a use of force."[22] Gow has also described how Rose's successor, Gen Rupert Smith, precipitated a hostage crisis for the UN that ultimately helped to make a NATO air campaign in Bosnia a viable option.[23] Chapter 7 of this study builds on the foundation set by Gow.

In contrast to Gow, Jane Sharp, a senior research fellow in the Centre for Defence Studies at King's College in London, England, took a highly critical view of General Rose in her report: *Honest Broker or Perfidious Albion.* For Sharp, Rose consistently acted as a surrogate for the British government, and, together their concern for British peacekeepers in Bosnia and alleged sympathy toward the Serbs led them to do everything within their power to block NATO air strikes.[24] Though Gow and Sharp believed General Rose played an important role in reducing the likelihood of the UN's use of airpower, Sharp saw greater continuity in Rose's reluctance to take enforcement action against the Bosnian Serbs. Sharp's praise for General Smith reinforced Gow's argument about Smith's role in paving the way for NATO air strikes in Bosnia.[25] Overall, however, Sharp downplayed the dangers UN forces faced whenever NATO used airpower, and she did not address legitimate concerns of UN commanders responsible for those forces.

Two works on political-military interaction during Deny Flight shed a little light on the influence of theater-level commanders in affecting policy and the use of airpower in Bosnia. Brigadier Graham Messervy-Whiting of the British army served as Lord Owen's first military advisor in Geneva. Although Messervy-Whiting left his post in Geneva in August 1993, just after NATO authorized air-to-ground operations in Bosnia, he recorded General Cot's role in establishing a NATO liaison element to compensate for the lack of airpower expertise within the UN.[26] In a broader look at civil-military relations, Michael Williams argued that "France and the UK, rather than the UN Secretariat, tended to define UNPROFOR's operational mission."[27] Williams, who served as director of information and senior spokesman for UNPROFOR, also claimed that "British and French officers effectively restricted UNPROFOR's mission to humanitarian assistance."[28] Williams was in a good position to draw his conclusions but gave few details to support them.

The second category of literature on intervention in Bosnia describes the UN's peacekeeping efforts in Bosnia, thus providing a ground view of events rather than an airman's perspective. Firsthand accounts by commanders during the early stages of the UN's presence in Bosnia give excellent insights into the ad hoc workings of UNPROFOR and the scope for initiative and influence afforded to commanders by the UN headquarters' lax oversight and its inability to manage events so far away from New York.[29] UNPROFOR's first commander, Gen Satish Nambiar of India, particularly praised the French for bringing to Bosnia five times the number of armored personnel carriers authorized by the UN.[30] Canada's Maj Gen Lewis MacKenzie, the first UN commander in Bosnia, recounted his July 1992 role in securing extra firepower for Canadian peacekeepers by working around the UN bureaucracy and dealing with his own government:

> The UN never did authorize us to bring the missiles for the TOW [antitank weapon]. We were authorized to bring the vehicle [it was mounted on]. In the end, *we cheated* and brought the missiles anyway. Can you imagine telling soldiers to bring the weapon but not the ammunition? We were also told we could bring mortars, but not high-explosive ammunition—only illuminating rounds to help us see at night. *We ignored that order also.* (Emphasis added)[31]

Interestingly, these early UN commanders had next to nothing to say on the topic of airpower, even though a public debate about using airpower in Bosnia was underway during their tours of duty in late 1992 and early 1993. When they did comment on possible air operations, their views were mixed. In July 1992, MacKenzie urged Nambiar to refuse offers for close air support, writing "the use of air power on our behalf would clearly associate us with the side *not* being attacked, and thereafter we would very quickly be branded an intervention force, as opposed to an impartial peacekeeping force."[32] Gen Philippe Morillon of France commanded UN troops in Bosnia after they had been given a more muscular mandate under chapter 7 of the UN Charter. In his memoir, Morillon's only remark about airpower was more positive than MacKenzie's. "It is not sufficient to be passively protected against the threats, it is necessary to be able to make them stop by responding to them . . . against artillery, the use of aviation is essential."[33] However, Morillon, like the other early commanders, left the former Yugoslavia before NATO airpower was ready for air-to-ground missions in Bosnia.

Lt Gen Francis Briquemont of Belgium succeeded General Morillon, and Briquemont had much more to say about NATO airpower in his memoir, *Do Something, General!* [34] The title of his book characterized the specificity of the political guidance given to Briquemont and his superior, General Cot of France, during most of their time in Bosnia.[35] They were the first UN generals to exercise some influence on the use of airpower in Bosnia, as is discussed in detail in chapters 4 and 5 of this study. However, no bombs fell while either of them served with the UN. Briquemont's replacement, General Rose, also wrote about his experiences as head of the UN's Bosnia-Herzegovina Command.[36] Though generally restrained in his remarks about the limitations of airpower[37] during and just after his tour in Bosnia, in his memoir Rose vented some of the frustration from his run-ins with the theater-level commanders in NATO who wanted to use airpower more aggressively.[38] Rose's book also gave his version of the large role he played in shaping NATO air action through the end of 1994—a topic addressed in chapters 5 and 6 of this study.

In *Srebrenica: Record of a War Crime,* Jan Honig and Norbert Both revealed the divergence of views between the two principal UN commanders, French general Bernard Janvier and his subordinate British commander in Bosnia, Gen Rupert Smith, during 1995.[39] During the spring of 1995, UN commanders disagreed over whether to take more forceful action in Bosnia, including air strikes. Of special interest were the authors' revelations about the role of Rupert Smith in helping statesmen in the UN and NATO confront the impossibility of simultaneously attempting to do peacekeeping and enforcement.[40] Though Honig and Both provided excellent evidence and analysis on

Lt Gen Francis Briquemont, Belgian army, commander of Bosnia-Herzegovina Command from July 1993 to January 1994

Photo by Tim Ripley

Gen Jean Cot, French army, commander of UNPROFOR from July 1993 to March 1994

the role of UN commanders in influencing the use of airpower in Bosnia, that was not the principal focus of their book. They did not discuss the role of NATO commanders, and in the final footnote of the book, the authors erroneously concluded, "air attacks, which the Clinton administration so favoured and executed, proved relatively ineffective in September 1995. The NATO air forces quickly ran out of targets and, in 750 attack missions, bombed the same 56 targets over and over again."[41] Such a misconception by these otherwise well-informed scholars was indicative of the paucity of information on NATO air operations available at the time they wrote. Another book on Srebrenica by investigative journalist David Rohde, provided supplementary evidence and worthwhile analysis of the roles played by the top UNPROFOR officials in decisions over the use of airpower during the summer of 1995.[42]

Hans-Christian Hagman's PhD thesis, "UN-NATO Operational Cooperation in Peacekeeping, 1992–1995," examined the efforts by the two international organizations to work together in Bosnia.[43] In 1994, Hagman was a staff officer with UNPROFOR. For that reason he was an authoritative source on UNPROFOR's views on the use of airpower, and he marshaled some of the staff analysis he himself produced as evidence for his research. Because his focus was on peacekeeping rather than on enforcement, he devoted very little attention to NATO's responsibility to enforce the no-fly zone over Bosnia. Moreover, throughout the thesis, the term *air strike* is often preceded by the word *punitive* or followed by the word *retribution*. Air attacks, other than close air support requested by the UN, were virtually illegitimate in Hagman's view, because one of his key assumptions was that NATO air operations were subordinate to UNPROFOR's mission. As such, airpower was really meant to be supporting UN peacekeeping. That was one view of what NATO should have been doing in Bosnia, but, as Hagman noted, NATO officers held different views.

Only a handful of works have focused specifically on airpower in Bosnia; however, in research theses and reports produced after Deny Flight, several air force officers took an alternative view from the one taken by Hagman of NATO's role over Bosnia. According to Maj George Kramlinger, in "Sustained Coercive Air Presence (SCAP)," from February 1994 onward, NATO was in a struggle with the UN over whether to coerce the Bosnian Serbs.[44] As with the other researchers, Kramlinger captured the high points of Deny Flight, but did not dwell on or analyze decisions over the use of airpower. Norwegian commentator Per Erik Solli also saw Deny Flight as an exercise in coercion rather than as a peacekeeping venture.[45] Similarly, in *Bombs over Bosnia: The Role of Airpower in Bosnia-Herzegovina*, Maj Michael O. Beale aimed to provide an account within the political and historical context of the war in Bosnia of Deny Flight's evolution from constrained deterrence to more proactive coercion.[46] By going out of his way to consider the Serb viewpoint, Beale revealed many of the complexities of using force in Bosnia. Finally, a pair of research reports on airpower in coalition operations built on the assumption that NATO airpower was over Bosnia for coercion and that the UN was largely in the way.[47] In addition to their informative texts, these reports contained useful bibliographies.

One of the earliest treatments of airpower in Bosnia appeared as a book chapter in Air Vice-Marshal Tony Mason's *Air Power: A Centennial Appraisal.*[48] The air vice-marshal's description of the airpower debates at the policy-making level was informative, and he documented the debate in Britain particularly well. At the time of the book's writing though, NATO and the UN had used airpower primarily to enforce the no-fly zone over Bosnia, and NATO attempts to affect the fighting on the ground were just beginning. Mason's later contributions on the use of airpower over Bosnia have been mostly theoretical—extracting the broader lessons about using airpower in peace-support operations.[49] Therefore, while Mason identified and discussed issues such as proportionality, impartiality, and consent—which lay at the heart of the airpower disputes—he did so in an attempt to generalize from the experiences of Bosnia, rather than to document the actions of the theater-level commanders.

Tim Ripley, a journalist and photographer who covered military operations in the former Yugoslavia, purveyed a solid overview of Deny Flight in his book, *Air War Bosnia.*[50] The book supplemented Ripley's many magazine articles,[51] providing a wealth of detailed information about air operations during Deny Flight.[52]

Col Robert Owen headed a team of researchers to produce the "Balkans Air Campaign Study" (BACS) sponsored by Air University, the center for professional military education in the US Air Force. The BACS report is the most comprehensive work on the planning and execution of Operation Deliberate Force—the brief NATO bombing campaign in late August and September of 1995. Though the study deals primarily with Deliberate Force, which was technically a part of Deny Flight, it also reveals many previously unpublished aspects of Deny Flight stretching back to 1993. The message of the report is that airpower played a significant role in coercing the Bosnian Serbs to comply with UN and NATO demands, thus ending the three and one-half-year siege of Sarajevo and paving the way for the Dayton peace talks. Because the study was directed by and for the US Air Force, its strengths are its practical focus and its wealth of information from American sources. These

Photo by Tim Ripley

Lt Gen Bernard Janvier, French army, commander of UN Peace Forces, 1995

strengths, however, tend to eclipse the role played by UN advisors and commanders in influencing the use of airpower, and the study does not analyze events before the Pale air strikes in May 1995. Two summary articles appeared in *Airpower Journal*,[53] and a final report was published in 2000.[54]

Method

This study employs a single case study method befitting a contemporary history. The techniques of identifying, accessing, ordering, and evaluating evidence that one would employ for writing history were enriched with interviews and firsthand observations.[55] This single case was addressed because the use of airpower over Bosnia fits what Robert Yin called an "extreme or unique case"—to be used when a situation is "so rare that any single case is worth documenting and analyzing."[56] Deny Flight is worth documenting and analyzing for a number of reasons. Others have studied it in order to draw theoretical lessons about the employment of airpower in peace support activities,[57] but no one has yet studied the roles of the theater-level commanders and their influence on the use of airpower. Deny Flight was unique in that divisions at the political level within the UN, within NATO, and between the UN and NATO made it impossible for political authorities in either the UN or NATO to give clear instructions to their theater commanders about the objective for employing airpower. As is argued at the outset of chapter 4, this left the operational commanders a great deal of leeway in helping their political masters sort out who would control NATO airpower, and to what end. Moreover, the divided command chain between the UN and NATO left army generals serving with the UN to contend with senior NATO airmen about how to use airpower—a struggle for control that has been ongoing for many years.

To test the hypotheses on the influence of theater-level commanders, this study endeavors to find the origins of the plans they used, the objectives served by those plans, and the commanders' methods of and success in promoting their plans. For uses of airpower that were responses to provocations rather than planned operations, this study attempts to determine who made the targeting decisions and how targeting choices were constrained in advance. To determine the role that expertise and command responsibility played in affecting the actions and decisions of commanders, commanders were asked to explain their concerns and frustrations. They also were asked if there were any actual or potential issues over which they considered resigning. More importantly, in evaluating commanders' actions, this study looks for patterns reflecting their approaches to using airpower and checked for changes over time. Interviews and documentary evidence sought to establish the causes of the apparent patterns and any changes. In analyzing evidence, the focus is on cases where command responsibilities and military expertise were likely to lead to courses of action different from those predicted if other factors were driving the commanders' decisions; for example, national political pressures, peacekeeping doctrine, personal advancement, and UN or NATO organizational biases.

Evidence for this case study was gathered from press accounts, secondary studies of Deny Flight and UNPROFOR, investigative journalists' accounts, memoirs, and transcripts from press conferences and press releases from the White House, the Pentagon, NATO headquarters in Brussels, and Allied Forces Southern Europe (AFSOUTH) in Naples. The academic version of Lord Owen's encyclopedic CD-ROM companion to *Balkan Odyssey* provided useful data, as did the archival holdings for the BBC/Discovery Channel program, *Yugoslavia: Death of a Nation*, held at the Liddell Hart Archives, King's College, University of London. Sources included UN documents, including records of Security Council debates, resolutions, and reports from the secretary-general.[58] Also information was drawn from US congressional and United Kingdom (UK) parliamentary reports, unclassified portions of military studies (mainly US), organizational histories, briefings, and reports. Extensive travel in Britain, Belgium, Germany, France, Italy, and the US to interview diplomats, NATO and UN staff officers, and participants—peacekeepers and pilots—allowed identification of important events, major decision points, and actors involved in shaping Deny Flight. Theater-level commanders and other senior officials in the US, UK, France, and Belgium were interviewed. Accessing French sources and securing and conducting interviews in Paris meant learning French. In all, over 60 separate interviews were conducted, roughly half of them with general officers or admirals. Two separate two-week-long visits to the US Air Force Historical Research Agency (AFHRA) were made to conduct documentary research and to review oral histories held in the BACS collection. The second of those trips netted over 100 pages of notes from classified sources, which were reviewed for classification and then declassified as necessary.

In five of the interviews conducted, including the interviews with General Janvier and Air Force general James "Bear" Chambers, the limitations of interview data were reduced somewhat because the interviewees kept journals and other documentary evidence from their tours of duty, and they referred to those notes during the interviews. In addition, an interview with the commander of NATO air forces for the southern region, Lt Gen Joseph Ashy, was based on a detailed classified briefing, and the redacted transcript of the interview contained 66 pages of text accompanied by more than 40 overhead slides. It included a verbatim mission statement from the North Atlantic Council, concepts of operations for different types of missions, and air orders of battle for the Balkan states. Interviews with principal decision makers also revealed information unlikely to be captured in documents, such as details of important meetings, briefings, and phone calls. When several individuals from different organizations with potentially different interests at stake provided similar accounts of events that were also consistent with publicly available information, the information was considered reliable. Where accounts differed, interviewees were invited to explain the apparent contradictions or to elaborate on the differences in perspective. Sometimes this helped to clarify what took place. In other cases this resulted in conflicting or incomplete versions of what had occurred. The text and endnotes throughout this study indicate where differing accounts of the same events were not reconciled or where alternative explanations should be considered. Unfortunately, some of the officials interviewed spoke only on the condition of anonymity. Others asked to see the work before agreeing to be cited by name. Both the anonymous interviewees and those who might be named later are cited in the endnotes as Military Official A, MOD Official B, and so on. Regrettably, Gen Rupert Smith, the UN commander in Bosnia during 1995 was not interviewed. Given General Smith's pivotal role, the absence of an interview may have implications for the absolute reliability of certain

Lt Gen James "Bear" Chambers was the first director of NATO's Combined Air Operations Center as a theater-level commander.

judgments. However, General Smith's NATO counterparts were consulted and, at his suggestion, so were some of his subordinates. The consistency of these supporting interviews lends credence to the findings.

This study assumes that all theater-level commanders were subjected to political pressures from their respective national capitals.[59] All of the commanders in the UN and NATO were sure that other commanders were receiving guidance from home, though most of them denied receiving explicit orders themselves.[60] In NATO, direct political pressure probably did not reach below the regional commander, the four-star admiral in charge of Allied Forces, South (AFSOUTH). However, this study also assumes the two- and three-star Air Force generals who were subordinate to the AFSOUTH commanders would have been aware of guidance from Washington.

Structure

Chapter 2 discusses background theory concerning military influence on the use of airpower. It first explores the findings of Betts and Petraeus on the subject of military influence on the use of force and then goes on to propose a theoretical basis for military demands for autonomy in operational matters, focusing on the special expertise and responsibility commanders have for managing violence. Chapter 2 also examines the countervailing political controls that constrain a commander's autonomy when using airpower. The chapter ends with a brief discussion of the traditional division between soldiers and airmen over the utility and control of airpower.

Chapter 3 briefly describes the background to Deny Flight, giving special attention to the national policies of the US, the UK, and France for using airpower in Bosnia. The organizing principle of chapters 4 through 9 is chronological, with the break points between chapters determined by changes of UN commanders in Bosnia or turning points in the missions of either UNPROFOR or the Deny Flight air forces. Those chapters present the case study evidence and analysis. The final chapter states conclusions, answering the questions set out above and addressing the hypotheses of whether and why theater-level commanders influenced the use of airpower in Bosnia.

Notes

1. Richard K. Betts, *Soldiers, Statesmen, and Cold War Crises* (Cambridge, Mass.: Harvard University Press, 1977; reprinted with new preface and epilogue, New York: Columbia University Press, 1991), 1.

2. Ibid., 11–12.

3. David H. Petraeus, "Military Influence and the Post–Vietnam Use of Force," *Armed Forces and Society* 15, no. 4 (summer 1989): 495; and David H. Petraeus, "American Military and the Lessons of Vietnam: A Study of Military Influence and the Use of Force in the Post–Vietnam Era" (PhD diss., Princeton University, 1987), 249–53.

4. Petraeus, "American Military," 255.

5. Some observers believed legislation went too far in empowering theater commanders. See Robert Previdi, *Civilian Control versus Military Rule* (New York: Hippocrene Books, 1988), 123; and Christopher Bourne, *Unintended Consequences of Goldwater-Nichols: The Effect on Civilian Control of the Military, Essays on Strategy XIV*, ed. Mary A. Sommerville (Washington, D.C.: National Defense University Press, 1997), 249–56.

6. The UN side focuses on the overall force commanders headquartered in Zagreb and their subordinate commanders for operations in Bosnia. For NATO, the focus is on officers filling the positions of Supreme Allied Commander, Europe (SACEUR), Commander in Chief Allied Forces Southern Europe (CINCSOUTH), and Commander of Allied Air Forces Southern Europe (COMAIRSOUTH). This study also includes General Chambers, the first director of NATO's Combined Air Operations Center as a theater-level commander, because he was the US joint force air component commander until his departure in November 1994.

7. Joint Publication 3-0, *Doctrine for Joint Operations*, 1 February 1995, III–4 and III–5. The UK's Defense Doctrine, published after Deny Flight, envisioned the planning function taking place at a higher level, though still with input from the operational commanders. JWP 0-01, *British Defence Doctrine*, 1.8–1.9.

8. Previdi, 91; Peter D. Feaver, *Civil–Military Conflict and the Use of Force*, eds. Don M. Snider and Miranda A. Carlton-Carew (Washington, D.C.: Center for Strategic and International Studies, 1995), 114 and 122; Richard H. Kohn, "Out of Control: The Crisis in Civil-Military Relations," *The National Interest*, no. 35 (spring 1994): 3–17; Edward N. Luttwak, "Washington's Biggest Scandal," *Foreign Affairs* 74, no. 3 (May/June 1995): 109–22.

9. Michael R. Gordon, "Powell Delivers a Resounding No on Using Limited Force in Bosnia," *New York Times*, 28 September 1992; Colin L. Powell, "Why Generals Get Nervous," *New York Times*, 8 October 1992. For claims of a crisis in civil-military relations, see Russell F. Weigley, "The American Military and the Principle of Civilian Control from McClellan to Powell," *The Journal of Military History*, Special Issue 57 (October 1993): 27–58; Kohn, 3–17; and Luttwak, 29–33. For examples of commentators uncomfortable with Powell's actions but who stop short of declaring a crisis, see Andrew J. Bacevich, "Civilian Control: A Useful Fiction?" *Joint Forces*

Quarterly, no. 6 (autumn/winter 1994–1995): 76–79; and Thomas E. Ricks, "The Widening Gap Between the Military and Society," *The Atlantic Monthly* 280, no. 1 (July 1997): 66–78.

10. Petraeus, "American Military," 258.

11. David Owen, *Balkan Odyssey* (London: Indigo, 1996).

12. Ibid., 264–65.

13. Owen, 329.

14. Dick A. Leurdijk, *The United Nations and NATO in Former Yugoslavia, 1991–1996: Limits to Diplomacy and Force* (The Hague: The Netherlands Atlantic Commission, 1996).

15. The London Conference of August 1992 established the ICFY, which was cochaired by a UN and an EC/EU negotiator. The UN chairman was Cyrus Vance until 1 May 1993, then Thorvald Stoltenberg. The EC/EU chairman was Lord Owen until 12 June 1995, then Carl Bildt. For an overview of NATO's role and perspective, see Gregory L. Schulte, "Former Yugoslavia and the New NATO," *Survival* 39, no. 1 (spring 1997): 19–42.

16. For instance, Leurdijk provides little discussion on the "dual key" command and control arrangements whereby NATO and the UN jointly controlled the authority to authorize air strikes.

17. Richard Holbrooke, *To End a War* (New York: Random House, 1998), 146.

18. James Gow, *The Triumph of the Lack of Will: International Diplomacy and the Yugoslav War* (New York: Columbia University Press, 1997), 1–7.

19. Ibid., 137–39 and 149–54.

20. Ibid., 136 and 146.

21. Ibid., 151.

22. Ibid.

23. Ibid., 267–69.

24. Jane M. O. Sharp, *Honest Broker or Perfidious Albion: British Policy in Former Yugoslavia* (London: Institute for Public Policy Research, 1993), 32–34 and 42–46.

25. Ibid., 50–54.

26. Brigadier Graham Messervy-Whiting, *Peace Conference on Former Yugoslavia: The Politico–Military Interface,* London Defence Studies 21 (London: Brassey's for the Centre for Defence Studies, 1944), 16.

27. Michael C. Williams, *Civil–Military Relations and Peacekeeping* (Oxford and New York: Oxford University Press for the International Institute for Strategic Studies, 1998), 46.

28. Ibid.

29. Maj Gen Lewis MacKenzie, *Peacekeeper: The Road to Sarajevo* (Vancouver: Douglas and McIntyre, 1993); Gen Philippe Morillon, *Croire et Oser: Chronique de Sarajevo* (Paris: Bernard Grasset, 1993); Lt Gen Satish Nambiar, "A Commander's Perspective on the Role of the Developing States in Peace Operations," in *Meeting the Challenges of International Peacekeeping Operations: Assessing the Contribution of Technology,* ed. Alex Gliksman (Livermore, Calif.: Center for Global Security Research, June

1998); and Col Bob Stewart, *Broken Lives: A Personal View of the Bosnian Conflict* (London: HarperCollins, 1993).

30. Nambiar, 89.

31. MacKenzie, 310.

32. Ibid., 428.

33. Morillon, 213.

34. Lt Gen Francis Briquemont, *Do Something, General! Chronique de Bosnie-Herzégovine, 12 juillet 1993–24 janvier 1994* (Bruxelles: Éditions Labor, 1997).

35. Gen Jean Cot, "Dayton ou la Porte Etroite: Genese et Avenir d'un Désastre," *Dernère Guerre Balkanique?* ed. Jean Cot (France: Éditions L' Harmattan, 1996), 113–38; Gen Jean Cot, "L'Europe et l'Otan," *Défense Nationale* 53, no. 4 (October 1997): 89–97; and Gen Jean Cot, "Les Leçons de l'ex-Yugoslavie," *Défense*, no. 65 (March 1995): 85–86.

36. Lt Gen Sir Michael Rose, *Fighting for Peace: Bosnia 1994* (London: The Harvill Press, 1998).

37. Lt Gen Sir Michael Rose, "Bosnia Herzegovina 1994 - NATO Support for UN Wider Peacekeeping Operations," *NATO's Sixteen Nations* 39, no. 3 (1994): 8–11; Idem, "A Year In Bosnia: What Has Been Achieved," *RUSI Journal* 140, no. 3 (June 1995): 22–25; Idem, "A Year in Bosnia: What Was Achieved," *Studies in Conflict and Terrorism* 19, no. 3 (July–September 1996): 221–28.

38. Rose, *Fighting*, 177.

39. Jan Willem Honig and Norbert Both, *Srebrenica: Record of a War Crime* (New York: Penguin Books, 1997).

40. Ibid., 141–59.

41. Ibid., 186.

42. David Rohde, *A Safe Area, Srebrenica: Europe's Worst Massacre Since the Second World War* (London: Pocket Books, 1997).

43. Hans-Christian Hagman, "UN–NATO Operational Co-operation in Peacekeeping 1992–1995" (PhD diss., King's College, University of London, 1997).

44. George D. Kramlinger, *Sustained Coercive Air Presence (SCAP)* (Maxwell Air Force Base [AFB], Ala.: Air University, Air Command and Staff College, School of Advanced Airpower Studies, 1996), 48–76.

45. Per Erik Solli, "In Bosnia, Deterrence Failed and Coercion Worked," in *Use of Air Power in Peace Operations*, ed. Carsten F. Ronnfeldt and Per Erik Solli, NUPI Peacekeeping and Multinational Operations Report no. 7 (Oslo: Norwegian Institute of International Affairs, 1997); and Solli, *UN and NATO Air Power in the Former Yugoslavia*, NUPI Report no. 209 (Oslo: Norwegian Institute of International Affairs, 1997).

46. Maj Michael O. Beale, *Bombs over Bosnia: The Role of Airpower in Bosnia-Herzegovina* (Maxwell AFB, Ala.: Air University Press, 1997).

47. Group Capt Stuart W. Peach, Royal Air Force (RAF), *Air Power in Peace Support Operations: Coercion versus Coalition*, MPhil thesis (Downing College, University of Cambridge, 1997), 70–76; and Maj Peter C. Hunt,

Coalition Warfare Considerations for the Air Component Commander (Maxwell AFB, Ala.: Air University Press, 1998), 48–65. Also see Matthew C. Waxman, "Coalitions and Limits on Coercive Diplomacy," *Strategic Review* 25, no. 1 (winter 1997): 38–47.

48. Air Vice-Marshal Tony Mason, RAF, *Air Power: A Centennial Appraisal* (London and Washington: Brassey's, 1994), 168–97.

49. Air Vice-Marshal Tony Mason, RAF, "Operations in Search of a Title: Air Power in Operations Other than War," in *Air Power Confronts an Unstable World*, ed. Dick Hallion (London: Brassey's, 1997), 157–77.

50. Tim Ripley, *Air War Bosnia: UN and NATO Airpower* (Osceola, Wisc.: Motorbooks International, 1996).

51. The articles by Ripley include: "Operation Deny Flight," *World Airpower Journal* 16 (spring 1994): 20–29; "Blue Sword over Bosnia," *World Airpower Journal* 19 (winter 1994): 18–25; "NATO Strikes Back," *World Airpower Journal* 22 (autumn/winter 1995): 18–27; "Operation Deliberate Force," *World Airpower Journal* 24 (spring 1996): 20–29; "Airpower Vindicated," *Flight International*, 1–7 January 1995, 31–35; "Reasons for Being," *Flight International*, 24–30 January 1996, 25–28; "A 'Deliberate Force' on the Mountain," *International Defense Review* 28 (October 1995): 27–30; "NATO's Air Command—Backing Up the Blue Helmets," *International Defense Review* 28 (November 1995): 61–62; and "Bosnia Mission Stretches Airborne Eyes and Ears," *International Defense Review* 27, no. 1 (1994): 54–56.

52. In 1999, Ripley published a book on intervention in Bosnia. The book presents a lot of new information on the ground campaigns in Bosnia and Croatia during 1995. Tim Ripley with foreword by Nik Gowing, *Operation Deliberate Force: The UN and NATO Campain in Bosnia 1995* (Lancaster, England: Centre for Defence and International Security Studies, 1999).

53. Robert Owen, "The Balkans Air Campaign Study: Part 1," *Air Power Journal* 11, no. 2 (summer 1997): 4–24; and idem, "The Balkans Air Campaign Study: Part 2," *Air Power Journal* 11, no. 3 (autumn 1997): 6–26 (hereafter cited as Owen, "Balkans: Part 1," and Owen, "Balkans: Part 2)."

54. Col Robert C. Owen, USAF, *Deliberate Force: A Case Study in Effective Air Campaigning* (Maxwell AFB, Ala.: Air University Press, 2000).

55. Robert K. Yin, *Case Study Research: Design and Methods* (London: Sage Publications, 1984), 18–20.

56. Ibid., 44.

57. For instance, see Mason, *Operations in Search of a Title*, 157–78; and Group Capt Andrew Lambert and Arthur C. Williamson, eds., *The Dynamics of Air Power* (RAF Staff College, Bracknell, UK: HMSO, 1996), 105–73.

58. A valuable compendium of UN Security Council resolutions, debates, and UN secretary-general reports prior to May of 1994 is contained in Daniel Bethlehem and Marc Weller, eds., *The 'Yugoslav' Crisis in International Law, General Issues Part I*, Cambridge International Documents Series, vol. 5 (Cambridge, Mass.: Cambridge University Press, 1997).

59. Williams, 46.

60. General Briquemont appears to have been the exception, though he was pressured by the European Community (EC) at a time when his country, Belgium, filled the rotating post of EC president.

Chapter 2

Military Influence
on the Use of Airpower

The military in the post–Vietnam period have exercised considerable influence over how force has been used— particularly in those cases in which the missions have been especially demanding and complex, thereby increasing the dependence of civilian policy makers on military judgment, expertise, and information.

> —David H. Petraeus
> "Military Influence and the
> Post–Vietnam Use of Force,"
> PhD diss.,
> Princeton University, 1987

Airpower was the central military component in the US policy for intervention in Bosnia. Airpower has also been at the core of a long-running debate in the United States over how much influence the military should exercise vis-à-vis their civilian masters when it comes to using force.[1] To frame the discussion in this study about the influence of theater-level commanders on the use of airpower in Bosnia, the first section of this chapter briefly addresses the larger issue of military influence on the US use of force. The second section narrows the focus to look at political controls on the use of airpower, namely targeting controls, bombing pauses, and rules of engagement. In addition to the political-military dimension of controls on the use of airpower, soldiers and airmen have traditionally held contending beliefs about how best to employ this type of military force.[2] The third section, therefore, highlights the major causes and consequences of the disparate military views on airpower. This chapter provides a theoretical construct for analyzing the various dimensions of the struggle by theater-level commanders to influence the use of airpower in Bosnia between the summers of 1993 and 1995.

27

Influence and Autonomy:
The US Military and the Use of Force

This section explores American military influence after 1945 on when, how, and with what constraints on military autonomy force has been used. Since World War II, American military leaders have usually played only a minor role in decisions over whether the United States should employ military force. Once decisions to use force have been made, military influence over how force is used has been relatively more significant. Furthermore, when force has been called for, military officers have lobbied hard to preserve their autonomy in operational matters. Two elements of military professionalism—expertise and responsibility—create the foundation for military demands for autonomy. Contrary to the military's desire for autonomy, American political leaders have felt the need to constrain or even control the use of force in military operations since 1945. Balancing the imperatives of policy against the demands for military autonomy has often led to tension in civil-military relations.

This study uses the word *influence* in a rather ordinary sense. Influence is the "power to sway or affect based on prestige, wealth, ability, or position."[3] This avoids unnecessary restrictions found in more technical definitions. For instance, Roger Scruton excludes coercion from the definition of influence. However, if a military commander attempted to coerce other military or political authorities in order to shape the use of airpower, that would certainly be of interest here.[4] Dennis Wrong makes a distinction between intended and unintended influence. The focus here is on intended influence though adopting Wrong's definition would be impractical since intended influence is what Wrong calls "power"—the definition of which takes up two chapters of his book.[5] Richard Betts defines influence as "causing decision makers to do something they probably would not have done otherwise."[6] Though generally compatible with the definition used in this study, Betts's definition could be interpreted to mean that military influence had to be causal. This would exclude military influence that served merely as a catalyst, enabler, or shaper of action that decision makers would have taken anyway. Finally, the ordinary definition adopted for this study is somewhat broader than Samuel Finer's concept of influence, which, in his typology, is the lowest level of military intervention into politics for countries with developed political cultures.[7] For Finer, influence meant "the effort to convince the civil authorities by appealing to their reason or their emotions." This level is the constitutional and legitimate one, entirely consistent with the supremacy of the civil power.[8] However, Finer's definition would exclude influence within military organizations themselves and would presuppose the legitimacy of military influence. For this study, the simple definition of influence will work best.

Deciding to Use Force: Military Reluctance and Influence

In the period since World War II, the American military has been neither as belligerent nor as influential in intervention decision making as popular stereotypes suggest.[9] In fact, the military has become quite the opposite of the hawkish image once popularized in movies and books. Writing in 1960, Morris Janowitz described and decried this stereotype in his classic sociological portrait of the American military elite, *The Professional Soldier.*[10] But in the recriminations over Vietnam, the limitations of the "military mind" and the military stereotype found renewed outlet in the United States.[11] Writing in 1973, Bernard Brodie argued that a "Chief of Staff is one who shares with his colleagues a great belief in the efficacy of force in dealing with recalcitrant peoples or regimes abroad."[12] Though the stereotype was certainly exaggerated and far from universal, the pugnacious attitudes of certain military leaders of the early 1960s, especially the Air Force generals at the top of Strategic Air Command, tended to lend credence to the popular images.[13]

Contrary to the view of American military leaders as bellicose elites who have pushed their reluctant civilian masters unwillingly into foreign interventions, military leaders have not been particularly warlike or influential when it comes to decisions over whether or not to use force.[14] That professional military officers would normally caution against using military force was a point argued by Samuel Huntington in *The Soldier and the State,*[15] and subsequent research has tended to confirm

Huntington's claim.[16] In the first systematic study of the military's role in intervention decision making, Richard Betts examined decisions during the period from 1945 until 1972. He discovered that American military leaders tended to be less bellicose than the most aggressive civilian advisors to the presidents.[17] Moreover, military leaders tended to be least effective when they advocated the use of force and most effective when they united in opposition to armed intervention.[18] A decade after Betts debunked the myth of military warmongering, David Petraeus found that the Vietnam War had had a chastening effect on the American military.[19] By the late 1980s, US military leaders were even less likely to advocate the use of force than either their predecessors or the senior civilian advisors of the day. Thus, Petraeus concluded that "In short, the military since 1973 had conformed more closely to the Huntington view (originally presented in 1957) than they had during the period of Betts's analysis."[20]

How to Use Force: Options, Influence, and Overwhelming Force

As Richard Haass has argued, decisions about whether to use force should be inextricably linked to considerations about what force is available and how that force is to be used.[21] Betts's study countered the "bureaucratic revisionists" who suggested that military capabilities drove foreign policy.[22] He also noted that the traditional theoretical model—whereby clearly articulated foreign policy served as a basis for military strategy—was too neat for the real world.[23] Describing the military role in foreign policy making, Betts observed that

> military officials' task was not simply to study a policy, deduce the appropriate strategy and forces to implement it, and recommend the results to political leaders. Instead they were often in the position where their advice on what could be achieved was to determine what would be achieved.[24]

As American involvement in Vietnam began to escalate, senior officers saw untested theories of limited war substituted for their professional advice on the use of force.[25] This was especially true of the bombing of North Vietnam, where a strategy of graduated pressure was employed to convince Hanoi's leaders to abandon their support for the insurgent Vietcong guerrillas fighting in South Vietnam.[26] A vignette from the outset of the bombing operations illustrated the disparate civilian and military views:

> In early 1965, Chief of Naval Operations David McDonald had returned from a White House meeting where, over the objections of the Joint Chiefs who favored heavy and decisive bombing, the civilian policy makers were planning the program of limited and graduated bombing. He reportedly told his aide that graduated response was militarily senseless and that when the war was over, the civilians responsible would no longer be in office and the only group left answerable for the war would be the military.[27]

Air Force plans called for hitting the entire list of 94 strategic targets in North Vietnam within a month.[28] Regardless of one's views on the wisdom of either bombing strategy, the point to be noted here is that even when the questions of whether and how to use force were considered together, the answers did not always reflect the preferred military options. This left military commanders to implement a strategy that they believed could not succeed.[29]

As Petraeus studied the period after Vietnam, he found that military influence over *how* force was used surpassed the influence that uniformed leaders exercised on decisions over *whether* force was to be used. Petraeus concluded that

> the military have exercised the most influence, however, once the decision to use force has been made—when the focus has become *how* to use force, and when decision makers have turned to consideration of the options available to accomplish the objectives established by the president. Options are the military's area of expertise, and expertise, particularly when concentrated in one institution, yields influence.[30]

Thus, with responsibility for formulating plans, the military gains influence. In describing the military's unique expertise in this area Petraeus averred that

> the development of military options is a complex undertaking that requires knowledge, experience, and creativity. Detailed and timely information about one's own forces is essential, as is current intelligence on the target of the military action. An understanding of the systems established for planning, coordination, and command and control of military operations is necessary as well. Military operations

are complicated affairs, and only senior military officers fully master their conduct.[31]

These observations are axiomatic rather than lessons of any particular conflict, but they again underscore the importance of expertise in giving the military influence over how force gets used.

From the Vietnam War, Army and Air Force officers drew somewhat different lessons about the use of force. Petraeus found that the American military emerged from Vietnam with an acute and lasting awareness of (1) the "finite limits of public support for protracted military operations," (2) "doubts about the efficacy of military force in solving certain international problems," and (3) "greater disillusionment with, and heightened wariness of, civilian officials."[32] The Army and Marine Corps bore the deepest scars, according to Petraeus, while the Navy was the least affected service.[33] However, Petraeus did not elaborate on the US Air Force. Mark Clodfelter has argued that Air Force leaders concluded from Vietnam that "since Linebacker II demonstrated bombing effectiveness, political leaders *must* realize that bombing can win limited wars if unhampered by political controls."[34] This suggested that senior Air Force officers might be just as wary of civilian officials as their Army counterparts, but they were less pessimistic about the utility of airpower. Edward Marks's study of the Vietnam generation of professional military officers found that career officers from all of the services firmly supported civilian supremacy, insisted on clear-cut political decisions and clear objectives for using force, and wanted to know that risks taken with American lives would "be for a worthwhile purpose."[35] Marks's study also found that the Vietnam generation of officers believed that once the military was given clear objectives, it should then be free from political interference in achieving those aims; that is, the officers believed they should be given operational autonomy.[36] So, while soldiers and airmen drew different conclusions about the effectiveness of airpower in Vietnam, both groups agreed the military should control decisions about how to use force in future operations.

The lessons of Vietnam were reinforced by American experiences in Lebanon, Operation Desert Storm, and Somalia. These combined experiences produced a military culture averse to engaging in small wars, and committed to ensuring rapid success whenever and wherever military force was to be employed.[37] As Frank Hoffman has pointed out, the articulation of this military "doctrine" owed much to Gen Colin Powell, who formally propounded the ideas in the 1992 National Military Strategy.[38] This preferred approach to employing force was called "Decisive Force" by its authors. Less charitably, Cong. Les Aspin labeled it the "all-or-nothing" school of thought.[39] Aspin, who was then chairman of the House Armed Services Committee, claimed the most important tenet of the all-or-nothing school stipulated that "military force should be used only in an overwhelming fashion."[40] He criticized the all-or-nothing school, which he associated with Colin Powell, and stated that his own views were more closely aligned with what he called the "limited objectives" school.[41] For Aspin, compellence and airpower lay at "the heart of the limited objectives argument," and Operation Desert Storm had demonstrated airpower's potential to deliver limited political objectives through precise applications of force.[42] Aspin's comments about how to use force, especially airpower, were made with an eye toward US intervention in Bosnia. For now, one should note that as US policy makers considered whether to get involved in Bosnia, they were dealing with a generation of military officers who expected the freedom to decide *how* to use force once the decision to use it was made.

Theoretical Bases of Demands for Operational Autonomy: Expertise and Responsibility

Military commanders demand autonomy in operational matters because they are experts in the employment of force and are held accountable for their actions. Autonomy enables them to influence how force is used.

While acknowledging the prerogative of political authorities in questions of when and how to intervene, military officers have resented infringements into the area of operational control of military forces.[43] Tensions in political-military relations have arisen when political authorities have dispensed with military advice and entered the professional military domain of managing violence. Clausewitz testified to the abiding condition of problems arising when nonexpert political authorities attempt to control military force:

> When people talk, as they often do, about harmful political influence on the management of war, they are not really saying what they mean. Their quarrel should be with the policy itself, not with its influence. . . . Only if statesmen look to certain military moves and actions to produce effects that are foreign to their nature do political decisions influence operations for the worse. In the same way as a man who has not fully mastered a foreign language sometimes fails to express himself correctly, so statesmen often issue orders that defeat the purpose they are meant to serve. Time and again that has happened, which demonstrates that a certain grasp of military affairs is vital for those in charge of general policy.[44]

Thus, military expertise has long been recognized as a basis for effective control over operational matters. Samuel Huntington went so far as to say that military disobedience of political orders would be justified in cases where a "military officer . . . is ordered by a statesman to take a measure which is militarily absurd when judged by professional standards and which is strictly within the military realm without any political implications."[45] The final qualification, "without any political implications," was as crucial to Huntington's argument as it was unlikely to pertain in the limited military operations following World War II. Moreover, at the time Huntington wrote, the advent of nuclear weapons was already rendering traditional military expertise largely irrelevant.[46] Still, for Huntington, the superior expertise of soldiers and statesmen in their respective military and political domains served as the basis for a civil-military division of labor, and it fortified military demands for autonomy.[47]

Writing in 1960, Morris Janowitz argued for more integrated civil-military relations, and he was far less deferential toward military expertise than Huntington.[48] For Janowitz, the military had to forego its absolutist tendencies and accept the blurring of civilian-military responsibilities.[49] For the world to survive in the nuclear age, the management of violence could no longer be governed by military logic; rather, the military needed to develop new expertise in ways of limiting the use of force.[50] Janowitz warned that until the military became imbued with a "constabulary force" outlook, it threatened to transgress the boundaries of civilian control.[51] He foresaw this as a likely problem in limited wars and wars against insurgency.[52] So, while Janowitz accepted the connection between expertise and professionalism, he was not sanguine about giving the military autonomy to use its expertise until the military profession could be rid of the outdated and dangerous influences of the "absolutist" heroic leaders and transformed into a profession led by "pragmatic" military managers. Moreover, he perceived the greatest need for change to be in the US Air Force, dominated as it was by generals from the Strategic Air Command.[53]

Betts showed how expertise could be used by the military to help preserve autonomy in operational affairs.[54] Sometimes, limitations in military capabilities impose constraints on what can be achieved in a given situation. This is known as *tactical determinism*, where the means more or less determine the ends. In the past, military leaders have falsely asserted tactical determinism or built plans around real limitations in military capabilities so as to prevent political authorities from interfering in operational matters. A classic example, cited by Betts, occurred at the outset of World War I when "General Moltke falsely claimed the rigidity of plans as an excuse to refuse a last-minute change in strategy to concentration on the Russian front."[55] However, tactical determinism is not merely a ploy used by experts to maximize their control over the use of force. It is often a real and important factor in decisions over when and how to use force. As an example, Betts showed that Graham Allison was wrong to accuse military leaders of falsely asserting the limits of airpower during the Cuban missile crisis in order to strengthen the chances of a more robust bombing operation or a full-scale invasion.[56] The limitations of airpower were all too real. This example highlights an important point: in the absence of mutual respect and trust, political leaders might dismiss relevant and accurate military advice, or come to believe that their own judgments on the use of force can substitute for military expertise.

Petraeus found that critics of military advice have suspected false claims of tactical determinism, while military planners have supposed that the critics were willing to ignore real-world limitations if they clashed with the critics' preferred solutions.[57] The point to note here is that special military expertise is needed to judge the limits of what military means can accomplish, and that the same expertise can give the military leverage in gaining autonomy.

Another element of professionalism, responsibility, serves as a basis for the military insistence on autonomy in operational matters. The unique requirement for the military to manage violence on behalf of the state implies certain responsibilities. Huntington discussed three forms of military responsibility: representative, advisory, and executive.[58] This study focuses mainly on executive responsibility, because theater-level commanders are primarily responsible for executing policy. Huntington argued that in its executive capacity the military profession's first duty was obedience, even when a professional officer disagreed with a policy he was tasked to fulfill. Two military ethicists, Kenneth Kemp and Charles Hudlin, examined the limits of the obligation for military obedience.[59] They analyzed the possible moral, legal, political, and private bases for disobedience, and they concluded there was almost no scope for either passively refusing orders or for positively acting in defiance of orders, unless the orders were clearly illegal or grossly immoral.[60] However, for Kemp and Hudlin, as with Huntington, the rigid distinction between obedience and disobedience mirrored an equally inflexible division of labor between policy making and policy implementation that seldom, if ever, exists.[61] Moreover, the responsibilities faced by a commander are more complex than the one-way model—from the military to the political authority—posed by Huntington.

Commanders are also responsible for and to the people who serve under them.[62] As James Toner argued, to command is to exercise moral and military competence in fulfillment of extraordinary responsibilities.[63] Furthermore, he claimed that the foremost sign of military incompetence is being careless or wasteful with the lives of the people under one's command.[64]

A competent commander, then, would be one who sought to fulfill military and policy objectives with the least risks and losses to his forces.[65] A more explicit statement of this connection between responsibility and command was put forth by Martin Edmonds. Edmonds pointed out that military organizational structures linked rank with authority; rank, in turn, was linked to responsibility—not just to the state, but also "responsibility to the individuals within the military for whom operations mean risking their lives."[66] "Above all," asserted Edmonds, "the dominant consideration affecting armed services as organizations is the prospect of their members being killed in the course of fulfilling their duty; it is this that dominates their organizational practices."[67] Military organizations link operational responsibility and accountability in a clear chain of command. And, Edmonds noted, a commander's responsibility "must include the *responsibility for both the operational effectiveness of the unit under his or her command and the lives of the people in it* in difficult and dangerous situations" (emphasis added).[68]

Military demands for autonomy in operations are a logical outgrowth of these responsibilities and the clear accountability that commanders face. Theater-level commanders are primarily responsible and accountable for both mission accomplishment and the lives of the people under their command. The responsibilities of command are lightened for a commander who is free to pursue a course of action that fulfills his mission and poses the least amount of risk to his forces. However, when circumstances demand a trade-off, a commander has to have a clear objective and some sense of its worth before being able to strike an appropriate balance between mission accomplishment and force protection. Moreover, a commander must also have the means to accomplish his mission, and control over those means, to sensibly manage the risks his forces will face in fulfilling the mission. Without autonomy, a commander cannot work the often delicate balancing act needed to best achieve his given objective with the least risk of getting his people killed.

Like expertise, responsibility is not only a basis for military demands for autonomy, it can also work as a tool for obtaining autonomy. Despite suspicions that military leaders might exaggerate the risks involved in a given military operation—not just of failure, but of losing lives—it is politically risky to order operations which the military advises against. Political leaders can order operations despite military objections; however, as Edward Luttwak noted,

> If they choose to go ahead, they must accept both the inherent political risk of the envisaged action and the added political risk of having overruled military advice—not something that is likely to remain secret for very long in the aftermath of failure. . . . Understandably in the circumstances, prime ministers and presidents rarely overrule military chiefs to order action. That, too, is a diminution of civilian control.[69]

To the extent civilian political leaders take control over operational matters, they become accountable for the consequences. This leads back to the issue of expertise. For as Luttwak observed, "micro-management . . . implies responsibilities that prudent leaders must strive to avoid" because the ability and authority to control does not confer the expertise to manage successfully.

To summarize, in the military tradition of Western democracies, promotion in rank is ostensibly based on one's ability to handle increased responsibility. The highest ranking officers selected for operational command are expected to use their professional expertise to fulfill their responsibilities for achieving mission success with the least risk and cost to their forces. Demands for operational autonomy are a natural consequence of holding a person accountable for human lives and for the accomplishment of a mission for which that person possesses a special expertise. Therefore, military commanders demand autonomy in operational matters because they are experts in the employment of force and because they expect to be held accountable for both mission success and the lives of the people under their command. They can also use their expertise and the responsibility inherent in command to obtain operational autonomy. To the extent theater commanders are given or can otherwise get autonomy, they can influence how force is used.

Political Constraints on Airpower: Targeting and Rules of Engagement

We turn now from the broader issues of whether and how force is used to the means of constraining military autonomy in the use of a particular form of military force—airpower. For the purposes of this study, "airpower" is defined as that component of military power derived from aerospace vehicles capable of sustained and controlled flight. More specifically, this study is concerned with the use, or threatened use, of conventional force,[70] rather than with the variety of military services or support functions that airpower can perform.[71] Constraints on the use of force can take many forms, and they have been a common feature in limited wars and military operations other than war since World War II. For NATO member states, all uses of military force since 1945 have been limited in the sense of the term offered by Robert Osgood—that is, limited in the means employed and the objectives pursued.[72] According to Christopher Gacek, the difficulty in reconciling military means with limited political ends stems from the nature of military force itself. Drawing heavily from Clausewitz, Gacek describes the "logic of force" as that "powerful tendency of war to reach for higher levels of violence."[73] Political constraints on the use of force serve the "logic of policy," which seeks "to subordinate all means including force to its own purposes."[74] The primacy of policy operates regardless of the impact on the means that serve it—that is, regardless of the effect it might have on the military.[75] In contrast to Gacek's view, Bernard Brodie and other observers have ascribed the escalatory nature of conflict to the professional military's unmitigated urge to "win at any cost."[76] Unsurprisingly, those observers valued tight political controls over military autonomy.[77] The degree to which American political authorities have sought to control military force and inhibit operational autonomy has varied greatly from the hands-on techniques employed during the Vietnam War to the relatively hands-off approach adopted during the Gulf War.[78] However, in all conflicts, the political controls on airpower have generally come in three forms: direct control over targeting, bombing pauses, and rules of engagement (ROE).[79]

Political controls on airpower can be meant to serve either a positive or a negative objective. Political authorities can limit military autonomy and exercise control over airpower so that force becomes part of policy in helping to achieve a desired positive political objective. The types of positive objectives for which force might be used include signaling, coercion, retribution, or destruction through bombing (e.g., the Israeli attack on Iraq's Osirak nuclear facility in 1981).[80] In contrast to these positive objectives, negative objectives, as Mark Clodfelter has called them,[81] are likely to come into play in all wars but especially in limited wars and operations other than war where traditional military objectives may compete with, rather than complement, important policy aims.[82] In highly constrained uses of force, what gets bombed—if bombing occurs at all—is often determined less by the positive aim for using force than by what is left over after satisfying all of the negative objectives. The negative objectives that might be served by political controls on bombing include preventing the spread of a conflict outside its current boundaries, preventing escalation of a conflict within its given boundaries, avoiding collateral damage, and avoiding friendly losses. Significantly, this last negative objective—casualty avoidance—overlaps with a commander's responsibility to protect his forces. Thus, external pressure to limit friendly casualties can serve to reinforce a commander's own internal pressures to minimize the losses to his forces. If any of these negative objectives are set too firmly—thus becoming absolute prohibitions—they can interfere with achievement of the positive objective for which force is being used. As discussed under ROE below, that might be an acceptable price to pay, and it will be up to political authorities to decide whether the negative objectives that constrain force outweigh the positive objectives for using force.

Targeting as Air Strategy: What to Attack, What Not to Attack

Civilian political authorities have exercised control over targeting in order to keep the military means of airpower in line with their policy objectives. Controls over targeting extend beyond decisions on what targets to bomb to include the rapidity with which targets are struck, their geographical locations, the sequence in which they are to be hit, the weight of effort assigned to each target, and the weapon systems and types of ordnance employed against the targets. Shortly after World War I, Guilio Douhet averred that strategy in air warfare was no more than the sum of these targeting factors: "The selection of objectives, the grouping of zones, and determining the order in which they are to be destroyed is the most difficult and delicate task in aerial warfare, constituting what may be defined as aerial strategy."[83] In 1995, Col Phillip Meilinger, then dean of the US Air Force School of Advanced Airpower Studies, demonstrated that Douhet's idea still had currency when he wrote "In essence, air power is targeting;" and "selecting objectives to strike or influence is the essence of air strategy."[84] Direct controls on targeting, then, constitute one of the greatest infringements on the autonomy of airmen.

The nadir in US military autonomy over targeting in air operations came during the Vietnam War. According to the prevailing theories of limited war, a nuanced approach to using force was needed to send the right message to Hanoi, and military considerations about what was to be struck were decidedly secondary. As Richard Betts put it,

> Orchestration of the use of force was a political tool, a signaling device. Whether the United States bombed a surface-to-air missile site or oil depot near Hanoi would communicate a message to the enemy and was hence a political decision that had to be made by political authority; it was not a purely military decision to be made by a subordinate commander.[85]

President Johnson's personal control over target selection was summed up in his boast that "I won't let those Air Force generals bomb the smallest outhouse north of the 17th parallel without checking with me."[86] Significantly, up until mid-1967, Johnson operated without the benefit of any direct military advice.[87] After congressional intervention, Gen Earl Wheeler, then chairman of the Joint Chiefs of Staff, was permitted to attend weekly White House targeting sessions.[88] Later, during the Nixon administration, bombing of the North was significantly curtailed.[89] However, up until 1972, targets in North Vietnam were still being selected by civilians in Washington.[90]

41

When political authorities are using military force for signaling, they are likely to demand more direct control over targeting in order to ensure that the intended signal is sent. Moreover, when signaling is a positive aim, negative objectives will usually play a strong role in determining what does or does not get bombed. Such was the case in the air strikes against Libya in April 1986, which, according to the chairman of the Joint Chiefs of Staff at the time, Adm Bill Crowe, was meant to "send an unequivocal signal that Washington was serious and that terrorist actions would not go unpunished."[91] Crowe later wrote that "In the final analysis, our tactical decisions were based on political considerations. . . . We did not want casualties . . . and the other major political goal was to minimize Libyan civilian casualties."[92] The final target selection list included "about half" of what Crowe had recommended, but it also included suspected terrorist targets that were not on the admiral's list but were added in order to send a signal about terrorism.[93] Because of concerns over potential collateral damage, the decision makers in Washington "sacrificed a number of the best targets."[94] When signaling rather than achieving military results is the positive aim, political authorities will take a more direct role in targeting decisions, and those decisions can easily be driven more by negative objectives than by the positive purpose for the bombing.

Bombing Pauses: When to Bomb or Not Bomb

The ultimate targeting control is the ability to stop or start bombing. When bombing forms part of coercive diplomacy, military commanders will likely find themselves competing with diplomats for control over decisions about how to regulate bombing. Whether bombing should be halted to permit negotiations or continued to enhance leverage during negotiations is clearly a matter for political authorities to decide.[95] However, they should expect their commanders to resist bombing cessation whenever a pause might erase the gains for which the military has already paid a significant price or whenever the pause is expected to increase the costs of operations once bombing is resumed.[96]

In Vietnam, American political leaders ordered bombing pauses in futile attempts to win similar restraint from Hanoi.[97] President Johnson did not consult with the military before suddenly ordering the first bombing halt of the Rolling Thunder campaign in May of 1965.[98] Had he done so, he would have met resistance from his top commanders. Commander in chief of the Pacific theater Admiral Sharp later wrote, "We had enough experience in negotiating with the Communists to know that military pressures must be sustained throughout the negotiating period."[99] The Johnson administration ordered subsequent cessations in the bombing of North Vietnam despite warnings from commanders in the field that the North "exploited them to resupply, prepare for attacks, redeploy forces and commit violations."[100] To Admiral Sharp, "It seemed pointless to allow the enemy the luxury of such respites, which, in the end, would only translate to higher casualties on our side."[101] The bombing of North Vietnam had been drastically reduced before the Nixon administration came to Washington. However, Henry Kissinger, Nixon's chief negotiator noted: "Hanoi bargained only when it was under severe pressure—in particular, whenever America resumed bombing."[102]

Political authorities may wish to turn bombing off or on to suit their strategies for coercive diplomacy. But, as Alexander George has noted, "If pushed too far, the civilian authority's effort to transform military force into a highly refined, discriminating instrument of diplomacy and coercive bargaining will eventually break down."[103] Such breakdowns, George noted, leave negotiators with one of two unpalatable choices: make major negotiating concessions or escalate.[104] Controls that regulate bombing in conjunction with coercive diplomacy are meant to serve positive objectives; however, they seriously infringe upon a commander's autonomy, and commanders will likely oppose them, especially if the pauses increase costs to friendly forces.

Rules of Engagement: Circumstances for Force

Rules of engagement have also served as a powerful constraint on military autonomy in air operations. The US

Department of Defense defined rules of engagement as "directives issued by competent military authority which delineate the circumstances and limitations under which United States forces will initiate and/or continue combat engagement with other forces encountered."[105] Academic instruction given by the US Air Force to its newly recruited lawyers explained that ROE "are the primary means by which political authorities . . . provide guidance to deployed forces in peacetime for handling crises and, in wartime, to help control the level of violence."[106] Rules of engagement have usually been derived from legal, political, and operational considerations.[107] The following discussion does not examine the legal dimension of ROE, but instead addresses political considerations then operational concerns.[108] In general, ROE serves negative objectives. The tension between positive objectives for using force and negative objectives served by ROE was reflected in an analysis by Scott Sagan:

> Rules of engagement . . . are designed to balance two competing goals: the need to use force effectively to achieve the objective of an offensive or defensive mission and the desire *not* to use military force in unnecessary circumstances or in an excessively aggressive manner.[109]

Rules of engagement can constrain the use of force so much that it becomes militarily ineffective. Sagan referred to this as a "weakness error."[110] Alternatively, lax ROE can lead to too much force being used for a given situation, resulting in what he called an "escalatory error."[111] The trick, as Sagan noted, was to set the ROE between these two errors. Recognizing that this demands an act of judgment on which political and military authorities might differ, Sagan observed, "ROE decisions, involving trade-offs between military effectiveness and broader political objectives, are legitimately the province of senior political authorities."[112] Sagan's analysis and conclusions were sound, yet he failed to give adequate attention to the responsibility commanders have for protecting their forces.

Highly restrictive rules of engagement, useful for preventing unwanted escalation, can also increase the risks to the forces involved in an operation. In Vietnam, the aerial rules of engagement significantly increased the risks to American aircrews and prevented them from taking appropriate measures for self-defense. The rules of engagement prohibited attacks against surface-to-air missile (SAM) sites and other air defense targets except in reaction to an immediate threat.[113] Because the North had networked its radar, SAM batteries could get firing cues without turning on their own radar, thus allowing them to shoot with little or no warning to US aircraft. By forcing the aircrews to wait for clear indications of a threat, the ROE greatly reduced the chances that the crews could take effective defensive actions.[114]

In the spring of 1972, Gen John Ryan, Air Force chief of staff, relieved Gen John Lavelle, commander of US Air Forces in Vietnam, when subordinates in Lavelle's command were found to be falsifying reports to cover up the fact that Lavelle had ordered preplanned strikes against the North's air defenses.[115] It frustrated Lavelle, as it had other commanders before him, to operate under complex rules that seemed to needlessly jeopardize the lives of his men.[116] In his testimony before the House subcommittee investigating the unauthorized bombings, Lavelle jokingly told the congressmen, "We have a saying we used in Vietnam, that we finally found out why there were two crew members in the F-4. One is to fly the airplane and one is to carry the briefcase full of the rules of engagement."[117] However, it was no joking matter for the aircrews involved, as one study later explained:

> To many aircrews, it seemed impossible to find a way to do what was ordered and not get killed by the enemy or hanged by the United States government in the process. The ROEs made many aircrews feel as if they were fighting two enemies: the North Vietnamese and American leaders in the White House.[118]

Lavelle's solution was to interpret the rules of engagement in a way that allowed strikes against elements of the North's air defenses even in the absence of a clear indication that the air defenses were about to engage US aircraft.[119] Although officers on the joint staff at the Pentagon apparently sympathized with what Lavelle was trying to do, authorities in Washington did not change the rules until after—and perhaps as a result of—Lavelle's dismissal.[120] Despite giving guidance that led to the ROE violations, Lavelle was praised by several congressmen during the hearings on the unauthorized bombings for trying to protect American airmen.[121] In Cong. William Dickinson's words to General Lavelle, "I think if I had been in your position, . . . I would have done exactly what you did. I think you would be less than a man if you were not trying to do all you could, and if stretching the rules [of engagement] is part of it, then good for you."[122] The Lavelle case demonstrated the dilemma commanders faced in Vietnam, where overly restrictive ROE were costing US airmen their lives.[123]

The principle of civilian control of the military dictates that commanders abide by political restrictions even if that means failing to achieve the desired positive objective for using airpower. Commanders are still obliged to apply their expertise in an effort to fulfill their responsibilities for mission success and force protection within the bounds of the constraints set by their political masters. When political restrictions jeopardize the safety of a commander's forces, he must decide how far to go in risking the lives of the people under his command since losing friendly forces will be an undesired side effect of a restriction, rather than an intended consequence. The problem for the commander is that it may take expertise, which those above him setting the restrictions lack, to recognize that the constraints are increasing the risks to friendly forces. If a commander balks at political constraints, he might be perceived as falsely exaggerating the dangers they cause, just as military advisors are sometimes suspected of making false claims of tactical determinism. A commander's difficulties are compounded if his mission is not in pursuit of a clearly defined objective because he will be unable to judge even for himself whether or not the risks to friendly forces are justified by the expected outcome. Little of the foregoing discussion is unique to airpower, but the problems can be especially acute for airpower because of its potential to cause collateral damage, the inordinate stigma that goes with losing an aircraft and its crew, and the political sensitivities over dropping bombs.[124] Moreover, the complexities of electronic warfare and aerial tactics required for self-defense are not as easily grasped as are requirements for self-defense by ground forces.

Soldiers and Airmen:
Efficacy and Control of Airpower

One of the main justifications for firm civilian political control over the use of force, according to Bernard Brodie, was the parochial mindset of senior military officers married to their unbalanced commitment to victory.[125] The down side of the expertise officers gained from combat experience and professional study was that it tended to create a situation where "the services are normally not strategy-minded but rather means-minded."[126] Moreover, Brodie asserted,

> Military officers have usually spent their entire careers perfecting their skills with respect to some *means* of war, whether those means be battleships, or carriers, or bombers, and they become deeply attached emotionally to those means.[127]

In examining the American uses of force from World War II through the end of the Vietnam War, Richard Betts found support for Brodie's assertion, especially on the issue of airpower.

> Since World War II the debates have pitted the air force, a majority of the Navy, and right-of-center civilians against the army, a minority of the navy, and left-of-center civilians. The former coalition has argued that bombing is more decisive and economical than a strategy based on ground forces and has been decisive except in those instances where civilian authorities refused to let it be so by curtailing the scope and intensity of the air campaigns. The latter group has argued that bombing can only support the achievement of a military decision, which must be done primarily on the ground by occupying territory and controlling population and that air campaigns are not cost-effective. Both theories have become articles of faith.[128]

Soldiers, though doubtful about what independent air operations can achieve, have generally recognized the value of air support. As Hal Winton has pointed out, soldiers on the battlefield usually depend on air support in a way that is not balanced by a reciprocal need amongst airmen for Army support: "The asymmetry of this dependence lies at the root of many of the tensions that exist between the Army and the Air Force regarding air-ground operations."[129] Principal manifestations of these tensions have been the doctrinal and operational contests over who should control airpower and to what ends.

Despite the relative surfeits of airpower American forces have enjoyed in the conflicts since 1945, the struggle within the US military to control airpower has, at times, been intense. Army and Marine Corps officers have long felt, with justification, that their needs for close air support would fare poorly if left entirely to the Air Force.[130] Conversely, Air Force officers have traditionally believed, also with justification, that soldiers tend not to appreciate airpower's potential to influence events beyond the battlefield.[131] As a consequence of these competing views, centralized control of airpower by an airman has long been a leading tenet of Air Force doctrine:

> Aerospace forces should be centrally controlled by an airman to achieve advantageous synergies, establish effective priorities, capitalize on unique strategic and operational flexibilities, ensure unity of purpose, and minimize the potential for conflicting objectives.[132]

Steve McNamara has detailed the resulting soldier-airman struggle to control airpower.[133] When the US military reorganized in the mid-1980s, airmen succeeded in having the position of an "air boss" written into joint doctrine. In 1986 the concept of a joint force air component commander (JFACC) was officially sanctioned in doctrine on counterair operations.[134] The idea gradually gained wider currency in the joint arena and was applied to all airpower missions. Of course establishing and defining the position of an air boss in US doctrine did not eliminate the services' different approaches to warfare or their desires to control airpower.[135] The concept was first tested in the Gulf War, where it was criticized by ground commanders who felt that the targets they nominated were too often ignored by the Air Force officers running the air war.[136] In addition, the Marine Corps had difficulty accepting infringement on control of its airpower.[137] The issue was finally settled after the Gulf War and after more than a little friction. The second C in JFACC stood for "commander," which implied the authority to control air assets, and not "coordinator"—as the Marines had argued—which implied a much weaker position.[138]

The relative control that an airman or a soldier exercises over airpower will depend largely on who is supporting whom. In US military doctrine, the "supported" commander and forces are the focus of an operation; they have the predominant role to play and they command priority when it comes to resources. Supporting forces, on the other hand, give aid, assistance, resources, firepower, and so on, to the supported elements.[139] This concept applies across military theaters as well as within a given theater of operations. As applied in its intra-theater sense, the supported-supporting concept determines which forces (e.g., air, land, or maritime) play the predominant role, and which ones assist.[140] Col John Warden has argued that airpower ought to be the key instrument or force (i.e., the supported force) in operations where "ground or sea forces are incapable of doing the job because of insufficient numbers or inability to reach the enemy military centers of gravity."[141] His prescription for theater commanders was to identify a key (or supported) element for each phase of a campaign and ensure that competing service viewpoints did not interfere with their campaign plans.[142] As obvious and logical as this sounds, Warden noted that in joint military operations theater commanders often "failed to identify a key force, and . . . each [component] either thought it was dominant or didn't realize what its role was in producing a coherent performance."[143]

The concept of supported and supporting forces is relevant to military operations other than war, but, as this study demonstrates, that concept was not easily or well applied in Bosnia. The problems were due, in part, to the different views held by soldiers and airmen on the uses and control of airpower. This problem was compounded by the lack of an overall theater commander, with the added complexity of having soldiers from European nations commanding UN forces on the ground while airmen from the United States commanded NATO air operations overhead. This created problems due to competing national agendas typical of coalition operations without the compensating benefits of unity of command and establishment of a common coalition objective. When NATO was contemplating intervention in the spring of 1993, Field Marshal Sir Richard Vincent, chairman of NATO's Military Committee, warned: "For God's sake, decide what you're trying to achieve before you go out."[144] However, after Deny Flight ended, Gen Joe Ashy, the first commander of NATO air operations over

Bosnia observed, "The bottom line was we did not have unity of command and unity of purpose."[145]

Summary

There are at least four dimensions to military influence on the use of airpower that might come into play once military forces are committed in a situation where airpower is likely to be used. First, there is the logic of force or the urge for military victory, which is in tension with the logic of policy; that is, the necessity to make sure the ends dictate the means and not vice-versa. Second, while acting under political constraints, a commander must try to balance his responsibilities for both mission success and force protection. Third, one must consider the competing views that soldiers and airmen are likely to hold on the proper uses of airpower. Fourth, in multinational operations there are likely to be different definitions of success stemming from different views of the conflict and different organizational doctrines. These various dimensions of military influence should be borne in mind as we turn now to the question of the theater-level commanders' roles in influencing the use of airpower in Bosnia.

Notes

1. For recent contributions to the debate, see Richard Holbrooke, *To End a War* (New York: Random House, 1998), 60–152; and Edward N. Luttwak, "From Vietnam to Desert Fox, Civil-Military Relations in Modern Democracies," *Foreign Affairs* 74, no. 3 (May/June 1995): 99–112.

2. Richard K. Betts, *Soldiers, Statesmen, and Cold War Crises* (Cambridge, Mass.: Harvard University Press, 1977), 203; Lt Col Stephen McNamara, *Air Power's Gordian Knot: Centralized versus Organic Control* (Maxwell AFB, Ala.: Air University Press, 1994), 81–85; and Harold R. Winton, "An Ambivalent Partnership: US Army and Air Force Perspectives on Air-Ground Operations" in Col Philip S. Meilinger, ed., *The Paths of Heaven: The Evolution of Airpower Theory* (Maxwell AFB, Ala.: Air University Press, 1997), 399–442.

3. *The American Heritage Dictionary of the English Language*, 3d ed. (New York: Houghton Mifflin Co., 1992).

4. Roger Scruton, *A Dictionary of Political Thought*, 2d ed. (London: Macmillan, 1982; Pan Books, 1996), 262.

5. Dennis H. Wrong, *Power: Its Forms, Bases, and Uses* (New York: Harper and Row, 1995), 1–32.

6. Betts, 5.

7. S. E. Finer, *Man on Horseback* (London: Pall Mall Press, 1962; revised edition, Peregrine Books, 1976), 86.

8. Ibid.

9. Betts, 1–2.

10. Morris Janowitz, *The Professional Soldier: A Social and Political Portrait* (London: Collier and Macmillan, 1960; reprinted with new prologue and preface, 1971), 3–5.

11. Karen A. McPherson, "The American Military in Fiction Since 1945," *Armed Forces and Society* 9, no. 4 (summer 1983): 650; and David H. Petraeus, "The American Military and the Lessons of Vietnam: A Study of Military Influence and the Use of Force in the Post-Vietnam Era" (PhD diss., Princeton University, 1987), 3. Brodie is particularly critical of the "military mind." See Bernard Brodie, *War & Politics* (New York: Macmillan Press, 1973), 479–96.

12. Brodie, 486.

13. Betts, 116–17, 120, and 127–28.

14. Ibid., 5–6.

15. Samuel P. Huntington, *The Soldier and the State: Theory and Practice of Civil-Military Relations* (Cambridge, Mass.: Harvard University Press), 68–69.

16. Petraeus, 258.

17. Betts, 5–6.

18. Ibid., 11–12 and 96.

19. Petraeus, 6; and David H. Petraeus, "Military Influence and the Post-Vietnam Use of Force," *Armed Forces and Society* 15, no. 4 (summer 1989): 493.

20. Petraeus, "American Military," 6.

21. Richard N. Haass, *Intervention: The Use of American Military Force in the Post-Cold War World* (Washington, D.C.: Brookings Institution for the Carnegie Institution for International Peace, 1994), 68.

22. Betts, 103.

23. Ibid., 96.

24. Ibid., 97.

25. Stephen Peter Rosen, "Vietnam and the American Theory of Limited War," *International Security* 7, no. 2 (fall 1982): 84–94.

26. H. R. McMaster, *Dereliction of Duty: Lyndon Johnson, Robert McNamara, The Joint Chiefs of Staff, and the Lies That Led to Vietnam* (New York: HarperCollins, 1947), 40–47.

27. Betts, 11.

28. Earl H. Tilford Jr., *Setup: What the Air Force Did in Vietnam and Why* (Maxwell AFB, Ala.: Air University Press, 1991), 104; Mark Clodfelter, *The Limits of Air Power; the American Bombing of North Vietnam* (New York: Free Press; Collier Macmillan, 1989), 76–77; and McMaster, 143.

29. McMaster, 106.

30. Petraeus, "American Military," 249–50.

31. Petraeus, "Military Influence," 495.

32. Petraeus, "American Military," 104.

33. Ibid., 104 and 276.

34. Clodfelter, 208. Also see Guenter Lewy, "Some Political–Military Lessons of the Vietnam War," *Parameters* 14, no. 1 (spring 1984): 9–13.

35. Edward Marks, "The Vietnam Generation of Professional American Military Officers," *Conflict* 5, no. 1 (1983): 51.

36. Ibid.

37. F. G. Hoffman, *Decisive Force: The New American Way of War* (Westport, Conn.: Praeger, 1966), 5–12, 100–102, and 103–5.

38. Ibid., 100.

39. Les Aspin, "The Use and Usefulness of Military Forces in the Post-Cold War, Post-Soviet World," address to the Jewish Institute for National Security Affairs, Washington, D.C., 21 September 1992, excerpted and reproduced as Appendix D in Haass, 185.

40. Ibid.

41. Ibid., 185–87.

42. Ibid., 188–89.

43. Betts, 9.

44. Carl Clausewitz, *On War*, ed. and trans. Michael Howard and Peter Paret (Princeton, N.J.: Princeton University Press, 1976), 608.

45. Huntington, 77.

46. Bernard Brodie, *Strategy in the Missile Age* (Princeton, N.J.: Princeton University Press, 1959), 400–409.

47. Huntington, 11–14 and 71.

48. Janowitz, 418–23.

49. Ibid., 426–30.

50. Ibid., 266–77 and 418–20.

51. Ibid., 343 and 420–21.

52. Ibid., 305–11 and 343.

53. Ibid., 304–7, 315–18, and 430.

54. Betts, 12–13. Also see Petraeus, "Military Influence," 495; and "The American Military," 249–50.

55. Betts, 155.

56. Betts, 155–56; and Graham T. Allison, *Essence of Decision: Explaining the Cuban Missile Crisis* (n.p.: HarperCollins, 1971), 124–26 and 205–6.

57. Petraeus, "American Military," 231 and 246.

58. Huntington, 14–16 and 72.

59. Kenneth W. Kemp and Charles Hudlin, "Civil Supremacy over the Military: Its Nature and Limits," *Armed Forces and Society* 19, no. 1 (fall 1992): 7–26.

60. Ibid.

61. Ibid., 8; and Huntington, 72. On the lack of clear boundaries between policy making and implementation, see Betts, 14; Allison, 162–63; and

Michael Clarke, "Foreign Policy Implementation: Problems and Approaches," *British Journal of International Studies* 5 (1979): 114.

62. Michael Walzer, "Two Kinds of Military Responsibility," in *The Parameters of Military Ethics*, eds. Lloyd J. Matthews and Dale E. Brown (London: Pergamon-Brassey's, 1989), 67–68; and Lewis S. Sorely, "Competence as Ethical Imperative: Issues of Professionalism," in *Military Ethics and Professionalism: A Collection of Essays*, eds. James Brown and Michael J. Collins (Washington, D.C.: National Defense University Press, 1981), 39–40 and 47–48.

63. James H. Toner, *True Faith and Allegiance: The Burden of Military Ethics* (Lexington, Ky.: University Press of Kentucky, 1995), 43–44.

64. Ibid. The point of departure for Toner's discussion on military competence is Norman Dixon's list of 14 aspects of military incompetence. See Norman Dixon, *On the Psychology of Military Incompetence* (London: Pimlico, 1976), 152–53.

65. Ibid.; and Sorely, 39–40 and 47–48.

66. Martin Edmonds, *Armed Services and Society* (King's Lynn, England: Leicester University Press, 1988), 30–31.

67. Ibid., 31.

68. Ibid., 33.

69. Luttwak, 102.

70. Nuclear operations will not be addressed because they are irrelevant to the case of Bosnia.

71. For a discussion of *airpower* in the broader sense of the term, and its use in peace support operations, see Air Vice-Marshal Tony Mason, "Air Power in the Peace Support Environment," in *The Dynamics of Air Power*, eds. Group Capt Andrew Lambert and Arthur C. Williamson (Bracknell, England: HMSO, 1996), 112–25; and idem, "Operations in Search of a Title: Air Power in Operations Other than War," 157–77.

72. Robert Osgood, *Limited War Revisited* (Boulder, Colo.: Westview Press, 1979), 3.

73. Christopher M. Gacek, *The Logic of Force: The Dilemma of Limited War in American Foreign Policy* (New York: Columbia University Press, 1994), 295.

74. Ibid.

75. Ibid.

76. Janowitz, 264; Brodie, *War & Politics*, 191–92; and Townsend Hoopes, *The Limits of Intervention* (New York: David Mckay Co., 1969), 62.

77. Janowitz, 343 and 435; Brodie, *War & Politics*, 496; Hoopes, 62.

78. Lt Col John G. Humphries, "Operations Law and the Rules of Engagement in Operations Desert Shield and Desert Storm," *Airpower Journal* 6, no. 3 (fall 1992): 25–26 and 39.

79. Sanctuaries are distinct from ROE, but often the two are treated together. For the purposes of this study, the distinction is not of great enough importance to warrant a separate discussion of sanctuaries. For more on the topic of sanctuaries, see Brodie, *War & Politics*, 67–68; Maj Ricky James Drake, *The Rules for Defeat: The Impact of Aerial Rules of*

Engagement on USAF Operations in North Vietnam (Maxwell AFB, Ala.: Air University Press, 1993), 4–5 and 25–26; Adm U.S. Grant Sharp, *Strategy for Defeat: Vietnam in Retrospect* (Novato, Calif.: Presidio Press, 1978), 204; Rick Atkinson, *Crusade: The Untold Story of the Persian Gulf War* (New York: Houghton Mifflin, 1993), 288–90; Richard P. Hallion, *Storm Over Iraq; Air Power in the Gulf War* (Washington, D.C.: Smithsonian Institute Press, 1992), 199; Michael R. Gordon and Gen Bernard E. Trainor, *The Generals' War: The Inside Story of the Conflict in the Gulf* (New York: Little, Brown and Co., 1995), 326–29; and Wayne W. Thompson, "Al Firdos: The Last Two Weeks of Strategic Bombing in Desert Storm," *Air Power History* 43, no. 2 (summer 1996): 52.

80. For a more thorough discussion of the types of positive objectives that might be served by using force, see Haass, *Intervention*, especially chap. 3; and idem "Military Intervention: A Taxonomy of Challenges and Responses" in *The United States and the Use of Force in the Post-Cold War Era* (Queenstown, Md.: Aspen Institute, 1995), 1–18.

81. Clodfelter, 141.

82. David Gates, "Air Power and Aspects of Civil-Military Relations," in *Perspectives on Air Power: Air Power in Its Wider Context*, ed., Stuart Peach (London: HMSO, 1998), 28; Also Mason, "Operations in Search," 158–60; Michael Clarke, "Air Power and Force in Peace Support Operations," 173; Sabin, "The Counter-Air Mission in Peace Support Operations" in *The Dynamics of Air Power*, 158.

83. Giulio Douhet, *The Command of the Air*, trans. by Dino Ferrari (New York: Coward-McCann, 1942; reprinted, Washington: Office of Air Force History, 1983), 50.

84. Col Philip S. Meilinger, *Ten Propositions Regarding Air Power* (Washington, D.C.: Office of Air Force History, 1995), 20–21.

85. Betts, 14.

86. Johnson is quoted in Rowland Evans and Robert Novak, *Lyndon B. Johnson: The Exercise of Power* (New York: New American Library, 1966), 538–39, cited in Betts, 10.

87. McMaster, 208–9.

88. Betts, 8.

89. Tilford, 153.

90. House Committee on Armed Services, *Unauthorized Bombing of Military Targets in North Vietnam: Hearing Before the Armed Services Investigating Subcommittee*, 12 June 1972, 46 (hereafter cited as House, *Bombing Hearing*).

91. Adm William J. Crowe with David Chanoff, *The Line of Fire: From Washington to the Gulf, the Politics and Battles of the New Military* (New York: Simon & Schuster, 1993), 132. Also see Caspar Weinberger, *Fighting for Peace: Seven Critical Years in the Pentagon* (New York: Warner Books, 1990), 97.

92. Crowe with Chanoff, 134.

93. Ibid., 135.

94. Ibid., 134.

95. Henry Kissinger, *Diplomacy* (New York: Simon and Schuster, 1994), 684; Paul Seabury and Angelo Codevilla, *War: Ends & Means* (New York: Basic Books, 1989), 246.

96. Gen William W. Momyer, *Air Power in Three Wars (WWII, Korea, Vietnam)* (Washington, D.C.: US Air Force Office of History, 1978), 23–29; and Admiral Sharp, 81–83 and 145.

97. Kissinger, 684; and Seabury and Codevilla, 246–53.

98. McMaster, 283–85; and Admiral Sharp, 81–82.

99. Admiral Sharp, 83. Also see Kissinger, 488 and 684; Seabury and Codevilla, 246–53.

100. Admiral Sharp, 145.

101. Ibid.

102. Kissinger, 684.

103. Alexander L. George, "Crisis Management: The Interaction of Political and Military Considerations," *Survival* 26, no. 5 (September/October 1984): 226–27.

104. Ibid., 227.

105. Joint Chiefs of Staff, *U.S. Department of Defense Dictionary of Military Terms* (London: Greenhill Books, 1991), 341.

106. "Operations Law Deployment Deskbook," vol. 2 (Maxwell AFB, Ala.: International and Operations Law Division, Office of the Judge Advocate General, Department of the Air Force, 1996), H–1 and H–2.

107. For excellent primers on ROE, see Capt J. Ashley Roach, "Rules of Engagement," *Naval War College Review* 36, no. 1 (January/February 1983): 46–55; and Bradd C. Hayes, *Naval Rules of Engagement: Management Tools for Crisis* (Santa Monica, Calif.: The RAND Corp., 1989), 1–34.

108. For an authoritative discussion of the legal dimension, see Col W. Hays Parks, USMCR, "Air War and the Law of War," *The Air Force Law Review* (1990): 1–225.

109. Scott D. Sagan, "Rules of Engagement," *Security Studies* 1, no. 1 (autumn 1991): 88.

110. Ibid.

111. Ibid.

112. Ibid., 87.

113. House Committee on Armed Services, *Unauthorized Bombing of Military Targets in North Vietnam*, report of the Armed Services Investigating Subcommittee, 15 December 1972, 2–4, 8, and 9 (hereafter cited as "House, *Unauthorized* report").

114. Ibid.

115. House, *Bombing Hearing*, 4, 35, 45, 48–49, and 52.

116. Ibid., 50–51; Col Jack Broughton, *Going Downtown: The War Against Hanoi and Washington* (New York: Orion Books, 1988), 10 and 173–74; Sharp, 4, 13, and 102–3; and Drake, 14–15.

117. House, *Bombing Hearing*, 51.

118. Drake, 15.

119. House, *Bombing Hearing*, 7.

120. House, *Unauthorized* report, 2–4, 8, and 9.

121. For words of praise from four congressmen, see House, *Bombing Hearing*, 45, 48, 49, and 50.

122. Ibid., 45.

123. For an essay on leadership, integrity, and ROE, which focuses on the Lavelle case, see Maj Lee E. DeRemer, "ROE: Leadership Between a Rock and a Hard Place," *Air Power Journal* 10, no. 3 (fall 1996): 87–94.

124. Luttwak, 108; Gates, 30; and Michael Clarke, "Threats and Challenges in the UK's Security Environment," in *Perspectives on Air Power: Air Power in Its Wider Context*, ed. Stuart Peach (London: HMSO, 1998), 16–17.

125. Brodie, *War & Politics*, 475 and 492.

126. Ibid., 465.

127. Ibid., 471–72.

128. Betts, 203.

129. Harold R. Winton, "An Ambivalent Partnership: US Army and Air Force Perspectives on Air-Ground Operations," in *The Paths of Heaven: The Evolution of Airpower Theory*, ed. Col Philip S. Meilinger, USAF (Maxwell AFB, Ala.: Air University Press, 1997), 401–2.

130. James A. Winnefeld and Dana J. Johnson, *Joint Air Operations: Pursuit of Unity in Command and Control* (Annapolis, Md.: Naval Institute Press, 1993), 10–11; and Michael Leurs, "Joint Doctrine: New Pubs: Old Controversies," *Joint Forces Quarterly*, no. 10 (summer 1994), 111.

131. Betts, 203.

132. Air Force Manual 1–1, *Basic Aerospace Doctrine of the United States Air Force*, vol. 1 (Washington, D.C.: Government Printing Office, 1992), 8.

133. McNamara, 103–13.

134. See for instance, Gordon and Trainor, 310–12.

135. Ibid., 310–12, 330–31, and 410–11.

136. Winnefeld and Johnson, 163–64; and McNamara, 2–3.

137. Leurs, 12; and Joint Pub 3-0, *Doctrine for Joint Operations*, II–11 and 12; and II–20.

138. Joint Pub 3–0, GL–12.

139. Joint Pub 1, *Joint Warfare of the US Armed Forces*, 58.

140. Col John A. Warden III, USAF, *The Air Campaign: Planning for Combat* (Washington, D. C.: National Defense University Press, 1988; Pergamon-Brassey's, 1989), 126.

141. Ibid., 124–27.

142. Ibid., 127.

143. Michael Evans, "RAF Prepares for NATO Bombing Raids on Serbs," *Times*, 28 April 1993.

144. Gen Joe Ashy, interviewed by author, 3 July 1998, Fairfax, Va., tape recording, author's personal collection.

145. Ibid.

Chapter 3

Background on the Use of
Airpower in Bosnia: 1992–April 1993

*The one cliché as popular as "air power can do anything" is
"bombing doesn't work."*

—Richard Betts
*Soldiers, Statesmen
and Cold War Crises*

The long-lived debates over the utility of airpower could
have gone on without the crisis in the former Yugoslavia in the
1990s, but the war in Bosnia emerged as a useful foil for anyone wishing to caution against drawing too many lessons from
the experiences of the Gulf War.[1] For some observers, high-
technology airpower, showcased in the 1991 Gulf War, offered
a politically attractive option for intervention.[2]

Precision-guided munitions and the survivability of modern
aircraft seemed to provide a means for threatening or using
force while simultaneously minimizing risks and costs. However,
the majority view amongst senior military officers in three of
the most influential NATO nations—the United States, Britain,
and France—was one of deep skepticism about the prospects
for using airpower to quell the violence in Bosnia.[3]
Notwithstanding these military misgivings, NATO airpower
was gradually added to the Balkan equation. Air campaign
planning modeled on the Gulf War began shortly after United
Nations peacekeepers started arriving in Bosnia under a mandate that authorized "all measures necessary" for getting
humanitarian aid to victims of the war. To establish the background necessary for analyzing the role of theater-level commanders in influencing the use of airpower in Bosnia, this
chapter describes United States, United Kingdom (UK), and
French national policies for using airpower in Bosnia and
reveals the actions of the American commanders who set up
Operation Deny Flight in NATO.

Airpower and Policy Making in the United States, France, and the United Kingdom

By late June of 1992, having "exhausted virtually all possible political and diplomatic measures" for a solution to the situation in Bosnia, US Secretary of State James Baker went to National Security Advisor Brent Scowcroft, and the two men agreed to propose "the use of force for the sole purpose of delivering humanitarian assistance."[4] To support this limited objective, a team of State Department advisors produced a two-page outline plan calling for, *inter alia*, "multilateral air strikes (e.g., against artillery in hills) as necessary to create conditions for delivery of humanitarian relief."[5] Even though the plan specified that there would be no US combat troops on the ground, Baker was chary enough about opposition from Gen Colin Powell and Secretary of Defense Dick Cheney that he took his proposal and "went directly to George Bush to try to work around the interagency process and pre-cook the result."[6] Baker's efforts paid off; on Friday, 26 June 1992 after a vigorous debate amongst the administration's top policy makers, Baker noted that President Bush "squarely backed the game plan I had outlined."[7] By 10 July US Secretary of Defense Dick Cheney had gone public with a proposal for US airpower to support the delivery of humanitarian aid in Bosnia.[8] Presumably, this would have accelerated the planning already being conducted by the US Air Force.

In France, air strikes apparently were not given serious consideration by the military. President François Mitterand opposed the idea of air strikes,[9] and Roland Dumas, the French foreign minister until April of 1993, was reportedly sympathetic toward the Serb cause.[10] With French foreign and security policy traditionally dominated by the "Quai," or foreign ministry, any military initiative for air strikes would likely have been blocked.[11] The French air force chief of staff, Gen Vincent Lanata, believed that airpower could have imposed an end to the fighting, not by threatening the Bosnian Serbs, but by giving an ultimatum to the Serb leaders in Belgrade to restrain their forces in Bosnia, or face bombing in Serbia.[12] However, the French military in general viewed intervention in Bosnia as a job for the army.[13] As long as the French peacekeepers in the

Balkans remained vulnerable to reprisals, there was no serious thought of conducting air strikes.[14] Adm Jacques Lanxade, the chief of defense staff, ruled out the use of force in November only to do an about-face in December by speaking in favor of either using force in Bosnia or getting out.[15] However, this apparent change of heart did not signal a change in French opposition to air strikes in Bosnia.[16]

The British military and government appear to have gone slightly further than the French in considering the possibility of air action. The UK's military leaders, like observers elsewhere, were concerned that Bosnia was the most unpropitious environment for attempting limited precision air strikes.[17] Among the challenges to be overcome in Bosnia were its rough terrain and frequent poor weather, the lack of clear front lines, and the potential for simple countermeasures against airpower such as hiding artillery, mortars, and tanks, or placing them near schools, hospitals, or religious buildings.[18] In contrast to the limited objective of using air strikes in support of humanitarian aid delivery as proposed by the Bush administration, the British military produced plans with the more ambitious aim of compelling Belgrade to stop fomenting the war.[19] Senior British officers were convinced that for airpower to be used effectively, it would have to be used in a big way, not in small doses.[20] The strategic bombing campaign envisioned by the UK focused on targets in Serbia proper, and executing it was within the capabilities of the Royal Air Force, provided certain intelligence, command and control, and electronic warfare assets were made available through NATO.[21] Though the strategic air attacks were deemed politically unacceptable, the option was at least considered.

Early USAFE Planning

Senior American Air Force officers began planning in December 1992 for an air campaign in the Balkans, and they initially modeled their plan on Gulf War air operations. Though the first plan was shelved and never implemented, it helped to initiate a continuous cycle of US planning that would coexist alongside NATO efforts to enforce the no-fly zone over Bosnia.

During the first week of December 1992, senior officers within the US Air Forces Europe (USAFE) command, based at Ramstein Air Base in Germany, began developing an air campaign plan for Bosnia. The detailed work fell to Col Bob Lushbaugh, chief of operations on the USAFE staff, who began his Air Force career by flying 200 night missions as a forward air controller over Vietnam.[22] Lushbaugh had arrived at Ramstein six months before Saddam Hussein invaded Kuwait, and during Operation Desert Storm he served as chief of staff for Joint Task Force Proven Force (Proven Force included the quasi-independent bombing missions against Iraq conducted under USAFE leadership from Incirlik Air Base in Turkey).[23] Early in December 1992, the vice commander of USAFE tasked Lushbaugh to "draft a CONOPS [Concept of Operations] for an air campaign in Bosnia like we did in Desert Storm."[24] A few days later when the USAFE commander approved Lushbaugh's concept for an air campaign, Lushbaugh was assigned to work under the direction of Maj Gen James "Bear" Chambers, commander of the US Seventeenth Air Force.[25]

Besides commanding an American numbered Air Force, Chambers also "wore a NATO hat"; that is, his position made him simultaneously responsible to both US and Allied authorities. However, at this stage planning for an air campaign in Bosnia was conducted strictly within US channels.[26] With a strong build, and a gruff, aggressive manner, Bear Chambers had a reputation within the Air Force for possessing great tactical expertise. He had begun his Air Force career as a flying instructor when Dwight Eisenhower was president, and he later served two combat tours as a fighter pilot flying missions over North Vietnam. As a two-star general, he flew fighters again in combat during Desert Storm, and he would continue to log combat flying hours over Bosnia until he retired in late 1994. During his career, Chambers amassed an astounding number of flying hours for a fighter pilot—topping 5,500 even before NATO air operations began over Bosnia.[27] Thus, the American officers who conducted the initial planning for air operations in Bosnia had learned their profession in the skies over Vietnam and had recently been involved in the Desert Storm air campaign.

Around mid-December 1992, shortly after planning began at USAFE, Lt Gen Joseph Ashy took command of Allied Air Forces Southern Europe (AIRSOUTH), making him the senior Air Force officer in NATO's southern region. Like most of the Air Force's senior leadership, Ashy was a fighter pilot who had flown in Vietnam. As a general officer, Ashy had commanded the prestigious 57th Fighter Weapons Wing, and later the Tactical Fighter Weapons Center. He was well known within the Air Force fighter community for his direct, no-nonsense, and sometimes abrupt style. Though Ashy was responsible for NATO air operations in the southern region and outranked Chambers, it would have been inappropriate for Ashy to run the US-only planning because he was not directly in the US chain of command.[28]

NATO Involvement in Bosnia

General Ashy became involved in planning air operations for the Balkans on his first day on the job, and he quickly became aware of the planning being done by USAFE. NATO foreign ministers meeting in Brussels on 17 December agreed to support a UN call to enforce the Bosnia no-fly zone, which the UN had declared in October.[29] General Ashy recalled being at the NATO officers' club at Naples just after his change of command and still greeting guests in the reception line when "I got a tap on the shoulder and [they] said, 'We really need you over at Admiral Boorda's office ASAP [as soon as possible].'"[30] Adm Jeremy M. Boorda was the American commander of NATO's southern region, or Allied Forces Southern Europe (AFSOUTH). In Admiral Boorda's office, General Ashy and the other assembled officers were informed that they "needed to do some serious planning for an air operation in the Balkans . . . specifically over Bosnia, in response to a possible UN resolution and . . . NAC [North Atlantic Council] guidance, to police a no-fly zone."[31]

Chambers and Lushbaugh flew to Naples the next morning, and they briefed their concept of operations for an air campaign to General Ashy and a small group of American planners from Boorda's command.[32] The objective of the nascent plan was "to cause the Bosnian Serbs to cease and desist, and to

61

get them to the bargaining table."[33] The plan consisted of three phases and, like its Gulf War progenitor, the first phase was designed to achieve control of the airspace over the area of operations—this served as a starting point for AFSOUTH planning of the no-fly zone.[34] However, NATO enforcement of the zone would not begin until April 1993. In the meantime, Chambers and Lushbaugh continued to work on an air campaign plan as part of a larger US joint-service effort, and they kept General Ashy informed about it.[35] By the end of January 1993, Chambers's team had completed their plan, and General Chambers briefed it in Washington; then "it got put on the shelf," never to be implemented.[36] However, General Chambers's plan was the first air plan built within the theater, and General Chambers perceived a similarity between this first plan and plans later built by General Ashy for NATO air strikes.[37]

Enforcing the No-Fly Zone

On 13 March, aircraft flying from Serbia bombed the Bosnian villages of Gladovici and Osatica.[38] The flights from Serbia were observed by UN military monitors, and the attacks were condemned by the UN Security Council.[39] On 31 March 1993 the Security Council passed Resolution 816 citing Chapter VII of the UN Charter and authorizing "all necessary measures" for enforcement of the six-month-old no-fly zone over Bosnia.[40] The ban covered "flights by all fixed-wing and rotary-wing aircraft in the airspace of the Republic of Bosnia and Herzegovina" other than those authorized by the UN.[41] Responses to violations were to be "proportionate" and "subject to close coordination with the secretary-general and UNPROFOR."[42]

Originally, General Chambers was named the joint force air component commander for US air operations in the Balkans, but the advent of the NATO no-fly zone caused Ashy's responsibilities to overlap with Chambers's.[43] Sometime around February 1993, with preparations well under way for enforcement of the ban on military flights over Bosnia, France demanded that the operation be directed by a non-British European.[44] Plans to run air operations from Aviano Air Base in Italy—a base long used by the Americans—were scuttled, because planners felt that using Aviano would tend to cut America's allies out of the operation.[45] In the end, NATO's 5th Allied Tactical Air Force (5ATAF) Headquarters at Vicenza was selected as the site from which to direct the no-fly zone enforcement, and its commander, Lt Gen Antonio Rossetti of Italy, was to head the operation.[46] Because Rossetti worked for General Ashy, the NATO chain of command in the southern region ran from Admiral Boorda, to General Ashy, to General Rossetti, to General Chambers, who quickly began directing the day-to-day operations from Vicenza's combined air operations center (CAOC).[47] This arrangement increased General Ashy's role in controlling the air operations over Bosnia; however, the command relations were a bit muddled, because General Chambers retained both his title as a US JFACC and commander of the non-NATO, US air operations in the region, such as the Provide Promise humanitarian airdrops.[48]

The way NATO commanders in the southern region dealt with helicopters violating the no-fly zone illustrated the influence of these theater-level commanders on the use of airpower. In order to maintain tight control over Operation Deny Flight, NATO authorities decided that orders to shoot down aircraft caught violating the no-fly zone could *not* be made by anyone below the CAOC director, General Chambers.[49] The no-fly zone resolution banned unauthorized flights by helicopters, as well as by fixed-wing aircraft.[50] Initially NATO had some success at curtailing helicopter flights. By intercepting the helicopters and making warning passes, NATO pilots got many of the helicopters to land during the first weeks of Deny Flight.[51] But, as General Chambers later recalled, it only worked for about the first 100 intercepts, after which the unauthorized helicopters began to heed NATO's warnings less and less, eventually flouting the no-fly zone openly.[52] Though no one below Chambers knew it at the time, he and his superiors, Ashy and Boorda, were not going to authorize the downing of helicopters over Bosnia.[53] However the mounting number of violations by helicopters soon drew criticism from above.[54] In defending the decision, Chambers later explained that if NATO did shoot down a helicopter (1) it would turn out to be the wrong helicopter; (2) it would be the right helicopter, but it would fall on the wrong spot, perhaps killing innocent people on the ground; or (3) failing (1) or (2) the downing of a helicopter would not have an appreciable effect on the military operations of the faction using the helicopter—and all sides were conducting unauthorized helicopter flights.[55] In Chambers's view, despite some high-level discontent with the helicopter violations, no one wanted to take the responsibility for overriding the commanders in the field by ordering that helicopters be shot down.[56]

"Safe Areas" and "Lift and Strike"

On Wednesday, 20 January 1993, Bill Clinton was inaugurated as the 42d president of the United States, and his National Security Council soon took up the issue of military intervention in Bosnia. Gen Colin Powell, in describing his advice to the council about using airpower in Bosnia, claimed

> I laid out the same military options that I had presented to President Bush. Our choices ranged from limited air strikes around Sarajevo to heavy bombing of the Serbs throughout the theater. I emphasized that none of these actions was guaranteed to change Serb behavior. Only troops on the ground could do that. Heavy bombing might persuade them to give in, but would not compel them to quit. And, faced with limited air strikes, the Serbs would have little difficulty hiding tanks and artillery in the woods and fog of Bosnia or keeping them close to civilian populations. Furthermore, no matter what we did, it would be easy for the Serbs to respond by seizing UN humanitarian personnel as hostages.[57]

It was during one of these early meetings that General Powell's protestations prompted Madeleine Albright, then ambassador to the UN, to ask her now famous question: "What's the point of having this superb military that you're always talking about if we can't use it?"[58] The Joint Chiefs of Staff chairman replied by explaining the need for a clear political objective, much as he had argued months earlier in print.[59] The national security advisor, Tony Lake, who had served on the National Security Council staff as a young man during the Vietnam War, sided with General Powell, saying: "You know Madeleine . . . the kinds of questions Colin is asking about goals are exactly the ones the military never asked during Vietnam."[60] By 10 February, the new administration had completed a policy review, and it soon became clear that American military intervention was not in the offing.[61]

However, by the beginning of May 1993 the situation in Bosnia had worsened, and the Clinton administration settled on the "lift and strike" policy that it pursued over the next two and one-half years. Lift and strike referred to lifting the arms embargo on the Bosnian government, and conducting air strikes against Serb military targets. The US ambassador to the UN, Madeleine Albright, advocated unilateral US action "under existing United Nations authority."[62] But President Clinton decided he was not ready to act without allied participation.[63] Under intense media and public pressure to "do something" in Bosnia, both London and Paris expressed a willingness to consider using airpower in Bosnia.[64] However, France and Britain remained firmly opposed to any lifting of the arms embargo because they feared such action would lead to increased fighting in Bosnia, which, in turn, would jeopardize the safety of French and British peacekeeping forces in Bosnia as part of the UN Protection Force.[65] Neither Britain nor the United States was willing to send troops to intervene in the ground fighting, and France would not take tougher measures on the ground in Bosnia without the other two countries.[66] Unless something were done to affect the balance of power on the ground, there seemed little point in conducting air strikes.[67] When US Secretary of State Warren Christopher toured European capitals in early May, he failed to win support for the administration's lift and strike policy. Throughout the month of May, NATO nations continued to mull over the idea of using military force, especially airpower, either to implement the moribund Vance-Owen peace plan or to help protect the six newly created "safe areas."[68]

On 6 May 1993, just after the Bosnian Serb Parliament rejected the Vance-Owen peace plan, the UN Security Council passed Resolution 824 declaring Bihac, Sarajevo, Tuzla, Zepa, and Gorazde safe areas.[69] Altogether there were six safe areas, because Srebrenica had been made a safe area in April, but they were not *safe havens*—a label which, under international law, would have implied far greater responsibilities for the UN in seeing that they were indeed safe.[70] Significantly, Resolution 824 invoked Chapter VII of the UN Charter, and in paragraph 4 of the resolution, the council called for

> the immediate cessation of armed attacks or any hostile act against these safe areas, and the withdrawal of all *Bosnian Serb* military or paramilitary units from the towns to a distance where from they cease to constitute a menace to their security and that of their inhabitants. (Emphasis added)[71]

Hopes for the Vance-Owen plan dwindled, and in early June the Security Council tried to make the safe areas safe, by giving UNPROFOR a tougher mandate and by supporting the force with NATO airpower.[72]

Conclusion

The Gulf War had a big impact on the debates over whether to use airpower in Bosnia. By the time the Gulf War ended in March 1991, high-technology airpower had acquired an image as a near antiseptic instrument capable of destroying without killing, and winning without risking. Most military professionals in the United States, United Kingdom, and France recognized the limitations as well as the capabilities of airpower, and they knew that expectations were running ahead of capabilities. Informed commentators tended to highlight airpower's limitations and the challenges of using it in Bosnia, but public debates on the issue were often ill informed.[73] Furthermore, the well-known difficulty of measuring the effectiveness of airpower only served to confound efforts, even by informed observers, to separate the enduring and general lessons of the Gulf War from observations applicable only to fighting an inept dictator in a desert environment. A less obvious, though not surprising, consequence of the Gulf War was that it created a cadre of airmen—especially in America—who were confident in airpower's abilities and schooled in its application.

By May of 1993, the American and British policies for using airpower in Bosnia had been set and would change little until 1995. Consistent with the findings of Betts and Petraeus, the US military had relatively little influence in shaping that policy. Despite Powell's protestations, the Clinton administration adopted a policy of "lift and strike." The weak commitment to this policy owed less to military reluctance to get involved in Bosnia than to internal divisions within the administration, objections from America's European allies, and the president's tendency to focus on domestic programs, such as nationalized health care.[74] The British and French governments preferred to dampen the effects of the war through the presence of lightly armed, impartial UN peacekeepers, who were obviously vulnerable to retaliation should the Serbs respond thus to being attacked from the air. Over the next two years, the ebb and flow of the war in Bosnia, and the consequent media attention on human rights violations, generated undulating pressure behind US ambitions for launching air attacks against the Serbs. British and French resistance to air strikes rose and fell as necessary to head off such US action, but the policies in Washington, London, and Paris hardly changed.[75] With policies set, the influence of senior military officers in America, the United Kingdom, and France diminished, and the influence of theater-level commanders serving in NATO and the UN gradually increased.

Notes

1. Lawrence Freedman, "The Future of Air Power," *Hawk Journal* (The Independent Journal of the Royal Air Force Staff College, 1993), 44; and Air Vice-Marshal Tony Mason, *Air Power: A Centennial Appraisal* (London: Brassey's, 1994), 137–97.

2. Edward N. Luttwak, "Toward Post-Heroic Warfare," *Foreign Affairs* 74, no. 3 (May–June 1995): 109–22; Les Aspin, "The Use and Usefulness of Military Forces in the Post-Cold War, Post-Soviet World," address to the Jewish Institute for National Security Affairs, Washington, D.C., 21 September 1992; and David Owen, *Balkan Odyssey* (London: Victor Gallancz, 1995; Indigo, 1996), 15–16.

3. In addition to the evidence given below, see the testimony by Gen John Shalikashvili, then Supreme Allied Commander Europe: Senate, *Department of Defense Authorization for Appropriations 1994*, 1, 20, 21, and 22 April; 19 May; 17 and 23 June 1993, 222–53.

4. James A. Baker III and Thomas M. DeFrank, *The Politics of Diplomacy: Revolution, War and Peace, 1989–1992* (New York: G. P. Putnam's Sons, 1995), 648.

5. Ibid., 648–49.

6. Ibid., 649.

7. Ibid., 649–50.

8. Mason, 169.

9. Lord David Owen, 27; and Pia Christina Wood, "France and the Post-Cold War Order: The Case of Yugoslavia," *European Security* 3, no. 1 (spring 1994): 142.

10. Philippe Guillot, "France, Peacekeeping and Humanitarian Intervention," *International Peacekeeping* 1, no. 1 (spring 1994): 38.

11. William T. Johnsen and Thomas-Durell Young, "France's Evolving Policy Toward NATO," *Strategic Review* 23, no. 3 (summer 1995): 18.

12. Gen Vincent Lanata, chief of staff of the French air force, interviewed by author, 8 September 1998, Paris, and tape recording, author's personal collection.

13. Lanata interview; Gen Jean Cot, interviewed by author, 30 September 1998, Paris, transcription and translation of tape recording, author's personal collection; Lt Gen François Régnault, French air force, chief of Employment of Forces Division of the Joint Services Headquarters, 1 October 1992–1 October 1993, interviewed by author, 9 September 1998, Paris, tape recording, author's personal collection; and Oliver Lepick, "French Perspective," in *International Perspectives on the Yugoslav Conflict*, eds. Alex Danchev and Thomas Halverson (London: Macmillan, 1996), 80–81.

14. Cot interview; Lanata interview; Régnault interview. The French government provided peacekeepers for operations in former Yugoslavia from March 1992, when the UN Protection Force mission began. A battalion of British peacekeepers were first sent to Bosnia in October 1992.

15. Wood, 143.

16. Lepick, 81–82.

17. MOD Officials B and D. MOD stands for the British Ministry of Defence.

18. MOD Officials B and E. Also see congressional testimony by the USAF chief of staff Gen Merrill M. McPeak warning of these problems: Senate, *Department of Defense Appropriations for Fiscal Year 1994, Part 1*, 20–22, 28, and 29 April 1993, 213–14.

19. MOD Official G.

20. Ibid., and MOD Official D.

21. MOD Official G.

22. Col Robert Lushbaugh, USAF, retired, interviewed by author, Langley Air Force Base (AFB), Va., 9 July 1998, author's notes, author's personal collection.

23. Ibid.

24. Ibid.

25. Ibid.; and Lt Gen James E. Chambers, USAF, retired, interviewed by author, Fairfax, Va., 10 February 1998, author's notes, author's personal collection.

26. Chambers interview.

27. Ibid.

28. Gen Joseph W. Ashy was deputy commander in chief of USAFE for the Southern Region. That was a titular position without much real author-

ity. Gen Joseph W. Ashy, USAF, interviewed by Lt Col Rob Owen, 29 April 1996, unclassified version redacted by the Air Force Historical Research Agency for the Director of History at Air Force Space Command, October 1997, Peterson AFB, Colo.

29. United Nations Security Council Resolution (UNSCR) 781, 9 October 1992; and *Facts On File Yearbook 1992* (USA: Facts on File, Inc., 1993), 761 and 988.

30. Ashy interview.

31. Ibid.

32. Lushbaugh interview.

33. Chambers interview.

34. Ibid.

35. Lushbaugh interview; and Gen Joseph W. Ashy, USAF, interviewed by author, Fairfax, Va., 3 July 1998, author's notes, author's personal collection.

36. Chambers interview; Lushbaugh interview; and Ashy interview by author.

37. Chambers interview.

38. Daniel Bethlehem and Marc Weller, eds., "The Yugoslav Crisis in International Law," *General Issues* Part 1, Cambridge International Documents Series, vol. 5 (Cambridge, Mass.: Cambridge University Press, 1997), 45; and Jan Willem Honig and Norbert Both, *Srebrenica: Record of a War Crime* (London: Penguin Books, 1996), 89.

39. Honig and Both, 89; and Bethlehem and Weller, 32 and 45.

40. UNSCR 816, 31 March 1993, par. 4.

41. Ibid.

42. Ibid.

43. Dr. Thomas S. Snyder and Dr. Daniel F. Harrington, USAFE Office of History, *USAFE Historical Highlights, 1942–1997: Fifty-fifth Anniversary Edition* (Ramstein Air Base, Germany: Headquarters USAFE, 1997), 159.

44. Lushbaugh interview.

45. Chambers interview.

46. Lushbaugh interview; and Ashy, interview by Colonel Owen. Note: General Rossetti took over command of 5ATAF on 7 April 1993, replacing Lt Gen Giuseppe Degli Innocenti.

47. Ashy interview by Colonel Owen; Chambers interview; and Lushbaugh interview.

48. Ashy interview by Colonel Owen; Chambers interview; and Lushbaugh interview. Under Operation Provide Promise, the US began air-dropping food in Bosnia in March 1993, shortly after the Clinton administration took office.

49. Col Robert Owen, *Deliberate Force: A Case Study in Effective Air Campaigning* (Maxwell AFB, Ala.: Air University Press, 2000), 381.

50. North Atlantic Treaty Organization Airborne Early Warning Force, *Operation Deny Flight: A History* (U), February 1997, n.p., 17-page unit history, History Office, NATO CAOC, Vicenza, Italy, 9.

51. Chambers interview.

52. Ibid.; and Lt Col Lowell R. Boyd Jr., USAF, AFSOUTH staff officer, Naples, Italy, April 1993–December 1995, interviewed by Lt Col Rob Owen, 6 December 1995, Naples, Italy, transcript of taped interview, Balkans Air Campaign Study (BACS) Collection, Air Force Historical Research Agency, Maxwell AFB, Ala. Colonel Boyd recalled the issue of intercepting helicopters coming to a head and being resolved in the first two weeks of Deny Flight operations.

53. Chambers interview; Ashy interview by author; and Lowell Boyd interview.

54. Chambers interview.

55. Ibid.

56. Ibid. The wisdom of AFSOUTH's policy on helicopters was validated a year later when USAF F-15s accidentally downed two US Army Blackhawk helicopters in the no-fly zone over northern Iraq, killing 26 people.

57. Colin Powell with Joseph E. Persico, *My American Journey* (New York: Random House, 1995), 576.

58. Ibid.

59. Ibid., 576–77; Colin Powell, "Why Generals Get Nervous," *New York Times,* 8 October 1992, A35; and Colin Powell, "US Forces: Challenges Ahead," *Foreign Affairs* 72, no. 5, (winter 1992–1993): 32–45.

60. Powell, *My American Journey,* 577.

61. Susan L. Woodward, *Balkan Tragedy: Chaos and Dissolution after the Cold War* (Washington, D.C.: Brookings Institution, 1995), 306; and Owen, *Balkan Odyssey,* 123.

62. Michael R. Gordon, "12 In State Department Ask Military Move Against Serbs," *New York Times,* 23 April 1993, sec. A1 and A12.

63. Gwen Ifill, "Clinton Considers Bosnia Air Strikes; Sees Allied Accord," *New York Times,* 24 April 1993, sec. A1 and A6.

64. Ifill; and Robert Morgan, "Hurd Warns of Dangers in Air Strikes Against Serbs," *Times* (London), 20 April 1993, 8.

65. James Gow, "British Perspectives," in *International Perspectives on the Yugoslav Conflict,* eds. Alex Danchev and Thomas Halverson (London: Macmillan, 1996), 95; and Oliver Lepik, "French Perspective," in *International Perspectives on the Yugoslav Conflict,* eds. Alex Danchev and Thomas Halverson (London: Macmillan, 1996), 83.

66. Peter Riddell and Martin Ivens, "Hurd Presses on for Quicker Response to Global Ills," *Times* (London), 21 April 1993, 9; and Thomas Halverson, "American Perspective," in *International Perspectives on the Yugoslav Conflict,* eds. Alex Danchev and Thomas Halverson (London: Macmillan, 1996), 13.

67. Michael Evans, "West Weighs Risks and Rewards of Air Strikes," *Times* (London), 29 April 1993, 12; Elaine Sciolino, "US Military Split on Using Air Power Against the Serbs," *New York Times,* 29 April 1993, A1 and A6; and Michael Gordon, "NATO General Is Reticent About Air Strikes in Bosnia," *New York Times,* 23 April 1993, A1 and A12.

68. Edward Mortimer, "Twin Track to Bosnia Peace: Air Attacks and Military Aid Are Complimentary, Not Alternatives," *Financial Times* (London), 12 May 1993, 18; David White, "NATO Backs Vance-Owen," *Financial Times* (London), 26 May 1993, 3; and David White, "NATO Wavers on Bosnia," *Financial Times* (London), 27 May 1993, 3. Former US secretary of state Cyrus Vance and former British foreign secretary Lord David Owen had crafted a peace plan under the auspices of the International Conference on the Former Yugoslavia (ICFY). ICFY was a joint UN-EU effort. Vance was the representative of the UN Secretary General, and Owen was the European Community (later the European Union) representative. Vance and Owen began to work together in September 1992, and their proposed peace deal became known as the Vance-Owen Peace Plan.

69. UNSCR 824, 6 May 1993.

70. Laura Silber and Allan Little, *Yugoslavia: Death of a Nation* (n.p.: TV Books, Inc., 1996), 274; Honig and Both, 104; Dick A. Leurdijk, *The United Nations and NATO in Former Yugoslavia, 1991–1996: Limits to Diplomacy and Force* (The Hague: The Netherlands Atlantic Commission, 1996), 33–34.

71. UNSCR 824, par. 4.

72. UNSCR 836, 4 June 1993.

73. Mason, *Air Power,* 168.

74. James A. Gow, *Triumph of the Lack of Will: International Diplomacy and the Yugoslav War* (New York: Columbia University Press, 1997), 213.

75. The French policy seemed to migrate slightly toward that of the US in February 1994 when the French proposed a heavy weapons exclusion zone around Sarajevo, a measure long sought by the Bosnian Muslims, and one that would be enforced through air strikes. In August and September, when limited air strikes took place, they were in the vicinity of Sarajevo, for which the French were primarily responsible. However, it was French opposition in the UN and NATO which first limited, then blocked, more robust air strikes in November 1994. British opposition to air strikes was much more uniform and resolute, at least until 1995.

Chapter 4

NATO Air Support and Air Strikes: May–December 1993

The politicians had a great deal of difficulty understanding the problems faced by the military in operations.

—Gen Francis Briquemont
Do Something, General!

During the second half of 1993, UNPROFOR's commanders could not strike an acceptable balance between mission accomplishment and force protection. In part, their difficulties lay in the muddle of conflicting political guidelines governing UNPROFOR's mission and the failure or inability of UN political authorities to provide their commanders with clear, prioritized aims. In part, UNPROFOR's problem lay in its lack of ground forces needed to fully accomplish the enforcement elements of its mission. This shortage of means was exacerbated by three factors. First, UN and EC political authorities repeatedly pressed the commanders to take risks for which the commanders felt they alone would be held accountable should things go wrong. Second, UN political authorities refused, or were unable, to give their commanders control over the airpower, which was supposed to make up for the shortfall in UN ground forces. Third, American Air Force generals in NATO's southern region were pressing UNPROFOR's top commanders to support air strikes that would have endangered UN forces and wrecked UNPROFOR's prospects for fulfilling the humanitarian elements of the UN mission. Deprived of a clear objective and lacking the means and authority to accomplish the tasks thrust upon them, the UNPROFOR commanders had nothing against which to balance the weight of responsibility for protecting their forces.

In contrast to their UN counterparts, solving the conundrum over using airpower in Bosnia was less of a challenge for NATO's commanders. Because General Ashy had been working on air campaign plans since December 1992, he and Admiral Boorda were able to quickly meet the needs of NATO political authorities during the crisis in August at Mount Igman near Sarajevo. The political-military tension that might have resulted from the struggle to control such a campaign remained in the background because no bombs were dropped. The AFSOUTH commanders also smoothly discharged their responsibilities for supporting UNPROFOR with close air support but, again, with no bombs dropped and with self-restraint from the Serb air defenses, the AFSOUTH commanders were not subjected to the same challenges that actual operations would have imposed.

UNSCR 836: "Safe Areas" and Airpower—Expanding the UNPROFOR Mandate and the Role of NATO: May–July 1993

On 4 June 1993, after the Bosnian Serbs had repeatedly rejected the Vance-Owen Peace Plan, the UN Security Council resolved, in Resolution 836, to protect the populations in the safe areas by expanding UNPROFOR's mandate and by allowing UN member states to use airpower to support UNPROFOR. However, Resolution 836 was not a political compromise between governments for and against using airpower in Bosnia; it was in fact a failure to compromise, which shifted the focus of the airpower debate from the political arena to the military. It embodied contradictions and vague language that reflected the divisions between Security Council members—not least those who had sponsored it: France, Russia, the United States, the United Kingdom, and Spain.[1] One of the Security Council's leading proponents of safe areas in Bosnia, Amb. Diego Arria of Venezuela, felt compelled to abstain from voting for 836, which he described as a charade cloaking inaction.[2] He reproached the council for failing to address fundamental questions, such as: "What would be the United Nations's responsibility if the aggressors were to accept the establishment of safe areas but later refused to withdraw from their surroundings? Would the United Nations then be obliged to use force in order to make them withdraw? Would the

Security Council be prepared to authorize military action in order to meet this objective?"[3] In the weeks following the passage of Resolution 836, comments by the UN representatives from the US and the UK would make clear that nothing had changed in their nations' stances toward the use of airpower in Bosnia.[4] Indeed, immediately after the vote on 836, Madeleine Albright told the council, "The United States voted for this resolution with no illusions. It is an intermediate step—no more, no less."[5] And, in an allusion to the Clinton administration's lift and strike policy, she added that the Security Council had agreed to "keep open options for new and tougher measures. . . . My government's view of what those tougher measures should be has not changed."[6]

Resolution 836 represented a wobbly step toward peace enforcement. Adopted under Chapter VII of the UN Charter, it was designed "to ensure full respect for the safe areas referred to in Resolution 824."[7] Until that time UNPROFOR had only been mandated to use force to guarantee the delivery of humanitarian aid in Bosnia.[8] In paragraph 5 of Resolution 836, the Security Council charged UNPROFOR with four tasks which, depending on interpretation, might have required UNPROFOR to use force other than in self-defense. They were (1) "deter attacks against safe areas"; (2) "promote the withdrawal of military or paramilitary units *other than those of the Government of the Republic of Bosnia and Herzegovina;*" (3) "occupy some key points on the ground"; and (4) participate "in the delivery of humanitarian relief" (emphasis added).[9] The first three of these four tasks were new.[10] To discharge these new responsibilities, the resolution authorized UNPROFOR to use force, and it allowed UN member states to use airpower in support of UNPROFOR.[11] But these authorizations were half-hearted and unclear.

In long, convoluted sentences, Resolution 836 spun a web of connections and conditions that would confound those military officers whose duty it would be to implement it. While the Security Council clearly decided to vest UNPROFOR with added responsibility for protecting the safe areas, it simultaneously— though less clearly—made it difficult for the force to fulfill that responsibility. In paragraph 9, the resolution authorized

UNPROFOR "to take the necessary measures, including the use of force, in reply to bombardments against the safe areas . . . or to armed incursion into them or in the event of any deliberate obstruction in or around those areas to the freedom of movement of the Force or of protected humanitarian convoys."[12] This authorization circumscribed the range of possible interpretations open to UNPROFOR and, for example, precluded its commanders from *proactively* using force against the Bosnian Serbs as a means to fulfill the task to "promote the withdrawal of military or paramilitary units" from around the safe areas. More importantly, at the insistence of the British, French, and Spanish,[13] the debilitating clause "acting in self-defence" appeared just before the authorization to use force,[14] and rendered the new authorization meaningless, because UNPROFOR had always had the right to use force in self-defense.[15] Permission to use force in self-defense was not something the Security Council needed to grant to UNPROFOR, nor could the council properly proscribe it.[16] Indeed, the clause *acting in self-defence* could have been seen as a step backwards from the authority UNPROFOR already possessed because, from its inception, the force in Bosnia had been allowed to use "all necessary measures" to assist in the delivery of humanitarian aid.[17] Thus, while paragraph 9 ostensibly added to UNPROFOR's authority to use force in Bosnia, it also contained a clause undermining that same authority.

Paragraph 10 of Resolution 836 added airpower to the mix, but in a way that was open to conflicting interpretations.[18] It stated that "Member-states, acting nationally or through regional organizations may take . . . all necessary measures, through the use of air power . . . to support the force in the performance of its mandate."[19] Airpower had not been specifically included or excluded in the paragraph authorizing UNPROFOR to use force (para. 9), and UNPROFOR had no airpower of its own. This seemed to imply a division of labor whereby UNPROFOR was only authorized to use force "acting in self-defence," but NATO—or indeed any individual UN member state acting alone or in cooperation with others—could potentially use airpower to pursue options barred to UNPROFOR. The freedom to use airpower was, however, constrained in two ways. First, any use of airpower had to be "subject to close coordination with the secretary-general and the Force."[20] And second, the use of airpower was meant to support UNPROFOR "in the performance of its mandate set out in paragraphs 5 and 9 above."[21] By requiring close coordination with the UN and linking the use of airpower to both UNPROFOR's expanded mandate and its convoluted authority for using force (when "acting in self-defence"), the authors of Resolution 836 left open the possibility for two very different interpretations of how airpower could be used in Bosnia. One way to interpret this constraint was to give precedence to the objective of the resolution—protecting the people in the safe areas— and to argue that airpower could be used *proactively* for air strikes in order to execute the tasks spelled out in paragraph 5, which UNPROFOR was proscribed from accomplishing by paragraph 9 (e.g., bombing the Bosnian Serb forces in order "to promote the withdrawal of military or paramilitary units" from around the safe areas). In addition, this first interpretation would permit airpower to be used in support of UNPROFOR forces when they lacked adequate means for self-defense. Alternatively, another interpretation—which appealed to those objecting to the widespread use of airpower—was to say that paragraph 9 of Resolution 836 clarified UNPROFOR's status as a peacekeeping force by limiting it to the use of force only when "acting in self-defence."[22] Since airpower was intended to support UNPROFOR, it could only be used legitimately for air support. Rather than resolving conflicting agendas through compromise, Resolution 836 merely served as a vehicle for transferring the struggle to a new stage—a stage where theater commanders in UNPROFOR and AFSOUTH would play important roles.

UNSCR 844: Implementing an Ambiguous Policy

The ambiguity over airpower continued as the Security Council took steps to implement its safe areas policy. On 14 June, Boutros Boutros-Ghali submitted a report advising the Security Council on the implementation of Resolution 836 in which he noted, "NATO confirmed its willingness to offer 'protective air power in case of attack against UNPROFOR'"[23]

Most of the references to airpower in the report dealt with close air support for UNPROFOR, not air strikes. However, several remarks alluded to the possibility for broader air action. These included "emphasis must be placed on a credible air strike capability" to help UNPROFOR "resist a concentrated assault on any of the safe areas."[24] Despite an assessment by UNPROFOR's commander, Lt Gen Lars Eric Wahlgren, that some 34,000 troops would be needed to implement the safe areas policy, Boutros-Ghali justified recommending a "light option" of only 7,600 reinforcements because "while this option cannot, in itself, completely guarantee the defence of the safe areas, it relies on the threat of air action against any belligerent."[25] On 18 June 1993, the Security Council passed Resolution 844, approving Boutros-Ghali's report, authorizing 7,600 reinforcements for UNPROFOR and reaffirming "its decision in paragraph 10 of Resolution 836 (1993) on the use of airpower in and around the safe areas to support the force in the performance of its mandate."[26] In brief speeches to the Security Council made immediately after passing Resolution 844, the representatives from the US, France, Russia, and the UK emphasized their own national spins on implementing the safe areas policy.[27] Nothing had changed. Much was being left to the interpretations of those who would have to implement these resolutions.

According to Michael Williams, a former director of information and senior UNPROFOR spokesman who has written about the UN's troubled political-military relations, Generals Wahlgren and Morillon "had little idea how to proceed" with the implementation of the safe areas resolutions.[28] Honig and Both have shown that on 5 June, the day before the Security Council authorized enforcement of the safe areas, General Wahlgren prophetically warned UN political authorities in New York, "If one allowed no controls of the military or paramilitary units of the Bosnian government, one would create a scenario which would encourage the use of the safe areas as havens, where forces could refit, rearm, train and prepare for further military operations."[29] Moreover, after 836 was issued, General Wahlgren worried that the safe areas concept jeopardized the impartiality of his forces in Bosnia, who were supposed to enforce its one-sided restrictions.[30] General Morillon's memoir refers to the safe areas only obliquely.[31] However, he seems to have favored using airpower when necessary to ensure the success of UNPROFOR's mission.[32] Though Wahlgren wrote to the UN's undersecretary-general for peacekeeping, Kofi Annan, proclaiming the importance of airpower in compensating for the inadequate number of ground reinforcements,[33] the force commander's successor believed Wahlgren was fundamentally opposed to the more forceful bent of his new mandate and, in consequence, wanted nothing to do with NATO airpower.[34] In any event, Generals Wahlgren and Morillon left their UN posts just a few weeks after Resolution 844 was passed and before NATO made aircraft available for air support. Thus, it fell to their successors to sort out what to do about airpower and to try to extract a coherent mission from the tangled verbiage of Resolutions 836 and 844.

New Leadership for UNPROFOR

Weaknesses in the UNPROFOR chain of command were complicated, not rectified, by changes made in May of 1993. At the beginning of May, former Norwegian foreign minister Thorvald Stoltenberg took over from Cyrus Vance as the UN co-chairman to the peace conference in Geneva.[35] Unlike Vance, however, Stoltenberg was designated the UN Secretary-General's special representative for the former Yugoslavia, thus making Stoltenberg the civilian head of UNPROFOR.[36] To assist him in the discharge of his military responsibilities, Stoltenberg recruited his fellow countryman Gen Vigliek Eide, who had recently retired from NATO's most senior military post—chairman of the military committee in Brussels.[37] By August, General Eide was based in Zagreb, heading a team of three officers who were to act as the liaison between Stoltenberg and the commander of UNPROFOR.[38] Also in early May, around the time of Warren Christopher's trip to sell the Clinton administration's lift and strike policy, Boutros-Ghali received support from Paris in insisting that the UN, rather than NATO, should oversee the implementation of any peace plan in the Balkans.[39] However, in early May, the French government also agreed to a chain of command for implementing a Yugoslav peace plan, which put NATO's Admiral Boorda at the top, a French general as second in command, and the general commanding NATO's Allied Rapid Reaction Corps in charge of operations in Bosnia.[40] Though the Vance-Owen Peace Plan—for which this chain of command was originally intended—was never implemented, the French government secured the top UNPROFOR billet in Zagreb for Gen Jean Cot, the man designated as Boorda's number two for implementing the peace plan.[41] Whether the UN or NATO led the effort in the former Yugoslavia, General Cot was poised to play a central role. Had the UN and NATO worked together to implement a peace plan, this might not have been a bad arrangement. But adding a layer of civilian authority that was geographically separated from the UN military commanders (Stoltenberg was based in Geneva) only complicated matters for the UNPROFOR generals as they later tried to interpret their mission.

Two months after Stoltenberg was installed, the UN replaced the top two commanders in UNPROFOR with senior infantry generals whose backgrounds and experiences suggested they would be likely to hold the traditional army view of airpower. On 1 July 1993, General Cot, the only four-star general to command UNPROFOR, replaced General Wahlgren—the latter having lasted just four months in his UN post. Cot, at 59 years of age, had spent nearly 40 years of his life in uniform and was one of the most senior generals in the French army.[42] In April 1990, General Cot was promoted to four-star general and named commander of the French 1st Army. He had been in his post for more than a year by the summer of 1991 when he was tasked to lead secret Western European Union (WEU) planning for possible military intervention in Yugoslavia.[43] After being designated as the ground commander under Admiral Boorda for implementing the Vance-Owen plan, Cot traveled to Naples at least twice to discuss implementation planning before taking up command of UNPROFOR; during these visits he was briefed on the US-authored air campaign plan, and he was not impressed.[44]

Though France contributed the largest number of troops to UNPROFOR, it could not expect to retain the two leading command billets, so General Morillon had to give up his post in Sarajevo.[45] In late June, General Morillon learned that an old friend, Lt Gen Francis Briquemont of Belgium, would replace him.[46] General Briquemont was a 58-year-old infantry officer who had recently received his third star and was about to take command of the 1st Belgian Corps headquartered in Cologne, Germany, when another of his French colleagues, General Cot, phoned and invited him to come to work in the former Yugoslavia.[47] Briquemont was at the zenith of his career in the Belgian army and had already commanded at the brigade and division levels in units earmarked for NATO.[48] Before going to Bosnia, he had not been privy to details of the US-built air campaign plan. On Monday, 12 July 1993, General Cot presided over the change of command in Sarajevo between Generals Morillon and Briquemont. The French generals then departed for Zagreb, leaving Briquemont in Sarajevo with his new and ill-defined responsibilities.[49] The two francophone army generals at the top of UNPROFOR had not participated in the Gulf War, and their familiarity with airpower was limited mainly to close air support. Nor were they experienced at peacekeeping or peace support operations. Yet both now held command in organizations virtually devoid of airpower expertise,[50] and they would soon find themselves caught up in negotiations with the Bosnian Serbs whilst outsiders attempted to bring pressure to bear on the Serbs by threatening air strikes. It was the perfect setup for the traditional soldier-airman split over how to use airpower, reinforcing the political tensions between France and Britain on one hand and the US on the other.

NATO Air-to-Ground Missions: June–August 1993

The need for air support to compensate for UNPROFOR's inadequate ground forces led the UN's new commanders to avail themselves of NATO's airpower expertise and resources; however, from the outset, Cot and Briquemont were highly skeptical of the utility of NATO air strikes. NATO agreed to provide unspecified air support to UNPROFOR on 10 June, and Admiral Boorda tasked planners at the CAOC to develop a concept of operations for adding close air support to Operation Deny Flight.[51] Under the direction of Colonel Lushbaugh, the CAOC staff quickly produced this concept of operations, and General Chambers and Admiral Boorda took it to Zagreb for UN coordination.[52] However, while NATO forged ahead with plans to implement close air support procedures under Change-1 to its Deny Flight plan, OPLAN 40101,[53] UNPROFOR did nothing to capitalize on its access to NATO airpower prior to General Cot's arrival in July.[54] When he showed up in Zagreb, General Cot's official link to NATO air operations was through a NATO lieutenant colonel who had been dispatched to Zagreb to help coordinate activities for the no-fly zone.[55] Cot quickly made arrangements to have a French-speaking general officer from the UK's Royal Air Force who had experience in air-to-ground operations assigned to his headquarters to head up a NATO liaison team.[56]

Adding air support to the mission in Bosnia also led NATO political authorities to give some clear guidance to the military on how to interpret the Security Council resolutions. Though NATO had agreed in general terms to provide air support in June, it was not until mid-July that the North Atlantic Council (NAC), NATO's highest political deliberative body, specifically offered the UN secretary-general aircraft for the new mission.[57] NATO ambassadors decided to limit the use of air support to the protection of UNPROFOR; it was not to be used for the wider mission of protecting the safe areas.[58] Furthermore, although the two resolutions authorizing airpower (836 and 844) stated that it could be used "in and around the safe areas," NATO ambassadors decided close air support would be made available to UNPROFOR throughout Bosnia.[59] These two NATO interpretations of the Security Council resolutions reflected the French, but more so the British, desires to both avoid escalation and to protect their troops in Bosnia. Unlike the French, who were deployed mainly in and around the safe areas of Bihac and Sarajevo, British soldiers were spread out across central Bosnia, where there were no safe areas.[60] Furthermore, a Bosnian Serb commander had already threatened the British that if NATO jets attacked the Serbs, then the Serbs would target British troops.[61] Through their interpretations, NATO's political authorities were reducing the chances of Serb reprisals.[62] These NATO interpretations were driven as much by objections, or negative objectives—avoiding escalation and friendly casualties—as by the positive aim of assisting in the delivery of humanitarian aid; though, in this case the positive and negative objectives complemented each other well.[63]

In August 1993, Bosnian Serb Army (BSA) pressure on Sarajevo led NATO to threaten the Bosnian Serbs with air strikes. Because American commanders in NATO had been planning for air strikes already, they were able to move NATO policy toward the sort of forceful use of airpower preferred by the US government. However, NATO political authorities established procedures for controlling the amount of force used and the rules for initiating air strikes. The potential for friction between the American theater-level commanders, who favored robust air action, and NATO political authorities, who wished to restrain airpower, did not materialize in 1993 because air strikes were blocked by UN commanders, particularly General Briquemont. However, tensions quickly peaked at the military level, where the vulnerability of UNPROFOR ground forces helped to push the UN commanders even further toward those political authorities who were opposed to air strikes.

Increasing Bosnian Serb pressure on Sarajevo during June and July of 1993 led the US government to push its allies for air strikes against the Serbs. The assault on Sarajevo began with increased shelling at the end of May, and by late July, BSA units were systematically taking government territory around the Bosnian capital.[64] By early August, the Serbs took Mount Bjelasnica south of Sarajevo and were threatening to capture nearby Mount Igman, creating a crisis for the international community.[65] If left unchecked, Serb forces encircling Sarajevo looked set to take control of all land routes into and out of the city.[66] As General Briquemont attempted to negotiate a cease-fire with the Bosnian Serbs, the US government pressed its allies to accept a broad interpretation of Resolution 836 by endorsing air strikes to relieve the strangulation of Sarajevo.[67] The American government even suggested it was ready to act alone, according to Dick Leurdijk.[68] Some of

America's allies remained opposed to air strikes due to concerns for their soldiers in Bosnia;[69] however, following 10 hours of debate on 2 August, the alliance issued the following warning:

> The Alliance has now decided to make immediate preparations for undertaking, in the event that the strangulation of Sarajevo and other areas continues, including wide-scale interference with humanitarian assistance, stronger measures including air strikes against those responsible, Bosnian Serbs and others, in Bosnia-Herzegovina.[70]

NATO air forces could mount these air strikes quickly because of earlier US planning and because air strikes did not require the complex system for air-ground coordination like the one needed for close air support.

Commanders in AFSOUTH quickly responded to calls from Brussels for a plan of action. The mission statement from the NATO Council to its military authorities directed them "to assist with the relief of the siege of Sarajevo and, if directed, help relieve sieges of other safe areas in Bosnia-Herzegovina," and in addition "when authorized conduct expanded air strikes elsewhere in B-H."[71] Working from the planning materials that had been accumulated and refined since General Chambers first built his air campaign plan at the start of the year, General Ashy and a few members of his staff in Naples quickly put together a list of targets for a robust set of air strikes aimed at crippling the BSA.[72] Admiral Boorda liked the plan, and a colonel from General Ashy's staff was dispatched to Belgium to brief the air strike plan to Gen John Shalikashvili, the Supreme Allied Commander, Europe (SACEUR).[73] General Shalikashvili accepted the plan, so that within just a few days of the order from Brussels to get ready for air strikes, AFSOUTH had a plan it could execute.

To ensure flexibility and control over air strikes, NATO ambassadors ordered their military authorities to consult with UNPROFOR and then to report back with some options.[74] In response to this tasking, staff officers in Brussels and at SHAPE produced a memorandum titled "Operational Options for Air Strikes."[75] A slim document of about 10 pages, "Operational Options" spelled out, in broad terms, how air strikes were to be authorized.[76] Among other things, the memorandum directed

NATO military authorities to prioritize and group together proposed targets by target type and by location in order to facilitate political oversight and decisions.[77] On 9 August NATO ambassadors approved the "Operational Options" memo, but the alliance softened the tone of its threat to use air strikes,[78] noting,

> Air strikes foreseen by the Council decisions of August 2 are limited to the support of humanitarian relief, and must not be interpreted as a decision to intervene militarily in the conflict. . . . [Furthermore], NATO's actions take place under the authority of the United Nations Security Council, within the framework of the relevant UNSC resolutions, including the UN Security Council Resolutions 770, 776, and 836, and in support of UNPROFOR as it carries out its overall mandate.[79]

The NAC also agreed "with the position of the UN Secretary-General that the first use of air power in the theatre shall be authorized by him," and the council reserved for itself the political authority within NATO to launch air strikes, rather than delegating that authority to the NATO secretary-general.[80] In this way, France and the UK could counter any unwanted pressure from the US to initiate air strikes, either indirectly (as permanent members of the UN Security Council), by pressuring Boutros Boutros-Ghali, or directly, by blocking the NAC authorization.[81]

Despite NATO's tight political controls over air strikes and the limited nature of its stated aims for conducting them, the air strike options approved by the NATO council allowed for militarily significant attacks in graduated steps. "Operational Options for Air Strikes" envisaged an escalating application of force in three phases: an initial demonstrative response to a provocation; a slightly more robust follow-on phase; and an expanded phase of air strikes.[82] These graduated steps allowed political authorities to work their way up through the phases as necessary to increase the coercive pressure on the Bosnian Serbs. NATO and UN authorities—both political and military—continued to reference these options for air strikes until the end of Deny Flight. However, analyses of NATO air strikes in Bosnia have been plagued by attempts to draw more clarity about the distinctions between the three phases—or options as they came to be called—than the words of the NATO document could provide.[83] While the title of the document referred to options, the guidance on targeting contained in it spoke of phases.[84] The options stemmed from being able to choose how far to go when executing the phases. Thus, the options, or phases, originally referred to coherent groups of targets rather than a means of differentiating between individual targets for one-off attacks—an interpretation later adopted by UNPROFOR.[85]

Considering the confusion that has grown up around Option 1, 2, and 3 targets and their discussion later in this study, it is worth pausing to examine them. For each of the three phases in the "Operational Options" memo, the document's authors offered examples, "for illustrative purposes only," of the types of targets military authorities should consider grouping together when proposing strikes.[86] The initial response option, or phase I, could include any militarily significant target threatening a safe area, and a "smoking gun" (a weapon which had recently fired on UNPROFOR or a safe area) was seen as an ideal target for phase I.[87] There was, however, never a requirement to hit only smoking guns in phase I. Targets outside of Bosnia would not be hit except in phase III of a response. But, distinguishing between phases II and III targets inside Bosnia sometimes required an act of judgment because similar examples and words were used to describe appropriate targets for these phases.[88] In general, the closer a target was to a threatened safe area and the more direct its contribution to the threat to that safe area, then the more likely it was to be hit in phase II of a response to a provocation. Conversely, targets located farther from a threatened safe area and bearing a less direct connection to the threat against it would not be hit unless bombing were expanded to phase III. Accordingly, a weapons depot near Sarajevo might be hit in phase II of an operation if Sarajevo were threatened. But the same target, if it were struck at all, would be attacked in phase III of a response to a threat against Bihac.[89] By the time NATO executed its first air strike—a year after NATO approved "Operational Options"—the idea of conducting strikes against groups of targets in escalating phases of a coercive bombing campaign had given way to the practice of one-off attacks against individual targets which were labeled as Options 1, 2, or 3.[90] It was not until operation Deliberate Force in the summer of 1995 that the original concept of linking groups of targets to options, or phases, was reapplied. However, by then the safe areas were lumped together in two wider "zones of action," thus further blurring the distinction between some Option 2 and 3 targets.[91] On 13 August 1993, NATO published Change-2 to the plan governing Deny Flight, CINCSOUTH OPLAN 40101, incorporating new procedures and ROE for air strikes.[92]

Airpower and Coercion at Mount Igman: August 1993

In his reaction to NATO pressures for air strikes, General Briquemont demonstrated his traditional army views on airpower. With America pushing NATO toward air strikes against the Bosnian Serbs, General Cot suggested to General Briquemont that he should go to Vicenza to learn about allied plans for employing airpower; however, General Briquemont already held strong convictions about the use and limitations of airpower in Bosnia.[93] As General Briquemont saw the situation,"These ambiguous resolutions (836 and 844), which everyone could interpret as he liked," were the cause of UNPROFOR's difficulties, and in his judgment

> the UN, lacking the means for these resolutions, turned to NATO and air support to compensate for the shortages of means on the ground. After Vietnam and Afghanistan, and considering the terrain in Bosnia, how could anyone still persist in this mistaken thinking about operational strategy?[94]

To General Briquemont, the appeal to airpower was a political gambit based on the minimal risks to NATO airpower and unrealistic beliefs held by NATO politicians about high-tech aerial warfare.[95] Moreover, he claimed,"What troubled me the most was that this mission was the responsibility of NATO (M. Boorda) and of M. Cot and that, at least initially, the UNPROFOR commander in Bosnia seemed to be considered a secondary player."[96] Enroute to Vicenza, General Briquemont resolved to himself and told his staff, "Nothing happens in Bosnia without my consent, and if it does, I will be returning to Brussels immediately."[97] Thus, before he had arrived at Vicenza, General Briquemont already held serious doubts about the ability of NATO airpower to compensate for the inadequacies of his ground forces, and he was disturbed that other senior officers might be infringing on his command prerogatives.[98]

At Vicenza, Briquemont showed the sort of authority and control he expected to exercise as *the* commander in Bosnia. On 11 August, General Briquemont met with Generals Ashy and Chambers at Vicenza, where a NATO staff officer briefed the UN commander on "the concept of an air campaign . . . with different phases, and lists of targets for each phase: their type, their location, their proximity to UNPROFOR troops and their potential for collateral damage."[99] After 20 minutes, General Briquemont interrupted the briefing to point out that this was not what he wanted.[100] While the NATO airmen seemed to be focused exclusively on bombing Bosnian Serb targets, General Briquemont's concerns also included the fighting in central Bosnia between the Bosnian Croats and the mostly Muslim Bosnian government forces.[101] The UN commander went on to tell the NATO officers that he wanted close air support only, and not "a wide ranging air campaign."[102] According to General Briquemont, Generals Ashy and Chambers understood his situation, but they claimed that they had their orders from NATO.[103] Briquemont responded by reminding them he was the supported commander in Bosnia, and that "NATO should be supporting me, rather than trying to impose its vision of operations on me."[104] Briquemont went on to discuss and approve potential air support targets including Bosnian Croat and Bosnian Serb targets.[105] Before General Briquemont left Vicenza on 12 August, General Ashy told him that one day they would execute the US-authored air campaign, to which Briquemont replied, "As long as I am the commander in Bosnia, I don't think so."[106]

The next day, Briquemont used the press to explain his views and to dampen enthusiasm for air strikes; the fallout from his comments illustrated the weakness in the UN chain of command.[107] On 13 August, when General Briquemont and his chief of staff, Brigadier Vere Hayes, voiced their criticisms of the American push for air strikes, Madeleine Albright, the

US ambassador to the UN, demanded that they be disciplined.[108] In Briquemont's view, what really bothered Mrs. Albright was that "everyone knew" that Briquemont had said, "If an aircraft of NATO is firing above Bosnia, without my permission, I am going back to Brussels immediately."[109] In making this assertion, Briquemont was appealing to a fundamental principle of war—unity of command—and as the commander in Bosnia, he expected control over all forces within his areas of responsibility.[110] Belgian political and military authorities backed their general, and said, furthermore, that since he was working for the UN, any punishment would have to be pursued through the UN.[111] Through all of this, General Briquemont felt he had the support of Mr. Stoltenberg.[112] However, an unnamed aide of Kofi Annan, acting without his boss's permission and apparently on his own imagined authority, sent a letter, bypassing General Cot, directly to General Briquemont admonishing him.[113] The failure of senior UN political authorities to clearly support or censure their commander in Bosnia highlighted a lack of coherence and efficiency within the UN hierarchy that would continue to plague UNPROFOR operations.

Generals Briquemont and Cot were skeptical of the US-sponsored air campaign plan, and as they themselves testified, their disagreements with Generals Chambers and Ashy over the utility of airpower owed much to the traditional soldier-airman split. Looking back on the meeting in Vicenza, General Briquemont recalled,

> I had seen the confrontation of two different strategic concepts. On the one hand, there were the American airmen who were convinced that the air force could win the war alone—on the other, there were the ground-pounders, to which I belonged, convinced that only the close coordination of actions between forces on the ground and in the air would permit the attainment of the final objective, and convinced that in this kind of internal civil war, the air forces could only be a supporting force.[114]

General Cot held similar views, noting,

> I have endured, in Naples and Vicenza, briefings in the style of a High-Mass, where only the Americans knew the business. One could characterize it as directly transposed from the Gulf War, the successive phases of total war . . . I admit having been concerned, as were other

> UN military chiefs, about this excitement amongst airmen dreaming of "breaking the Serbs," and [who] were uninformed about the situation in Yugoslavia, which they had only seen from their supersonic flights over the country.[115]

There were other reasons for Generals Cot and Briquemont to oppose air strikes but, clearly, their outlook as soldiers was an important factor.

Despite General Briquemont's refusal to countenance NATO air strikes, the threat of such strikes seemed to play an important role in coercing the Serbs into halting their encirclement of Sarajevo and relinquishing the territory they had captured. The Bosnian Serbs had continued their advance around Sarajevo in violation of their own promises in late July to halt the offensive.[116] As Dick Leurdijk later explained,

> On 18 August 1993, Boutros-Ghali informed the Security Council that the UN now had the "initial operation [sic] capability for the use of air power in support of UNPROFOR in Bosnia-Herzegovina." On that same day, NATO carried out its first air support exercise. On the ground, the Bosnian Serbs stopped their attack on Mount Igman. The area came under UNPROFOR control. It was the first time that the UN—through NATO—really threatened to use force and the Bosnian Serbs gave in. This outcome would have important consequences for later decisions on air strikes in the context of NAC's decisions on Sarajevo, Gorazde, and the other safe areas.[117]

Though this reasoning is essentially correct, the timing is in error. Bosnian Serb troops began to withdraw from Mount Igman and Mount Bjelasnica a week before the date cited by Leurdijk, and they were reportedly gone completely two days before it.[118] Moreover, if it was NATO airpower that coerced the Serbs, then it was probably the threat of air strikes, rather than air support, that had motivated them to give in. General Briquemont, who ran the military negotiations for the BSA's withdrawal, recorded that the real Bosnian Serb willingness to pull back came in the wake of the two NATO decisions to allow air strikes.[119] The first Bosnian Serb overture came from Karadzic in Geneva just after the NATO Council's decision to authorize air strikes on 2 August.[120] Following that, General Mladic negotiated and signed the military agreement to withdraw his troops from Mount Igman on 10 August, the day after NATO announced its approval of "Operational Options for Air

Strikes."[121] Finally, the threat of NATO air strikes was kept alive as the terms of the Mount Igman agreement were implemented.[122] Though the sequence of events does not prove that the threat of airpower worked, it would have been reasonable for NATO ministers to conclude that there was a connection between their threats and Serb compliance, as Leurdijk asserted.

Contrary to the NATO view described by Leurdijk, General Briquemont believed the threat of air strikes was counterproductive to his endeavors to negotiate a solution to the Mount Igman crisis, and that air strikes exacerbated the risks to his troops.[123] General Briquemont knew that the Serbs had other reasons to quit Mount Igman; in particular, General Mladic was short on manpower and wanted to use UNPROFOR to help consolidate his gains.[124] With ambiguous Security Council resolutions to work from and *Do Something, General!* as his guidance from Mr. Stoltenberg, General Briquemont began trying to calm the situation in Bosnia by negotiating an end to the fighting around Sarajevo.[125] He hoped that the Sarajevo agreement would, in turn, enhance negotiations in Geneva and reduce the suffering amongst the people in Bosnia.[126] However, the threat of NATO air strikes, ostensibly in support of UNPROFOR, jeopardized the UN's impartiality in Bosnia, especially since the threats were being directed only at the Serbs.[127] The NATO threat, he felt, hindered his negotiations and, if carried out, would endanger his forces.[128] Briquemont did not see how NATO air strikes could help him, and he did not credit them for securing the Serb withdrawal from Mount Igman. Just as Betts had observed, proponents and opponents of airpower could find justification for their opposing beliefs in the same evidence.[129]

Command without Control: September–December 1993

The crisis over Mount Igman brought General Briquemont face-to-face with his responsibilities as a commander and forced him to choose between mission accomplishment and force protection. The crisis occurred within six weeks of his taking command. And in that time, General Briquemont had come to see a "strange dysfunction in the strategy of the international community," whereby nations advocating air strikes—especially the US—were unwilling to take risks associated with putting troops on the ground; and those nations taking such risks were unwilling to endorse air strikes.[130] The UN commander in Bosnia was acutely aware of the risks he himself was taking by putting soldiers on Mount Igman, and he felt the weight of his responsibilities.

> I had never experienced quite as profoundly what it meant to be responsible for the lives of so many men. The vast majority of them were the age of my children, because at 58 I was undoubtedly the oldest military man in the field. I have always acted with the thought that a drop of blood of one of my men was a drop of my own blood, and I am convinced that every officer worthy of the name thinks this way.[131]

He knew that in war it was necessary to take casualties, but this was not war.[132] Though Briquemont's civilian political advisor, Viktor Andreev, assured him that the Security Council resolutions were so unclear that the general could always justify his decisions and his actions,[133] General Briquemont himself worried that what he was doing at Mount Igman was both dangerous and beyond the mission mandated to UNPROFOR by the Security Council.[134] As he later wrote, "I knew that I was engaging in an operation which did not conform at all with the mandate of UNPROFOR, but, on the other hand, I had decided to do everything in order to help restart the negotiations in Geneva."[135] Five years after sending UN troops onto Mounts Bjelasnica and Igman, General Briquemont recalled that

> it was a military mission. If I had thirty casualties or dead soldiers on Mount Igman, I'm sure that I [would have been] before the [court-martial] in my country, because it was [outside] of the mandate of the United Nations—but Stoltenberg asked [me to do it].[136]

In fact, though, moving the French onto Mount Igman was entirely consistent with the mandate established in Resolution 836, which tasked UNPROFOR to "promote the withdrawal of military or paramilitary units other than those of the Government of the Republic of Bosnia Herzegovina," and to "occupy some key points on the ground."[137] The real problem for General Briquemont was doing it without taking casualties. Recounting a discussion with his civilian political advisor at the outset of Briquemont's tenure in Bosnia, the general recalled that

> I said: "Okay, I have understood. The resolutions of the Security Council cannot help me in my mission." And the rules of engagement were foreseen for peacekeeping operations. We had no peace. It was the war between the three parties, and I was there with a few "blue helmets," and it was impossible to respect the rules of engagement. I have said: "Bon. *We shall never speak about the rules of engagement. We shall do our best to avoid casualties*—point [period, full-stop]" (emphasis added).[138]

Thus, General Briquemont uneasily confronted the contradictory tasks and restrictions bequeathed to him by the Security Council. Avoiding casualties among UNPROFOR's peacekeepers, easing the suffering of the Bosnian people, and facilitating negotiations in Geneva became his priority tasks.[139] Protecting the safe areas, the principal objective stated in Security Council Resolution 836 defining UNPROFOR's mandate in Bosnia, was impossible with the means available to Briquemont. He simply could not attempt to accomplish this mission within the bounds of acceptable risks to his forces.

In late August and September, Admiral Boorda assuaged the UN commanders' concerns about air strikes and obtained UNPROFOR approval for a joint UN-NATO target list. It had bothered General Briquemont that he had been left out of the decision making and planning for air strikes until senior NATO officers had tried to pressure him into approving an air campaign.[140] And General Ashy had been very direct in attempting to get the UN commander in Bosnia to accept an air campaign.[141] On 21 August, Admiral Boorda attended a dinner hosted by General Cot in Zagreb during which he conveyed to Generals Cot and Briquemont a sense that he understood their situation and,[142] more importantly, he shared their concerns about the risks involved with air strikes.[143] However, General Briquemont seems to have been left out of further discussions on air strikes.[144] In September, General Cot met again with Admiral Boorda for the first UN-NATO joint targeting board in order to review and approve a list of air strike targets.[145] The list included targets for all three warring factions in Bosnia—though the Serb military possessed by far the most targets suitable for air strikes.[146] The list did not, however, attempt to designate targets in terms of options or phases; it was just one list of potential targets.[147] Presumably, if the need arose, they would have been grouped into phases to meet the needs of a given contingency, and then proposed to UN and NATO political authorities for approval. General Cot remained opposed to air strikes, but he recognized NATO's need to plan, and he saw no harm in maintaining his input into the air strike planning process.[148] Furthermore, General Cot had an incentive to maintain a good working relationship with Admiral Boorda since he was to be Boorda's deputy under UN-NATO arrangements to implement the latest peace pro- posal for Bosnia—the Union of Three Republics plan, which seemed close to being signed during the third week in September 1993.[149]

UNPROFOR Commanders Strive to Control NATO Close Air Support

By the end of September, NATO and UN military command- ers had a workable system for close air support, but the UN apparatus for authorizing close air support rendered the sys- tem ineffective. Generals Cot and Briquemont had agreed that General Briquemont should be the one to initiate any request for air support.[150] By the end of the month, staff officers at Vicenza, using rules of engagement approved by NATO politi- cal authorities, had written a set of procedures for conducting close air support.[151] Just as with the air-to-air missions for enforcing the no-fly zone, the procedures for air-to-ground missions stipulated that ordnance could be expended over Bosnia only with clearance from one of five senior NATO com- manders, with General Chambers, the CAOC director, being the lowest level of approval authority.[152] Senior commanders in NATO's southern region ensured that all aircrews rotating into the region for Deny Flight operations were thoroughly briefed and trained to follow these rules of engagement.[153] As General Ashy described the arrangements, "We had a briefing that was promulgated by me and approved by Admiral Boorda that had to go to every aircrew before [they] flew . . . you had to be personally certified by your unit commander to me . . . we didn't want anybody out there winging it."[154] It was a tightly controlled operation.

On the UN side, air support was also tightly controlled, but at such a high level that it was useless to UNPROFOR's commanders. Only Boutros Boutros-Ghali could approve an air attack. According to General Briquemont, early exercises designed to test the UN's command and control system demonstrated that, "Between Cot and myself, no problem. It was very rapid, very quick reaction."[155] However, the UN commander in Bosnia found that the approval process stalled once it got above General Cot.

> In the most favorable circumstances, before having the release [approval for an attack], I needed four to six hours. And we had aircraft in the sky permanently. And I said to General Cot: "But, it's impossible. We have the aircraft above our heads, and I must wait six hours to have the release to . . . engage one tank, or two tanks."[156]

Concerned about the security of his troops, General Briquemont urged General Cot to obtain the authority to approve close air support missions; the UN commander in Bosnia later recalled arguing, "I can't have casualties. I have not enough troops on the ground. I have so many aircraft in the sky, and I cannot use the aircraft to defend my own troops!"[157] But, General Cot needed no prompting; the two senior UN commanders were of the same mind about air support.[158] As General Cot later wrote,

> The Secretary-General personally reserved for himself the decision for each possible attack. Yet the delay in the process, between Zagreb and New York and back, of around four hours, was totally incompatible with the urgency of such missions. Furthermore, it appeared *unacceptable to me that someone could decide in New York what ought to have been left solely to my authority: the security of my units* (emphasis added).[159]

General Cot's petition went unanswered,[160] and Boutros-Ghali did not delegate the authority to approve air support to UNPROFOR's military commanders until 1995.[161] Frustrated at this lack of control, General Briquemont suggested that the UN commanders would be justified in by-passing their political authorities in order to save the lives of their troops:

It's very strange for generals to say that, but when you are responsible for the lives of your soldiers on the ground, you don't react as in peace-time. Eh? I said to General Cot, but, if I am engaged by the Serbs, or the Croats, or the Muslims, I shall not ask the release of the political side.[162]

However, the UN commanders realized that Admiral Boorda would block any request for air support unless he knew that the UN commanders had political approval for an attack.[163] Unlike air strikes, the UN generals wanted close air support. But, without the means to approve requests for air support in a timely manner, UNPROFOR could make little use of NATO airpower.

General Briquemont was also concerned about the vulnerability of Belgian troops, who were not under his command but were stationed in Croatia where close air support had not yet been authorized.[164] Briquemont pressed General Cot to solicit authority from New York for close air support in Croatia; though again, Cot needed no urging.[165] On 19 September, Boutros-Ghali wrote to the president of the Security Council informing him of General Cot's desire to have close air support in Croatia.[166] And in early October the Security Council renewed the UNPROFOR mandate in Croatia for six months—this time under Chapter VII of the UN Charter.[167] However, the council postponed authorizing air support there, and the extension of close air support to the territory of Croatia did not come until the end of March of 1994, two weeks after General Cot relinquished command of UNPROFOR.[168]

Without effective air support, which the UNPROFOR commanders were unable to acquire, the logic of the "light option" broke down and so, too, did the whole safe areas policy. But the logic of the light option was suspect to begin with. At first blush, it seemed logical to assert that the weaker UNPROFOR was on the ground, then the more it would have to rely on NATO airpower. The presence of UN forces would deter attacks on the safe areas, and if the deterrence broke down, then UNPROFOR soldiers could call on NATO airpower for close air support. This assumed the Bosnian Serbs—the most likely target of air attacks by the very nature of the UN's safe areas policy—would tolerate CAS if the BSA attacked first, but might respond to other air attacks by taking hostages or by retaliating against UNPROFOR.[169] As discussed earlier in this chapter, NATO ambassadors had interpreted Resolutions 836 and 844 to take this into account. However, BSA tolerance for UN self-defense was likely to evaporate if UNPROFOR's need for self-defense was provoked by UN soldiers aggressively trying to fulfill their mandate and then counting on NATO air support to back them up. Thus, the weaker UNPROFOR was, the less likely it was to deter BSA attacks on the safe areas, and the less aggressive it could afford to be in helping to deliver humanitarian aid in Bosnia.

The "Operational Options" approved by the NAC in August were also of questionable utility. As long as NATO political authorities remained self-deterred by fears of Bosnian Serb retaliation, they would have difficulty choosing one of the first two options: the demonstrative phase or the follow-on phase.[170] Those options would have served merely as a signal to the Bosnian Serbs to begin taking hostages.[171] While it was far from certain that a robust air campaign would succeed in compelling the Serbs to quit attacking a safe area, the dangers of trying to get to phase III in a graduated fashion seemed to rule out the possibility of ever making an attempt. Thus, somewhat paradoxically, the weaker UNPROFOR was on the ground, the less it could afford to have NATO airpower attempting to enforce Serb compliance with the safe areas policy. By keeping UNPROFOR in place and weak, and by refusing to give its commanders timely access to NATO air support, the responsible political authorities practically guaranteed that airpower would not be used effectively and that UNPROFOR could not succeed in helping to enforce the safe areas policy. Air strikes and more robust enforcement on the ground could only come at the price of increased risks to UNPROFOR's soldiers. Thus, under the circumstances, the light option became a prescription for paralysis.

Absent Political Guidance

Without clear political objectives or guidance, UNPROFOR commanders were left to interpret the ambiguous Security Council resolutions and to decide for themselves what their mission was. In doing so and in light of their meager resources, they were driven by their responsibilities as commanders to give priority to force protection. At the same time they were pressing for more control over NATO airpower, the senior UNPROFOR commanders vainly solicited clearer political direction from their political authorities. General Briquemont recalled,

> I have never had terms of reference for my mission. I've asked [for] that. [Brigadier Vere] Hayes asked [for] that. I have said to Mr. Stoltenberg: "Yes, but you asked me to go to Mount Igman, and it was probably the most dangerous mission that we have ever fulfilled with 'blue helmets.' The Security Council has never approved this mission— Mount Igman."[172]

General Cot recalled meeting with similar frustration:

> I was never able to get Stoltenberg to give me written orders. Stoltenberg, as well as Boutros-Ghali, always told me: "There are the UN resolutions which were made by the Security Council; you know how to read the Security Council resolutions as well as I do, therefore we have nothing more to tell you." And that was very distressing. Very, very distressing.[173]

General Briquemont later said: "I think it's very important for the generals to understand what [are] the political objectives. The problem was that we had no politicians to explain that to us."[174] While General Briquemont believed that he had excellent civilian political advisors, and a well-intentioned political representative, he noted that they possessed no real political authority: "It was impossible for them to take a decision. They were permanently reporting to New York for anything."[175] To rectify this situation, the UNPROFOR generals repeatedly asked New York to send them a full-time political representative.[176] But, by the time Boutros-Ghali designated one, both Generals Briquemont and Cot were on the verge of leaving.[177]

With poor ties to the UN's civilian hierarchy, the senior UNPROFOR commanders fell out of step with the shifting UN diplomacy in Geneva and the career peacekeepers in New York. From mid-June until late September, negotiators in Geneva sought agreement from the warring factions on the Union of Three Republics peace plan, also known as the Owen-Stoltenberg Plan.[178] Authored by the Serbs and Croats, the plan embodied the de facto partition of Bosnia into three ethnically oriented republics.[179] Though General Briquemont supported the plan, he did so while holding the somewhat incoherent conviction that "the political objective was to save Bosnia; and to save Bosnia means that the three communities in Bosnia—the Serb community, the Croatian community, and the Muslims—can live together."[180] Unlike Briquemont, General Cot was critical of the Geneva-based diplomacy, believing it was premature to negotiate while there was still fighting.[181] He later blamed the negotiations—including the tactics allegedly used by Owen and Stoltenberg in the second half of 1993—for inciting some of the fighting in Bosnia and for prolonging the war.[182] Furthermore, the UNPROFOR generals were not inclined to take directions from the UN peacekeeping department in New York.[183] In contrast to some previous commanders in UNPROFOR, notably Gen Lewis MacKenzie and Gen Lars Wahlgren, Cot and Briquemont did not have backgrounds as peacekeepers. Generals Cot and Briquemont were not part of a UN peacekeeping culture. They and most of their staff officers were NATO officers in blue helmets.[184] Absent clear political direction or a firm commitment to UN peacekeeping doctrine to guide them, Generals Cot and Briquemont were left to set their own course.

Responsibility, Risks, and Accountability

Even as they tried to interpret their mission, the top UN commanders in the former Yugoslavia discovered they did not have the authority needed to fulfill their responsibilities as commanders. As partial fulfillment of the European Union pledge to support the UN's light option, the Danish, Norwegian, and Swedish governments sent a joint Nordic battalion to Bosnia. When General Briquemont protested that he did not need the Leopard tanks that the Danish were preparing to send, the Danish military informed him that the tanks would be coming anyway.[185] After the well-armed Nordic battalion arrived at Tuzla, General Briquemont ordered it to leave that quiet part of Bosnia and to go to Srebrenica where it was needed—twice he gave the order.[186] On both occasions, as General Briquemont recounted: "The colonel said: 'General I cannot execute. The governments refuse to deploy any units in

Srebrenica. It's too dangerous.' A safe area too dangerous!"[187] Rather than receiving support from the UN headquarters, officials there complained to General Briquemont about the friction he had created amongst the ambassadors in New York.[188]

General Cot was not in a good position to help General Briquemont, for as Cot remembered,

> Stoltenberg in Geneva was very much afraid that I would take a decision, which would be contrary to the diplomatic negotiations that he was conducting in Geneva. Therefore Stoltenberg often told me that: "I don't want you to move a single section of soldiers without my authorizations." And me, I always responded: "I will move whoever I would like to, without your authorization." Therefore we have had difficult relations.[189]

In order to surmount such difficulties, General Cot would typically ask the French Chief of Defense Staff, Admiral Lanxade, with whom he often spoke, to grant UNPROFOR the resources he needed or to have the French government put pressure on Boutros Boutros-Ghali to get him to approve the course of action Cot wanted.[190] However, the French were primarily responsible for the safe areas of Bihac and Sarajevo, and the French government had already declined to provide additional soldiers to implement the safe areas policy elsewhere in Bosnia.[191] So, Generals Cot and Briquemont could only wait until another troop-contributing nation volunteered forces for Srebrenica.[192] Despite being commanders, they were deprived of the requisite authority for controlling the forces under their respective commands. Without that control, they were unable to execute their mission, which was supposed to include providing protection to the safe areas.

By November 1993, General Briquemont had had enough of commanding in a situation where he had insufficient means and inadequate authority to meet the responsibilities of his mission. Generals Cot and Briquemont, who had not been invited to visit New York or Brussels to discuss their situation with political leaders,[193] were delighted to be asked to attend a meeting of European Union foreign ministers in Luxembourg on 22 November 1993.[194] Belgium held the presidency of the EU during the second half of 1993, so its foreign minister, Willy Claes, ran the meeting.[195] However, Briquemont's hopes turned to frustration a week later when it became clear that the European ministers, who were determined to have UNPROFOR guarantee the security of several humanitarian aid routes in Bosnia, were not going to provide the additional 4,000 troops that General Briquemont estimated would be needed to do the job.[196] After a second EU meeting, which took place in Geneva on 29 November, General Briquemont decided he had had enough: "At the end of the day, no European country has said one word about my reinforcements. And that day I said to my minister of foreign affairs, 'No. No, I don't play ball. I go back to Belgium.'"[197] The UN commander in Bosnia maintained that generals have a stronger obligation in time of war to obey their political authorities than in military operations where no vital interests are threatened.[198] Furthermore, according to Briquemont:

> The generals must dare to say "no" to the politicians. I went out of Bosnia, because in November of '93 I have said: "No. It's impossible to play that. *I don't accept to risk the lives of so many soldiers with such a mandate, with such a mission, without the means [which] are necessary to fulfill the mission.* It's impossible." (Emphasis added)[199]

Both Generals Cot and Briquemont were irked by UNPROFOR's flawed command chain that seemed to invite unaccountable officials to try to usurp the generals' command authority. For Cot, Stoltenberg's absence from Zagreb, and the primacy of his negotiating duties in Geneva, was a particular problem.[200] The UNPROFOR commander rejected the notion that Stoltenberg's chosen representative, General Eide, had any legitimate role in the UN chain of command.[201] As Cot later explained,

> I never accepted that Eide could give me orders, therefore we had very big difficulties with Stoltenberg in Zagreb. I had asked to be the deputy, and he sent me a boss. If you like, Stoltenberg made or designated Eide his assistant, his deputy, and I did not want to be under the orders of that general.[202]

General Briquemont resented politicians pushing for him to act, since he believed that he himself, and not those urging the action, would be held accountable if things went wrong. He stated,

101

It was not a problem to take decisions. It was not a problem. Because nobody was criticizing my decisions. So long as you have no casualties, you can take all the decisions for the politicians; it's good. You take the decisions in place of the politicians. When you have casualties, it's another problem. Because then they ask you: "Why have you done that?" or "Why have you not done that?"[203]

In contrast to the clear military chain of accountability, the diffuse nature of the political pressures to "do something" in Bosnia left Briquemont feeling exposed: He went on to say that

there was no political leadership . . . General Cot was alone in Zagreb, there was nobody in Sarajevo . . . I can say we were alone there, and we tried to do our best to solve the problems. And it is the reason why we must answer all of the questions of the Tribunal of The Hague. Because the Tribunal of The Hague cannot speak with the politicians who were responsible in Bosnia. There were so many politicians who were responsible for something in Bosnia that it is impossible to say that: "You were responsible for that, or that, or that."[204]

Though he would remain at the head of Bosnia-Herzegovina Command until late January of 1994, General Briquemont decided at the end of November to leave rather than be pushed into accepting ever-greater risks and responsibilities by political officials who, for the most part, were unaccountable themselves.[205]

By the beginning of 1994, with the UN safe areas policy failing, General Cot precipitated his own departure by pushing even harder for the UN to grant him control over NATO airpower. The average number of artillery and mortar rounds falling on the safe area of Sarajevo had climbed to over 1,000 per day, sniping was rampant in the capital, and UNPROFOR had received fewer than 3,000 of the 7,600 reinforcements authorized six months earlier.[206] The Bosnian Serbs also refused to allow Tuzla airport to be opened.[207] At Zepa and Srebrenica, the Bosnian Serbs controlled access to the safe areas, and blocked the rotation of UNPROFOR units.[208] Though UN Secretary-General Boutros-Ghali had named Mr. Yasushi Akashi to be his full-time special representative in Zagreb, this was cool comfort for General Cot if all decisions to use air support still had to be referred to New York.[209] As General Briquemont recalled, "General Cot has said: 'We are not discussing with the representatives of Mr. Boutros-Ghali.

They are functionaires [functionaries]. . . . They were . . . part of the administration, but they had no responsibilities.'"[210] At the beginning of 1994, General Cot began to complain publicly about the problems with the UN operation, including the secretary-general's refusal to give Cot control over NATO airpower.[211] By Cot's account this caused Boutros Boutros-Ghali to seek his removal.

> After having tried in vain, for six months, to obtain the delegation of decision [for approving air support] through normal channels, I chose to speak publicly of my requirement, which immediately led the Secretary-General to ask the French government for my dismissal.[212]

Though the French government agreed to remove General Cot, its foreign minister and defense minister registered their dissatisfaction with the UN's management of UNPROFOR which, as Philippe Guillot phrased it, "consumed generals at an immodest rate" rather than fixing problems within the UN hierarchy.[213] Indeed, only one of the six generals who served in UNPROFOR's top two posts had, by that time, managed to complete his full tour of duty.[214] To the diplomats in Geneva, General Cot's bid for control was part of an attempt to bypass even the secretary-general and to open direct communications with the Security Council.[215] To UNPROFOR's commanders it seemed that they were on their own, with all of the responsibility, deprived of the means and authority for accomplishing their mission, and at times they did not even know how to get in touch with the political authorities who could make decisions.[216]

Conclusion

The responsibilities of command and the expertise born of service affiliation shaped the actions of the theater-level commanders who were attempting to find a way to use NATO airpower in Bosnia during the second half of 1993. General Cot, and to a greater degree General Briquemont, struggled under the weight of their responsibilities in circumstances that forced them to make trade-offs between accomplishing their mission and protecting their forces. Though their NATO counterparts, Admiral Boorda and Generals Ashy and Chambers, often had to work fast and work hard to fulfill their duties as commanders, their responsibilities were much lighter because they did not have to make a similar trade-off between mission and men. In addition to their different responsibilities, the UN and NATO commanders came from markedly different backgrounds and had different service expertise. Generals Ashy and Chambers had solid expertise for planning the conventional air operations called for by NATO, and they were confident that airpower could be used to coerce the Bosnian Serbs. Conversely, Generals Briquemont and Cot held the traditional army view that airpower was best used for supporting ground forces, and they were skeptical of plans to coerce the Serbs through bombing.

To a remarkable degree, the factors affecting the commanders on either side of the airpower debate were mutually reinforcing. On one side, senior US airmen serving in a traditional military alliance—NATO—pushed for a US-backed air campaign, which entailed little risk to the forces under their command. On the other, European army generals working for the UN strove to fulfill a largely humanitarian mission favored by the European governments with vulnerable ground forces in UNPROFOR. Of these multiple, mutually reinforcing factors, the clash of cultures between the UN and NATO played the least significant role in shaping the decisions and actions of the theater-level commanders. They all considered themselves NATO officers, none had any peacekeeping experience, and the UNPROFOR commanders were driven toward a peacekeeping-like mission by the limitations of their means, rather than starting with traditional peacekeeping doctrine to guide their thoughts and actions.

National ties were stronger than organizational associations, and they played an important role in influencing how the theater commanders viewed plans for using airpower. However, it is difficult to disentangle the national political pressures from the responsibilities of the commanders, since they were all bound up together. The French government's approach to Bosnia was part and parcel of General Cot's. Paris helped him to obtain resources and UN permission for his actions, and both Cot and the French government were concerned for the lives of the French soldiers in UNPROFOR.

Similarly, on the US side, the Clinton administration's desire to minimize the risks to US forces led it to adopt a lift and strike policy; therefore, political pressure, mission accomplishment, and force protection all pointed in the same direction. General Briquemont was the exception. Briquemont was from Belgium, and he was under political pressures from the EC—led by Belgian foreign minister Willy Claes—to take actions that would have entailed serious risks to the people under his command. These EC pressures were not matched by resources, and the people urging the action were largely unaccountable for the consequences should things go wrong. Unable to strike a satisfactory balance between accomplishing the tasks being thrust upon him and an acceptable level of risk to his forces, Briquemont quit—just as he had threatened to do in August when looming NATO air strikes promised a similar inability to manage his command responsibilities.

Notes

1. United Nations (UN) Security Council Provisional Verbatim Record 3228 (S/PV.3228), 4 June 1993 (hereafter cited as S/PV.3228).

2. Ibid. Also see Richard Caplan, *Post-Mortem on UNPROFOR*, London Defence Studies, no. 33 (London: Brassey's for the Centre for Defence Studies, 1996), 8–9.

3. Caplan, 287; and S/PV.3228.

4. UN Security Council Provisional Verbatim Record 3241 (S/PV.3241), 18 June 1993 (hereafter cited as S/PV.3241).

5. S/PV.3228.

6. Ibid.

7. UN Security Council Resolution (UNSCR) 836 (1993) (S/RES/836), 4 June 1993 (hereafter cited as S/RES/836).

8. Ibid.; and Report of the Secretary-General pursuant to UN Security Council Resolution 836 (1993) (S/25939), 14 June 1993 (hereafter cited as S/25939).

9. S/RES/836, par. 5; and S/25939. Note that UNSCR 836 also tasked UNPROFOR "to monitor the cease-fire." However, it would have been difficult to justify the use of force other than in self-defense to fulfill this task.

10. S/25939.

11. S/RES/836, par. 9.

12. Ibid.

13. Jan Willem Honig and Norbert Both, *Srebrenica: Record of a War Crime* (London: Penguin Books, 1996), 114.

14. S/RES/836, par. 9.

15. L. C. Green, *The Contemporary Law of Armed Conflict* (Manchester, England: Manchester University Press, 1993), 323–24.

16. Ibid.

17. UN Security Council Resolution 776 (1992) (S/RES/776), 14 September 1992 (hereafter cited as S/RES/776).

18. For other interpretations and discussions, see Dick A. Leurdijk, *The United Nations and NATO in Former Yugoslavia, 1991–96* (The Hague: The Netherlands Atlantic Commission, 1996), 35–36; Caplan, 7–9; Honig and Both, 5–6; and James Gow, *Triumph of the Lack of Will: International Diplomacy and the Yugoslav War* (New York: Columbia University Press, 1997), 135–36 and 270–71 n. 9.

19. S/RES/836, par. 10.

20. Ibid.

21. Ibid.

22. This "objectives v. objections" manner of expression comes from James Gow's, "British Perspectives," in *International Perspectives on the Yugoslav Conflict*, eds. Alex Danchev and Thomas Halverson (London: Macmillan, 1996), 88 and 97. It is roughly equivalent to Clodfelter's positive objectives and negative objectives introduced in chap. 2. Mark Clodfelter, *The Limits of Airpower; the American Bombing of North Vietnam* (New York: Free Press; Collier Macmillan, 1989), 141–42.

23. S/25939.

24. Ibid.

25. Ibid. Lt Gen Lars Eric Wahlgren of the Swedish army was the second commander of UNPROFOR. He took up his post at the beginning of March 1993 and was replaced just four months later.

26. UN Security Council Resolution 844 (1993) (S/RES/844), 18 June 1993 (hereafter cited as S/RES/844).

27. S/PV.3241.

28. Michael Williams, *Civil-Military Relations and Peacekeeping*, Adelphi Paper 321 (London: International Institute for Strategic Studies), 25. Maj Gen Philippe Morillon of the French army began his assignment in the Balkans as the first chief of staff for UNPROFOR. In October 1992, he took command of Bosnia-Herzegovina Command.

29. Honig and Both, 115–16.

30. Brigadier Graham Messervy-Whiting, *Peace Conference on Former Yugoslavia: The Politico-Military Interface*, London Defence Studies 21 (London: Brassey's for the Centre for Defense Studies, 1994), 40 n. 27.

31. Gen Philippe Morillon, French army, *Croire et Oser: Chronique de Sarajevo* (Paris: Bernard Grasset, 1993), 202.

32. Ibid., 213.

33. Wahlgren to Annan, "Provision of Air to Ground Support—Safe Areas," 23 June 1993, cited in Hans-Christian Hagman, "UN-NATO Operational Co-operation in Peacekeeping 1992–1995," (PhD diss., King's College, University of London, 1997), 171.

34. Gen Jean Cot, French army, UNPROFOR force commander, July 1993–March 1994, interviewed by author, 30 September 1998, Paris. Transcript and translation of tape recording. Author's personal collection.

35. David Owen, *Balkan Odyssey* (London: Victor Gollancz, 1995; Indigo, 1996), 157–59.

36. Ibid., 189 and 264; and Gow, *Triumph*, 101.

37. Messervy-Whiting, 15.

38. Ibid., 28.

39. Michael Littlejohns, "Bosnia on the Brink: UN Weighs New Measures," *Financial Times* (London), 7 May 1993.

40. Messervy-Whiting, 14–15 and 41; and Owen, 161–62.

41. General Morillon says he learned about the shake-up in June, but, Philippe Guillot has implied that Morillon may have actually found out about it in May when "he went back to France for a weekend for family reasons but reportedly also secretly met the new Minister of Defence, M. Léotard." Morillon, 202; and Philippe Guillot, "France, Peacekeeping, and Humanitarian Intervention," *International Peacekeeping* 1, no. 1 (spring 1994): 38.

42. Cot's longtime friend, and subordinate commander in UNPROFOR, Gen Francis Briquemont claimed Cot was *the* oldest general in the French army. Lt Gen Francis Briquemont, interviewed by author, 11 August 1998, Brussels, transcript of tape recording, author's personal collection.

43. Gen Jean Cot, French army, "L'Europe et l'Otan," *Défense Nationale* 53, no. 3 (July 1997): 94; and idem, "Dayton ou la Porte Etroite: Genese et Avenir d'un Désastre," in *Dernière Guerre Balkanique?* 2d ed., ed. Jean Cot (France: Éditions L'Harmattan, 1996), 113. Cot's chief of staff at the time was Maj Gen Philippe Morillon. Morillon, *Croire*, 11.

44. Cot interview; and idem, "Dayton," 113 and 124.

45. Morillon, *Croire*, 202.

46. Ibid.

47. Lt Gen Francis Briquemont, *Do Something, General!: Chronique de Bosnie–Herzégovine, 12 juillet 1993–24 janvier 1994* (Bruxelles: Éditions Labor, 1997), 17–20.

48. Briquemont interview.

49. Ibid.; and Briquemont, *Do Something*, 34.

50. Messervy-Whiting, 16.

51. Lushbaugh.

52. Ibid.

53. Lt Col Lowell R. Boyd Jr., USAF, AFSOUTH staff officer, February 1993–1996, interviewed by Lt Col Robert Owen, 6 December 1995, Naples, Italy. Transcript of taped interview. Balkans Air Campaign Study (BACS) Collection, Air Force Historical Research Agency, Maxwell AFB, Alabama.

54. Messervy-Whiting, 16; and Cot interview.

55. Messervy-Whiting, 16.

56. Ibid.

57. David Owen and Laura Silber, "Hurd Hints at Croatia Sanctions;" *Financial Times* (London), 15 July 1993, 2; and George Graham, "Aspin Orders Military Support to the Adriatic," *Financial Times* (London), 16 July 1993, 2.

58. Gow, *Triumph*, 136.

59. *Atlantic News*, No. 2542, 9 July 1993, cited in Leurdijk, 37.

60. Col Bob Stewart, *Broken Lives: A Personal View of the Bosnian Conflict* (London: HarperCollins, 1993), 86.

61. Ibid., 303.

62. Serb leaders expected UNPROFOR to shoot back in self-defense and apparently accepted this. See Briquemont, *Do Something*, 94.

63. Gow, "British Perspective," 95–97.

64. *Facts On File Yearbook 1993* (USA: Facts on File, Inc., 1993), 401 and 570.

65. Ibid., 570.

66. Leurdijk, 37.

67. Ibid., 37–38.

68. Ibid., 37.

69. Notably Canada and Britain, but also Denmark and, to a lesser degree, France. Leurdijk, 38; and *Facts On File Yearbook 1993*, 605.

70. Statement of the North Atlantic Council, 2 August 1993, cited in Leurdijk, 38.

71. Gen Joseph W. Ashy, USAF, interviewed by Lt Col Robert Owen, 29 April 1996, Washington. Unclassified version of General Ashy's Oral History Interview (66 pp.) redacted by the Air Force Historical Research Agency, October 1997. Office of History, Air Force Space Command, Peterson AFB, Colo.

72. Ibid.; and Lt Gen James E. Chambers, USAF, director of NATO's Combined Air Operations Center (CAOC), Vicenza, Italy, interviewed by author, 10 February 1998, Fairfax, Va., author's notes, author's personal collection.

73. Ashy interview by Owen; and Gen Joseph W. Ashy, USAF, interviewed by author, 3 July 1998, Fairfax, Va., author's notes, author's personal collection.

74. Leurdijk, 38; and Lt Gen Nicholas B. Kehoe, USAF, assistant chief of staff, Operations and Logistics, Supreme Headquarters Allied Powers Europe, Mons, Belgium, July 1992–October 1994, interviewed by author, 18 November 1997, Brussels, transcript of tape recording, author's personal collection.

75. Kehoe interview.

76. MCM-KAD-084-93, "Operational Options for Air Strikes," Memorandum for the Secretary-General, North Atlantic Treaty Organization, NAC Decision Statement, 8 August 1993 (hereafter cited as MCM-KAD-084-93).

77. Ibid.

78. Leurdijk, 38–39.

79. NATO, Press Release (93)52, 9 August 1993.

80. Ibid.

81. Since NAC decisions required unanimity, each individual member state had veto power.

82. MCM-KAD-084-93.

83. Various descriptions of the options can be found in Col Robert Owen, *Deliberate Force: A Case Study in Effective Air Campaigning* (Maxwell AFB, Ala.: Air University Press, 2000), 99, 283–85, 399–400, and 471. Of these, the one on page 99 is, perhaps, the best, though it inexplicably lists CAS as an example of a target to be hit under Option 3. For examples of flawed descriptions, see Per Erik Solli, *UN and NATO Air Power in the Former Yugoslavia*, NUPI Report no. 209 (Oslo: Norwegian Institute of International Affairs, 1996), 52–53; and Hagman, 229.

84. MCM-KAD-084-93.

85. Ibid.

86. MCM-KAD-084-93.

87. Ibid.

88. Ibid.

89. Col Robert Owen, *Deliberate Force*, 99.

90. Hagman gets this evolution backward, mistakenly concluding that, "Air Strikes were rarely aimed at a specific violating weapon system (or a "hot barrel") but rather evolved to include any military target decided by NATO/UN." Hagman, 131.

91. This is discussed further in chap. 9.

92. Col Robert Owen, *Deliberate Force*, 471.

93. Briquemont, *Do Something*, 114 and 122; and Cot interview.

94. Briquemont, *Do Something*, 122.

95. Ibid.

96. Ibid., 123.

97. Ibid., 123–24.

98. Ibid., 110–11 and 120. Extracts from letters General Briquemont sent to his wife during the week before he went to Vicenza clearly show that he was already seriously concerned about air strikes before his trip to Italy.

99. Ibid., 121 and 124.

100. Ibid., 124–25.

101. Ibid., 125.

102. Ibid.

103. Ibid.

104. Ibid.

105. Ibid. General Ashy saw this meeting with Briquemont as a joint targeting board (JTB), and Ashy believed General Briquemont validated AFSOUTH's master target list. However, Briquemont's memoir makes no mention of this. During General Briquemont's interview, he seemed to have been unaware of a JTB, or a list of approved air strike targets. It seems General Briquemont approved a list of targets he thought was meant for air support, while General Ashy believed he had obtained approval for a list of air strike targets. Other sources put the date of the first JTB in September,

at a meeting between Admiral Boorda and General Cot, as discussed in the next section of this chapter.

106. Ibid., 126.

107. Ibid., 128; and *Facts On File Yearbook 1993*, 606.

108. Briquemont, *Do Something*, 129; Briquemont interview; and Laura Silber and Gillian Tett, "Fighting Threatens Talks on Bosnia," *Financial Talks* (London), 11 August 1993.

109. Briquemont interview.

110. Ibid.; and Briquemont, *Do Something*, 125.

111. Laura Silber, Gillian Tett, and George Graham, "Sarajevo Accord Puts UN In Charge," *Financial Times* (London), 19 August 1993; and Briquemont interview.

112. Briquemont interview.

113. Briquemont, *Do Something*, 131.

114. Ibid., 126.

115. Cot, "Dayton," 124.

116. Briquemont, *Do Something*, 103; and *Facts On File Yearbook 1993*, 570.

117. Leurdijk, 39.

118. "World News in Brief," *Financial Times* (London), 12 August 1993; Laura Silber, "Bosnia Factions Agree UN Control of Sarajevo," *Financial Times* (London), 17 August 1993; and Briquemont, *Do Something*, 108.

119. Briquemont did not credit the threat of NATO air strikes for the Serb withdrawal. However, his detailed recounting of events between 4–15 August 1993 provide evidence that Serb concessions in negotiations followed each successive threat of air strikes by NATO.

120. Briquemont, *Do Something*, 103.

121. Ibid., and 113–18.

122. Laura Silber and Gillian Tett, "Karadzic Warns of War if NATO Air Strikes Go Ahead," *Financial Times* (London), 11 August 1993; and idem, "Serbs Agree to Pull Back Their Forces," *Financial Times* (London), 14 August 1993.

123. Briquemont, *Do Something*, 109–11, 126–28.

124. Ibid., 104.

125. Ibid., 103 and 122; and Briquemont interview.

126. Briquemont, *Do Something*, 112 and 119.

127. Ibid., 119; and Briquemont interview.

128. Briquemont, *Do Something*, 110, 120, and 138.

129. Richard K. Betts, *Soldiers, Statesmen, and Cold War Crises* (Cambridge, Mass.: Harvard University Press, 1977; reprint with new preface and epilogue, New York: Columbia University Press, 1991), 203.

130. Ibid., 110 and 127–28. Note: This is nearly a direct translation of what Briquemont himself has written, *Do Something*, 127.

131. Ibid., 112.

132. Ibid.

133. Ibid.

134. Ibid., 111–12.

135. Ibid., 112.

136. Briquemont interview. General Briquemont's interview was conducted in English. The bracketed comments in the quotation correct the general's grammar without changing the meaning.

137. S/RES/836, par. 5.

138. Briquemont interview.

139. Briquemont, *Do Something,* 133.

140. Ibid., 123–24.

141. Ashy interview.

142. Briquemont, *Do Something,* 177.

143. Cot interview; Briquemont interview; and Briquemont, *Do Something,* 198.

144. In his memoir, General Briquemont notes the meeting with Admiral Boorda on 22 September, but makes no mention of air strikes. In his interview General Briquemont claimed to be unaware of a JTB list of targets for air strikes. Briquemont, *Do Something,* 198–99.

145. "Operation Deliberate Force Factual Review," 2.2, BACS Collection; Cot interview; and Col Robert Owen, *Deliberate Force,* 99.

146. Ashy interview; Briquemont, *Do Something,* 125; and Laura Silber, Gillian Tett, and George Graham, "Bosnian Peace Plan Under Fire," *Financial Times* (London), 25 August 1993.

147. Ashy interview.

148. Cot interview; Cot, "Dayton," 124; and Cot, "Les Leçons de l'ex-Yougoslavie," *Défense,* no. 67 (March 1995): 85.

149. David Owen, *Balkan Odyssey,* 234–35; and Briquemont, *Do Something,* 198–99.

150. Briquemont, *Do Something,* 127.

151. In addition to the previously mentioned changes to OPLAN 40101, new close air support and air strike procedures were written into Commander Fifth Allied Tactical Air Force Operations Order 45101.5, Deny Flight, 30 September 1993. Col Robert Owen, *Deliberate Force,* 399 n. 78; and Brig Gen William Peck, USAF, chief of plans, Deny Flight CAOC, Vicenza, Italy, July 1993–June 1994, "Plans Directors' Thoughts," undated contemporaneous notes.

152. Col Robert Owen, *Deliberate Force,* 381. The five command positions (commanders) were SACEUR (Shalikashvili/Joulwan), CINCSOUTH (Boorda/Leighton Smith), COMAIRSOUTH (Ashy/Ryan), 5ATAF commander (Rossetti/Fornesiero), and, finally, the CAOC director (Chambers/Hornburg).

153. Brig Gen William Peck, USAF, chief of plans, Deny Flight CAOC, Vicenza, Italy, July 1993–June 1994, interviewed by author, 9 July 1998, Langley Air Force Base, Virginia, tape recording, author's personal collection; idem, "Deny Flight: A Joint and Combined Operation," unpublished article dated 2 May 1994; Lowell Boyd interview; and Lushbaugh interview.

154. Ashy interview by Owen.

155. Briquemont interview.

156. Ibid.

157. Ibid.

158. Ibid.; Briquemont, *Do Something,* 127; and Cot interview.

159. Cot, "Dayton," 122.

160. Ibid.

161. Leurdijk, 77.

162. Briquemont interview.

163. Ibid.

164. Ibid.

165. Ibid.; and Cot, "Dayton," 122.

166. Letter from the secretary-general to the president of the Security Council, 19 September 1993 (S/26468, 30 September 1993).

167. The United Nations (UN), *The Blue Helmets: A Review of United Nations Peacekeeping,* 3d ed. (New York: United Nations Reproduction Section, 1996), 518; and UN Security Council Resolution 871 (S/RES/871), 4 October 1993.

168. UN, *Blue Helmets,* 518–19; UN Security Council Provisional Verbatim Record 3286 (S/PV.3286), 4 October 1993; and UN Security Council Resolution 908 (1994) (S/RES/908), 31 March 1994. Even though close air support for Croatia was authorized by the UN on 31 March 1994, NATO authorities did not agree to allow such missions until December 1994. The new NATO authority was to be spelled out in Change 3 to OPLAN 40101, but delays caused by negotiations with the Croatian government prevented Change 3 from being issued. NATO aircrews finally received authority for CAS in Croatia with Change 4 to the plan, promulgated in May 1995.

169. Philip Sabin, "Peace Support Operations—A Strategic Perspective," in *The Dynamics of Air Power,* ed. Group Capt Andrew Lambert and Arthur C. Williamson (Bracknell, England: HMSO, 1996), 105–11.

170. The first air strikes conducted by NATO, derisively called "pin pricks," managed to avoid the logic problem described here because the UN commander in Bosnia ensured that the Bosnian Serbs were warned in advance and that targets were insignificant. The first significant air strike in Bosnia by NATO took place in May 1995 at Pale, with predictable results.

171. The argument is not that it had to happen this way (i.e., that hostages had to be taken). Nothing was predetermined. The point is that if NATO political authorities were convinced that bombing would lead to intolerable risks or costs, as seemed to be the case, then their logic for demanding graduated options broke down.

172. Briquemont interview.

173. Cot interview.

174. Briquemont interview.

175. Ibid.; and Briquemont, *Do Something,* 137–38 and 142–43.

176. Briquemont interview.

177. Ibid.; and Cot, "Dayton," 122.

178. David Owen, *Balkan Odyssey,* 204 and 232–37; and Gow, *Triumph,* 254–56.

179. The partition, which violated the principles laid down by the first London Conference establishing the Geneva-based negotiations, motivated Lord Owen to resist efforts by the warring factions to call it the Owen-Stoltenberg plan. David Owen, *Balkan Odyssey*, 204.

180. Briquemont interview.

181. Cot, "Dayton," 127 and 129.

182. Ibid.

183. General Cot opined that: "The civilian component of the UN is controlled by mandarins, whose careers depend primarily on the suppleness of their spines." Cot, "Dayton," 127. In his interview General Cot noted that Kofi Annan was an exception—that Annan knew when to stand up and say no.

184. Briquemont, *Do Something*, 127.

185. Ibid., 138; and Briquemont interview.

186. Briquemont interview; and Briquemont, *Do Something*, 282–83.

187. Briquemont interview.

188. Ibid.; and Briquemont, *Do Something*, 283.

189. Cot interview.

190. Ibid.

191. Honig and Both, 118.

192. Ibid. As the Dutch reluctantly agreed to do in November 1993.

193. Briquemont, *Do Something*, 127.

194. Ibid., 277–78; and Briquemont interview. Also see David Owen, *Balkan Odyssey*, 249–50.

195. Briquemont, *Do Something*, 92 and 278.

196. Ibid., 286–87; and Briquemont interview.

197. Briquemont interview.

198. Ibid.

199. Ibid.

200. Cot interview; and Briquemont interview.

201. Cot interview.

202. Ibid.

203. Briquemont interview.

204. Ibid.

205. Ibid. General Briquemont noted that the French foreign minister, Alain Juppé, whose country had the greatest number of peacekeepers on the ground in the former Yugoslavia, was one exception to this generalization.

206. Report of the secretary-general submitted pursuant to paragraph 29 of General Assembly Resolution 48/88 (A/48/847, 7 January 1994) (hereafter cited as A/48/847); and Gen Sir Michael Rose, *Fighting for Peace: Bosnia 1994* (London: The Harvill Press, 1998), 1.

207. A/48/847.

208. Letter from the secretary-general to the president of the Security Council, 28 January 1994 (S/1994/94, 28 January 1994).

209. Cot, "Dayton," 122.

210. Ibid.

211. Guillot, 39.

212. Cot, "Dayton," 122.

213. Guillot, 39.

214. General Nambiar, the first UNPROFOR commander, served a full one-year tour. General Morillon's case is ambiguous since he was ostensibly replaced to make room for General Cot; however, it seems that he was on the verge of being dismissed in April 1993 but was instead kept on until July when Cot took the top position in UNPROFOR. For various reasons, Generals Cot, Wahlgren, Briquemont, and MacKenzie left prematurely. On the same subject, see Gow, *Triumph*, 139.

215. David Owen, *Balkan Odyssey*, 264–65.

216. Briquemont interview.

Chapter 5

Airpower Threats, Uses, and Disappointments: January–June 1994

Hitting one tank is peacekeeping. Hitting infrastructure, command and control, logistics, that is war.

> —Lt Gen Sir Michael Rose
> Roger Cohen, "UN General Opposes
> More Bosnia Force," *New York Times*,
> 29 September 1994

And then the business of low passes and flying around scaring people with noise—Rose was trying to use the threat of airpower, and the Bosnian Serbs knew, after a very short period of time, that Rose wasn't going to carry through on that threat.

> —Adm Leighton W. Smith
> Interviewed by author
> 10 February 1998

During the first half of 1994, new UN military commanders in the former Yugoslavia aided their civilian superiors in redefining UNPROFOR's mission. In the process, UNPROFOR began to discard the elements of its mandate relating to the enforcement of the safe areas policy. This would bring UNPROFOR's mission, as the UN commanders interpreted it, in line with UNPROFOR's capabilities. It was tactical determinism—where the limitations of the means available determine the ends one pursues—working at the implementation level.[1] The new approach reduced the need for the UN commanders to make some of the more difficult trade-offs between mission accomplishment and force protection that their predecessors had faced. It also enjoyed political support from the United Kingdom (UK) and was much more in line with traditional peacekeeping activities favored by UN headquarters in New York. But, redefining the mission came at the price of abandoning the safe areas policy. UNPROFOR's approach not only

115

prevented UN forces from taking enforcement action, it also meant that NATO airpower had to be restrained as well.

This chapter shows that commanders in NATO's southern region were moving in the opposite direction from their UN counterparts, but for the same reason: tactical determinism. The problems associated with finding heavy weapons, hitting them, and getting coercive leverage by attacking them reinforced the allied commanders' preferences for targeting larger and more militarily significant targets in Bosnia. A previously unnoticed aspect of the Sarajevo ultimatum in February shows how NATO commanders sought to preserve their autonomy in case they were given the opportunity to bomb. Later this chapter highlights the importance of timely decisions for the effective employment of NATO airpower over Bosnia. It also demonstrates that when commanders are accountable for the consequences of military action, they are much more likely to demand operational autonomy. After disappointing attempts to use airpower around Gorazde in April 1994, the biggest obstacle to the effective employment of airpower came from the civilian and military leaders in UNPROFOR. The chapter further argues that Gorazde was a turning point, after which opposing camps in the contest to control NATO airpower hardened their positions. Commanders in the UN and NATO found that their responsibilities for balancing mission accomplishment and force protection pulled them in opposite directions and added to the mutually reinforcing factors on both sides of the struggle over the use of airpower in Bosnia.

Commanders and Command Relationships

Near the end of January 1994, Lt Gen Francis Briquemont relinquished command of UN operations in Bosnia and was replaced by British army officer Lt Gen Sir Michael Rose. A week later, Lt Gen Joseph W. Ashy was named commander of the US Sixteenth Air Force headquartered in Italy. Prior to that, General Ashy had not been part of the US chain of command, and he therefore had not controlled US operations over Bosnia. These two changes would strengthen the opposing military camps vying for control of NATO airpower.

General Rose, Peacekeeping, and Airpower

British influence over the UN mission and the use of air-power in Bosnia increased markedly when Lt Gen Sir Michael Rose replaced UNPROFOR's Belgian commander in Bosnia, General Briquemont. In choosing General Rose, the British purposely picked a strong-willed individual.[2] While Rose has maintained that he was not under explicit instructions from London, that does not mean he was not pursuing British interests.[3] Stephen Hart's observation about Monty's "casualty conservation" approach to warfare during World War II seems apt:

> Montgomery's pursuit of British interests prompts consideration of whether he received any formal instructions from the British government concerning his conduct of the campaign. There is no evidence for any such instructions, but then they were probably unnecessary. It is inconceivable that a commander as senior as Montgomery . . . would not have been aware of the British government's agenda.[4]

General Rose was well aware of Britain's agenda. Shortly before going to Bosnia, Rose met with Britain's prime minister and later recalled,

> I left the meeting with a firm impression that John Major believed in the humanitarian role being played by the UN in Bosnia, and that Britain had a special contribution to make. He was not about to pull out the troops. . . . [And] in 1994, he never altered the peacekeeping basis upon which British troops were deployed.[5]

Throughout General Rose's time in Bosnia, his actions were in consonance with the UK's interests and the British interpretation of UNPROFOR's role there.[6]

From the outset of his tour in Bosnia, General Rose focused on the humanitarian and peacekeeping-like aspects of his mission to the exclusion of enforcing the UN's safe areas policy. Although UNPROFOR began as a peacekeeping force in Croatia, it never had a peacekeeping mission in Bosnia where there was no peace to keep.[7] The resolutions defining UNPROFOR's mandate in Bosnia—770, 776, and 836—were adopted under Chapter VII of the UN Charter dealing with enforcement measures.[8] However, in attempting to rescue what he saw as "a collapsing mission" in Bosnia, General Rose determined that he would concentrate "on the three main elements of the mission, which were, in order of priority: the

117

delivery of humanitarian aid, the creation of conditions for a political settlement of the war, and the prevention of the conflict from spreading beyond Bosnia."[9] While these mission elements might have required enforcement action, they left out the nettlesome safe areas aspect of UNPROFOR's mandate. Staff officers at the UK's Army Staff College in Camberley built a campaign plan around General Rose's three mission elements, and Rose went to New York to discuss his ideas about UNPROFOR's mission with some of the Security Council ambassadors and department of peacekeeping officials.[10] During this trip, he found support for his plans from Kofi Annan, head of the peacekeeping department. Thus, the mutually reinforcing political, military, organizational, and personal factors uniting the camp opposed to using robust airpower in Bosnia to enforce the safe areas policy grew stronger with General Rose's appointment to head UNPROFOR.

General Rose's interpretation of his mission in Bosnia was also a product of his expertise as a British army officer. He was well versed in the doctrinal discussions on peacekeeping then percolating within the UK's army, which would emerge during Rose's one-year tour in Bosnia in the form of official British army doctrine, "Wider Peacekeeping."[11] The doctrine of wider peacekeeping undoubtedly evolved as the British army drew lessons from events in Bosnia during Rose's tenure there,[12] but many of its fundamental concepts—such as the imperative for consent, and the strict boundary between peacekeeping and peace enforcement—were prefigured in the parliamentary report from July 1993, which had suggested that new peacekeeping doctrine was needed.[13] The British army's experiences in Northern Ireland, where Rose had served as a brigade commander in the 1980s, was the wellspring from which much of the British wisdom on peacekeeping flowed.[14] Like his predecessor in Bosnia, Rose, too, was an infantry officer and had missed the Gulf War. With a proud record from the Falklands War and as a former commander of British Special Forces, General Rose's military expertise and his outlook on the situation in Bosnia were, unsurprisingly, those of a soldier.

General Rose's views on airpower were fundamentally different from those of the NATO airmen with whom he would soon have to cooperate. He did not favor air strikes, though he believed some use could be made of close air support. Before leaving for Bosnia, General Rose told British prime minister John Major, "Although NATO air power certainly had an important role to play in Bosnia, it could not be applied much above a tactical level without collapsing the entire mission."[15] The day after expressing that view, Rose flew to New York, where US ambassador to the UN Madeleine Albright asked him what he thought of air strikes, to which he replied, "There was no case for mounting a strategic air campaign in Bosnia similar to the one in the Gulf War. The circumstances were entirely different. However, I had no problem with the use of close air support in self-defense or to support the mandate."[16]

Significantly, in this recollection of the discussion, published nearly five years after the event, Rose described two extremes for using airpower with no middle ground between those extremes. Lost by this elision was any discussion of a robust air campaign against the Bosnian Serb Army (BSA). By seeming to equate bombing other than for close air support (CAS) with a strategic air campaign akin to the one in the Gulf War, Rose was ruling out what was arguably the most effective airpower option. Even some of the staunchest critics of strategic bombing during the Gulf War praised airpower for its effect at the operational level of war, that is, for destroying the fighting potential of Iraq's army.[17]

Furthermore, the air strike options favored by General Ashy and approved at SHAPE, focused mainly on the Bosnian Serb Army, not Belgrade.[18] Whether Rose's apparent airpower astigmatism was real or affected was unknown, but it is apparent in the observation of a frustrated NATO airman who, during Rose's time in Bosnia, claimed that "General Rose either cannot, or will not, understand airpower."[19] What is clear, though, is that General Rose did not have the same view of airpower and its potential usefulness in Bosnia as did the senior American airmen in NATO.

Command Relationships, Air Strikes, and Close Air Support

In the two weeks leading up to General Rose's arrival in Sarajevo, the UN streamlined its chain of command and strengthened its civilian control over UNPROFOR. Mr. Yasushi Akashi arrived in Zagreb as the UN secretary-general's special representative and the first full-time civilian head of UNPROFOR.[20] Shortly after Akashi's arrival, Boutros-Ghali approached the French government about replacing General Cot, who had had difficulties with his previous civilian superior, Thorvald Stoltenberg.[21] On 2 February 1994, the UN secretary-general informed the Security Council that General Cot would be replaced by Lt Gen Bertrand de Lapresle.[22] Though it would be mid-March before de Lapresle took command of UNPROFOR, General Cot's authority over UNPROFOR had been curbed.

While the UN worked on replacing UNPROFOR's leadership, NATO again threatened air strikes to relieve the siege of Sarajevo, but obvious divisions between alliance members weakened the impact of the threat. On 10 and 11 January, NATO heads of state gathered in Brussels for a summit that the US had hoped would spotlight the launch of its Partnership for Peace proposal. However, with some instigation from Paris, NATO's role in Bosnia—and the absence of American ground forces there—became a major topic of discussion.[23] The summit ended with a communiqué reiterating the alliance's readiness "to carry out air strikes in order to prevent the strangulation of Sarajevo, the safe areas, and other threatened areas in Bosnia-Herzegovina."[24] Asked if NATO's commitment to use air strikes should be taken seriously after similar threats failed to produce any bombing the previous August, President Clinton said that he believed some members of the alliance were "more prepared to deal with this than they were in August."[25] Indeed, France was more willing to support air strikes, but the British were not.[26]

By mid-February, Boutros Boutros-Ghali had delegated to Mr. Akashi the power to authorize close air support, but not air strikes.[27] After the NATO summit, Mr. Akashi was instructed to work with NATO to plan for the use of airpower to overcome interference with UN operations in Srebrenica, Zepa, and at the Tuzla airport.[28] Though plans for using airpower were aimed ostensibly at all parties, it was obvious that the BSA was most in danger of becoming the target of NATO air action.[29] In late January, four days after General Rose took command in Bosnia, Boutros-Ghali informed the UN Security Council by letter that "for operations relating to Srebrenica and Tuzla, I have delegated to my Special Representative, Mr. Akashi, the authority to approve a request for close air support from the Force Commander."[30] Though UNPROFOR was ill prepared to protect these two safe areas, the secretary-general warned that

> the parties should, however, be aware that UNPROFOR's mandate for the safe areas has been adopted under Chapter VII of the United Nations Charter. Accordingly, UNPROFOR is not obliged to seek the consent of the parties for operations which fall within the mandate conferred upon it under Security Council Resolutions 836 (1993) and 844 (1993).[31]

In the same letter, the UN secretary-general made clear the distinction between close air support and air strikes, and noted that "NATO forces are not authorized to launch air strikes, which would require a further decision of the North Atlantic Council."[32] Finally, on 16 February, Boutros-Ghali wrote to the Security Council, stating, "I am delegating the necessary authority to my Special Representative . . . authority to approve a request from the Force Commander of UNPROFOR for close air support for the defence of United Nations personnel anywhere in Bosnia and Herzegovina."[33] Thus, within five weeks of his arrival in Zagreb as the new civilian head of UNPROFOR, Mr. Akashi was apparently vested with full authority to approve requests for close air support anywhere in Bosnia.

On 1 February 1994 General Ashy became a commander in the US chain of command, strengthening his position, but further tangling the awkward lines of responsibility below Admiral Boorda.[34] Back in September of 1993, the US Air Forces in Europe had created a new directorate for General Chambers, making him the US air component commander for the region.[35] By then, Chambers had received his third star, raising to three the number of lieutenant generals in Italy ostensibly responsible for air operations over Bosnia.[36] General Rossetti, the Italian commander of Fifth Allied Tactical Air Forces generally did not play much of a role in operational matters, but instead worked with his country's military and political superiors, keeping them informed and taking care of the many host-nation support issues.[37] General Ashy was senior to General Chambers, and higher up in the NATO chain of command, so Ashy and his staff worked on policy issues such as coordinating plans and rules of engagement with SHAPE and NATO Headquarters.[38] Meanwhile, General Chambers and the staff at the combined air operations center planned and ran the day-to-day flying activities.[39] Though Ashy's new title as a US commander did not change the working arrangements for air operations over Bosnia, it did give him easier access to US resources and strengthened his position. By the beginning of February, the two camps contending for control of airpower had fortified their positions at the operational level.

The Sarajevo Ultimatum: February 1994

An explosion in a Sarajevo market triggered a NATO threat to launch air strikes against the Bosnian Serbs, and it marked the beginning of increased military influence over the possible use of air strikes. On 5 February 1994, a shell exploded in an unusually crowded Sarajevo market, killing approximately 60 people and wounding more than 140 others.[40] Though the origins of the blast could not be confirmed, the presumption of Bosnian Serb guilt was strong.[41] Referring to Resolution 836, Boutros-Ghali informed the UN Security Council of the need to prepare for the use of airpower in Bosnia to forestall further attacks on Sarajevo.[42] He also asked NATO secretary-general Manfred Wörner to secure "a decision by the North Atlantic Council (NAC) to authorize the commander in chief of NATO's Southern Command [Admiral Boorda] to launch air strikes at the request of the United Nations, against artillery or mortar positions in and around Sarajevo which are determined by UNPROFOR to be responsible for attacks against civilian targets in that city."[43] This amounted to a very limited and specific request to get NAC approval for air strikes, if requested by the UN, and then only against smoking-gun-type targets designated by UNPROFOR.[44]

Despite British reluctance, NATO issued an ultimatum backed by the threat of air strikes to compel the Serbs to end the siege of Sarajevo. On 8 February the British Cabinet met in emergency session, and Foreign Minister Douglas Hurd reportedly urged his government to put alliance solidarity ahead of other British concerns by going along with the US and French-sponsored move in NATO toward tougher action.[45] Meanwhile, General Rose worked hard to finalize an agreement that would obviate any need for NATO air strikes.[46] Rose shuttled, mediated, and even coerced the Bosnian government and the Bosnian Serbs into a verbal agreement for defusing the situation around Sarajevo.[47] The media and the threat of air strikes were Rose's most potent weapons in forcing the two sides to accept his four-point plan for relieving the siege of Sarajevo.[48] But, as the council met in Brussels, General Rose had nothing but verbal assurances to show for his efforts.[49] The British were alone within NATO as they sought to dampen enthusiasm for enforcement action.[50] With France and the US in the fore, alliance ministers issued an ultimatum on 9 February 1994 establishing a heavy weapons exclusion zone around Sarajevo.[51]

Military Influence

The NATO ultimatum went beyond Boutros-Ghali's request in two significant ways: (1) it broadened the list of potential targets, and (2) it included restrictions on Bosnian government forces. The ultimatum called for the Bosnian Serbs to withdraw their heavy weapons from "an area within 20 kilometres of the centre of Sarajevo, and excluding an area within two kilometres of the centre of Pale."[52] Rather than removing their heavy weapons from the exclusion zone, the Serbs had the option of placing them "under UNPROFOR control."[53] Bosnian government forces were called upon to relinquish their heavy weapons[54] and put them under UNPROFOR control.[55] The real teeth to the ultimatum were contained in paragraph 10, which reads as follows:

> The Council decides that, ten days from 2400 GMT 10th February 1994, heavy weapons of any of the parties found within the Sarajevo exclusion zone, unless controlled by UNPROFOR, will, along with their direct and essential military support facilities, be subject to NATO air strikes which will be conducted in close coordination with the UN secretary-general and will be consistent with the North Atlantic Council's decisions of 2d and 9th August 1993.[56]

Significantly, paragraph 6 of the ultimatum expanded the potential list of targets by defining heavy weapons beyond the "artillery or mortar positions . . . responsible for attacks," which Boutros-Ghali had mentioned in his request. More importantly, paragraph 10 included the rather broad category of potential targets called "direct and essential military support facilities."

The terms of the NATO ultimatum reflected the influences of both General Rose and the commanders in NATO. Confirming his influence, General Rose wrote,

> Determined not to allow the UN peace process in Bosnia to be hijacked by NATO, I phoned an old friend who was involved in the discussions in Brussels, Lt Gen Rupert Smith, and told him it was crucial that the UN and NATO demands regarding the cease-fire and withdrawal of heavy weapons be completely aligned. . . . It was particularly important that the text of the NATO ultimatum being drafted that afternoon accurately reflected the wording of the negotiated agreement that had just been obtained in Sarajevo, and that the threat of NATO air strikes would be directed against any party that reneged on the Agreement. Fortunately, Rupert was able to introduce the necessary clauses into the document.[57]

The same sort of peacekeeping impartiality, in a situation where enforcement was called for, had gotten former UNPROFOR commanders Generals Lars Wahlgren and Philippe Morillon in trouble with the UN Security Council 10 months earlier at Srebrenica.[58] Moreover, it was, arguably, contrary to the intent of Resolution 836, which had mandated the use of airpower to support UNPROFOR to "promote the withdrawal of military or paramilitary units other than those of the Government of the Republic of Bosnia and Herzegovina."[59] However, as a commander, General Rose was responsible for both his mission and force protection. By inserting the reference to Bosnian government weapons in the ultimatum, General Rose strove to uphold the peacekeeping principle of impartiality necessary for preserving BSA consent for UNPROFOR. Thus, by hewing to peacekeeping, he was limiting his need to make the difficult trade-off between mission and men, which enforcing the safe areas policy entailed.

NATO military influence—mainly by Gen George Joulwan and General Ashy—affected the potential targets to be struck around Sarajevo, and reflected a desire to enforce the safe areas while limiting the risks to NATO aircrews. Greg Schulte, the civilian head of NATO's Bosnia Task Force at NATO headquarters, later explained, "From a military perspective, finding and attacking a specific smoking-gun was extremely difficult and risky for the aircraft involved. Therefore, NATO agreed to establish a 20 km 'exclusion zone' around Sarajevo."[60] Using NAC guidance from the previous summer's "Operational Options" memorandum, General Ashy developed several response options for attacking targets within the exclusion zone.[61] At least one of Ashy's options included "direct and essential military support facilities," which was a category of targets listed in "Operational Options."[62] General Ashy had also identified the wide range of heavy weapons spelled out in paragraph 6 of the ultimatum; however, it was Gen George Joulwan, the new SACEUR, who intervened at the end of the council meeting for formulating the ultimatum to suggest that the term *heavy weapons* be specified.[63] As a result, the NAC added tanks, rocket launchers, missiles, and antiaircraft weapons under the heavy weapons rubric, in addition to the artillery and mortars specified by Boutros-Ghali in his request for air strikes.[64] These inputs from NATO officers were significant because the terms of the exclusion zone around Sarajevo guided NATO policy on air strikes until the end of Deny Flight, and they served as a template for the exclusion zone created at Gorazde in April. Thus, NATO and UN theater-level commanders influenced the ultimatum in ways that made it safer for their forces and more favorable for the missions they preferred.

Airpower, Control, and Autonomy

The actions of General Rose as well as those of senior NATO officers during the ultimatum period demonstrated how military commanders sought to preserve autonomy and avoid outside "interference" in accomplishing their mission. General Rose knew that he had a hand on the UN key in the dual key arrangement for authorizing NATO air strikes,[65] and he resisted pressures to go along with NATO—including pressure from the United Kingdom's chief of defence (CHOD) staff, marshal of the Royal Air Force (RAF) Sir Peter Harding.[66] In taking this stand, Rose was fortified in knowing he enjoyed the support of Gen John Wilsey, who visited Rose in Sarajevo on the first day of the ultimatum period.[67] Wilsey was the UK-based joint commander of British Forces in the former Republic of Yugoslavia, and Rose noted,

> We spoke almost daily throughout my time in Bosnia as I felt it was important that there was someone in Britain who would defend, at the strategic and political level [sic], what I was trying to do at the tactical level. I had seen for myself how British lives had been unnecessarily lost in the Falklands because of political interference and John had suffered the same experience commanding in Northern Ireland. In John Wilsey I was fortunate to have someone who instinctively understood and supported the peace process. . . . It was also perhaps convenient for us both that as I was serving in a UN post, he could not directly give me orders.[68]

Thus, Rose used his UK connections to push his own aims, while shielding himself behind his status as a UN general to ward off unwanted national pressures. However, General Rose feared he might be overridden by higher authorities, thus losing control over military operations in his area of responsibility if the Bosnian Serbs did not comply with the ultimatum.[69] The Serbs were slow to show any sign of compliance, and once they began to move their heavy weapons, it remained unclear whether they would meet the NATO deadline.[70] Meanwhile, approximately 200 combat and support aircraft from four NATO nations—the US, Britain, France, and the Netherlands—stood ready to enforce the ultimatum.[71] As the deadline approached, General Rose's soldiers went to extraordinary lengths to verify Bosnian Serb compliance, even assisting the BSA in moving some of its equipment.[72] The reports from his soldiers were essential in the decision not to bomb.[73] Rose later remarked that in the end, "both sides concealed a substantial number of weapons within the TEZ [Total Exclusion Zone], but as long as they did not use them, this hardly mattered."[74] What mattered to General Rose was that air strikes were avoided, peacekeeping was not abandoned, "and that the UN controlled what was happening in Bosnia both from the air as well as on the ground."[75]

Commanders in NATO also wanted to control NATO airpower but, despite their efforts to maintain operational autonomy, their actions were subjected to detailed political supervision.[76] Admiral Boorda and General Ashy had been to Brussels with sample target folders to brief NATO ambassadors on plans for air strikes.[77] The commanders used the target folders to illustrate the types of targets they intended to strike and the care that had been taken to minimize chances for collateral damage.[78] By showing just a few sample targets and avoiding a detailed presentation on all of them, the commanders sought to earn the trust of NATO political authorities while inhibiting micromanagement from Brussels.[79] However, on the eve of the deadline, the defense ministers and chiefs of defense staff from the four nations providing aircraft for the strikes, plus the minister of defense (MOD) and chief of defense staff from Italy, gathered at Aviano Air Base with the principal NATO commanders, General Joulwan, Admiral Boorda, and General Ashy.[80] Under this high-level supervision, Admiral Boorda and General Ashy assessed the level of Bosnian Serb compliance being reported, mostly by General Rose.[81] As General Ashy recalled,

> When we got down to midnight that night, with Secretary Perry, Shali, Joulwan, and all the MODs and CHODs in that room, we were still verifying that the last of these was either in a holding point or was being observed under UN control or had been removed, or we would have been triggered to bomb this stuff. It was the damndest thing I've ever been through.[82]

Like General Rose, the NATO commanders had hoped to avoid political "help" in operational matters, and their control over information was a tool for maintaining their autonomy. However, unlike General Rose, they did not succeed.

As discussed in chapter 2, a commander will want control over forces and autonomy in using those forces if he is to be held accountable for the consequences of operations that take place under his command. General Rose had plenty of autonomy and control on the ground but no real control over NATO airpower. Conversely, the American commanders controlling

NATO airpower were so closely supervised that they might not have had autonomy if bombing operations had gone forward. The responsibility borne by the NATO commanders was lifted by higher military and political authorities who arrogated authority over the decision not to bomb. Because there was no bombing, commanders did not need to cope with infringements on their operational autonomy. Still, the actions of these UN and NATO commanders illustrated how commanders, convinced of their own expertise and charged with responsibility for their mission and their forces, might seek to control military operations and preserve their own autonomy—whether acting against or in concert with political pressures.[83]

General Cot's role in the run-up to the ultimatum deadline also suggested that open political support for a course of action reduces the weight of responsibility borne by a commander. During the ultimatum period, Cot was in close contact with General Rose and Admiral Boorda, and he was dependent on them for his information; moreover they, not he, were controlling the forces involved.[84] As a result, Cot lacked both control and autonomy. Yet, the UN force commander later denied being very apprehensive about the prospect of bombing and claimed that, while he was glad there was no bombing, he had been quite prepared to go along with it if the BSA had failed to comply.[85] In an interview, Cot professed, "You seem to think I was afraid of air strikes. No. I didn't want, and the UN didn't want, the Americans to make an American war in the former Yugoslavia. And if the Americans made an American war in Yugoslavia, then they needed to send battalions to Sarajevo, Bihac, and Mostar, eh?" However, unlike General Rose's situation, General Cot's government was comparatively supportive of air strikes, and Cot seems to have been more ambivalent about them, later recalling,

> Mitterrand telephoned me, and said to me: "Do we strike? Do we fire? Or do we not fire?" I said to him: "Boorda and I agree that the ultimatum is properly respected, therefore we are not going to strike." If the ultimatum had not been respected, we would have struck. That's obvious, eh?[86]

President Mitterrand's willingness to condone air strikes—not just in the phone call but also openly at the NATO summit in

January—reduced the weight of Cot's responsibility. The majority of UN soldiers on the ground in Bosnia came from France. Cot was a French general, and it was Mitterrand's prerogative to accept accountability for the consequences to French soldiers as a result of NATO bombing.

No-Fly Zone Enforcement and First CAS Approval: February–March 1994

Two events between the Sarajevo ultimatum and the crisis at Gorazde two months later illustrated the value of timely command decisions in the control of airpower over Bosnia. The first, the downing of four Serb aircraft caught violating the no-fly zone, showed how quickly a well-designed command and control (C^2) system could function while still maintaining tight control over operations. In the case of the no-fly zone enforcement, there was not much risk to the NATO forces involved, thus no real need for NATO commanders to make weighty decisions in choosing between mission accomplishment and force protection. Moreover, they enjoyed control and autonomy in their actions.

In the second event, a failed CAS mission at Bihac, the slow UN approval process caused the mission to fail. General Cot, who professed equanimity over the possibility of bombing as a result of the Sarajevo ultimatum, was outraged a month later when Mr. Akashi was slow to approve the CAS mission and French soldiers were under Bosnian Serb fire. Cot threatened to hold Akashi accountable for the consequences of the delays, clearly demonstrating the connection Cot saw between operational control and responsibility.

NATO Downs Serb Aircraft in the No-Fly Zone

A well-designed C^2 system and speedy decisions were needed to enforce the no-fly zone over Bosnia. On 28 February 1994, UN forces in Croatia saw Serb Galeb aircraft taking off from Udbina Airfield.[87] Soon afterwards, two American fighters over Bosnia picked up radar contacts on aircraft entering Bosnian airspace at low-level from Croatia and notified a NATO early warning aircraft.[88] With permission from the airborne warning and control system (AWACS), the flight lead of the two F-16s descended to low altitude to visually identify the radar contacts, and found six Galebs—small, single-seat jets used by the Serbs—in the ground attack role.[89] The F-16 flight lead managed to maneuver into a position behind the Galebs, apparently without his presence being detected.[90] While the F-16 pilot was waiting for guidance from the NATO AWACS, he saw the Galebs commit a hostile act—attacking a ground target in the central Bosnian town of Novi Travnik—and the pilot reported this to the AWACS.[91] When an officer in the CAOC informed General Chambers of the violation, Chambers immediately ordered the planes shot down.[92] In rapid succession the F-16 pilot downed three of the Serb jets.[93] A second flight of two American F-16s engaged and shot down a fourth Galeb.[94] Two of the Galebs were not thought to have been shot down, but it was suspected that one of the planes might have crashed in Croatia, perhaps due to fuel starvation.[95] At least one Galeb reportedly landed at an air base near Banja Luka in Serb-controlled northern Bosnia, further underscoring the military cooperation amongst the Serb communities in Croatia, Bosnia, and Serbia.[96] The entire operation, from the time NATO aircrews first detected the Galebs until the fourth one was shot down, lasted approximately 15 minutes.[97]

The downing of the four Galebs highlighted the importance of timely decisions for enforcing the no-fly zone, and the ease of decision making when mission accomplishment can be achieved with little risk to one's forces. Though Resolution 816, which authorized enforcement of the no-fly zone, stipulated that NATO air operations were "subject to close coordination with the secretary-general and the force," there was no dual-key control over decisions to take enforcement action against aircraft caught violating the zone.[98] A few minutes' delay in authorizing the F-16s to engage and the Galebs could have been safely on the ground somewhere in Bosnia or outside of Bosnian airspace.

Close Air Support

General Cot's actions during a failed NATO CAS mission illustrated how commanders deprived of control over operations by political decision makers might insist that individuals exercising control also take accountability for the consequences of the operations. The CAS request system in Bosnia worked on dual paths once a request reached the UN's Air Operations Control Center, and the NATO path required no real decision making—it operated on the assumption that UN approval would come in a timely manner.[99] The airplanes would be ushered to the area where CAS was needed while the request worked its way through the UN chain of command.[100] The NATO key was, in effect, in the "on" position. According to a February 1994 report by seasoned defense journalist Craig Covault, "the CAS system set up under UN/NATO agreement is designed to react so quickly that [Admiral] Boorda may not know the action is underway until it has commenced."[101] Though perhaps true in theory, this was a bit of an overstatement.[102] In practice, General Chambers had time to inform his superiors of the situation, and they would discuss the pending operation.[103] Typically, Chambers would then direct operations while General Ashy and Admiral Boorda monitored events closely by radio, by phone, and by a computerized aircraft situation display in Naples.[104] Chambers's superiors never overruled him, and NATO never refused a legitimate CAS request from the UN, though NATO commanders eventually became wary of the UN practice of using the threat of airpower as a bluff.[105]

While NATO could and did respond quickly to CAS requests, the UN approval process remained flawed. On 12 March 1994, French troops near Bihac came under fire from Bosnian Serb guns.[106] Within minutes, two A-10s were overhead the besieged French forces, awaiting clearance from the UN.[107] The A-10s were later replaced by an AC-130 gunship, which orbited near Bihac with an offending Serb weapon under the crosshairs of the plane's fire-control system, watching the Serb gun fire from time to time.[108] This situation, with NATO aircraft standing by for orders to attack, went on for several hours, while the UN hierarchy tried to reach a decision on whether to approve the CAS mission.[109] After French soldiers were injured, General Cot demanded that Akashi make a decision.[110] Despite having been delegated authority in mid-February to issue such approval, Akashi checked with Boutros-Ghali in

New York before finally giving the go ahead for close air support.[111] Moreover, Akashi caused further delays in an attempt to reach Bosnian Serb leader Radovan Karadzic by phone.[112] Finally, "Cot lost his temper," according to General Rose, who was present in the UN headquarters as Cot and Akashi spoke on a speaker phone:

> [Cot] told Akashi that the time for negotiation was over and he wanted either a yes or a no from him, warning him that if he said no, then he would bear all responsibility for the decision. Akashi ignored this and . . . Cot repeated that he wanted either a yes or a no, adding that if Akashi said no, then the press would hear about it the next day.[113]

At about midnight, when the mission was finally approved by the UN, execution was delayed because of problems with the weather and with communications between the ground-based forward air controllers and the gunship.[114] During the long delay, the AC-130 had left the target area, and upon returning, its crew needed to reacquire sight of the target.[115] When these problems were finally overcome, the forward air controllers withheld permission to expend ordnance because they had lost sight of the Serb weapon and could not verify that the crew aboard the AC-130 had reacquired the correct target.[116] As with the no-fly zone, timely decision making was needed for CAS to succeed. Unable to control the decision-making process, General Cot refused to be held accountable for the consequences of the delays.

The Bihac CAS episode made a strong impression on General Cot's replacement, Lt Gen Bertrand de Lapresle, who had arrived in Zagreb two days before the incident and was due to take command at mid-month.[117] General de Lapresle was an armored cavalry officer who had commanded an armored division in Germany, and he considered himself a NATO officer who happened to be assigned to the UN rather than a peacekeeper.[118] De Lapresle, who was present during the heated exchange between Cot and Akashi on 12 March, drew an important lesson from the incident: never to surprise Mr. Akashi with the need for an instantaneous decision.[119] In order for Mr. Akashi to respond favorably to any request to use force, General de Lapresle believed two things were necessary. First, Akashi had to be kept appraised of all military activities on the ground, and he had to be helped to anticipate decisions about the use of force.[120] Second, Akashi had to be confident that the UNPROFOR commanders were recommending the right course of action for the situation at hand.[121] This second condition required General de Lapresle to begin a process of earning Akashi's trust and educating him on airpower and procedures for controlling it—explaining to him how to stop air attacks if necessary and informing him of the likely consequences of using airpower.[122] Significantly, General de Lapresle was skeptical of the safe areas concept and even more doubtful about the logic behind the light option.

> I had the normal experience of a NATO officer, having served in the armored forces, and used close air support. And I knew how important it was in order to obtain some military effect on the ground—tactical effect, not strategic—to have this combination of infantry, tanks, helicopters, and aircraft. I knew very well that you can not have light infantry—which we had in the UN—and air support, without anything in this huge gap between light infantry and F-18s or F-16s. And I was horrified when, I was not yet in charge, this concept of safe areas was imposed to the UN, because in my mind it was completely clear that we would not, or the UN would not, be able to implement the mission as far as safe areas were concerned, if this gap was not filled. General Wahlgren . . . asked for 35,000 more men. . . . The "light option" was 7,500 men, and the gap between 7,500 and 35,000 being filled with the fact that aircraft would be overhead. . . . I was not very hopeful that airpower would really make the difference.[123]

Like the other UN army generals who had come to the former Yugoslavia, General de Lapresle started his tour with firm ideas about the utility of airpower in Bosnia. Unlike his predecessor, de Lapresle would work closely with the UN secretary-general's special representative and would thus have a greater impact on clarifying UNPROFOR's mission in Bosnia—lending military legitimacy to the UN secretariat's preferred interpretation of UNPROFOR's mission instead of combating the secretariat as Cot had done.

Turning Point: Gorazde, April 1994

The attempt by UN and NATO commanders to use airpower at Gorazde in April 1994 highlighted the bankruptcy of the light option and served as a turning point for the commanders and the organizations they represented. As the first anniversary of the resolution creating the safe areas approached, UNPROFOR leaders made their inputs to a UN report evaluating the safe areas policy. In light of their experiences at Gorazde and their inability to secure the full complement of reinforcements proposed for the light option, the UNPROFOR commanders began distancing themselves from the enforcement elements of their mandate. Meanwhile, the NAC took sides against the Bosnian Serbs and delegated more responsibility to the AFSOUTH commander. The experience at Gorazde taught the senior airmen in AFSOUTH that in order to fulfill their responsibilities as commanders, they needed to get tighter control on the use of NATO airpower. It also reinforced their preference for robust air strikes instead of CAS. In addition to the other mutually reinforcing factors at work, the responsibilities of command were driving commanders in AFSOUTH and UNPROFOR in different directions.

When the Bosnian Serb Army under General Mladic attacked Gorazde in early April 1994, UNPROFOR's commanders had no forces in the safe area and had to rely on NATO airpower to block the assault. On 6 April, General Rose sent a team of seven or eight special forces soldiers in the guise of UN military observers into the enclave; this small force doubled the meager UN presence in the safe area, which had previously consisted of just a few liaison officers.[124] These special forces soldiers were deployed to provide Rose with reliable information and to act as forward air controllers for NATO airpower.[125] It was General Rose's plan to send the forward air controllers into Gorazde with high-tech communications gear, and it indicated he was willing to try to use airpower to enforce the UN mandate to protect the safe areas. General de Lapresle had authorized the operation and,[126] in light of his lessons from the Bihac incident, his subsequent efforts to educate and gain the trust of Mr. Akashi, and the relative speed with which CAS was approved at Gorazde, it seems reasonable to conclude that Mr. Akashi also understood the nature and purpose of the soldiers deployed to the enclave.

On 8 April 1994, Admiral Smith took command of AFSOUTH from Admiral Boorda.[127] Smith was a Navy attack pilot who had flown 280 missions over North Vietnam during three combat cruises. The day of Admiral Smith's change of command, General Mladic "agreed in principle" to withdraw his forces to the line of demarcation between the Serbs and Muslims that existed in late March.[128] However, the next day the Serbs showed their true intentions by resuming the assault on Gorazde, which precipitated NATO's first real air attack.[129]

General Rose warned Mladic to stop or else face NATO air attacks, and he asked General de Lapresle and Mr. Akashi to approve a close air support mission.[130] When Rose was informed of an intelligence intercept revealing that Mladic had given orders to his commanders to raze Gorazde, Rose noted

> the time for diplomacy or negotiations was over and a great weight was lifted from my shoulders as I found myself back in the familiar business of war fighting. It did not cross my mind for a moment that the UN should refrain from using force. The lives of my soldiers and the civilians in Gorazde were being directly threatened.[131]

However, the only tools General Rose possessed for going to war were NATO aircraft and a handful of forward air controllers. Given the nature of the attacking Bosnian Serb forces, the poor weather he would confront, and his own lack of expertise in handling airpower, General Rose was not in a strong position from which to fight. UN political approval for close air support came shortly before 5:00 P.M., and with the attack on Gorazde intensifying, General Rose coordinated with Admiral Smith to have NATO attack a tank.[132] Because of poor weather, the first two flights of fighters failed to find the tank.[133] When a two-ship of F-16s arrived over Gorazde at 6:00 P.M., poor weather conditions forced the pilots to go below a cloud deck—with cloud bottoms at about 6,000 feet above sea level—in an attempt to find the tank.[134] In so doing, they increased their risk of being shot down; for although they were at the upper limits of small arms fire, they were well within range of antiaircraft guns and surface-to-air missile systems. Unable to visually acquire the tank, the F-16 pilots moved to an alternate target selected by General Rose—a group of vehicles and tents reportedly serving as an artillery command post on the high ground overlooking Gorazde.[135] At approximately 6:25 P.M. on Sunday, 10 April 1994, the F-16s dropped their

500-pound Mk-82 bombs on the command post, marking NATO's first-ever air-to-ground mission.[136] According to General Rose, some senior BSA officers were killed in the attack, including friends of Mladic, and the BSA commander threatened Rose that "no UNPROFOR would leave their territory alive."[137]

The BSA assault ended shortly after the bombing, but the Serbs resumed their attack the next day, 11 April.[138] CAS was quickly approved, but before authorizing actual attacks, General Rose had the planes conduct dramatic air presence passes in the target area.[139] Describing the activities for the press in Washington, director of operations for the Joint Chiefs of Staff Gen Jack Sheehan said,

> The F-18s did not attack the targets immediately. They went through a series of what I would call controlled flight profiles at the request of General Rose. They did a couple of high speed, supersonic runs against the target set, just to make sure the Serbs knew that they were there, that this was a serious activity.[140]

The threats had no effect, so shortly before noon General Rose again called for close air support.[141] A British forward air controller directed a pair of F/A-18s to hit some armored vehicles, but once again poor weather created problems.[142] The bomb attacks against the vehicles did not go well; out of four bombs, one failed to release from its aircraft, and two others impacted without detonating.[143] The lead F/A-18 pilot then proceeded to make low-altitude strafing attacks on the vehicles.[144] This was even more dangerous to the attacking aircraft than the previous day's CAS mission because the F/A-18 pilot was not only vulnerable to antiaircraft guns and surface-to-air missile systems but he was also within range of small arms fire and was repeatedly making passes near BSA forces he had just bombed. Though unnoticed by most observers then, and since, NATO's first two air-to-ground missions set off alarm bells within AIRSOUTH.[145] The attacks demonstrated that NATO aircrews could become so engrossed in successfully accomplishing their missions that they would violate the most basic tactical principles and endanger themselves in an attempt to destroy relatively insignificant targets.[146] Such risks might be justified if friendly forces needed immediate relief, or if the air missions were the only way to halt a ground attack. However, AFSOUTH commanders believed there were safer ways and more appropriate targets if the goal was to signal Mladic that the UN and NATO meant business.

The BSA assault on Gorazde tapered off after General Rose threatened another air attack, but Bosnian Serb president Radovan Karadzic claimed his forces would shoot down NATO aircraft, and the Bosnian Serbs broke off all contacts with UNPROFOR.[147] During the lull in fighting from 12 to 14 April, General Mladic's forces took approximately two hundred UN peacekeepers as hostages or detained them as virtual hostages.[148] This was the first instance of what would become the standard Bosnian Serb response to NATO air attacks. As with subsequent bombings, four things happened: 1) the Bosnian Serbs interfered with humanitarian aid deliveries, 2) they broke off negotiations with the UN, 3) they took hostages, and 4) they became more aggressive about firing on NATO aircraft.[149]

On the 15th, Mladic renewed his assault. That night, in Gorazde two British special forces soldiers were injured when the Bosnian government forces defending the city withdrew precipitately, leaving the British soldiers exposed to fire from onrushing BSA forces.[150] General Rose in Sarajevo phoned Mr. Akashi who was in Pale meeting with Radovan Karadzic.[151] Rose desperately wanted immediate approval for close air support to halt the attack, but Akashi demurred.[152] One of the soldiers died from the wounds suffered that night, but Akashi's delay most probably was not a factor in the soldier's death.[153] However, as Gow has argued, what seemed to matter most to General Rose was that in the heat of combat—with soldiers he had put in harm's way wounded and still taking fire—the general had called upon Mr. Akashi to deliver NATO airpower, and Mr. Akashi had balked.[154]

With UN peacekeepers as hostages, Mladic's forces began hitting back at NATO airpower. On 15 April, a reconnaissance version of the French Etendard fighter-bomber flying over Gorazde was hit by a heat-seeking surface-to-air missile, but managed to land safely back aboard the carrier *Clemenceau*.[155] It was the first NATO combat aircraft to be hit during Deny Flight. The next day, with the Serb assault still in progress, the UN leadership once again authorized close air support. A British Sea Harrier was called in to find a tank, but the Sea Harrier was not optimized for such a mission, and the weather was again poor. After several passes at low altitude in the target area, the Sea Harrier was shot down by a shoulder-launched surface-to-air missile.[156] The pilot ejected sustaining only minor injuries and was able to join his special forces compatriots in Gorazde.[157] When later asked by Admiral Smith's aide why he had made multiple passes in the target area when he knew he was being shot at, the Sea Harrier pilot explained that he did it because his countrymen were in trouble.[158] However, Gorazde was a city of approximately 60,000 people, and there were only a half dozen soldiers, whose movement within the enclave was not restricted. If the soldiers really were in harm's way, it would have been because they had gone there intentionally—possibly looking for targets for NATO airpower. Later on 16 April, American A-10s were tasked to provide air support for the British special forces in Gorazde, but poor weather prevented them from accomplishing their mission.[159] That evening, Russian mediator Vitaly Churkin arranged for Mr. Akashi to suspend further air action in exchange for Bosnian Serb pledges to release the UN hostages and to meet for negotiations the next day.[160] While Karadzic met with Akashi on 17 April, the UN hostages were supposed to be freed, but only a few of them were, and more than a hundred were still being detained by the BSA at day's end.[161] Meanwhile the attack on Gorazde continued, and as NATO readied for air strikes, General Rose ordered his special forces troops out of the enclave.[162]

North Atlantic Council Decisions and the Gorazde Ultimatum

On 18 April, the same day General Rose's forward air controllers left Gorazde, Boutros-Ghali sent a letter to Manfred Wörner asking for "a decision by the North Atlantic Council to authorize the commander in chief of NATO's Southern Command to launch air strikes, at the request of the United Nations, against artillery, mortar positions or tanks in or around [any] . . . of the safe areas."[163] President Clinton strongly endorsed the UN request, and on 20 April the NAC met to consider it.[164] However, council members adjourned without taking a decision, reportedly because they wanted military commanders to assess the targeting options and the probable effectiveness of air strikes.[165] Two days later, after the Bosnian Serbs repeatedly made and broke pledges for cease-fires around Gorazde, the council met again in emergency session.[166] Subsequently, NATO issued two statements on decisions taken by the NAC that day. The first dealt with the immediate relief of the situation at Gorazde, and the second established conditions under which NATO air strikes might take place for all of the safe areas in Bosnia. Significantly, the list of potential targets once again included direct and essential support facilities, and it also reflected the broader definition of heavy weapons stemming from General Joulwan's input during the establishment of the exclusion zone for Sarajevo.

Of immediate consequence, the decisions established a pair of ultimatums for the Bosnian Serbs with respect to Gorazde: one ultimatum demanded that the Bosnian Serbs—and only the Bosnian Serbs—demilitarize the area within three kilometers of the center of the town and that they grant the UN unimpeded access to the enclave by 0001 GMT on 24 April 1994;[167] the other ultimatum established a 20-kilometer heavy-weapons exclusion zone around Gorazde, with a deadline of 0001 GMT on 27 April 1994.[168] Of greater long-term significance, the NAC removed itself almost completely from the decision-making process needed to authorize air strikes around the safe areas. Council decisions would no longer be necessary for air strikes within 20 kilometers of the safe areas so long as the strikes were against Bosnian Serb heavy weapons and "their direct and essential military support facilities, including but not limited to fuel installations and munitions sites."[169] It was left for "NATO Military Authorities to initiate air attacks . . . in coordination with UNPROFOR" and in accordance with the NAC "decisions of 2d and 9th August 1993."[170] NATO's military authorities would only require further decisions from the NAC if they wanted to conduct air strikes beyond the parameters spelled out in these two NAC decisions (i.e., beyond the vicinity of the safe areas or against targets of any faction other than the Bosnian Serbs). Furthermore, the NAC decided that

> once air attacks have been carried out against a specific target set pursuant to these decisions, the NATO military authorities may continue to carry out, in coordination with UNPROFOR, the attacks against that target set until NATO military authorities judge the mission to be accomplished (emphasis added).[171]

These NAC decisions were a mixed blessing for NATO commanders. While granting the commanders some autonomy and room for initiative, they also left it to the military to work out arrangements for air attacks with reluctant UNPROFOR leaders.

On the night of 22 April, Mr. Akashi received a briefing on the proposed NATO air strikes, and he and his advisors were convinced that hitting the dozen or so targets proposed by NATO would only upset the Bosnian Serbs without compelling a positive change in their behavior.[172] The Bosnian Serbs missed the first deadline, but Mr. Akashi, who was with General de Lapresle in Belgrade for negotiations with Bosnian Serb leaders, blocked NATO air action.[173] The BSA grudgingly, and only partially, withdrew in accordance with the NATO ultimatums, burning and destroying sections of Gorazde as they pulled back.[174] Hundreds of Bosnian Serb combatants remained within three kilometers of the center of Gorazde by posing as police officers, and UN forces continued to find Serb heavy weapons within the 20-kilometer exclusion zone.[175] However, the BSA ground advance and heavy-weapons fire on Gorazde had stopped. On 26 April, UN officials announced that Bosnian Serb progress toward compliance was sufficient to drop the threat of air strikes.[176] Though the enclave did not fall, and NATO publicly joined the UN in declaring success, the events around Gorazde marked a turning point in UN-NATO relations and seriously challenged the utility of NATO airpower in Bosnia.[177]

UN and NATO Missions in Bosnia: A Matter of Interpretation and Political Guidance

As a result of the experience at Gorazde and the continued vulnerability of UN forces, Generals Rose and de Lapresle virtually gave up trying to use airpower as a means to help protect the safe areas.[178] By General Rose's account, "Peacekeepers had to believe that any risks they took or sacrifices they made would be justified by results. No one is prepared to sacrifice himself or his comrades for a failed mission."[179] Losing a highly skilled soldier due to apparent Bosnian army malfeasance undoubtedly colored General Rose's view of the government whose people he was trying to protect at Gorazde.[180] Furthermore, if Mr. Akashi could not be counted on to authorize air support and NATO pilots could not find their targets when air support was authorized, then General Rose could not ensure that the risks and sacrifices of his forces "would be justified by the results."[181] Gorazde apparently changed General Rose from being rather punchy about using NATO airpower to help protect the safe areas, to virtually unwilling to call on it. Contrary to that impression, General Rose claimed that he remained willing to use airpower; he was just unwilling to go beyond the smoking-gun-type targets that he equated with option 1 air strikes. As Rose later said, "I was a great exponent of airpower, but I was not going to go to level two."[182] As the next chapter shows, General Rose was indeed unwilling to go to option 2 targets, but he also seemed to have lost his enthusiasm for airpower altogether.

General de Lapresle saw Gorazde as a turning point for himself and for General Rose. The UNPROFOR commander recalled, "We had this first experience in Gorazde, which unfortunately confirmed completely what Michael Rose and myself had in mind as to what Harriers and other aircraft could bring us in a very woody, and mountainous, and difficult terrain."[183] By all accounts, including their own, the UN commanders suffered no lack of confidence in what unrestrained airpower was capable of doing in a combat scenario.[184] However, UNPROFOR's vulnerability made a more robust use of airpower off limits.[185] Referring to the risks to the lives of UN soldiers, General de Lapresle said,

> What sort of explanation would we have to give to their children, or their wives, and so on? Was it really worth the lives of those soldiers

141

who came to keep peace and not to fight a war against the Serbs? This was a daily concern, of course.[186]

These concerns were undoubtedly heightened when the BSA took the first UNPROFOR hostages as a result of the air attacks on 10 and 11 April. It seemed that trying to employ airpower, even in a relatively passive or defensive mode of CAS for UN soldiers, exceeded the Bosnian Serbs' tolerance and consent for UNPROFOR's presence. Rather than compensating for the UN's shortage of ground forces as the light option envisioned, NATO airpower jeopardized UNPROFOR's security and its humanitarian mission with no compensating return in terms of protecting the safe areas. Although UN commanders had been aware of this potential problem, vivid affirmation of their beliefs at Gorazde came just as General de Lapresle and Mr. Akashi were making their inputs to a UN report on the status of the safe areas.[187] Thus, not only was Gorazde a personal turning point for General Rose, it was also a turning point in the UNPROFOR mission.

In a 9 May report to the Security Council, the UN secretary-general pointed out the difficulties of using force to secure the safe areas, the risks of retaliation against UNPROFOR, and the vulnerability of peacekeepers to hostage taking. Furthermore, he noted that member-states had failed to provide the 7,600 troops called for under the light option.[188] Given these difficulties and the ambiguities from the accretion of resolutions and reports concerning UNPROFOR, Boutros Boutros-Ghali conveyed UNPROFOR's interpretation of its mission with regard to the safe areas. The mission, as UNPROFOR interpreted it, was to deter attacks on the safe areas merely through its own presence.[189] If deterrence failed, UNPROFOR "could be required to resort to close air support to protect its own members or to request air strikes to compel an end to the attack on the safe areas."[190] Finally, Boutros-Ghali sought Security Council confirmation or clarification on UNPROFOR's interpretation of its mission[191] and closed his report with a recommendation that "the Security Council approve the statement of UNPROFOR's mission in relation to the safe areas as set out in the present report."[192]

Essentially, by this report, Generals de Lapresle and Rose received political support for their preferred interpretation of UNPROFOR's mission—one that reflected the limitations of their forces. This interpretation saw the safe areas as mechanisms to further an overall humanitarian mission aimed at alleviating suffering and promoting conditions for peace.[193] The UNPROFOR interpretation would prevent the safe areas from becoming an end in themselves that would drain away scarce UN resources, or worse still, serve as a mechanism for justifying enforcement action that might drag UNPROFOR into the fighting.[194] This interpretation of UNPROFOR's mission with regard to the safe areas was entirely consistent with the views long held within the UN secretariat.[195] Unlike Generals Briquemont and Cot, who quarreled with the UN staff in New York, and the secretary-general's special representatives, Generals Rose and de Lapresle added their endorsement and military legitimacy to Mr. Akashi's report. The shift away from enforcement was not just a change in policy; it was also a reflection of the reality of UNPROFOR's inability to take enforcement action. As General de Lapresle noted, "you can change every word of any Security Council resolution; if you do not have soldiers who have been sent there to fight, you cannot change their behavior on the field. So, what I meant when discussing with Akashi . . . [was] that if we were expected to behave differently, we would need some means."[196] Though UNPROFOR commanders increasingly took the position that their mission was peacekeeping and not peace enforcement, the Security Council never passed a resolution superseding 836, nor did it offer any clarification of UNPROFOR's mission in relation to the safe areas.[197] However, because the Security Council did not dispute UNPROFOR's interpretation, which obviously enjoyed the support of Boutros Boutros-Ghali, Generals de Lapresle and Rose had good grounds for adhering to their view of UNPROFOR's mission.

Trust, Expertise, and Forces at Risk

In May, just as UNPROFOR was seeking Security Council approval for its interpretation of its mission with regard to the safe areas, Gen George Joulwan and NATO's deputy secretary-general Sergio Balanzino visited UNPROFOR leadership in Zagreb and Sarajevo. General Joulwan expressed his concern that the UN had not been forceful enough in its use of air-power at Gorazde, and that it was unacceptable for the Serbs to maintain heavy weapons inside the exclusion zones.[198] General Rose assured SACEUR that any weapons inside the exclusion zones were broken down.[199] From Zagreb, the NATO visitors went with General Rose to Sarajevo. En route to the UN commander's headquarters, the group came under fire, which General Joulwan was convinced came from a mortar. General Rose suggested it was merely rocket-propelled grenade fire, hence not from a banned heavy weapon.[200] Inside General Rose's headquarters, General Joulwan asked the UN chief of intelligence if red pins dotting a map of the Sarajevo area and inside the exclusion zone represented broken-down heavy weapons. According to Joulwan, the intelligence officer assured SACEUR that they represented active heavy weapons, leading General Rose to explain that he had been away from his headquarters for a while.[201] From that point on, General Joulwan said he felt he could not trust General Rose. According to the NATO commander:

> It is important that when you commit forces, you must make sure that you have trust and confidence of those you're working with . . . [further-more,] it's not just right to be politically correct; you better be militar-ily correct when you have forces involved. And so I insisted upon bru-tal truth, brutal honesty when you're putting aircrews, and ground crews, and tank crews, and ships at risk. And I didn't get brutal hon-esty; I got a shaky answer from Rose.[202]

The lack of trust was mutual, for General Rose felt that, "Joulwan and his team tried to bounce the UN in May into using more force. And [the UN] just [said]: 'You're not doing it.'"[203] General Rose already had forces at risk, and he did not appreciate a NATO general pushing for risky actions when NATO was unwilling to deploy forces on the ground in Bosnia.[204] Compounding the difficulties was General Joulwan's tendency at this stage to treat the UNPROFOR commanders as his subordinates since they came from NATO nations.[205] Joulwan's motto as SACEUR was "one team, one fight"; however, the UN wanted neither to be on the team nor to join in the fight.[206]

Though Admiral Smith and General Ashy in Naples understood the difficulties the UN faced when it came to using force against the Serbs, the two senior airmen found that they could no longer blithely countenance the practice of using NATO airpower for "air presence" missions.[207] Restrictions against targeting anything other than smoking-guns or the actual forces threatening the UN was bad enough. Such constraints, however, could be justified in order to protect the lives of UN peacekeepers on the ground. What concerned NATO operational commanders was the UN practice of calling on airpower to intimidate one of the warring factions (almost always the Bosnian Serbs), apparently without having the intention or the political approval from within the UN to actually employ force.[208] Initially the mere presence of aircraft had been used by the UN as a show of force to strengthen its hand at road blocks, or to dampen heavy weapons fire.[209] But, "the UN became addicted to air presence," according to one NATO officer.[210] General Chambers noted that over time UNPROFOR found it necessary for the planes to fly lower and to make more noise in order to intimidate the warring factions. General Rose even requested some high-speed passes below an altitude of 500 feet, which would have made the aircraft vulnerable to ground fire.[211] As a matter of routine, NATO continued the practice of sending aircraft to the vicinity of UN peacekeepers whenever a situation began to develop that might require close air support.[212] Air presence missions continued to be flown, but with some restrictions.[213] However, in the wake of the Sea Harrier loss and the UN's refusal to employ airpower in a more robust manner, senior NATO airmen became extremely reluctant to give General Rose the same level of control over NATO aircraft that he had exercised at Gorazde.[214]

General Rose held fundamentally different views of NATO airpower and its role over Bosnia than did the senior airmen in AFSOUTH. From General Rose's perspective, the NATO commanders were presenting him with an all-or-nothing choice—either he had to be willing to go after something other than the smoking-guns, or he would get no air support at all.[215]

145

In his memoir, General Rose says that Admiral Smith "would only accept strategic-level targets, such as major HQs, communications sites, or logistic installations such as ammunition bunkers. I told him that neither NATO nor the UN had authority to escalate the use of air power in this manner."[216] In truth, these were precisely the sorts of targets spelled out under option 2 of NATO's "Operational Options for Air Strikes," and by labeling them "strategic level targets," Rose indicated the gulf between his view of airpower and that shared by NATO commanders.[217] More significantly, General Rose believed that NATO should be prepared to lose some aircraft, noting that the downing of the Sea Harrier "was unfortunate . . . but the incident should be considered a routine hazard of peacekeeping."[218] The American airmen in NATO disagreed with this on two counts: first, they did not see their mission as peacekeeping,[219] and second, they viewed the risks as unjustifiable and unnecessary. The principal reason for attempting to employ airpower in Bosnia was to make use of a tool for enforcement action, which carried minimal risks. That Admiral Smith felt the risks were unjustified and unnecessary is clear from General Rose's account. They were unjustifiable because the UN would halt the use of airpower as soon as the Bosnian Serbs stopped shooting;[220] thus, the results were ephemeral, and the Bosnian Serbs could, and did, resume their attacks when the weather worsened or after they had taken UN hostages. Under these circumstances, the risks were being taken for no discernible payoff. The rationale for going beyond smoking-gun-type targets during the Sarajevo ultimatum was to get more payoff for less risk.[221] In the days and months after the downing of the Sea Harrier, senior airmen in AFSOUTH and their political masters in Brussels would repeatedly demonstrate just how little risk to NATO aircraft they were willing to accept.[222] Furthermore, the risks were unnecessary in the eyes of the NATO commanders because they believed there was a better way to use airpower and that was to strike more significant targets that might actually compel the Bosnian Serbs to respect the UN safe areas and the NATO exclusion zones.[223]

Conclusion

The growing split between UN and NATO commanders can be viewed in terms of force protection and tactical determinism; that is, it was impossible to prosecute smoking-gun-type targets within the bounds of acceptable risk to NATO pilots and the capabilities of NATO airpower. Unfortunately the most realistic and safest way of employing NATO airpower clashed with the security needs of UNPROFOR. These disparate limitations and vulnerabilities of NATO and UNPROFOR were driving the commanders in the two organizations further and further apart. Yet NAC decisions increasingly left it to the operational commanders to try to find some workable middle ground to do something whenever political pressures mounted. AFSOUTH and UNPROFOR attempts to meet halfway, however, manifested themselves in the compromised safety of NATO pilots or UN peacekeepers. After Gorazde, theater-level commanders gradually began to accept the tactical determinism that pulled them toward the separate elements in what was supposed to be a cooperative effort. Rather than seeking political direction, Generals Rose and de Lapresle sought to help define their own mission. General Rose began the process with his campaign plan even before he arrived in Bosnia. After Gorazde, the UN generals made their input and added military legitimacy to the UN secretary-general's report of 9 May, which moved UNPROFOR away from responsibility for enforcing the safe areas policy. These were the first steps in creating a division of labor, whereby UNPROFOR conducted peacekeeping and NATO took responsibility for enforcement action.

The difficulties and dangers of providing air presence and close air support to UNPROFOR reinforced the AFSOUTH commanders' preference for more militarily meaningful air attacks. Moreover, it convinced the NATO commanders of the wisdom of having airmen controlling airpower. Likewise, the difficulties and dangers of having close air support at Gorazde reinforced the UNPROFOR commanders' desire to control airpower. The theater-level commanders in both the UN and NATO were trying to strike a proper balance between the risks to their forces and accomplishment of their missions. For

UNPROFOR, that meant reinterpreting the mission so as to avoid responsibility for the safe areas and the exclusion zones. For AFSOUTH, striking the right balance meant not putting forces at risk unless there was a commensurate payoff. That, in turn, led the commanders in AFSOUTH to favor air strikes over CAS, and to curtail the reflex of giving UNPROFOR air presence. As noted before, the commanders' responsibilities were reinforced by national political pressures, differing areas of expertise, and organizational biases. The next chapter further assesses the role of responsibility in motivating the commanders and shows their actions as part of a broader pattern of behavior.

Notes

1. Richard K. Betts, *Soldiers, Statesmen, and Cold War Crises* (Cambridge, Mass.: Harvard University Press, 1977; reprint with new preface and epilogue, New York: Columbia University Press, 1991), 154–56. Betts's discussion focused on tactical determinism working at the policy-making level while policy was still being formed. As this chapter demonstrates, the process can also work backward, reshaping policy after it has been made. And, in this case, military commanders in the field played an important role.

2. British Ministry of Defence Official F.

3. Gen Sir Michael Rose, British army, retired, *Fighting for Peace: Bosnia 1994* (London: The Harvill Press, 1998), 13, 16, and 53.

4. Stephen Hart, "Montgomery, Morale, Casualty Conservation, and Colossal Cracks: Twenty-First Army Group's Operational Technique in North-West Europe, 1944–45," *The Journal of Strategic Studies* 19, no. 4 (December 1996): 144.

5. Rose, 13.

6. Laura Silber and Allan Little, *Yugoslavia: Death of a Nation* (n.p.: TV Books, Inc., 1996), 310–17. For a spirited (if not spleenful) discussion of General Rose's role in pursuing British interests, see Jane Sharp, *Honest Broker or Perfidious Albion: British Policy in Former Yugoslavia* (London: Institute for Public Policy Research, 1997), 32–34 and 43–46. Also see Mark Almond, "A Far Away Country," in *With No Peace to Keep: United Nations Peacekeeping and the War in the Former Yuguslavia*, eds. Ben Cohen and George Stamkoski (London: Grainpress, 1995), 125–41.

7. The principal Security Council resolutions defining UNPROFOR's mandate, 770, 776, and 836, were all based on chap. 7 of the United Nations (UN) Charter, though Resolution 776's connection to chap. 7 was through Resolution 770 rather than an explicit reference in 776 itself. Richard Caplan incorrectly claimed that "Res. 776 imposed constraints on the use of

force; unlike 770, it was a chapter 6 resolution." Richard Caplan, "Post-Mortem on UNPROFOR," *London Defense Studies*, no. 33 (London: Brassey's for the Centre for Defence Studies, 1996), 11. Also see James Gow, *Triumph of the Lack of Will: International Diplomacy and the Yugoslav War* (New York: Columbia University Press, 1997), 270–71, n. 9.

8. Jerzy Ciechanski, "Enforcement Measures under Chapter 7 of the UN Charter: UN Practice After the Cold War," in *The UN Peace and Force*, ed. Michael Pugh (London: Frank Cass, 1997), 86–93.

9. Rose, 12.

10. Ibid., 14 and 24; and Military Official G.

11. Rose, 11.

12. John Gerard Ruggie, "The UN and the Collective Use of Force: Whither and Whether?" in *The UN Peace and Force*, ed. Michael Pugh (London: Frank Cass, 1997), 9–10.

13. House of Commons, Defence Committee, Fourth Report, *United Kingdom Peacekeeping and Intervention Forces*, 13 July 1993, 27 and 38–39.

14. Ibid., 28; and Army Field Manual (AFM) (UK),*Wider Peacekeeping* (London: HMSO, 1995), 12.

15. Rose, 13.

16. Ibid., 15.

17. See for example: Robert A. Pape, *Bombing to Win: Air Power and Coercion in War* (Ithaca, N.Y.: Cornell University Press, 1996), 240–53; and Maj Stephen T. Ganyard, USMC, "Where Air Power Fails," *U.S. Naval Institute Proceedings* 121, no. 1 (January 1995): 36–39. Also see United States Department of Defense, "Conduct of the Persian Gulf War: Final Report to Congress," (n.p.: Government Printing Office, April 1992), 158–59 and 179; and Lt Col William F. Andrews, USAF, *Airpower Against an Army: Challenge and Response in CENTAF's Duel with the Republican Guard*, CADRE Paper (Maxwell Air Force Base [AFB], Ala.: Air University Press, 1998).

18. As discussed in chap. 4.

19. Military Official W.

20. David Owen, *Balkan Odyssey* (London: Victor Gollancz, 1995; Indigo, 1996), 264. Akashi's predecessor as SGSR continued his duties as the UN cochairman of the International Conference on the Former Yugoslavia in Geneva.

21. Ibid.; and Philippe Guillot, "France, Peacekeeping and Humanitarian Intervention," *International Peacekeeping* 1, no. 1 (spring 1994): 39.

22. Letter from the Secretary-General to the President of the Security Council, 2 February 1994 (S/1994/121, 4 February 1994).

23. Alan Ridding, "France Presses U.S. for Stronger Stand on Bosnia," *New York Times*, 6 January 1994, A8; and Douglas Jehl, "In NATO Talks, Bosnia Sets Off A Sharp Debate," *New York Times*, 11 January 1994, A1 and A8.

24. North Atlantic Treaty Organization, "Declaration of the Heads of State and Government Participating in the meeting of the North Atlantic Council held at NATO Headquarters, Brussels, on 10–11 January 1994," *Press Communiqué* M-1(94)3, 11 January 1994, par. 25.

25. R. W. Apple Jr., "NATO Again Plans Possible Air Raids on Serbs in Bosnia," *New York Times*, 12 January 1994, A1 and A8.

26. Dick A. Leurdijk, *The United Nations and NATO in Former Yugoslavia, 1991–1996: Limits to Diplomacy and Force* (The Hague: The Netherlands Atlantic Commission, 1996), 40; Pia Christina Wood, "France and the Post-Cold War Order: The Case of Yugoslavia," *European Security* 3, no. 1 (spring 1994): 148; and Apple, A1.

27. Letter from the Secretary-General to the President of the Security Council, 28 January 1994 (S/1994/94, 28 January 1994) (hereafter cited as S/1994/94); and Letter from the Secretary-General to the President of the Security Council, 15 February 1994 (S/1994/182, 15 February 1994) (hereafter cited as S/1994/182).

28. S/1994/94.

29. Ibid.

30. Ibid.

31. Ibid.

32. Ibid.

33. S/1994/182.

34. The reorganization gave General Ashy command of the US Sixteenth Air Force, making him "dual hatted," since he retained his NATO position as commander Allied Air Forces Southern Europe (COMAIRSOUTH). Dr. Thomas S. Snyder and Dr. Daniel F. Harrington, USAFE Office of History, *USAFE Historical Highlights, 1942–1997: Fifty-fifth Anniversary Edition* (Ramstein Air Base, Germany: Headquarters USAFE, 1997), 168.

35. Ibid., 164–65.

36. The other two were General Ashy and the Italian commander of Fifth ATAF, General Rossetti.

37. Lt Gen James E. Chambers, USAF, director of NATO's Combined Air Operations Center (CAOC), Vicenza, Italy, interviewed by author, 10 February 1998, Fairfax, Va., transcript of taped interview, author's personal collection.

38. Gen Joseph W. Ashy, USAF, interviewed by Lt Col Robert Owen, 29 April 1996, Washington, D.C. Unclassified version of "General Ashy's Oral History Interview," (66 pp.) redacted by the Air Force Historical Research Agency, October 1997. Office of History, Air Force Space Command, Peterson AFB, Colo.; and Lt Col Lowell R. Boyd Jr., USAF, AFSOUTH staff officer, February 1993–1996, transcript of taped interview by Lt Col Robert Owen, 6 December 1995, Naples, Italy, Balkans Air Campaign Study (BACS) Collection, Air Force Historical Research Agency, Maxwell AFB, Ala.

39. Chambers interview; and Col Robert Lushbaugh, USAF, retired, chief of Operations for Provide Promise and Deny Flight, CAOC, Vicenza, Italy, February–June 1993, interviewed by author, 9 July 1998, Langley AFB, Va., author's notes, author's personal collection.

40. Silber and Little, 309; and the United Nations, *Blue Helmets: A Review of United Nations Peacekeeping*, 3d ed. (New York: United Nations Reproduction Section, 1996), 528.

41. Silber and Little, 309–31; *Blue Helmets*, 528; and Gen Sir Michael Rose, transcript of filmed interview, "The Death of Yugoslavia" collection, Box 18, File 4 (R-Z), 1 (Liddell Hart Archives, King's College, University of London).

42. *Blue Helmets*, 529.

43. S/1994/131, 6 February 1994, cited in *Blue Helmets*, 529.

44. Gregory L. Schulte, "Former Yugoslavia and the New NATO," *Survival* 39, no. 1 (spring 1997): 22–23.

45. BBC and the Discovery Channel, "Episode 5: No Escape."

46. Gen Sir Michael Rose, interview with author, 10 December 1997, London, transcript of tape recording, author's personal collection; Rose, transcript of filmed interview, 3; and Silber and Little, 310–15.

47. Rose, transcript of filmed interview, 1–6; Silber and Little, 313–15; and Rose, *Fighting*, 47–51.

48. Rose, *Fighting*, 47–48; and Silber and Little, 313.

49. Silber and Little, 315.

50. Ibid., 313.

51. Ibid., 313–14; and Wood, 148.

52. NATO, Press Release (94) 15, 9 February 1994, par. 6.

53. Ibid., par. 6.

54. Ibid., par. 7.

55. Senate, *Briefing on Bosnia and Other Current Military Operations*, 23 February 1994, 13.

56. NATO, Press Release (94) 15, 9 February 1994, par. 10.

57. Rose, *Fighting*, 51–52.

58. A report by a Security Council team that traveled to Bosnia and visited Srebrenica criticized the two UNPROFOR commanders for agreeing to disarm the government forces in Srebrenica and for pressuring the enclave's leaders into accepting terms dictated by General Mladic for surrendering the enclave. Report of the Secretary-General Pursuant to Security Council Resolution 819 (1993) (S/25700, 30 April 1993) (Reissued). Also see Jan Willem Honig and Norbert Both, *Srebrenica: Record of a War Crime* (London: Penguin Books, 1996), 106.

59. Security Council Resolution 836 (1993) (S/RES/836, 4 June 1993). Technically Rose's agreement did not violate the letter of the resolution. Because the Bosnian government was not being asked to withdraw its heavy weapons or any associated units, it merely had to turn them over to UNPROFOR. Arguably, it ran counter to the intent not to disarm the Bosnian government forces.

60. Schulte, 22. Obviously the exclusion zone created a mechanism for the sort of wider bombing advocated by the United States. However, Schulte's explanation accurately reflected the limitations of airpower, thus demonstrating the double nature of tactical determinism (i.e., as a real constraint and as a possible expedient for shaping policy).

61. General Ashy's interview with Colonel Owen indicated that there were three options based on the level of compliance with the ultimatum (not

counting option one, which was to simply monitor the exclusion zone in the event of full compliance). However, the redacted interview transcript was unclear as to what the range of options was and what criteria were to be used in selecting the appropriate option.

62. Ashy interview with Col Robert Owen.

63. Gen George Joulwan, interviewed by author, 11 February 1998, Washington, transcript of tape recording, author's personal collection. Joulwan replaced General Shalikashvili as SACEUR in October 1993, when Shalikashvili became chairman of the US Joint Chiefs of Staff.

64. Joulwan interview, 11 February 1998.

65. The term *dual key* may have entered the lexicon at a NATO meeting on 10 February, the day after the NAC ultimatum. Representing the military at the meeting, Vice Adm Norman Ray, the deputy chairman of NATO's Military Committee, described UNPROFOR's control over NATO airpower using the dual key analogy, thus easing the concerns of ambassadors who feared that the ultimatum had gone too far. The term would have been familiar to those in the room who understood nuclear safeguards, whereby two keys, far enough apart that one person could not activate them both, needed to be turned simultaneously in order to launch a nuclear missile. Vice Adm Norman W. Ray, USN, interviewed by author, 19 November 1997, Brussels, transcript of tape recording, author's personal collection.

66. Rose, *Fighting*, 55–56.

67. Ibid., 52.

68. Ibid., 52–53.

69. Ibid., 55–56; and Silber and Little, 314–17.

70. Gow, *Triumph*, 147–48; and Silber and Little, 316–17.

71. Leurdijk, 42–43; Craig Covault, "NATO Flights Accelerate for Sarajevo Recon," *Aviation Week and Space Technology*, 21 February 1994, 34.

72. Rose, transcript of filmed interview, 7; and BBC and Discovery Channel, "Episode 5."

73. Rose, *Fighting*, 56 and 61–62; and Senate, *Briefing on Bosnia*, 23 February 1994, 15–16.

74. Rose, *Fighting*, 57.

75. Ibid., 55.

76. Cot interview; Ashy interview by Col Robert Owen.

77. Ashy interview by Col Robert Owen; Lt Gen Nicholas B. Kehoe, USAF, assistant chief of staff, Operations and Logistics, Supreme Headquarters Allied Powers Europe, Mons, Belgium, July 1992–October 1994, interviewed by author, 18 November 1997, Brussels. Transcript of tape recording, author's personal collection; Ray interview; and Ashy interview by author. The date of Ashy and Boorda's visit to Brussels remains undetermined. In General Ashy's interview with Colonel Owen, Ashy seemed to indicate it took place around the time of the Sarajevo ultimatum; however, it might have been as early as some time in 1993. The timing would not affect the point made here about control of information and operational autonomy.

78. Ashy interview by author.

79. Ibid.

80. Senate, *Briefing on Bosnia*, 10 and 15; Ashy interview by Col Robert Owen; and Ashy interview by author.

81. Senate, *Briefing on Bosnia*, 15–16; Rose, *Fighting*, 56 and 61–62; Ashy interview by Col Robert Owen; and Ashy interview by author.

82. Ashy interview by Col Robert Owen.

83. The point here is to show that commanders *do* seek to preserve control and autonomy over operations and *how* they might do so. This chapter and subsequent chapters show that at times it is, in large part, because commanders have responsibility and expertise that they insist on control and autonomy. Obviously, these demands could be motivated by other factors, such as national political pressures or military doctrine. In the case of the Sarajevo ultimatum, the factors motivating the commanders were mutually reinforcing, so it is difficult to argue persuasively that any of them was most important.

84. Gen Jean Cot, French army, UNPROFOR force commander, July 1993–March 1994, interviewed by author, 30 September 1998, Paris, transcript and translation of tape recording, author's personal collection.

85. Ibid.

86. Ibid.

87. Per Erik Solli, *UN and NATO Airpower in the Former Yugoslavia*, NUPI Report no. 209 (Oslo: Norwegian Institute of International Affairs, 1996), 27. Within two weeks of the shooting down of the Galebs, the author acquired a copy of the cockpit video from the F-16 that shot down three of the Serb planes. The tape was used along with a talking paper to brief officers at the author's home unit.

88. Chambers interview; and Maj Mark A. Bucknam, USAF, talking paper on "Shootdown of Galebs over Bosnia," 29 April 1994, briefing notes, author's personal collection.

89. Bucknam.

90. Ibid.

91. Ibid.; and *Facts On File Yearbook 1994* (Facts on File, Inc., 1994), 134–35. The Galebs may have divided their formation and made two separate attacks: one on Novi Travnik and another a few miles to the west at Bugojno. See Air Vice-Marshal Tony Mason, Royal Air Force, *Air Power: A Centennial Appraisal* (London: Brassey's, 1994), 180; and Maj Michael O. Beale, USAF, *Bombs over Bosnia: The Role of Airpower in Bosnia-Herzegovina* (Maxwell AFB, Ala.: Air University Press, 1997), 1.

92. Bucknam; and Chambers interview.

93. Bucknam; and *Facts On File 1994*, 135.

94. Bucknam; and Ashy interview by author.

95. Bucknam; Chambers interview; and Ashy interview by author.

96. Bucknam; Mason reported two landed at Banja Luka. See *Air Power*, 180. General Rose claimed the Serbs held a funeral for the pilots in Belgrade the week after the downing. Rose, *Fighting*, 71.

97. *Facts On File 1994*, 135.

98. Chambers interview. Citation from Security Council Resolution 816, 31 March 1993 (S/RES/816, 31 March 1993).

99. Col Daniel R. Zoerb, USAF, director, Deny Flight Air Operations Center, HQ AFSOUTH, interviewed by author, 29 April 1997, Spangdahlem, Germany, transcript of tape recording, author's personal collection; and Covault, 35.

100. Brig Gen Charles F. Wald, USAF, interviewed by author, 7 May 1997, Aviano, Italy, tape recording, author's personal collection; Zoerb interview; and Covault, 35.

101. Covault, 35.

102. Ashy interview by author.

103. Covault, 35; Wald interview; and Chambers interview.

104. Ashy interview by author; and David Miller, "NATO Command and Information Systems," *International Defense Review* 27, no. 6 (1994): 57–64.

105. Chambers interview; and Adm Leighton W. Smith, USN, interviewed by author, 10 February 1998, Arlington, Va., transcript of tape recording, author's personal collection. The next chapter addresses the aborted close air support mission at Bihac in November 1994.

106. The number and types of weapons firing on the French are uncertain. It seems that a mobile antiaircraft gun and possibly a tank were involved. Rose, *Fighting*, 85; Mason, 180; Lowell Boyd interview; Solli, 49–50; and Hans-Christian Hagman, "UN-NATO Operational Co-operation in Peacekeeping 1992–1995" (PhD diss., King's College, University of London, 1997), 123.

107. Chambers interview; and Zoerb interview.

108. Chambers interview.

109. Ibid.; Ashy interview by author; and Maj Gen James Chambers, "Outstanding Air Support of UNPROFOR," photocopy of electronic message, 13 March 1994, Vicenza, Italy [to participating NATO units], BACS Collection.

110. Gen Jean Cot, French army, "Dayton ou la Porte Etroite: Genese et Avenir d'un Désastre," in *Dernière Guerre Balkanique?*, 2e ed., ed. Jean Cot (France: Editions L'Harmattan, 1996), 123; Gen Bertrand de Lapresle, interviewed by author, 13 January 1998, Paris, transcript of tape recording, author's personal collection; and Rose, *Fighting*, 85.

111. Cot, "Dayton," 123; Rose, *Fighting*, 85; Ashy interview by author; and Chambers interview.

112. Cot, "Dayton," 123; and Rose, *Fighting*, 85.

113. Rose, *Fighting*, 85.

114. Lowell Boyd interview.

115. Solli claimed that NATO aircraft left at the request of the UN. Solli, *UN and NATO*, 49. NATO sources indicated that the AC-130 left to refuel in-flight. Lowell Boyd interview; and Zoerb interview.

116. Lowell Boyd interview; and Ashy interview by author.

117. De Lapresle interview.

118. Ibid.

119. Ibid.

120. Ibid.

121. Ibid.

122. Ibid.

123. Ibid.

124. Rose, *Fighting*, 100; Tim Ripley, "Blue Sword over Bosnia," *World Airpower Journal* 19 (winter 1994): 22; and Silber and Little, 327–28. Silber and Little asserted the soldiers were all from the British Special Air Service.

125. De Lapresle interview; Ashy interview by author; and Hagman, 125. Rose hints at the forward air controller status of these soldiers without directly saying that that is what they were. Rose, *Fighting*, 101.

126. De Lapresle interview.

127. *Facts On File 1994*, 96 and 207.

128. David Owen, *Balkan Odyssey*, CD-ROM version 1.1, Academic Edition (The Electric Company, 1995), reference 177.

129. Department of Defense (DOD), "Special DOD News Briefing," 11 April 1994.

130. Rose, *Fighting*, 106–7.

131. Ibid.

132. Ibid., 147. General Rose reported that the approval process took over an hour because Akashi, who was in Paris, had to check with New York before approving the mission.

133. Smith, press conference, 11 April 1994; and Ripley, 22.

134. Smith, press conference; and Zoerb interview.

135. DOD, "Special News Briefing," 11 April 1994; and Rose, *Fighting*, 107.

136. Snyder and Harrington, 170–71; DOD, "Special News Briefing," 11 April 1994; and *Facts On File 1994*, 253.

137. Rose interview by author; Silber and Little, 328; and Rose, *Fighting*, 107–8.

138. DOD, "Special News Briefing," 11 April 1994; and Rose, *Fighting*, 108.

139. DOD, "Special News Briefing," 11 April 1994; and Ripley, 23.

140. DOD, "Special News Briefing," 11 April 1994.

141. Ripley, 23.

142. Ibid.; Smith, press conference, 11 April 1994; and DOD, "Special News Briefing," 11 April 1994.

143. Ripley, 23; and Zoerb interview.

144. DOD, "Special News Briefing," 11 April 1994; Ripley, 23; and Zoerb interview.

145. Zoerb interview.

146. Ibid.

147. *Facts On File 1994*, 254.

148. Silber and Little, 328; and *Facts On File 1994*, 269.

149. These consequences did not follow the first NATO air strikes in August and September of 1994 because the Serbs had been warned in advance of the strikes, and UN commanders elected to strike symbolic, and militarily insignificant, targets.

150. Rose interview by author.

151. Silber and Little, 329.

152. Ibid.; BBC and Discover Channel, Episode 5; and Rose, *Fighting,* 111–13.

153. *Facts On File 1994,* 269; and Rose, *Fighting,* 112.

154. Gow, *Triumph,* 150–51.

155. AFSOUTH, "Operation Deny Flight Fact Sheet," 5 October 1995; Ripley, 23; and Tim Ripley, *Air War Bosnia: UN and NATO Airpower* (Osceola, Wisc.: Motorbooks International, 1996), 70 and 79.

156. Ripley, "Blue Sword," 23; and Zoerb interview.

157. Ripley, "Blue Sword," 23.

158. Cmdr Kevin M. Donegan, USN, interviewed by author, 29 April 1998, London, printout of E-mail, author's personal collection.

159. Ripley, *Air War Bosnia,* 70; and "Blue Sword," 23.

160. Silber and Little, 330; and David Owen, *Balkan Odyssey,* CD-ROM version 1.1, reference 177.

161. David Owen, *Balkan Odyssey,* CD-ROM version 1.1, reference 177.

162. Ripley, "Blue Sword," 23; and Silber and Little, 331.

163. Annex to Letter from the Secretary-General to the President of the Security Council, 18 April 1994 (S/1994/466, 19 April 1994).

164. *Facts On File 1994,* 269–70.

165. Ibid.

166. Ibid., 270 and 293.

167. NATO, Press Release (94)31, 22 April 1994.

168. NATO, Press Release (94)32, 22 April 1994.

169. Ibid.

170. Ibid.

171. Ibid.

172. Thomas Quiggin, military information analyst, UNPROFOR Headquarters, Zagreb, interviewed by author, 20 December 1998, printout of E-mail, author's personal collection; Ashy interview by author; Chambers interview; and Military Official Y.

173. Report of the Secretary-General Pursuant to Resolution 913 (1994) (S/1994/600, 19 May 1994).

174. Daniel Bethlehem and Marc Weller, eds., *The "Yugoslav" Crisis in International Law, General Issues Part I,* Cambridge International Documents Series, vol. 5 (Cambridge: Cambridge University Press, 1997), 56; and *Facts On File 1994,* 293–94 and 383.

175. S/1994/600, 19 May 1994.

176. Military Official Y.

177. Silber and Little, 332–34; and Leurdijk, 49–54.

178. De Lapresle interview; Gow, *Triumph,* 150–51; and Military Official W.

179. Rose, *Fighting,* 76.

180. Ibid., 111–15.

181. Gow, *Triumph,* 151.

182. Rose interview by author.

183. De Lapresle interview.

184. Ibid.; Rose interview by author; Ashy interview by author; and Zoerb interview.

185. De Lapresle interview; and Rose interview by author.

186. De Lapresle interview.

187. David Owen, CD-ROM reference 177, "UN-NATO disagreement over the use of air power." According to General de Lapresle, Akashi signed the report from Zagreb on which the secretary-general's report was based. However, Mr. Akashi came to Zagreb unschooled in the workings of airpower, and de Lapresle had mentored him. Moreover, they had spent a lot of time together during the Gorazde crisis. Gen Bertrand de Lapresle, UNPROFOR force commander, 15 March 1994–February 1995, interviewed by author, 8 September 1998, Paris, transcript of tape recording, author's personal collection.

188. Report of the Secretary-General Pursuant to Resolution 844 (1993) (S/1994/555, 9 May 1994).

189. S/1994/555, pars. 13 and 16.

190. Ibid., par. 17.

191. Ibid., par. 29.

192. Ibid., par. 32.

193. Ibid., pars. 13 and 24.

194. Ibid., pars. 16, 17, and 24.

195. See for instance, Report of the Secretary-General Pursuant to Security Council Resolution 836 (1993) (S/25939, 14 June 1993).

196. De Lapresle interview, 8 September 1998.

197. S/1994/1389, 1 December 1994.

198. Joulwan interview, 11 February 1998; and Rose, *Fighting*, 127–28.

199. Ibid., and Rose, *Fighting*, 125–27. In General Rose's account the weapons were five old artillery pieces barely 100 meters inside the exclusion zone, and that their range probably precluded them from threatening Sarajevo.

200. Joulwan interview, 11 February 1998; and Rose, *Fighting*, 128.

201. Joulwan interview, 11 February 1998.

202. Ibid.

203. Rose interview by author.

204. Rose, *Fighting*, 126. Since there were soldiers from NATO nations in UNPROFOR, I take General Rose's use of "NATO" to mean more specifically the United States.

205. Military Officials X and Z.

206. Rose, *Fighting*, 125–26.

207. Smith interview; and Donegan interview.

208. Smith interview; Chambers interview; Zoerb interview; and Wald interview.

209. Smith interview; and Chambers interview.

210. Lowell Boyd interview.

211. Chambers interview.

212. Chambers interview; Smith interview; and Wald interview.

213. Smith interview; Zoerb interview; and Wald interview.
214. Smith interview; Donegan interview.
215. Rose interview by author.
216. Rose, *Fighting*, 114.
217. See discussion in chap. 4 on "Operational Options." Targets NATO might have considered "strategic level" would have been part of phase 3, or option 3, as it came to be called.
218. Rose, *Fighting*, 114.
219. Smith interview. Also note the mission statement given to General Ashy in August of 1993 cited in chap. 4, the terms of the Sarajevo ultimatum, and the terms of the Gorazde ultimatum, which followed the loss of the Sea Harrier. Each of these directed NATO commanders to prepare for enforcement action in situations where Bosnian Serb consent was nonexistent.
220. Smith interview.
221. Schulte, 22–23.
222. The topic of limiting risks to NATO aircrew is discussed extensively in the next chapter.
223. Ashy interview by author; Smith interview; and Zoerb interview.

Chapter 6

Competing Missions and Demands for Force Protection: August–December 1994

The whole business of dual key again caused a certain amount of discussion. But when you've got two chains of command, slightly different mandates, you're going to have to have a dual key. There's no other way of running an operation.

—Gen Sir Michael Rose
Interviewed by author
10 December 1997

In the second half of 1994, NATO airmen believed the UN's piecemeal and highly restrained use of airpower held little prospect for affecting the behavior of the Bosnian Serbs. Furthermore, NATO commanders began to believe that the influence of UNPROFOR's commanders over the conduct of air attacks unnecessarily jeopardized the safety of NATO airmen. Conversely, commanders in UNPROFOR became convinced—especially after events at Gorazde in April 1994—that NATO airpower could easily create more problems than it was likely to solve. Though willing to accept air support *in extremis*, they harbored serious misgivings over NATO plans for air strikes. Under the "dual key" control arrangements, the UN could veto NATO's more muscular air options, and an unhealthy tension between soldiers and airmen and the organizations they represented grew during the summer and fall of 1994.

This chapter shows how military commanders in NATO and the UN clashed over their competing concerns for force protection and mission accomplishment. The first section addresses UN-NATO friction over the UNPROFOR practice of warning the Bosnian Serbs of pending air attacks. It also examines UN-NATO disputes over "proportionality" in responding to Bosnian Serb provocations around Sarajevo. The UN dimension of this struggle has been addressed elsewhere, but

159

the NATO perspective has been largely unrecognized or misinterpreted.[1] The second section shows how the commanders of UNPROFOR and AFSOUTH accepted short-term degradation of their missions during the air strike against the Serb-controlled Udbina airfield and how they cooperated in order to support each other's needs for force protection. The third section details some previously neglected issues concerning NATO's response in late 1994 to the growing Bosnian Serb surface-to-air threat. Though NATO commanders won formal political approval to change the rules of engagement (ROE) governing suppression of air defenses, the commander of UNPROFOR used the dual-key mechanism to prevent NATO airmen from acting on their new authority. This inhibited the ability of NATO airmen to act in self-defense, causing a serious split between UNPROFOR and AFSOUTH. Thus, despite some compromises on both sides, by the end of 1994 the divergent responsibilities of UN and NATO commanders contributed to a breakdown in cooperation between them, rendering Deny Flight virtually ineffective.

NATO Air Strikes and the Clash over Warnings and Control: August–October 1994

By the summer of 1994, commanders in UNPROFOR and AFSOUTH were working at cross-purposes in Bosnia even as they tried to cooperate to implement the same Security Council resolutions. The divided UN-NATO command arrangements reflected and were reinforced by conflicting national political pressures, different means available, different types of military expertise, and different responsibilities. With US support for the Bosnian government cause, commanders in AFSOUTH came under increasing political pressure to enforce Bosnian Serb compliance with the NATO-decreed exclusion zone around Sarajevo. The one-sided nature of this sort of intervention threatened to unhinge Serb consent for the UN forces, whose mandate the exclusion zone was meant to serve. Meanwhile, UNPROFOR commanders endeavored to preserve the humanitarian and peacekeeping focus of their mission, which meant remaining impartial and maintaining the consent of the warring factions. The division of labor—with the UN focusing on peacekeeping and NATO focusing on enforcement—led to radically different approaches to using airpower.

From the summer of 1994, planners in Naples worked on target matrices to guide NATO commanders should they wish to propose air strikes in response to provocations from any of the warring factions.[2] These matrices were to be used in conjunction with five thick target books maintained at the headquarters of the principal commanders in the region: AFSOUTH, AIRSOUTH, 5ATAF/CAOC, UNPROFOR, and Bosnia-Herzegovina Command.[3] Each book contained identical information—such as photographs and target descriptions—on targets approved by the UN-NATO joint targeting board.[4] Additionally, the books included copies of UN Security Council resolutions and NAC decisions relevant to air operations in the former Yugoslavia.[5] Targets were divided into categories according to the type of target and were also divided into five sets—one for each safe area, but with only one set for Zepa and Srebrenica combined.[6] Next to each typical provocation and suggested response, NATO planners identified the authorizing Security Council resolutions and NATO decisions as well as the appropriate ROE from Deny Flight plan 40101.[7] The target books incorporated targets for the three warring factions in Bosnia: the Bosnian Serbs, Bosnian Croats, and Bosnian government forces.[8] However, many factors—including the UN safe areas concept, the supporting NATO ultimatums, and the fact that the Bosnian Serbs possessed the preponderance of heavy weapons and other likely targets—made it easier for NATO planners to identify Bosnian Serb targets and more likely that those targets would be nominated for air strikes.[9] Officers working in the air component of Admiral Smith's headquarters went to great lengths to keep these books updated so UN and NATO commanders could react quickly and appropriately to a provocation.[10]

During the summer of 1994, General Rose proposed a new scheme for using airpower though the proposal convinced some airmen that the UN's commander in Bosnia did not understand the vulnerabilities of airpower or share their views on its proper employment.[11] Labeled Operation Antelope, the proposal called for NATO to respond to the unauthorized removal of heavy weapons from UN control points by striking the exact piece of equipment that had been illegally taken.[12] From an airman's viewpoint, this concept of operations was grossly inefficient and seemed quite risky for UN and NATO forces involved. The CAOC chief of plans who headed the project for NATO, Col Chuck Wald, recalled,

> [General Rose] wanted to hit the exact weapon or tank they took out of a cantonment area. And he'd asked us if we could get a C-130 gunship to work with their Lynx helicopters, with their special ops guys on them, with FLIR [Forward Looking Infrared] to go out and find, if we could, a tank that they [the Serbs] had stolen, follow it through towns if we had to, and then hit that particular tank. . . . We planned an operation to do that. I planned it. And we practiced it. . . . It was ludicrous.[13]

The large number of supporting aircraft required by such a mission—refueling tankers, defense suppression planes, standby close air support aircraft, and search and rescue assets—would create a signature, tipping off the Serbs that some air action was about to occur.[14] Furthermore, the helicopters and the relatively unmaneuverable AC-130 gunships would have been vulnerable to BSA air defenses.[15] It would have been simple for the Serbs to counter an operation like Antelope by seizing weapons from several sites at the same time or merely waiting for poor weather to steal heavy weapons from the United Nations.[16] No attempt was ever made to actually execute Operation Antelope, but General Rose apparently had it in mind when the Bosnian Serbs confiscated heavy weapons from UNPROFOR in early August; Rose later wrote, "My plan was to hit the vehicles and weapons with air strikes as they left the weapons collection point."[17] However, the plan did not work in this case; as one observer noted: "Once a UN helicopter, which was tracking the stolen weapons, was struck by ground fire, it was forced to give up the chase. NATO then launched 16 fighters."[18]

NATO's First Air Strike, 5 August 1994

NATO's first air strike demonstrated the large and growing gap between the UN and NATO over using airpower. On the morning of 5 August, Bosnian Serb forces injured a Ukrainian peacekeeper in a raid on the Ilidza weapons control point west of Sarajevo and took five heavy weapons.[19] Yasushi Akashi was away on vacation, and according to General Rose, General de Lapresle agreed with Admiral Smith "to authorize NATO to attack Gulf War-style targets, including Serb ammunition bunkers and communications sites."[20] However, General Rose intervened, asserted his rights as the responsible commander, and designated a new target for the attack, which turned out to be a derelict tank destroyer.[21] NATO launched over a dozen French, British, and Dutch aircraft, but after long delays and problems with weather, two US A-10s under the control of a French forward air controller made the attack.[22] NATO's first "air strike" involved no bombs. The A-10s made several strafing passes on the vehicle, which was miles from Ilidza and which AFSOUTH airmen only later realized had already been out of commission.[23] Throughout the attack, the UN commanders held tight control over events. While General Rose coordinated with General Chambers on which target to hit,[24] General de Lapresle held one phone to Chambers's NATO superiors in one hand, and in the other he held a phone through which he issued demands to Momcilo Krajisnik, president of the Bosnian Serb Assembly.[25] The Serbs agreed to return the weapons after the attack on the broken down vehicle, and General Rose later rejected notions that this was a "pin prick" strike, stating: "This air strike by NATO proved a textbook example of the precise use of force in a peacekeeping mission."[26] Admiral Smith had a different view:

> I was frustrated as *hell* when Michael Rose would give us one target, and drop the bomb, and that was it. And I tried my damndest to get him to understand that you've got to do more than go after some derelict tank in the middle of a field.[27]

The underlying problem was that the two commanders were pursuing different missions. The UN general was practicing peacekeeping, and the NATO admiral was attempting to enforce UN mandates and NATO ultimatums.[28]

Warnings

Compounding Admiral Smith's frustration over having the attack directed against a disused vehicle was his discovery that General Rose had given the Serbs a warning before the air strike.[29] While most observers appreciated the risks faced by peacekeepers in Bosnia, a continual point of frustration for senior NATO airmen was that few, if any, commentators seemed to recognize the dangers confronting NATO aircrews.[30] General Rose believed warning the Bosnian Serbs was necessary for limiting collateral damage, and that it was consistent with the peacekeeping principles of maintaining consent and the minimum use of force.[31] Moreover, the warnings minimized the chances of Bosnian Serb retaliation against Rose's peacekeepers. For Admiral Smith, warnings created an unjustifiable risk to the lives of NATO aircrews, and he became furious with General Rose over the issue.[32] Despite the admiral's remonstrations, though, General Rose would ignore Smith's concerns and continue to warn the Serbs.[33]

The warnings helped General Rose to lower the risks to his forces. UNPROFOR did not just warn the Serbs in general that they were about to be attacked but told them specifically what would be attacked just prior to each strike.[34] The practice of giving the Serbs warning served the needs of the UN mission in Bosnia and was intended to head off Bosnian Serb retaliation against UNPROFOR peacekeepers. By warning the Bosnian Serbs of NATO air attacks, UN commanders reduced the chances of killing any BSA soldiers, thus helping to maintain the consent of the Serbs for the UN's presence and its mission in Bosnia. This, in turn, reduced Serb motivations to take revenge against UNPROFOR forces. Therefore, tactical warnings prior to air strikes helped to maximize both mission success and force protection for UNPROFOR. General Rose considered warnings a principle of peacekeeping,[35] and he continued to issue warnings despite Admiral Smith's strenuous protests.[36] Recounting a discussion with Admiral Smith, General Rose recalled,

> He [Admiral Smith] said: "If you issue a warning, you're hazarding my pilots." And I would say: "Sure there is a risk to your pilots, because they're coming down quite low to deliver their ordnance, and these guys could be ready for them. But the fact is they're only coming into the theater of operations for minutes at a time." I said: "We live, you know, within the range of these weapons all the time, so what's the

problem? What's the big deal? When you're a peacekeeper you ought to take risks."[37]

Moreover, General Rose claimed his intent was to give the Serbs only 20 or 30 minutes' warning—enough time for them to evacuate their own forces and to help minimize collateral damage but not enough time to organize their air defenses against the attack.[38]

Warning the Serbs, however salutary for UNPROFOR, mitigated the effects of air strikes and put NATO aircrews at increased risk of being shot down. The UN warnings gave the Bosnian Serbs an opportunity to move or protect whatever NATO was going to attack, and to prepare any available air defenses already in the area of the intended target. Combined with other factors detracting from airpower's effectiveness— such as poor weather, mountainous and wooded terrain, the inherent difficulties of spotting individual weapons, and UN reticence to authorize more robust air attacks—the warnings helped to soften whatever signal air strikes were meant to send. As the Bosnian Serb surface-to-air threat increased during the summer of 1994, warnings of NATO attacks heightened the likelihood the BSA would shoot down another NATO aircraft. So while warnings improved mission accomplishment and force protection for UN peacekeeping, it had the opposite effect on NATO's enforcement action.

NATO's Second Air Strike, 22 September 1994

NATO's second air strike again highlighted the UN and NATO disagreements over targeting and warning, but it also demonstrated that nations with troops on the ground in Bosnia were involved in the air strikes. Maintenance of alliance cohesion was an implied objective for NATO commanders, and participation by as many nations as possible in any air strike was one of NATO's stated goals.[39] However, by September 1994, only American aircraft had prosecuted NATO air attacks, thus distorting the image of Deny Flight by masking its multinational character.[40] Commanders in AFSOUTH were anxious to include non-US allies in the next use of NATO airpower, and they got their chance when General Rose's deputy, Maj Gen André Soubirou, called for an air strike on 22

165

September 1994.[41] In the CAOC at Vicenza, General Chambers sat with the French and British senior national representatives and orchestrated the NATO response; over the next several hours, the CAOC team would endeavor to make this particular air strike more overtly multinational than previous allied air attacks.[42]

As with NATO's first air strike, General Rose once again intervened to warn the Serbs and to redirect the attack against a target of lesser military significance than the one agreed to by his UNPROFOR superior, General de Lapresle. On 22 September, French peacekeepers around Sarajevo came under direct fire from Bosnian Serb forces at several different locations, and at least two Frenchmen were injured.[43] General Rose had just returned to the UK temporarily, and his French deputy, General Soubirou, was in charge in Bosnia.[44] Generals Soubirou and de Lapresle were preparing to strike an ammunition depot at Pale in response to this latest provocation[45] when General Rose was alerted of the pending operation by his staff in Sarajevo.[46] Working with General Wilsey in the UK, General Rose was able to halt the planned attack and then redirect it toward a target of Rose's choosing—a T-55 tank in the Sarajevo exclusion zone.[47] Moreover, General Rose again ensured the Serbs were warned about the planned attack, later stating, "Adm Leighton Smith had ordered that no warning be given to the Serbs prior to the attack in order to avoid giving them time to alert their air defense system, putting NATO pilots at greater risk. I told my chief of staff in Sarajevo, Brinkman, to ignore that order."[48]

Though a pair of US A-10s were the first aircraft on scene and the pilots could see the target, NATO commanders withheld the A-10s in favor of non-US aircraft.[49] Two French Mirage 2000s were brought in, but the pilots had difficulty finding the target and eventually departed the target area for in-flight refueling.[50] After about an hour's delay, the situation grew tense at the CAOC.[51] The airmen in the CAOC, who were aware the Serbs had been warned, worried that NATO would lose credibility if they were unable to follow through with the attack and that the Serbs might shoot down an attacking aircraft.[52] RAF Jaguars were available for the attack, but General

Chambers consulted with the British and French senior national representatives, and opted for the French Mirages.[53] However, as soon as the Mirage pilots reported the target in sight, they also announced they were low on fuel and needed to depart.[54] Late in the day and with NATO credibility on the line, General Chambers ordered the A-10s to attack the tank.[55] At about 6:20 P.M., an A-10 strafed the tank, and the dust kicked up highlighted the vehicle's location for the orbiting Jaguars.[56] The British pilots were then called in to drop 1,000-pound bombs on the tank, and one of the bombs reportedly scored a hit.[57] The British bombs demonstrated the multinational nature of Deny Flight, boosting the apparent legitimacy of the operation and deflating concerns that only the United States—with no troops on the ground—was doing all of the bombing in Bosnia.[58]

Proportionality

NATO's second air strike also revealed problems UN and NATO commanders had in agreeing to what represented a "proportionate" response to Serb provocations. In General Rose's view: "By using force in a proportionate way and by not attacking the targets proposed by Adm Leighton Smith, the route to a peaceful resolution of the war in Bosnia still lay open."[59] However, NATO commanders did not subscribe to General Rose's judgment on proportionality, and the frustration this issue caused among NATO airmen was evident in a comment later made by Gen Mike Ryan, who replaced General Ashy in September 1994:

> Proportionality is an awful word and I never want to hear it again. . . . All of us in our own minds understand proportionality, but none of us would agree on what it is when we come to a certain situation. If we do use it, then we ought to spell out very, very clearly what we mean by proportionality.[60]

However, even if commanders in AFSOUTH and UNPROFOR had agreed upon a definition of proportionality, they were still bound to disagree over how to apply the concept, given the differences in the vulnerability of their forces and in their interpretations of their missions.

In part, problems with the word *proportionate* may have arisen from its connection to an important concept from laws of armed conflict—one with which the airmen would have been especially familiar. According to Green, the principle of proportionality is one of the most basic concepts in the laws of armed conflict that "prohibits military action in which the negative effects (such as collateral civilian casualties) clearly outweigh the military gain."[61] In applying this principle, much is left to "the discretion of the commander of the forces involved," for he must judge whether the military advantage from the attack warrants the likely unintended effects or "incidental injuries" it might cause.[62] In making this determination, the commander must consider the military gain "to the whole operation and not merely the particular attack contemplated."[63] Although the principle of proportionality guided targeting decisions in Bosnia, it was not the primary cause for disagreement between UN and NATO commanders.

The term *proportionate,* as used to describe Deny Flight air attacks, had to do with responding to provocations by the warring factions with an amount of force commensurate with both the provocation and the desired objective, without escalating the level of violence.[64] However, UNPROFOR and AFSOUTH were pursuing different objectives; and, more importantly, UNPROFOR's judgment of a proportionate response was dictated by its vulnerability—especially to Bosnian Serb reprisals.[65] The scope for disagreement over the definition of proportionate can be illustrated by considering the following questions first from the viewpoint of a UN commander, then second, from the perspective of a NATO commander: (1) Was the objective of the air strike to get the BSA to return a stolen weapon, or was it to change Bosnian Serb behavior toward greater respect for the "safe areas"? (2) Was the air strike to be proportionate to today's provocation, or should the provocation be taken as the cumulative weight of transgressions leading up to today's decision to respond with air strikes? (3) Which was more important—attaining the objective for the air strike or avoiding escalation?

UN and NATO commanders had different objectives and priorities. AFSOUTH's objective was to enforce the exclusion zone and coerce the Bosnian Serbs into respecting the safe areas.[66] Whenever an incident occurred that NATO officers believed merited a response, they would recommend the UN targets (selected from the target books using the target matrices) that were geographically near the provocation and could logically be linked to it.[67] NATO officers preferred fixed targets, which could be safely attacked in nearly any weather and by any type of aircraft, not just planes capable of dropping precision-guided munitions.[68] Thus, Serb military depots around Sarajevo, including the ammunition storage site near Pale, were attractive targets for NATO planners whenever there was a BSA provocation around Sarajevo.[69] Moreover, NATO airmen were relatively immune from retaliation; thus, their commanders had less to fear from escalation, making it easier for NATO commanders to prioritize their objective of coercion above their desire to avoid escalation. Since May 1994, UNPROFOR had been trying to shrug off responsibilities for the NATO-declared exclusion zones.[70] Enforcing the exclusion zones reduced UNPROFOR's ability to fulfill its other responsibilities, which were closer to peacekeeping.[71] When pressed to cooperate with NATO, the UN preferred smoking-gun-type targets because they could be directly linked to self-defense or protection of the safe areas, and attacks against them were less likely to jeopardize the UN's impartial status.[72]

In determining UN views on proportionality, UNPROFOR's vulnerability was more important than UN objectives for ordering air strikes; thus, the Bosnian Serbs exercised a powerful vote in deciding what was, or was not, a proportionate response.[73] As General de Lapresle explained,

> My main concern, of course, and so was Michael Rose's, was to avoid, first of all, that countries who had sent their boys and girls on a peace mission would find themselves with body bags coming back to their capital after a sort of military and war action which was not the point [of the mission]; and the second . . . concern, was *not* to obtain a military victory, but to come to a cease-fire, [and] to have this cease-fire standing as long as possible in Croatia and in Bosnia. And so when we tried to combine this first objective of no UN lives lost, and hostages, and so on, and so on, and then trying to keep the arms as silent as possible, of course we were not very much enticed into having a strong and efficient use of NATO airpower.[74]

General Rose echoed that sentiment: "My primary responsibility was to the countries that had contributed peacekeeping troops to the mission and I could not allow them to become combatants, hostages, or casualties in a war."[75] Through the dual key mechanism, the UN commanders exercised control in decisions over what constituted a proportionate response. In making their decisions, commanders in UNPROFOR were guided by their complementary concerns for force protection and for accomplishing their mission.

Attempts to Control Air Strikes

At the end of September, NATO defense ministers intervened to give their commanders in AFSOUTH more control over air strikes, but UNPROFOR's leaders resisted the move. The "Operational Options" memo, approved by the NAC in August 1993, stated that if commanders in AFSOUTH and UNPROFOR could not agree about air strikes, then they were to refer the matter to higher military and political authorities.[76] But UNPROFOR had no higher military authorities. Therefore, disagreements in the divided UN-NATO military command system could only be reconciled by higher political authorities. When NATO defense ministers met for an informal conference in Seville at the end of September, US officials, led by Secretary of Defense William Perry, urged ending the UNPROFOR practice of issuing tactical warnings in advance of NATO air attacks.[77] In addition, Perry advocated a process whereby once UNPROFOR requested an air strike, NATO commanders would decide which target to hit using a list of three or four preselected candidate targets that had been mutually agreed upon by UNPROFOR and NATO commanders.[78] Because this was an informal meeting, no decisions were taken, but Perry's proposal was referred to Brussels and New York for formal consideration. After leaving Seville, the American defense secretary went to visit UNPROFOR's leaders—Akashi, de Lapresle, and Rose—in Split, Croatia, to discuss air strikes in Bosnia.[79]

Before Perry's arrival at Split, and again after the meeting, UNPROFOR's leaders worked out the arguments against the Seville proposals and against more forceful air strikes. The UN force commander made clear his concern that a more robust use of airpower would create unacceptable risks to UN personnel on the ground.[80] Furthermore, he questioned whether the defense ministers really intended to make the use of NATO airpower a higher priority than the security of United Nations ground forces.[81] Implicit in the record of the discussions was the question of whether a few activist NATO states ought to be recommending policies that might jeopardize the safety of peacekeepers from over 30 troop-contributing countries.[82] The force commander believed a more forceful approach in Bosnia would require a redeployment of UN peacekeepers that would, in turn, change the nature of the tasks UNPROFOR could accomplish.[83] The message from the discussions was clear— unless UNPROFOR were given a new mandate by the Security Council, it would not support the proposals for stiffer enforcement action.

In talks with Secretary Perry at Split in early October, UNPROFOR leaders described the vulnerabilities of their forces, their inability to enforce the exclusion zones, and the importance of their humanitarian and peacekeeping mission.[84] UN leaders explained that as a consequence of UNPROFOR's situation they could not afford to have NATO doing the enforcing either.[85] General Rose averred, "Any force used had to be within the UN rules of engagement."[86] Since the UN rules stipulated force could only be used in self-defense, General Rose's claim virtually ruled out any use of air strikes to enforce the exclusion zones.[87] UNPROFOR leaders did not want NATO air strikes, and they did not want to loosen their control over them.

With support from high officials in the UN's department of peacekeeping, General de Lapresle managed to retain control over air strikes. Following the meeting in Split, NATO and UN officials conducted talks in New York about implementing new procedures that would end warnings of impending strikes and give NATO a stronger voice in selecting targets.[88] Formal adoption of these suggestions first raised at Seville was announced in a late-October joint UN-NATO press statement which read, in part,

> While general warning may be given to an offending party, tactical warning of impending air strikes, in principle, will not. Under normal

circumstances, several targets, where possible three or four, will be authorized for each air strike, which will be carried out by NATO in close coordination with UNPROFOR.

Dual-key arrangements remain in effect, ensuring that decisions on targeting and execution will be taken jointly by UN and NATO military commanders. The principle of proportionality in response to a violation will continue to be respected, as will the need to avoid unacceptable casualties.[89]

Though the agreement proscribed warnings "in principle," it did little else to affect UN control over air strikes. As General de Lapresle later described his view,

Of course, they [NATO] wanted to be master of the choice of the target, and I could not accept that, because I knew, and they did not know, who was in the proximity and the vicinity of these targets—UNMOs, CIVPOLs, civil affairs guys, and so on.[90]

It did not take long for NATO commanders to discover that nothing had changed; as Admiral Smith recounted,

De Lapresle goes back to Zagreb; I call him up and I said: "Well, I guess what I'm looking at is ain't nothing changed. You're still going to give me one target, and I get to bomb it, and that's about it?" He said: "That's exactly correct." He said: "My conscience is clear. I have gone back to New York; I have read the documents; I have gotten no new political guidance. My conscience is clear."[91]

Thus, the political intervention had failed to win NATO commanders greater control over air strikes; the UN was still firmly in charge.

After just two air strikes in the summer of 1994, UNPROFOR and AFSOUTH commanders deadlocked over whether and how to proceed with future strikes. The paralysis was a consequence of the commanders' competing efforts to maintain their chances for both mission success (as they had interpreted their different missions) and force protection. The UNPROFOR mission, once its commanders had abandoned attempts to enforce the safe areas policy, was one of peacekeeping and support for humanitarian aid agencies. Coupled with its modest military capabilities and its widely dispersed mode of deployment on the ground in Bosnia, UNPROFOR's mission dictated that its commanders adhere to peacekeeping principles by acting only with the consent of the warring factions, with minimum use of force, and with impartiality. In light of their responsibilities, the military commanders in UNPROFOR felt compelled to issue warnings to the targeted factions in Bosnia—invariably the Bosnian Serbs—prior to authorizing NATO air attacks. Conversely, the warnings endangered the lives of NATO airmen and weakened enforcement measures, so, commanders in AFSOUTH wanted some flexibility in targeting decisions and an end to the warnings. Though the issue was formally reconciled in NATO's favor, according to procedures proposed at Seville and thrashed out in New York, the UNPROFOR commanders in Zagreb and Sarajevo retained final control over air operations via the dual key arrangements. There were no more air strikes related to enforcing either the safe areas policy or the exclusion zones until May 1995 after new UN commanders replaced Generals Rose and de Lapresle.

Udbina: Mission Accomplishment Versus Force Protection

Subtle Bosnian Serb challenges to the no-fly zone in the summer of 1994 grew more blatant in the fall, prompting a NATO response and a serious split between UN soldiers and NATO airmen. NATO airmen were convinced of substantial support from Serbia for the summer buildup and continued functioning of the Bosnian Serb integrated air defense system.[92] In mid-July the United States suspended humanitarian airlift into Sarajevo after two C-141 transports sustained hits from small arms fire on consecutive days.[93] A month later, an American C-130 and a German C-160 cargo aircraft conducted the last airdrops of Operation Provide Promise by parachuting supplies to the isolated Muslim enclave of Bihac.[94] Though the needs of that enclave and others remained acute, the increasing Bosnian Serb surface-to-air threat made further airdrops in Bosnia too dangerous.[95] In a mid-September letter to General Mladic, General Rose warned him to stop menacing NATO aircraft, stating,

> I am deeply concerned about actions directed against NATO aircraft flying in Bosnia-Hercegovina airspace. Specifically, I refer to the MAN-PAD [shoulder launched surface-to-air missiles] missile firing on 8

> September and to repeated radar activity over Prijedor/Bihac areas, which include activation of target tracking radar modes. These activities are perceived to be acts of aggression, and I feel compelled to warn you of NATO's prerogative for response.
>
> NATO aircraft, having the inherent right of self-defence, can immediately and decisively exercise that right if challenged by your threat missile systems. This response is totally a NATO decision and does not require UN coordination.[96]

This implied that NATO aircraft could shoot in response to "hostile intent" from the Bosnian Serbs and that the UN had no control over such actions. Both implications were false.[97] In addition to the growing surface-to-air threat, by November the Serbs began flouting the no-fly zone, flying fixed-wing jets on bombing missions inside Bosnia to support a BSA counteroffensive around Bihac.[98] NATO commanders were losing the initiative in the airspace over Bosnia, and they were clearly failing in their responsibilities to enforce the no-fly zone. However, they could do little to respond to these Bosnian Serb challenges without additional authority from New York and Brussels, and consent from UNPROFOR's leaders for enforcement measures.

The Serbs used the sanctuary of Croatian airspace and their air defense network to good advantage, making it nearly impossible for NATO aircraft to engage Serb planes violating the no-fly zone. After an initially successful Bosnian Muslim ground offensive launched from within the safe area of Bihac in October, Croatian Serbs joined the BSA and the forces of rebel Muslim leader Fikret Abdic in a counteroffensive that quickly reversed the government forces' gains.[99] Serb pilots flew supporting missions from Udbina airfield in Serb-controlled eastern Croatia. So long as they remained in Croatian airspace, Serb aircraft could not be engaged by NATO pilots, whose authority to enforce the no-fly zone was limited to Bosnia. By monitoring NATO combat air patrols via the Serbian air defense network, the Udbina-based aircraft could time their flights into Bosnia whenever NATO aircraft were refueling or otherwise not in a position to respond.[100] Udbina was only a few minutes' flying time away from Bihac. Thus, it was fairly easy for the Serb pilots to make attacks into Bosnia and land before NATO aircraft could engage them. NATO commanders in the region could have mounted more no-fly zone patrols to narrow the window of opportunity for the Serb violations, but that would have required more aircraft, aircrews, and other resources.[101] More importantly, patrols near Bihac would put NATO aircraft in the midst of the Serbs' most lethal SAM coverage, which was concentrated in northwest Bosnia and eastern Croatia. In addition to the added costs and risks, any subsequent violation would have been all the more damaging to NATO's credibility. Until NATO commanders obtained authority to attack aircraft on the ground in Croatia, there was little they could do to stop the violations.

Udbina: November 1994

NATO commanders in the southern region, including the recently arrived commander of AIRSOUTH, Lt Gen Mike Ryan, wanted to stop the no-fly zone violations; and they examined options for disabling Serb air activity from Udbina.[102] Ryan, who had taken over from General Ashy in September, was also a fighter pilot who had flown 100 missions over North Vietnam. His father, Gen John D. Ryan, commanded all Air Force units in the Pacific during the time that his son Mike flew in Vietnam, and the senior Ryan had gone on to become chief of staff of the US Air Force. As discussed in chapter 2, Gen John Ryan was the man whose duty it had been to discipline Gen John Lavelle for his actions related to the unauthorized bombings against North Vietnamese air defense targets in late 1971 and early 1972.[103] Gen Mike Ryan arrived in Naples, having come from the Pentagon where he was an assistant to the chairman of the Joint Chiefs of Staff. Thus, the new AIRSOUTH commander would have been familiar not only with the political mood in Washington where he had just served but also particularly sensitive to political controls—such as ROE—that might interfere with a commander's responsibility to protect his forces.

On Friday, 18 November 1994, Serb jets from Udbina attacked the Bosnian army's 5th Corps headquarters near Bihac using cluster bombs and napalm.[104] Then on Saturday, a Serb aircraft making an attack on an ammunition factory crashed into an apartment building in Cazin, 10 miles north of Bihac.[105] Papers found amongst the dead pilot's possessions established his Serb identity.[106] With support from the Croatian government, the UN Security Council agreed that day to authorize a NATO air attack against Udbina.[107] The NAC met on Sunday to issue a decision, giving Admiral Smith permission to act on the new Security Council authority, provided he did so in close coordination with UNPROFOR.[108] Despite political pressures to strike Udbina, the UNPROFOR commander refused to turn his key that morning until he was given the details of the planned attack.[109] In addition to concerns over NATO targeting, there was a question within the UNPROFOR chain of command as to whether General de Lapresle needed Mr. Akashi, who was in Frankfurt en route back to Zagreb, to authorize the attack.[110] The scheduled time of attack was slipped back several times while UN commanders wrestled with these issues and took decisions about whether or not to evacuate potential hostages from around Udbina.[111] Shortly after noon, Mr. Akashi authorized the attack, but with NATO aircraft taxiing for takeoff at bases throughout Italy, the mission was scrubbed at the last minute.[112] High cloud cover over Udbina was the reported reason for canceling the mission that day.[113] However, the strike against Udbina may have been slipped a day because of the delays induced by the UN or because of the need for NATO to change targets or aircraft ordnance loads.[114]

Targeting Udbina

Concerned about retaliation against UN forces and civilian aid workers in the region, General de Lapresle wanted to minimize the chances of causing Serb casualties, and he insisted that only the runway at Udbina could be struck.[115] As Admiral Smith later recounted,

> We had looked at Udbina, and I had wanted to take out everything. I wanted to make a parking lot out of that place. I wanted to take out all of the buildings. I didn't want anything left standing. De Lapresle said: "No." He would only approve hitting the runway, because he didn't want to kill anybody.[116]

176

For General de Lapresle, destroying the buildings, maintenance facilities, and aircraft at Udbina, as Admiral Smith desired, would have been counterproductive to both UNPROFOR's mission and the security of UN peacekeepers.[117]

Admiral Smith agreed to forego attacks against the aircraft, buildings, and maintenance facilities, but he would not compromise on the need to aggressively suppress Serb air defenses at Udbina.[118] As General Ryan later explained, NATO commanders took the position that "We're not going to tie the hands of the force—to have them shoot at us first before we go after them. . . . So the issue was force protection versus the political fallout of having collateral damage."[119] Admiral Smith explained to General de Lapresle the need to attack certain radar-guided weapon systems, stating, "We don't hit that, [then] we don't fly."[120] General Rose was opposed to the attack on Udbina because of concerns it would lead to Serb reprisals in nearby Bosnia; in the end, though, the decision on how to advise the UN's political leaders rested with General de Lapresle.[121] As the UNPROFOR commander later recalled,

> This, I must say, was a very difficult decision—to give the green light for an air strike when you know you will have some CIVPOL, or some UNMOs, or some civil affairs people who will be held [as] hostages. And the first thing you have to do is give the go-ahead order, and then, second, immediately [make] contact with the Serbs . . . in order to get [back] those guys who are hostages.[122]

Despite his concerns, once General de Lapresle was convinced preemptive supression of enemy air defenses [SEAD] attacks were essential for protecting NATO airmen, he supported the demands of the AFSOUTH commanders.[123] Ultimately, NATO was allowed to execute a tactically sound attack, which included preemptively launching high-speed, anti-radiation missiles (HARM) at Serb air defense systems.[124]

On Monday, 21 November, 39 strike aircraft attacked the runway and taxiways at Udbina, and Dutch, American, British, and French aircraft took part in the raid.[125] The Serbs responded predictably with fresh provocations in Bosnia and by taking hostages in Croatia. Though publicly touted as a success, behind the scenes some high-level political authorities in Washington and Brussels were upset that NATO commanders—

especially Admiral Smith—had not ordered bombing against more lucrative targets at Udbina.[126] According to one high-ranking NATO official, the decision not to hit aircraft was a political one, and Admiral Smith had gone beyond the bounds of his military authority by making the decision to agree with General de Lapresle without first consulting Brussels.[127] Responding to a reporter's question at a press conference the day after the attack, Admiral Smith defended the UN rationale for limiting the attack and explained his own role as the supporting commander:

> General de Lapresle and I have had many conversations on this subject. He, and the other members of the United Nations Protection Force command structure with whom I talk, believe that *their principle [sic] concern is the safety of their forces and their mission, being peacekeeping.* So, response is going to be, in their view, proportional to the offense and measured, rather than what some of us might consider more militarily effective. General de Lapresle spoke with me several times before this strike and he specifically asked that we limit our strike to the runways, and I later added the taxiways, and the purpose was to ensure to the best that we could, that we would minimize the number of people on the ground that were injured as a result of this strike, and minimize collateral damage (emphasis added).[128]

Clearly, negative objectives drove the targeting at Udbina. Despite efforts to limit collateral damage and Serb casualties, Serb forces in Croatia threatened retaliation and took UN peacekeepers hostage—including two Czech soldiers stationed as observers near Udbina.[129] The day after the Udbina raid, Serb air defenses inside Bosnia fired the first radar-guided missiles at NATO jets patrolling the no-fly zone.

Interpreting the Results

Though not unrelated to the BSA ground offensive against Bihac, the attack on Udbina was designed primarily to stop violations of the UN-declared no-fly zone over Bosnia rather than to affect the BSA.[130] Therefore, it would be inappropriate to criticize the raid for failing to deter the Serb attack on Bihac, as some observers have done.[131] The bombing of Udbina came at political insistence, with urging from AFSOUTH officers, and against the desires of UNPROFOR.[132] NATO commanders insisted on the attack and wanted to destroy much more at

Udbina than they did, but they compromised mission accomplishment in deference to the UNPROFOR commanders' concerns for the safety of their soldiers. Some officials may have hoped the raid would deter the Serb assault on Bihac; but if they did, then UNPROFOR's efforts to limit attacks to the runway probably undermined that objective. UNPROFOR's open reluctance to risk casualties, even amongst Serb military personnel at Udbina, could only enfeeble any deterrent signal the attack might have conveyed. A NATO official later described the dilemma in using force for deterrent effect in Bosnia: Deterrence often depends on a credible threat to use a great deal of force, while peacekeeping operations are based on a minimum use of force.[133] And, as Sabin has noted, in peace support operations, "there is a . . . risk that a perceived paralysis of command could lead to a failure of deterrence and could encourage locals to challenge the intervening forces with impunity."[134] That pretty well describes what happened at Bihac and in the no-fly zone over Bosnia after the Udbina raid.

The Udbina attack forced both General de Lapresle and Admiral Smith to make trade-offs between accomplishing their missions and protecting their forces. As one might expect in an intervention where vital national interests were not engaged, mission accomplishment came in second behind force protection. Broadly speaking, UN and NATO commanders were supposed to be cooperating to achieve the same overall goal. However, practically speaking, the disparate capabilities and vulnerabilities of their forces and the discordant political voices telling the commanders what to do had driven them to a division of labor—with the UN doing peacekeeping, and NATO doing the enforcing.[135] Just as Admiral Smith compromised his mission by targeting only the runways and taxiways, the UNPROFOR commander accepted the inevitable disruptions to his peacekeeping mission in Croatia. However, both commanders stood firm when it came to the issues most likely to affect the safety of their forces; General de Lapresle refused to countenance attacks most likely to give the Serbs cause for retaliation while Admiral Smith demanded permission for preemptive attacks against air defenses. That both commanders resisted compromising on issues most likely to put their forces in danger while accepting a short-term degradation in their respective missions also indicated they not only took seriously their own responsibilities for protecting their people, but they also respected and honored, as best they could, each other's needs in this regard. Admiral Smith's decision to forgo more lucrative targets at Udbina angered some of his superiors,[136] leading General de Lapresle to note that: "Leighton Smith was rather alone in his clear understanding on what was [on] my mind and what was going on in the field."[137] General de Lapresle reciprocated. After Admiral Smith convinced the UNPROFOR commander of the need for preemptive SEAD, Admiral Smith recalled: "UN New York tried to disapprove the integrated air defense target, and de Lapresle said: 'No. Admiral Smith is exactly correct. He cannot go in there without taking those out first.'"[138] In peace support operations where vital interests are not at stake, a commander might expect to eventually recover from setbacks to the mission, but he cannot recoup a lost life. Thus, when trade-offs must be made between force protection and mission accomplishment in these types of interventions, protecting people will likely trump mission accomplishment.

"Retrospective SEAD" and the Growing UN-NATO Rift: November–December 1994

For AFSOUTH and UNPROFOR, the air strikes at Udbina began an eventful week that highlighted the growing concerns for force protection in NATO. For more than 18 months, NATO aircraft had flown combat air patrols, reconnaissance flights, and practice air support missions within range of Serb radar-missile defenses without being fired upon.[139] However, on Tuesday, the day after the Udbina airfield attack, a Serb surface-to-air missile site at Otoka in northwestern Bosnia fired two radar-guided SA-2 missiles at a pair of British Sea Harriers patrolling the no-fly zone.[140] Though the jets escaped unharmed, the Serb firing of radar-guided missiles signaled a serious new challenge to NATO.[141] Since the Serbs possessed more modern, more capable, and mobile radar-guided missiles such as the SA-6, NATO airmen had to assume that these too might be used against them. In response to this challenge,

General Ryan ordered the deputy director of the CAOC, Brig Gen Dave Sawyer, to locate the exact position of the offending SAM site and to set in motion plans to attack it.[142] Meanwhile, General Ryan worked on getting the UN and NATO keys turned for an air strike against the site.[143] Up until this point, SEAD was not an authorized mission for Deny Flight operations except as a defensive element in support of actual CAS or air-strike missions.[144] By autumn of 1994, the growing surface-to-air threat over Bosnia had generated efforts at NATO headquarters to change this policy even before the missile firings from Otoka.[145] Because it was already under active consideration in Brussels, AFSOUTH was able to get NAC approval the next day, 23 November, to conduct what became known as "retrospective SEAD."[146]

While the Deny Flight rules of engagement had always permitted NATO airmen to use force in self-defense, nearly all NATO aircraft flying over Bosnia were unsuited to respond to missile firings. Thus, when threatened, a NATO aircrew would take evasive action and leave the area covered by the missile system. Once away from the threat, NATO forces were prohibited by ROE from going back and attacking it.[147] Such operating procedures ceded the initiative to the Serb missile crews, who were tied into a larger air defense network and could pick on NATO aircraft that were least likely to be able to shoot back.[148] Within NATO, the British and French were reluctant to approve air defense suppression in response to the Serb practice of menacing NATO aircraft with target tracking radar.[149] So long as the Serbs were not firing missiles, NATO ministers from some of the troop-contributing nations remained unwilling to authorize a new mission that could lead to an escalating use of force in Bosnia.[150] Once the Serbs began firing radar-guided missiles, NATO commanders in the region wanted to take out the entire Serb integrated air defense system.[151] Barring that, they pushed to be able to go back "retrospectively" with an appropriately equipped force and eliminate an offending missile site.[152] For senior commanders in NATO's southern region, it was a matter of self-defense. On 23 November, the NAC authorized retrospective SEAD but stipulated that any response ought to be proportional, without

SUNDAY	MONDAY	TUESDAY	WEDNESDAY	THURSDAY	FRIDAY	SATURDAY
NOVEMBER	14	15	16	17	18 Serb jets from Udbina drop napalm and cluster bombs near Bihac	19 Serb jet from Udbina crashes during attack near Bihac UNSCR 958 okays air strikes in Croatia
20 NAC authorizes Udbina strike; UN balks —— Attack scrubbed	21 Largest NATO air strike to date hits runway, taxiways, and air defenses at Udbina	22 Two SA-2s fired from Otoka site at British Sea Harriers patrolling the no-fly zone	23 Two NATO attacks target Serb SAMs at Otoka, Dvor, and Bosanska Krupa	24 Bosnian Serbs fire a radar-guided SAM at British F-3s patrolling the no-fly zone —— New NAC-author-izations	25 Bosnian Serbs advancing on Bihac fire at UNPROFOR; Gen Rose calls for air support —— F-16s shot at	26 NATO recon-naissance package with SEAD escort aborted

Figure 1. Outline of Events around the Time of the Udbina Air Strike

collateral damage, and subject to the dual key arrangements with the UN.[153]

Udbina and Otoka: November 1994

As NATO aircraft approached Otoka on Wednesday morning, several Serb SAM sites in northwestern Bosnia threatened the strike package and fired missiles, thus fueling the escalating spiral of threats and uses of force from both sides. NATO jets responded by firing high-speed, antiradiation missiles at the Serb SAM batteries, including one which happened to be inside Croatia, 10 miles north of Otoka.[154] Unable to complete the planned destruction of the Otoka site because of the challenge from the other SAM sites, NATO commanders launched another strike package that afternoon to hit Otoka.[155] In retaliation, the Bosnian Serbs threatened war against UNPROFOR and took hundreds of peacekeepers hostage; three were reportedly made to lie on the runway at Banja Luka.[156] On Thursday, the Bosnian Serbs, operating from a previously undetected site near Danji Vakuf in central Bosnia, fired a radar-guided SAM at two British F-3 Tornado aircraft on a routine no-fly zone patrol.[157] Meanwhile, the ground offensive against Bihac continued with the Bosnian Serb forces pushing up from south of the enclave and overrunning the point at which they had promised UNPROFOR they would stop.[158] In Brussels, the NAC met and declared, inter alia, its willingness to activate the heavy weapons exclusion zone it had provisionally declared seven months earlier when it created the exclusion zone at Gorazde.[159] However, rather than unilaterally declaring a new heavy-weapons-free zone at Bihac via an ultimatum as it had with Gorazde, the Council made the activation of the new zone contingent on UNPROFOR agreement.[160] UNPROFOR found the task of policing the existing exclusion zones burdensome and declined the opportunity to create yet another.[161]

UNPROFOR's top military commanders opposed NATO air strikes, and, while they wanted air support to protect UN peacekeepers around Bihac, they refused to authorize NATO air operations needed to reduce the surface-to-air threat in northwestern Bosnia.[162] In a meeting on 25 November, the commander of UNPROFOR made it clear he viewed air strikes as being fundamentally incompatible with his peacekeeping mission.[163] The NATO officer sent to the meeting reported to General Ryan and Admiral Smith that so long as General de Lapresle commanded UNPROFOR, there was little hope the UN would turn its key for air strikes.[164] That night, however, when peacekeepers in the Bihac area came under fire, General Rose personally called the CAOC for air support.[165] The increased SAM threat around Bihac precluded NATO commanders from sending a pair of fighters already in the no-fly zone in response to the request; a larger package of aircraft capable of protecting itself against Serb air defenses needed to be assembled.[166] Because the peacekeepers in Bihac lacked forward air controllers, NATO and UN officers had had to work out a scheme whereby an ersatz forward air controller would clear NATO aircraft to attack Bosnian Serb forces within an improvised grid.[167] A couple of hours later when the requisite force was assembled, the situation had quieted and General Rose did not have a specific target for NATO to strike.[168] However, he still wanted NATO aircraft to fly into northwestern Bosnia.[169] NATO airmen demurred; they would put their forces at risk to fulfill a specific mission, but not, in this particular case, for air presence.[170]

Some UN officials were wary of retrospective SEAD, because they suspected that NATO airmen were more interested in retribution than self-defense.[171] Others accepted NATO's need for force protection but still believed the new air operations against the Serbs created a cycle of escalation that was detrimental to UNPROFOR's mission and the safety of its peacekeepers.[172] The Serbs again fired a SAM at a pair of F-16s at the end of the week; however, on Saturday, 26 November, General Ryan was thwarted in his efforts to send a heavily escorted reconnaissance package into northwestern Bosnia to pinpoint a SAM site that had fired at NATO aircraft.[173] As the force marshaled over the Adriatic, high-level French intervention through NATO headquarters[174] forced General Ryan to recall the reconnaissance package.[175] With some 250 UNPROFOR hostages, Britain and France, as well as the UN leadership in the former Yugoslavia, were uneasy about the escalating use of force in Bosnia.[176] Moreover, some ambassadors believed the AFSOUTH commanders were baiting the Serb air defenses, and intense discussions over ROE and hostile intent raged in Brussels.[177] The recriminations over the week of activities around Bihac were so intense that Lord Owen later described this point in time as "the nadir in UN-NATO and US-EU relations."[178]

NATO and UN Split over Airpower: December 1994

By early December, while NATO formalized new rules for protecting its aircraft in the no-fly zone, UNPROFOR pressed NATO to minimize its flights over Bosnia. Unable to take actions necessary for protecting NATO airmen, General Ryan and Admiral Smith briefly shifted the no-fly zone patrols to the relative safety of the airspace over the Adriatic.[179] The move made the patrols safer, but virtually ineffective. When NATO aircraft returned to the skies over Bosnia on 5 December, they were well escorted by SEAD aircraft.[180] In an effort to win the release of UNPROFOR hostages and ease Bosnian Serb concerns about NATO airpower, the UNPROFOR commander broached the subject of reducing NATO air operations over Bosnia with his NATO counterpart, CINCSOUTH.[181] Admiral Smith responded to the request by acknowledging his continued support for the UN, but emphasized repeatedly that, even if he were inclined to reduce NATO air activity, it would require a political decision that he was not empowered to take on his own.[182] On 8 December, the day of Admiral Smith's reply, the NAC agreed to change the rules of engagement for SEAD by authorizing it as a stand-alone mission (i.e., no longer limited to the support of CAS or air strike missions); this further codified the council's decision on retrospective SEAD from 23 November.[183] Two days later, UNPROFOR secured the release of the remaining hostages taken during the week following the Udbina air strike.[184] That same day, 10 December, in a letter to the Bosnian Serb president, Dr. Karadzic, Mr. Akashi explained that NATO operated only in support of the UN mission and that the alliance had four "primary missions in the airspace over Bosnia": no-fly zone enforcement, CAS for UNPROFOR, enforcement of the heavy weapons exclusion zones around the safe areas, and deterrence of armed attacks against the safe areas.[185] Mr. Akashi tried to assuage Serb fears of NATO airpower by stating,

> Except for self-defense, NATO aircraft will not conduct air-to-ground operations without advance authorization from the Special Representative of the Secretary-General. NATO will not use force except in pursuit of these missions, or in self-defense when aircraft are directly threatened by antiaircraft fire, surface-to-air missiles, locking on of antiaircraft weapon tracking radars, or attack by aircraft. No automatic firing of missiles will occur. If the armed forces in conflict respect the terms of Security Council resolutions and the North Atlantic Council decisions of 9 February 1994 and 22 April 1994, do not attack UNPROFOR, and do not threaten NATO aircraft, they will have nothing to fear from NATO.[186]

Mr. Akashi's letter sent mixed signals, for it implied NATO aircrews might act if merely threatened but not fired upon; at the same time it stated that, "no automatic firing of missiles will occur." In fact, NATO ROE did not allow aircraft patrolling the no-fly zone or performing other routine missions such as reconnaissance or CAS training to use force in response to "hostile intent" such as lock-ons by Serb target-tracking radar.[187] That was why the heavy escorts were needed, so that NATO airmen could shoot back right away in response to a hostile act. The NAC decision of 8 December 1994 merely recognized the need for stand-alone SEAD missions in response to hostile acts against UN or NATO aircraft. Even with this new authorization, NATO commanders needed dual key approval to conduct strikes against offending surface-to-air weapon sites. The Serbs would have to fire first, then NATO commanders in AFSOUTH would have to coordinate with UNPROFOR over a proportional response.

UNPROFOR-AFSOUTH agreement on proportionality was most unlikely for SEAD because, unlike air strikes, SEAD had nothing to do with the UN commanders' responsibilities, and everything to do with the responsibilities of NATO commanders. From General Ryan's perspective, the debates on proportionality reached the point of absurdity over SEAD: "Proportionality by some said that if they shoot at you with a SAM missile and they miss, then you can shoot a missile back, but you have to miss them!"[188] In contrast to those urging a minimum use of force, the US chairman of the Joint Chiefs of Staff had recently published new *Standing Rules of Engagement for US Forces* (SROE), which included guidelines on proportionality for the use of force in self-defense:

> *Proportionality.* The force used must be reasonable in intensity, duration, and magnitude, based on all facts known to the commander at the time, to *decisively counter* the hostile act or hostile intent and to ensure the continued safety of US forces (emphasis added).[189]

Although General Ryan was part of an alliance operation, that did not free him from following the new ROE guidance. Page one of the SROE contained a notice that forces under multinational control would remain so, "only if the combatant commander and higher authority determine that the ROE for that multinational force are consistent with the policy guidance on unit self-defense and with rules for individual self-defense contained in this document."[190] However, even after NATO ROE changed to reflect a more robust approach to dealing with the Bosnian Serb SAM threat, NATO commanders could not make the UN accept the US view of proportionality. Unlike enforcement of the exclusion zone around Sarajevo, UNPROFOR had no responsibility to enforce the no-fly zone or to do anything else in the airspace over Bosnia. Moreover, its forces were not threatened by SAM firings. Conversely, freedom from the SAM threat was the sine qua non for NATO operations.

Suppressing Bosnian Serb air defenses was an issue of self-defense for the commanders in AFSOUTH, and they could not tolerate dual-key controls over their aircrew's right to self-defense. The dual-key concept was embedded in the Security Council resolutions and supporting NATO decisions that authorized the use of airpower in Bosnia. It reflected the ground commanders' need to have control over air actions affecting the security of ground forces. Although the term *dual key* was new for air operations, the same fundamental concept had always governed close air support, and was not something unique to Bosnia. That is to say, the ground commander ultimately controlled the process for designating targets and approving attacks. However, two aspects of this dual-key principle were new in Bosnia. First, it applied to air strikes, which would normally fall under the purview of the air component commander rather than that of the ground commander.[191] Second, and more importantly, the rationale for the dual key stemmed from the ground commanders' responsibilities for force protection and mission success. In a combat scenario these responsibilities would normally be complementary, and airpower would support both the security of the ground forces and the accomplishment of a common mission. In Bosnia, however, when AFSOUTH commanders used airpower for enforcement, they endangered both UNPROFOR's forces and its primary mission. UNPROFOR commanders needed the dual-key mechanism to fulfill their command responsibilities. However, when the Bosnian Serb surface-to-air threat increased, the dual-key control over SEAD strikes interfered with the airmen's right to self-defense.

Nearly every NATO aircraft operating over Bosnia was incapable of an immediate riposte in self-defense to SAM firings. Even multirole aircraft, suitable for air-to-air and air-to-ground missions, were incapable of effectively responding to having a missile fired at them.[192] Unlike certain UN soldiers who had armored vehicles that were sufficiently well protected to drive through Serb roadblocks, the NATO airmen for their survival had to depend primarily on avoiding fire rather than withstanding it. An aircraft that had just dodged a missile would not be well positioned to return fire against the offending site. Therefore, NATO air forces needed specialized SEAD aircraft to cope with the Bosnian Serb SAM threat. These specialized aircraft were scarce resources and were generally not suitable for other missions such as close air support or enforcing the no-fly zone.[193] Moreover, the Bosnian Serb integrated air defense system allowed the launching of missiles with very little or no warning to the aircrews being fired upon. This tactic greatly reduced the time SEAD aircraft would have for responding to a threat, and this, in turn, would degrade the protection afforded by SEAD escort.

Commanders in AFSOUTH were responsible for missions to enforce Security Council resolutions and NATO decisions, and in practice these missions were directed almost exclusively against the Bosnian Serbs. Therefore, the Bosnian Serbs were most unlikely to consent to having NATO aircraft overhead the parts of Bosnia where enforcement might be needed. This situation left NATO with five possible courses of action: (1) conduct a SEAD campaign to destroy the Bosnian Serb air defenses; (2) make forceful responses through retrospective SEAD to induce self-restraint from the Bosnian Serbs; (3) provide SEAD escorts for missions over Bosnia; (4) avoid the Bosnian Serb air defenses; and (5) ignore the threat and continue to operate over Bosnia. This last option would have been a gross dereliction of duty by NATO commanders. Moreover, the US SROE clearly and repeatedly stated: "A commander has the authority and obligation to use all necessary means available and to take all appropriate action to defend that commander's unit and other US forces in the vicinity from a hostile act or demonstrated hostile intent."[194] The first option—conducting a SEAD campaign—was too extreme for UN authorities.[195] The second option—conducting retrospective SEAD—was permitted on one occasion and then blocked by UN commanders mainly because of the vulnerability of UN forces. The UN commanders did not like the third option—heavy SEAD escort over Bosnia—because it meant that NATO aircraft could only fly over Bosnia during brief periods when the specialized SEAD aircraft were available, thus greatly reducing the UN's ability to call on close air support. Moreover, in the eyes of the Bosnian Serbs, these escorted missions were indistinguishable from the large packages of aircraft used for air strikes. The more threatened the Serbs felt, the more they used their air defense system. The more they used their air defense system, the more NATO felt the need to actually attack the air defense. So, heavily escorted packages tended to feed the cycle of escalating force. The final option—avoiding Bosnian Serb air defenses—equated to abandoning NATO's responsibilities over Bosnia, in order to secure force protection. There were no good options that would permit both the UN commanders and the NATO commanders to accomplish their disparate missions within the bounds of acceptable risks to their forces.

Responsibilities for different missions and for the protection of different forces led to a temporary end in UN and NATO cooperation for using airpower over Bosnia. Senior UNPROFOR officials were unhappy with NATO's apparent attempts to hijack the mission in Bosnia and change its course from peacekeeping to war fighting.[196] The assessment of General Rose and his staff summed this up well:

> We all firmly believed that NATO should not act outside the principles of peacekeeping. If NATO was [sic] only able to respond to such incidents [as the SA-2 attack] in a way that risked collapsing the entire UN mission, then it would be better not to respond at all.[197]

General de Lapresle was of the same view:

> I could no longer call for . . . air support action because of this SEAD. . . . As these air defense systems appeared, it was more and more difficult for me to have this [air support]. And I could either have nothing

> . . . no aircraft over Bosnia, or thirty aircraft together, completely changing the spirit of my mission and the psychological perception of the Bosnian Serbs of what I was up to.[198]

By December, the UN generals no longer wanted air support on the terms NATO was offering.

The situation was equally vexing for NATO commanders who also saw their forces and their enforcement mission jeopardized by UNPROFOR's limitations on the use of airpower. As General Ryan reflected afterward,

> I was the commander of the air campaign in Bosnia and had lived with almost-Vietnam rules the first year that I was there, and it was the most frustrating thing that I have ever dealt with. . . . I may have been frustrated as an aircrewman by some of the stupidity in Vietnam, but I was doubly frustrated [in Bosnia] because . . . I guess I took it on myself to be frustrated for all our aircrews, when [the Bosnian Serbs] could shoot at us with SAMs and we had to go back and ask the UN's permission to come back and take out the same site.[199]

Despite the NAC authorization for stand-alone air defense suppression missions, in early December NATO commanders could not get their UNPROFOR counterparts to agree to air strikes or retrospective SEAD.

Conclusion

Dual key worked as intended for air strikes; however, it was seriously dysfunctional for other no-fly zone operations. By giving UNPROFOR commanders veto control over air strikes, the dual key permitted Generals Rose and de Lapresle the power to manage the risks to their forces. UN army generals used the dual key to influence targeting decisions so as to prevail with their concept of proportionality, thus helping them to maintain Bosnian Serb consent for UNPROFOR's presence. Because air strikes were supposed to be in support of UNPROFOR's mandate to deter attacks on the safe areas, Admiral Smith and General Ryan had little choice but to tolerate this aspect of the dual-key arrangement. Moreover, Admiral Smith sympathized with General de Lapresle's need to protect UN peacekeepers in Bosnia, so he did not push very hard for air strikes.

In contrast to AFSOUTH's unhappy tolerance for UN controls over enforcement measures relating to the safe areas, Admiral Smith and General Ryan refused to accept the dual-key factors that might endanger NATO airmen. Though the NATO commanders succeeded in winning support to end the UNPROFOR practice of issuing warnings before air strikes, their victory had little effect because Generals Rose and de Lapresle never asked for, or approved, another air strike related to the safe areas. When the dual key prevented effective self-defense of airmen flying over Bosnia, the NATO commanders' tolerance for the dual key ended. Unlike the responsibility to deter attacks on the safe areas, which was supposed to be shared by the UN and NATO, responsibility for the no-fly zone belonged exclusively to the commanders in AFSOUTH. Furthermore, only NATO airmen were endangered by the lack of effective SEAD. From the perspective of the army generals serving with the UN, SEAD strikes created the same adverse consequences as air strikes for safe area enforcement; they therefore blocked NATO's retrospective SEAD attacks. This deprived General Ryan and Admiral Smith of the ability to balance their responsibilities for force protection and mission accomplishment in an area where they alone were accountable. The dual key was not intended to interfere with NATO airmen's right of self-defense or with the enforcement of the no-fly zone. But that is what it did. The conflict engendered by the dual key has generally been misplaced. It was not inherently a bad thing as many NATO airmen came to believe. It was a necessary tool designed to help the supported commanders in the UN control risks to their forces on the ground. The dual key was merely symptomatic of the real problem, which was political disunity over the best approach to intervention in Bosnia. This situation in turn gave birth to two command chains with different missions and forces with different vulnerabilities.

Notes

1. For the United Nations's perspective, see Hans-Christian Hagman, "UN-NATO Peacekeeping 1992–1995" (PhD diss., King's College, University

of London, 1997), 140–42; and Gen Sir Michael Rose, *Fighting for Peace: Bosnia 1994* (London: The Harvill Press, 1998), 160–80.

2. Col Daniel R. Zoerb, USAF, director, Deny Flight Air Operations Center, Naples, Italy, January 1994–May 1996, interviewed by author, 30 April 1997, Spangdahlem Air Base (AB), Germany, transcript of tape recording, author's personal collection; and Gen Michael E. Ryan, USAF, commander Allied Air Forces Southern Europe (COMAIRSOUTH) and commander US Sixteenth Air Force, September 1994–April 1996, interviewed by author, 6 June 1997, Ramstein, Germany, transcript of taped interview, author's personal collection.

3. "Operation Deliberate Force Factual Review," draft edition, 14 November 1995, prepared by the CAOC, Balkans Air Campaign Study (BACS) Collection, Air Force Historical Research Agency (AFHRA), Maxwell Air Force Base (AFB), Ala. The first target books shared by the UN and NATO were built during the second half of 1993 after the Mount Igman crisis (see chap. 4). These were constantly updated to reflect changes, such as the creation of the exclusion zones at Sarajevo and Gorazde. Gen Joseph W. Ashy, USAF, interviewed by Lt Col Robert C. Owen, 29 April 1996, Washington, unclassified version of "General Ashy's Oral History Interview" (66 pp.), redacted by the AFHRA, October 1997, Office of History, Air Force Space Command, Peterson AFB, Colo.; and Lt Col Lowell R. Boyd Jr., USAF, AFSOUTH staff officer, February 1993–1996, interviewed by Lt Col Robert C. Owen, 6 December 1995, Naples, Italy, transcript of taped interview, BACS Collection.

4. Zoerb interview, 30 April 1997; and Ashy interview by Owen.

5. Ryan interview.

6. "Operation Deliberate Force, Factual Review," 2–2; and Zoerb interview. The targets were divided into six categories: heavy weapons in the Exclusion Zone (EZ); heavy weapons outside the EZ; weapons collection points; direct and essential support facilities; command and control facilities; and air defenses.

7. Zoerb interview; and Ryan interview.

8. Col Daniel R. Zoerb, USAF, interviewed by author, 29 April 1997, Spangdahlem AB, Germany, transcript of tape recording, author's personal collection; and Ashy interview by Owen.

9. Zoerb interview, 30 April 1997.

10. Ibid.; Lowell Boyd interview; Ashy interview by Owen; and Ryan interview.

11. Military Official W; and Brig Gen Charles F. Wald, USAF, CAOC chief of plans, (June–November 1994), commander, 31st Fighter Wing, Aviano AB, Italy, (May 1995–June 1997), interviewed by author, 7 May 1997, Aviano AB, Italy, taped recording, author's personal collection.

12. Wald interview. General Rose hints at this option in his memoir, *Fighting*, 144 and 160.

13. Wald interview.

14. Ibid.

15. Ibid.; Gen Sir Michael Rose, British army, retired, commander, Bosnia-Hercegovina Command, January 1994–January 1995, interviewed by author, 10 December 1997, London, transcript of taped interview, author's personal collection; and Rose, *Fighting*, 175.

16. Wald interview.

17. Rose, *Fighting*, 160.

18. "Maryland's 175th FG Pilots Go 'Hot' and Destroy Serb Target," *National Guard* 49, no. 3 (March 1995): 18.

19. Report of the Secretary-General Pursuant to Resolution 959 (1994) (S/1994/1389, 1 December 1994).

20. Rose, *Fighting*, 160; *Facts On File Yearbook 1994* (USA: Facts On File, Inc., 1994), 561; and S/1994/1389.

21. Rose, *Fighting*, 160–61; Rose interview by author; *Facts On File 1994*, 561; and S/1994/1389.

22. *Facts On File 1994*, 561; and "Maryland's 175th FG Pilots," 19. According to General Ashy, the A-10 pilots were not expecting to work with a forward air controller (FAC), because they were on an air strike mission. However, the FAC came up on the radio frequency used by the A-10 pilots and aborted an attack in progress. After that, the A-10s completed the mission under the FAC's control. Gen Joseph W. Ashy, commander, Allied Air Forces Southern Europe (AIRSOUTH), December 1992–September 1994, and commander, US Sixteenth Air Force, February–September 1994, interviewed by author, 3 July 1998, Fairfax, Va., author's notes, author's personal collection.

23. *Facts On File 1994*, 561; "Maryland's 175th FG Pilots," 18–19; and Zoerb interview, 29 April 1997.

24. Rose, *Fighting*, 160–61.

25. Gen Bertrand de Lapresle, UNPROFOR commander, 15 March 1994–28 February 1995, interviewed by author, 8 September 1998, Paris, transcript of tape recording, author's personal collection.

26. Rose, *Fighting*, 161.

27. Adm Leighton W. Smith, USN, interviewed by author, 10 February 1998, Arlington, Va., transcript of tape recording, author's personal collection.

28. Ibid.; Rose, *Fighting*, throughout. In his memoir, General Rose characterized NATO's goals, as pursued by Admiral Smith, as war-fighting rather than peace enforcement. Though the brand of peacekeeping General Rose was practicing allowed a greater use of force than traditional peacekeeping, it was based on peacekeeping principles. It also envisioned a definite divide between peacekeeping and peace enforcement that was not to be crossed. General Rose called this dividing line the Mogadishu line.

29. Military Official W; and Admiral Smith interview.

30. Admiral Smith interview; and Ryan interview.

31. Rose interview by author; and Rose, "A Year in Bosnia: What Has Been Achieved," *RUSI Journal* 140, no. 3 (June 1995): 24.

32. NATO Official W; and Admiral Smith interview.

33. Rose interview by author; and Admiral Smith interview.

34. Rose, *Fighting*, 177; Rose interview by author; Admiral Smith interview; Wald interview; and Military Official W.

35. Rose interview by author; and Rose, "Bosnia-Herzegovina 1994–NATO Support for UN Wider Peacekeeping Operations," *NATO's Sixteen Nations* 39, no. 3/4 (1994): 9. Elsewhere, General Rose referred to warning as one of the "rules for the use of force in peacekeeping" rather than a principle of peacekeeping, per se. See Rose, "A Year In Bosnia," 24.

36. Rose interview by author; Admiral Smith interview; and Military Official W.

37. Rose interview by author.

38. Ibid.

39. MCM-KAD-084-93, "Operational Options for Air Strikes," Memorandum for the Secretary-General, North Atlantic Treaty Organization, NAC Decision Statement, 8 August 1993. File B1c-2, BACS Collection.

40. For instance, at a press conference after the air strike on 6 August 1994, a reporter asked Admiral Smith, "Why does it seem that it's always American planes that do the bombing?" Admiral Smith, transcript of a news conference, 6 August 1994.

41. Wald interview; Lt Gen James E. Chambers, USAF, director of NATO's Combined Air Operations Center (CAOC), Vicenza, Italy, interviewed by author, 10 February 1998, Fairfax, Va., author's notes, author's personal collection; and Ashy interview by author.

42. Wald interview; and Chambers interview.

43. *Facts On File 1994*, 710–11; and Rose, *Fighting*, 176.

44. Rose, *Fighting*, 176.

45. General Rose has written that his commander, General de Lapresle, took a special interest in the event because he had a son commanding one of the units involved. Rose, *Fighting*, 176. Hagman claims that General Soubirou had a son-in-law in one of the participating French units. Hagman, 140.

46. De Lapresle interview; and Rose, *Fighting*, 176–77.

47. Rose, *Fighting*, 177.

48. Ibid.

49. Wald interview.

50. Ibid.; and North Atlantic Treaty Organization, "NATO Aircraft Attack Bosnian-Serb Tank," Press Release (94) 90, 22 September 1994.

51. NATO, Press Release (94) 90; Wald interview; and Chambers interview.

52. Wald interview.

53. Ibid.; and Chambers interview.

54. Wald interview.

55. Ibid.

56. NATO, Press Release (94) 90.

57. Ibid.; Wald interview; and Zoerb interview, 29 April 1997. There was some question as to whether the bombs actually hit the tank. See for instance, Rose, *Fighting*, 177.

58. In some accounts of the attack, only the Jaguar contribution was mentioned. See for instance, Tim Ripley, *Air War Bosnia: UN and NATO Airpower* (Osceola, Wisc.: Motorbooks International, 1996), 70; "The Jags Are Back," *Air Forces Monthly*, October 1995, 34; and Rose, *Fighting*, 177.

59. Rose, *Fighting*, 180.

60. Gen Michael E. Ryan, USAF, transcript of briefing to Air Power Conference, London, 13 September 1996.

61. L. C. Green, *The Contemporary Law of Armed Conflict* (Manchester, England: Manchester University Press, 1993), 120, citing Department of Defense (DOD), *Conduct of the Persian Gulf War*, 611.

62. Green, 120.

63. Ibid., 121.

64. Zoerb interview, 29 April 1997; and Hagman, 131–32, citing *NATO Doctrine for Peace Support Operations* (Draft, 20 October 1993, Annex D, Rules of Engagement).

65. De Lapresle interview; Rose, *Fighting*, 160–61 and 180; Admiral Smith interview; and Zoerb interview, 29 April 1997.

66. Admiral Smith interview; and Hagman, 198.

67. Zoerb interview, 29 April 1997.

68. Ibid.

69. Ibid.

70. Report to the Secretary-General Pursuant to Resolution 844 (1993) (S/1994/555, 9 May 1994), par. 10.

71. Ibid.

72. Hagman, 126, 131–32, and 182–83; Rose, *Fighting*, 15; and Zoerb interview, 29 April 1997.

73. Zoerb interview, 29 April 1997; Ashy interview by author.

74. De Lapresle interview, 8 September 1997.

75. Rose, *Fighting*, 235–36.

76. MCM-KAD-084-93.

77. "Record of Discussions: Meeting SRSG, FC and Staff to Review Fixed Targets, and the Implications of NATO Defence Ministers," Meeting—Seville—30 September 1994, c. 8 October 1994, File B4-2, BACS Collection; and Admiral Smith interview.

78. Gregory L. Schulte, "Former Yugoslavia and the New NATO," *Survival* 39, no. 1 (spring 1997): 27–28; and Admiral Smith interview.

79. "Record of Discussions: Meeting SRSG, FC and Staff;" Schulte, 27–28; and Rose, *Fighting*, 182.

80. "Record of Discussions: Meeting SRSG, FC and Staff," 3.

81. Ibid.

82. Ibid.

83. Ibid.

84. Rose, *Fighting*, 182–83.

85. Ibid.

86. Ibid., 183.

87. Despite such constraints, General Rose himself threatened the Bosnian government with air strikes against its forces in mid-August and again in September 1994. Rose, *Fighting,* 163 and 184; and *Facts On File 1994,* 562 and 711. In his memoir, Rose erroneously claimed that on the occasion of his threat in September, Bosnian government forces were violating a September 1993 NATO ultimatum making them subject to NATO air strikes. There was no such NATO ultimatum.

88. "Discussion between the United Nations and NATO," 27 October 1994, File B4-2, BACS Collection.

89. NATO, "Press Statement Issued Jointly by UN and NATO," Press Release (94)103, 28 October 1994.

90. Gen Bertrand de Lapresle, interviewed by author, 13 January 1998, Paris, transcript of tape recording, author's personal collection.

91. Admiral Smith interview.

92. Zoerb interview, 29 April 1997; Military Official U; and Senate, "Briefing on F-16 Shootdown in Bosnia and Current Operations: Hearings before the Committee on Armed Services," 104th Cong., 1st Sess., 13 July 1995, S. Hrg. 104–421, 33.

93. Dr. Thomas S. Snyder and Dr. Daniel F. Harrington, USAFE Office of History, *USAFE Historical Highlights, 1942–1997: Fifty-fifth Anniversary Edition* (Ramstein AB, Germany: Headquarters USAFE, 1997), 175.

94. Ibid., 176.

95. S/1994/1389; and Chambers interview.

96. Lt Gen Sir Michael Rose, Sarajevo, TLS (photocopy), to Gen Ratko Mladic, Han Pijesak, 18 September 1994, BACS Collection.

97. As is discussed in the next section.

98. Alan Warnes, "The Battle for Bihac," *Air Force Monthly,* January 1995, 40–41; *Facts On File 1994,* 874–75; and Ryan interview.

99. *Facts On File 1994,* 849–50; and Tim Ripley, "NATO Strikes Back," *World Airpower Journal* 22 (autumn/winter 1995): 18–27.

100. Wald interview; Ryan interview; Admiral Smith interview; and Senate, "Briefing on F-16 Shootdown," 32–33 and 52.

101. Adm Leighton Smith, USN, commander in chief NATO Allied Forces Southern Europe, briefing to US Air Force Air War College, Maxwell AFB, Ala., 9 November 1995, videocassette of briefing, file MISC–19, folder H–4, BACS Collection; and Gen Michael E. Ryan, USAF, "NATO Air Operations in Bosnia-Herzegovina: 'Deliberate Force,' 29 August–14 September 1995," transcript of briefing to Air Power Conference, London, 13 September 1996.

102. Admiral Smith interview; Ryan interview; Chambers interview; Zoerb interview, 30 April 1997; and Brig Gen David A. Sawyer, USAF, deputy director, Combined Air Operations Center, Vicenza, Italy, interviewed by Maj Tim Reagan and Dr. Wayne Thompson, 11 October 1995, Vicenza, Italy, BACS Collection.

103. See chap. 2, ROE discussion.

104. The United Nations, *The Blue Helmets: A Review of United Nations Peace-keeping,* 3d ed. (New York: United Nations Reproduction Section, 1996), 535.

105. Warnes, 41; and Ryan interview.

106. Ibid.

107. UN Security Council Resolution 958 (1994) (S/RES/958, 19 November 1994).

108. Admiral Smith, transcript of press conference, 21 November 1994; and NAMILCOM, "Implementation of Council Decision on Subsequent Air Attacks against an Identified Surface-to-Air Weapons System," Message to SHAPE, 230800Z NOV 94, File B4-2, BACS Collection.

109. Military Official U.

110. Ibid.; and Admiral Smith interview.

111. Military Official U.

112. Ibid.

113. "Jags Are Back," 34; and *Facts On File 1994,* 874.

114. De Lapresle interview, 13 January 1998; and Rose, *Fighting,* 201. Both UN generals indicated targeting decisions made on 20 November caused the one-day slip. Any changes in targets at that point would have necessitated replanning and possibly reconfiguring the ordnance loads on the jets. The following discussion, however, is not based on the supposition that the delay was for any reason other than the one given—high cloud coverage over the target.

115. De Lapresle interview, 13 January 1998; and Admiral Smith interview.

116. Admiral Smith interview.

117. De Lapresle interview, 13 January 1998.

118. Adm Leighton W. Smith, USN, "NATO Air Strike Against Udbina Airfield," transcript of news conference, Naples, 21 November 1994 (3:30 P.M.).

119. Ryan interview.

120. Admiral Smith interview.

121. De Lapresle interview, 13 January 1998; and Rose, *Fighting,* 200–203.

122. De Lapresle interview, 13 January 1998.

123. Adm Leighton W. Smith, USN, "NATO Air Strike Against Udbina Airfield—Mission Assessment," transcript of news conference, Naples, 22 November 1994 (5:00 P.M.); and Admiral Smith interview.

124. Ryan interview.

125. Admiral Smith, transcript of news conference, 22 November 1994.

126. NATO Official C; Gen George A. Joulwan, USA, Supreme Allied Commander Europe, 22 October 1993–11 July 1997, interviewed by author, 11 February 1998, Washington, transcript of tape recording, author's personal collection; and Admiral Smith interview.

127. NATO Official C.

128. Admiral Smith, transcript of news conference, 22 November 1994.

129. Ripley, "NATO Strikes Back," 23; and *Facts On File 1994*, 889.

130. Admiral Smith interview; Ryan interview; Zoerb interview, 30 April 1997; and Rose, *Fighting*, 201–2.

131. For instance, see Hagman, 147. In his analysis, Hagman correctly notes the strike had "no effect on the Serb encirclement of Bihac" but incorrectly concludes that was the raid's purpose, saying he found "no indication that enforcement of the 'no-fly zone' was the primary aim." My research indicates that because of no-fly zone violations by aircraft flying from Udbina, planners in AFSOUTH began looking at options for attacking Udbina around mid-1994. This was before the Bosnian government offensive from Bihac and the ensuing Bosnian Serb counteroffensive. Zoerb interview, 30 April 1997; and Chambers interview.

132. De Lapresle interview, 8 September 1998; Rose, *Fighting*, 169 and 200–202; Ryan interview; and Wald interview.

133. Charles Skinner, political-economic advisor to USNATO, interviewed by author, 28 April 1997, Brussels, notes and tape recording, author's personal collection.

134. Philip Sabin, "Counter-Air Mission in Peace Support Operations," in *The Dynamics of Air Power*, eds. Group Capt Andrew Lambert and Arthur C. Williamson (Bracknell, England: HMSO, 1996), 165.

135. Admiral Smith interview; and De Lapresle interviews, 13 January 1998 and 8 September 1998.

136. NATO Official C; Military Official X; Military Official U; and Richard Holbrooke, *To End A War* (New York: Random House, 1998), 61.

137. De Lapresle interview, 8 September 1998.

138. Admiral Smith interview. Also see Admiral Smith, transcript of news conference, 22 November 1994.

139. Sawyer interview. General Chambers left the CAOC earlier in November and retired from the US Air Force; his replacement, Maj Gen Hal Hornburg, did not arrive until the end of November.

140. NATO Press Release (94)111, 23 November 1994; and Warnes, 42.

141. Prior to this incident, only heat seeking surface-to-air missiles (SAM) had been fired at aircraft over Bosnia. The SA-2 radar-guided SAMs could engage NATO aircraft at much greater ranges than could heat seeking missiles. Moreover, radar-guided missiles such as the SA-2 and SA-3 carried a much larger warhead, and they could engage aircraft at any altitude (recall that an early version of the SA-2 shot down Gary Powers in a high-flying U-2 over the Soviet Union in 1960).

142. Sawyer interview.

143. Ibid.

144. Annex E: "Rules of Engagement (ROE)," to CINCSOUTH OPLAN 40101, Change 2, 13 August 1993, File B3e, NPL-21, BACS Collection.

145. MCM-KAE-090-94, "Operation Deny Flight ROE," 22 November 1994, File D2 a-c, BACS Collection.

146. NAMILCOM, "Implementation of Council Decision," Message to SHAPE, 230800Z NOV 94.

147. Ryan interview; and Chambers interview.

148. Ryan interview; Admiral Smith interview; and Senate, "Briefing on F-16 Shootdown," 32–33 and 52.

149. A variety of radar types is used in most radar-guided SAM systems. The different radar types perform different functions, such as early warning, surveillance, target acquisition, and target tracking. Once a target tracking radar is locked onto an aircraft and the aircraft is in range of the missile site, the missile crew can shoot at the aircraft.

150. Vice Adm Norman W. Ray, USN, deputy chairman of NATO's Military Committee, July 1992–December 1995, interviewed by author, 19 November 1997, Brussels, transcript of tape recording, author's personal collection.

151. Admiral Smith interview; Zoerb interview, 29 April 1997.

152. Ryan interview; and Zoerb interview, 29 April 1997.

153. NAMILCOM, "Implementation of Council Decision," Message to SHAPE, 230800Z NOV 94.

154. Warnes, 42.

155. NATO, Press Release (94)111, 23 November 1994; and NATO, Press Release (94)112, 23 November 1994.

156. Warnes, 42; and *Facts On File 1994*, 889.

157. Sawyer interview.

158. Military Official U.

159. NATO Press Release (94)114, 24 November 1994.

160. Ibid.

161. S/1994/555, 9 May 1994, par. 10; and Report of the Secretary-General Pursuant to Resolution 987 (1995) (S/1995/444, 30 May 1995), pars. 49 and 50.

162. *Facts On File 1994*, 889.

163. De Lapresle interview, 8 September 1998; and Maj Gen Eldon W. Joersz, USAF, message to CINCSOUTH (Adm Leighton W. Smith, USN) and COMAIRSOUTH (Gen Michael E. Ryan, USAF), 25 November 1994, File B4-2, BACS Collection.

164. Joersz, message to CINCSOUTH. General de Lapresle later confirmed this was an accurate reading of his position. De Lapresle interview, 8 September 1998.

165. Rose interview by author; and Sawyer interview. In his memoir, General Rose placed this event on 24 rather than 25 November. He also implied the claim he made about his forces being under fire may have been a ruse to get NATO aircraft to the area when General Ryan might otherwise have balked at Rose's request for planes. Rose, *Fighting*, 209.

166. Sawyer interview.

167. Zoerb interview, 27 May 1998. This type of CAS is known as "procedural control," and it is inherently riskier, in terms of collateral damage and danger of friendly fire, than close control CAS, because the forward air controller cannot see the targets, the aircraft, or the friendly forces that

might be near the target area. Under close control the forward air controller typically can see all three.

168. Sawyer interview. Jane Sharp, citing a newspaper article by E. Vulliamy, claimed that "CIA interceptions of SAS communications later revealed, however, that as NATO planes took off from Aviano in Southern Italy, Rose (who had recently learned that Belgrade had supplied the Bosnian Serbs with new SAM antiaircraft missiles) was ordering his SAS spotters in the field not to identify any targets." Jane M. O. Sharp, *Honest Broker or Perfidious Albion: British Policy in Former Yugoslavia* (London: Institute for Public Policy Research, 1997), 43. Whether or not the report is true, it gives an indication of the intensity of the split between AFSOUTH and UNPROFOR in late November 1994.

169. Admiral Smith interview; and Sawyer interview.

170. Admiral Smith interview; and Sawyer interview.

171. Military Official U, and Hagman, 131, 133, and 148.

172. Rose interview by author; and de Lapresle interview, 13 January 1998. For a discussion of the political-military trade-offs when dealing with air defense suppression in peace support operations, see Philip Sabin, "Counter-Air Mission in Peace Support Operations," in *The Dynamics of Air Power*, eds. Group Capt Andrew Lambert and Arthur C. Williamson (Bracknell, England: HMSO, 1996), 169–71.

173. Sawyer interview; and Ryan interview.

174. David Owen, *Balkan Odyssey* (London: Victor Gollancz, 1995), 327; and NATO Official C.

175. Military Official U; Ryan interview. General Ryan and others were less specific about the origins of the order to recall the package.

176. Military Official U; NATO Official C; and Hagman, 150–51.

177. Ray interview; and Lt Gen Patrick K. Gamble, USAF, assistant chief of staff, Operations and Logistics, SHAPE, interviewed by author, 2 July 1998, Washington, tape recording, author's personal collection.

178. Owen, 331.

179. Sawyer interview; Zoerb interview, 27 May 1998; and Lt Gen Hal M. Hornburg, USAF, interviewed by author, 17 July 1998, tape recording of telephone interview, author's personal collection.

180. Sawyer interview; Hornburg interview; and Tim Ripley, "Silence of the SAMS," *Aircraft Illustrated* 28, no. 1 (November 1995): 25. Ripley claimed NATO's move out of Bosnian airspace was requested by UNPROFOR in order to facilitate peace talks. It seems likely that visits by high-level diplomats to Sarajevo on 4 December may have prevented the resumption of flights over Bosnia before that date. However, research (including the sources cited here) revealed that the reason for the pullback to the air space over the Adriatic was because NATO could not defend itself adequately.

181. Gen Bertrand de Lapresle, Zagreb, TLS (photocopy), to Adm Leighton Smith, Naples, 7 December 1994, File B1a, BACS Collection.

182. Adm Leighton Smith, Naples, TLS (photocopy), to Gen Bertrand de Lapresle, Zagreb, 8 December 1994, File B1a, BACS Collection.

183. "Operation Deliberate Force Factual Review," 2–1.

184. *Facts On File 1994*, 995.

185. Note that the first and third missions are *not* consent-based peace-keeping activities. Yasushi Akashi, Zagreb, TLS (photocopy), to Dr. Radovan Karadzic, Pale, 10 December 1994, BACS Collection.

186. Ibid.

187. Gamble interview. The NAC decision of 8 December 1994 allowed stand-alone SEAD missions in response to hostile acts against UN or NATO aircraft.

188. Ryan, transcript of Air Power Conference.

189. CJCSI 3121.01, *Standing Rules of Engagement for US Forces* (Washington: Office of the Chairman of the Joint Chiefs of Staff, 1 October 1994), A–5.

190. Ibid., A–1.

191. Under US doctrine, the ground commander and the air commander work for a common superior, the Joint Task Force commander. In Bosnia, there was no equivalent overall commander, no unity of command, and no unity of purpose guided by a common objective. See Admiral Smith's comments in, "The Jane's Interview: Admiral Leighton W. Smith, USN," *Jane's Defence Weekly*, 28 January 1995, 32.

192. The "Block 50" variant of the F-16C was somewhat of an exception to this generalization; however, these aircraft were just being fielded, and were not readily available in Europe. "SEAD Role for F-16 Comes Closer," *Jane's Defence Weekly*, 20 August 1994, 14.

193. Again, certain fighters adapted for SEAD missions are rare exceptions, and even these generally have to be fitted with weapons for a particular mission, rather than being able to go out equally well prepared to perform SEAD and another mission. Given their scarcity and the high demand for them worldwide, commanders in AFSOUTH could not expect to employ them in such an inefficient way for very long.

194. CJCSI 3121.01, A–3, A–4, and A–6. For further discussions on SROE, see Lt Col Ronald M. Reed, "Chariots of Fire: Rules of Engagement in Operation Deliberate Force," in *Deliberate Force: A Case Study in Effective Air Campaign Planning*, ed. Col Robert C. Owen (Maxwell AFB, Ala.: Air University Press, 2000), 381–430; and Richard Grunawalt, "The JCS Standing Rules of Engagement: A Judge Advocate's Primer," *The Air Force Law Review* 42 (1997): 245–58.

195. Admiral Smith interview; Rose, *Fighting*, 200.

196. Military Official U; Rose interview by author; and de Lapresle, interview, 13 January 1998.

197. Rose, *Fighting*, 203.

198. De Lapresle interview, 8 September 1998.

199. Gen Michael E. Ryan, USAF, cited in Tirpak, "The Chief Holds Course," 39 (bracket comments in original).

Chapter 7

Paving the Way to Enforcement: January–June 1995

Our field commanders carry out political decisions; they do not make them. Soldiers can prosecute war when ordered to do so; they cannot declare war.

—Kofi Annan, November 1994

Through their planning, initiative, and insistence on operational autonomy in the first half of 1995, theater-level commanders in the UN and NATO paved the way for enforcement action later in the year. The first section of this chapter describes the origins of two key NATO plans for airpower: Dead Eye and Deliberate Force. Created at General Ryan's initiative, these plans later defined the shape of NATO air actions against the Bosnian Serbs. Another step in the process of clearing the way for NATO air action in Bosnia took place when General Rose's successor, Gen Rupert Smith, precipitated a hostage crisis for the UN. Though other researchers have analyzed General Smith's role in that regard, the second section presents evidence showing that making airpower more useable in Bosnia was probably an element in Smith's calculations rather than a coincidence.[1] The third section argues that the shooting down of a US F-16 in the no-fly zone had a major impact on furthering AFSOUTH plans to use airpower in Bosnia. The F-16 downing was important because it highlighted for Western political leaders the dangers to NATO airmen posed by the Bosnian Serb air defense system, thus helping AFSOUTH commanders acquire material resources and broader political support for their Dead Eye and Deliberate Force plans. This chapter's final section shows how Admiral Smith helped raise European political awareness—particularly within NATO—of problems with the no-fly zone. Fortified by his expertise and sense of responsibility to his forces, the AFSOUTH commander refused pressures that would have increased the risks to NATO pilots. This precipitated a NATO review of operation Deny Flight and lowered political resistance to the type of forceful SEAD operations favored by senior airmen in AFSOUTH.

Air Campaign Plans and
UNPROFOR Changes: Winter 1994–1995

From late December 1994 until June 1995, two key plans were developed to change the status quo. The first was designed to win back the airspace over Bosnia; the second to attrit the BSA's military capability.

Dead Eye

Planning for an air campaign that was eventually executed in the summer of 1995 owed something to plans developed at the CAOC to neutralize the Bosnian Serb surface-to-air threat. In the autumn of 1994, planners at the CAOC in Vicenza began looking at ways to deal with the new Serb surface-to-air threat.[2] They solicited and received approval from the new CAOC director, Maj Gen Hal Hornburg, to build a plan aimed at destroying the Serb air defense system.[3]

By mid-December they had put together a plan called *Dead Eye* that would win back control of the airspace over Bosnia by systematically attacking the entire Bosnian Serb integrated air defense system.[4] When this plan was presented to General Ryan, he expanded the initiative and ordered that an air campaign plan be built—one aimed at attriting the BSA's military capability.[5]

Deliberate Force

The wider air campaign plan was developed under the direction of Col Daniel R. "Doc" Zoerb, an American on General Ryan's staff in Naples, and it eventually was given the title "Deliberate Force."[6] Zoerb had worked on various air plans and targeting schemes at Naples since his arrival in January of 1994.[7] Between December 1994 and June 1995, his team drew from existing target lists to craft an air campaign plan to take away the BSA's military advantage over its adversaries.[8]

The idea behind the planning was to level the playing field by attriting certain BSA military capabilities so that the Bosnian Serbs would see it as in their best interest to cease military operations and genuinely seek a negotiated settlement in Bosnia.[9] As General Ryan later explained,

> that was the premise of the bombing operation. That was the heart of the bombing operation—you'd heard about lift and strike. . . . Lift wasn't going to occur. So if you're going to level the playing field, you do it the other way around by attriting.[10]

Ryan and his planners had studied the BSA and had seen how it depended upon maneuvering its better armed but less numerous forces to dominate the Bosnian government forces.[11] During the fighting around Bihac in the autumn of 1994, NATO planners observed that General Mladic had taken two and one-half weeks to maneuver his forces and equipment through the Posavina corridor into western Bosnia.[12] Once in place, the BSA forces drew from local caches of ammunition and rapidly reversed the gains made by the Bosnian government forces.[13] By taking away the command, control, and communications facilities on which Mladic depended for directing his forces and by hitting certain arms caches and targets that would limit the BSA's mobility, Ryan believed he could go a long way toward leveling the playing field.[14]

General Ryan had not been given political direction to initiate plans for a wider air campaign, nor did he seek political approval for the planning; he simply believed it prudent to have such a plan because the course of events in Bosnia indicated that it might be needed.[15] Though mildly concerned that some NATO nations might object to military planning that had not been directed by the NAC, General Ryan saw it as part of his responsibility as a commander to order the planning.[16] Later he observed,

> If we didn't do the planning, I think we would have been as remiss as the UN was in not upholding the mandates they were supposed to. . . . I never did get called on that. We planned it, and I briefed it to Joulwan and briefed it to—we started briefing it [in] March [or] April.[17]

Thus, the need to properly defend NATO air forces over Bosnia served as a catalyst for wider air campaign planning, and activities for both issues fell under General Ryan's responsibilities.

Through the winter and into the early spring of 1995, planners at Naples and Vicenza returned the focus of air-strike planning to its original, robust form. By the time General Ryan had arrived in theater, the accretion of political restrictions and lessons about what air-strike options the UN would accept had driven air-strike plans to become little more than a series of disjointed target lists associated with the safe areas or with specific attacks like the one at Udbina.[18] General Ryan reversed that trend and became involved in the planning. He spent many hours pondering what it was that constituted the Bosnian Serb's center of gravity and how to use airpower to affect that center of gravity in a way that would compel the Serbs to quit fighting.[19] Ryan also brought in various outside experts and agencies in an attempt to identify which of over 150 possible targets to strike in order to produce the desired effect on the BSA.[20] Meanwhile, planners at the CAOC attempted their own analysis of the Bosnian Serb air defense system.[21] After their initial effort, they received (from Kelly Air Force Base in San Antonio, Texas) a visit by US Air Force experts who specialized in command, control, and communications warfare.[22] The planning General Ryan ordered in late 1994 was not entirely different from earlier efforts; in fact, it reversed the evolution that had led to air strikes for one-off attacks against individual symbolic targets. General Ryan's initiative returned the planning focus to a more comprehensive view of air operations similar to those envisioned in 1993.[23]

NATO air campaign planning could also support plans to reinforce or withdraw the UN from Bosnia.[24] By December 1994, NATO planners in Belgium had been tasked to develop a plan to extricate UNPROFOR from the former Yugoslavia, and the withdrawal from Bosnia was expected to be messy.[25] When senior NATO officers saw the magnitude of the effort that would be needed to withdraw UNPROFOR, they raised the question of whether such a large force might be better used to reinforce the UN in the former Yugoslavia, rather than to consummate its failure.[26] By consequence, allied chiefs of defense staff meeting that winter in The Hague decided that plans for reinforcing UNPROFOR should be drawn up.[27] Thus, by early

1995 NATO military staffs were actively planning for several options ranging from the complete withdrawal of UNPROFOR to its reinforcement.[28] The broad-ranging air campaign aimed at the Bosnian Serbs could have been used to support several options, including the one for the withdrawal of UNPROFOR.[29] However, should UNPROFOR try to withdraw, it was not at all clear that the Bosnian Serbs would pose the greatest risk to the departing peacekeepers.[30] AFSOUTH planners continued to maintain active lists of potential Bosnian government and Bosnian Croat military targets—though there were scarcely enough of these to warrant an air campaign plan.[31] The uncharacteristic speed with which Western governments implemented military options in response to crises during the spring and summer of 1995 underscored the value of these early planning efforts.[32]

New UN Commanders and Redefining UNPROFOR

Early in 1995, the two top UNPROFOR commanders completed their one-year tours of duty in the former Yugoslavia. General Rose's replacement had a background that suggested he might have a better understanding of airpower and a more flexible approach to ground operations in Bosnia than the rigid peacekeeping formula followed by Rose. Near the end of January, Lt Gen Sir Rupert Smith arrived in Sarajevo to take over Bosnia-Herzegovina command from General Rose.[33] General Smith was known to be an innovative problem solver who had forged good relations with the US military during the Gulf War. As commander of the First (UK) Armored Division during Desert Storm, General Smith had witnessed first-hand how coalition airpower had prepared the battlefield before the ground war, and he had seen the difficulties of employing CAS.[34] In the two years prior to taking command of the UN forces in Bosnia, Smith served as the assistant chief of the defense staff (Operations and Plans) in London, so he was intimately familiar with the British contributions to both the UN and NATO for operations in the former Yugoslavia.[35] Thus, his recent joint-service responsibilities and his background probably gave Smith a less parochial view of the conflict than that of his predecessor.[36]

At the beginning of March, Lt Gen Bernard Janvier of France took over from his compatriot, General de Lapresle. Janvier, like Rupert Smith, had also worked well with American military officers during Desert Storm where Janvier commanded the "Daguet Division," or Sixth Light Armored Division. When asked after he had left Bosnia about the basis for his knowledge of airpower, Janvier cited first and foremost his experiences as a young officer in Algeria where in the early 1960s he had learned about close air support.[37] He held views similar to General de Lapresle's regarding the UN's role in Bosnia and the use of NATO airpower.[38] So, Janvier's arrival did not change the cordial but occasionally tense nature of the relationship between UNPROFOR and AFSOUTH.

Soon after General Janvier took over in Zagreb, the UN Security Council reorganized UNPROFOR. However, the move had no real impact on the responsibilities of UNPROFOR's principal commanders.[39] General Smith's command in Sarajevo took the name UNPROFOR, which had previously applied to the overall theater UN force headquartered in Zagreb. The theater force, commanded by Janvier, was renamed the United Nations Peace Force (UNPF), and it remained under Mr. Akashi's political direction.[40] Smith's command continued to be subordinate to Janvier's.

Calling the overall theater command a "Peace Force" aptly reflected the growing efforts by the UN secretariat to divest the force of any enforcement responsibility in the former Yugoslavia.[41] In December of 1994, Boutros Boutros-Ghali issued a report on the safe areas lamenting the failings of the light option and the difficulties experienced by the UN when trying to use airpower to compensate for UNPROFOR's inadequate ground forces.[42] He made it clear that UNPROFOR's ability "to *enforce* respect for the safe areas by *unwilling parties* is extremely limited, unless additional troops and the necessary weapons and equipment are made available" (emphasis added).[43] Though worried enforcement action would jeopardize the humanitarian portion of the UN's mission in Bosnia, Boutros-Ghali at least paid lip service to the idea of taking enforcement action if UNPROFOR were given the necessary forces.[44] A month later, when the UN secretary-general published his "Supplement to an Agenda for

Peace," he sounded a more pessimistic note about the UN's ability to conduct enforcement and the difficulties of subcontracting enforcement to regional organizations such as NATO.[45] Moreover, Boutros-Ghali expressed concern over "using force, other than in self-defense, in a peace-keeping context."[46] This was one step away from acknowledging the incompatibility of simultaneously conducting peacekeeping while taking enforcement action.

In late May, at Boutros-Ghali's insistence, General Janvier traveled to New York to brief the Security Council on, among other things, UNPF's inability to enforce the safe areas policy and to explain the requirement for a new, more realistic mandate if UN forces were to stay in Bosnia.[47] The US ambassador to the UN, Madeleine Albright, and others who viewed it as a call to abandon the UN's principal mission in Bosnia harshly criticized Janvier's presentation.[48] Nonetheless, on 30 May Boutros-Ghali submitted a report to the Security Council recommending a new mandate for UNPF that would limit the force strictly to peacekeeping duties.[49] Gone was the talk of early 1994, when Boutros-Ghali wanted to remind the warring factions in Bosnia that "UNPROFOR's mandate for the safe areas has been adopted under Chapter VII of the United Nations Charter. Accordingly, UNPROFOR is not obliged to seek the consent of the parties for operations which fall within the mandate conferred upon it under Security Council Resolution[s] 836 (1993) and 844 (1993)."[50] UN demands for more resources to carry out its enforcement duties in Bosnia had gradually yielded to an acceptance of the incompatibility of simultaneously attempting peacekeeping and enforcement.[51] Considering the limitations of UNPROFOR's means, the UN had little option but to choose peacekeeping.

While UNPROFOR adopted a peacekeeping posture, NATO picked up the enforcement mission in Bosnia. This division of labor made life increasingly difficult for theater commanders, especially Admiral Smith. The AFSOUTH commander recalled being at a high-level exercise at SHAPE in April 1995 during which the NATO secretary-general and an undersecretary-general from the UN gave speeches acknowledging the incompatibility of the UN and NATO missions. According to Admiral Smith, Willy Claes and the UN official agreed that

> "The problem that we have here is that NATO is in peace enforcement and the UN has been peacekeeping, and those are incompatible goals." And when they finished up, I thought: God, that's magnificent. They've finally realized the problem. I've been saying that for months.[52]

The admiral expected this recognition to lead to a resolution of the problem. However, the division of labor persisted and the two organizations continued to pursue their dichotomous agendas through their theater commanders. Admiral Smith concluded that the political authorities in NATO and the UN were ducking their duties and pinning the blame for failure in Bosnia on the military commanders:

> They were shirking their responsibility. . . . So why did they have to have a contact group? Why? Because two political bodies [the UN and NATO] that were involved in this thing couldn't talk to each other. They were getting absolutely nowhere, and they were just beating [up] their military leaders because that happened to be a lucrative target.[53]

The problem was especially acute for Admiral Smith because in addition to enforcing the no-fly zone and the heavy weapons exclusion zones, he was also supposed to support the UN commanders. Conversely, the UN commanders were not obliged to help NATO with enforcement, especially since the UN secretariat backed the move to peacekeeping, and the Security Council failed to insist on enforcement.

The Beginning of the End

Throughout early 1995, in Bosnia peace talks foundered, the cessation of hostilities agreement negotiated in December 1994 was repeatedly violated, and the rhetoric and actions of the warring factions prefigured a renewed bout of intensified fighting.[54] Fighting between Bosnian Serbs and Bosnian government forces continued around Bihac through January and February.[55] During the third week in March, Bosnian government forces launched a major offensive.[56] The Serbs shelled Tuzla, Gorazde,[57] and Sarajevo in reply, and the UN threatened air strikes to stop attacks on civilians. At the same time, Mr. Akashi condemned the Bosnian government for instigating the trouble.[58] In April—the third anniversary of the war in Bosnia—the downhill spiral continued as Bosnian Croat forces joined government forces against the Bosnian Serbs in central Bosnia, fighting continued around Bihac, and on two consecutive days near mid-month, sniper fire in Sarajevo claimed the lives of French peacekeepers.[59]

When the four-month cease-fire expired at the beginning of May, the most significant fighting was not in Bosnia but in eastern Croatia where Croatian government forces retook western Slavonia—one of four UN protected areas.[60] Serbs in Croatia launched rockets into Zagreb in retaliation for the Croatian government offensive.[61] The slide toward war continued in Bosnia as well, and, by the start of the second week in May, Bosnian Serb shelling of Sarajevo prompted Gen Rupert Smith to seek authorization for air strikes to silence the guns.[62] Smith's UN superiors rejected the request, but the starter's gun had been fired in the race by the warring factions to win their shares of Bosnia.

Rupert Smith on the Use of Airpower in Bosnia

As Bosnia stumbled toward open warfare, Gen Rupert Smith had a vision of how events might unfold and the role airpower might play. In June 1994, Smith had warned a US Senate committee that an all-out Bosnian Serb attack would be "most unlikely to be halted by airpower alone."[63] Furthermore, he cautioned, "The mission of the air forces to provide protection and support for UNPROFOR is different from that required for stopping the Serb attacks. It is unlikely that there would be sufficient resources to conduct both of those missions simultaneously successfully."[64] After describing the messy UN withdrawal that air strikes might provoke, General Smith rather presciently testified that the peacekeepers guarding the heavy weapons control sites would be vulnerable to being taken hostage and that the weapons would fall to whichever faction reached them first.[65] Later on the same day that Smith testified, Gen Mike Ryan spoke to the same committee with similar prophetic accuracy, pointing out that the first steps of a Serb attack would be directed against "the outlying regions that they could take very quickly."[66] A month after the Senate hearings, General Smith reportedly "spelled out the options of extending NATO air action to bombing a number of Bosnian Serb targets simultaneously" in a briefing to the foreign ministers of the contact group nations meeting in Geneva.[67]

During the winter of 1994–95, General Smith was exposed to elements of General Ryan's emerging air campaign plan, even though Smith might not have been fully aware of all of the details of it. In early 1995 NATO was busy planning to support a withdrawal of UNPROFOR, and the airpower portion of those plans was linked to Colonel Zoerb's air campaign plan.[68] As one AFSOUTH officer responsible for withdrawal planning later explained, "As we were writing the withdrawal plans, we were writing in the flexibility for an air campaign. Colonel Zoerb and the people in the Deny Flight Air Ops Cell were all heavily involved in writing a campaign plan but not calling it that" because of NATO political sensitivities.[69] General Joulwan recalled,

> There was a great hue and cry that the UN might have to withdraw. So my instructions were to plan a withdrawal option. So we had both a peace implementation option and a withdrawal option for Bosnia. Then in January [of 1995], all the CHODS [NATO Chiefs of Defense Staff] went to The Hague and talked about a reinforcement plan for the UN. So there was a series of plans by AFSOUTH that had hybrid pieces to it. *But the consistent part of that was a series of air targets.* We went through all of the detailed planning. Included were the targeting of air defense sites, of key installations, of all the associated sites. (Emphasis added)[70]

In February 1995, General Smith traveled to the NATO wargaming center at Ramstein, Germany (home of USAFE Headquarters), for a computer-assisted exercise of a possible UNPROFOR withdrawal from Bosnia.[71] From an air planner's perspective, preventing the BSA from interfering with UNPROFOR's withdrawal required the same initial actions as for Colonel Zoerb's campaign plan. Neutralizing the Bosnian Serb air defenses would be the first step. Next would come key BSA command and control sites that had not already been destroyed when the integrated air defense systems (IADS) were attacked. After that the courses of action might vary, but as General Joulwan noted, the core list of targets for a number of options was pretty much the same. In short, for at least 11 months prior to his request for air strikes in May 1995, General Smith had been contemplating future scenarios for UNPROFOR, and airpower seemed to be a recurring theme in those scenarios.[72] Therefore, it seems reasonable to conclude that General Smith's efforts to reinforce UNPROFOR and to use force proactively in Bosnia were made with the intention of including NATO airpower.

Pale Air Strikes and UNPROFOR Hostages: 25–26 May 1995

Gen Rupert Smith helped to keep UNPROFOR from getting further entangled in the war in Bosnia, and in the process he made the use of airpower a safer, hence more viable, option for the UN.[73] But to do so, he first took what at the time appeared to be an inordinate risk with the lives of his troops.[74] Research by Honig and Both has shown that by early March 1995 General Smith was pretty sure of Bosnian Serb intentions to go on a final offensive that year.[75] Furthermore, given the mutually exclusive options of making UNPROFOR a purely peacekeeping force or turning it into a force capable of taking enforcement action, Smith preferred enforcement.[76] James Gow suggests the same thing and argues further that it was British support for General Smith and the reinforcement of UNPROFOR that primarily shaped the Western response to the situation in Bosnia in 1995.[77] Smith asked for air strikes on Monday, 8 May, to curb Bosnian Serb shelling near Sarajevo but was turned down by Boutros-Ghali who was acting on advice from Akashi and Janvier.[78] As Honig and Both have revealed, in a move uncharacteristic for the British government, Foreign Secretary Douglas Hurd wrote a letter to Boutros-Ghali complaining about the decision to deny the air strikes.[79]

At a meeting in Paris a few days after the refused air strike, Generals Smith and Janvier told Boutros-Ghali that UN forces in Bosnia needed to be able to use force more decisively or stick exclusively to peacekeeping.[80] For either option, the UN generals wanted to redeploy their most vulnerable soldiers out of the eastern safe areas and away from weapons control points to more secure positions in central Bosnia.[81] The UN soldiers were potential hostages and, thus, a block to the more forceful option.[82] Yet, if the UN eschewed force and UNPROFOR were tasked strictly with peacekeeping, then there was no point in keeping UN soldiers in the safe areas, which seemed set to become the center of fighting between the factions.[83] After hearing the commanders' arguments, the UN secretary-general insisted that Janvier brief the Security Council on these military proposals.[84]

On 24 May while Janvier was at the UN headquarters in New York for his briefing, fighting intensified around Sarajevo, and the Bosnian Serbs removed some heavy weapons from a UN collection point.[85] General Smith issued a démarche to the Bosnian government and to the Bosnian Serbs warning them that "their forces would be attacked from the air if all heavy weapons did not cease firing by 1200 the next day."[86] In addition, Smith demanded the Bosnian Serbs return the heavy weapons they had recently confiscated from UN weapons control sites.[87] By this point, little had been done to reduce the risks to UNPROFOR from Bosnian Serb retaliation.[88]

On the afternoon of 25 May, after the Serbs failed to return the stolen heavy weapons by the UN deadline, NATO aircraft attacked an ammunition storage facility near the Bosnian Serb capital of Pale. The next day, the Bosnian Serbs failed to meet another deadline for returning the heavy weapons, and a second round of strikes destroyed the remainder of the ammunition bunkers at the same storage site near Pale. While still more demonstrative than militarily significant, the strike was considerably more robust than the two previous air strikes requested by the UN.[89] General Smith clearly had a different view of proportionality than his predecessor.[90] General Ryan later recalled,

> If we had an incident occur, we'd pull out the book, go to the matrix, and say: "What can we do under the current guidelines." And the guidelines kept getting piled on. . . . It was wacko, but those were the political rules that we were given. I don't know whether those books are still around, but it . . . was from that that we did things like the Pale raid. . . . And we stretched it a little bit actually on that one.[91]

General Janvier was in New York when the first démarche was issued, and he did not return to Zagreb until after the second air strike.[92] According to Janvier, Mr. Akashi consulted with Boutros-Ghali before the strikes.[93] However, Janvier criticized the UN's lack of forethought and its failure to give advance warning to its own forces and to the many aid workers in Bosnia.[94] Had Janvier been in Zagreb, he probably would have blocked the strikes or at least picked a less forceful bombing option. Moreover, given his criticism of the resulting hostage crisis, he would have been unlikely to approve the attacks without doing more to prevent UN peacekeepers from being taken hostage.

Gow, as well as Honig and Both, has suggested that Rupert Smith was intentionally trying to force the responsible officials in the international community to confront the choice between peacekeeping and enforcement in Bosnia because the UN could no longer go on pretending to do both.[95] General Ryan and his chief planner in Naples also believed that General Smith's decision to strike the Pale ammo dump was a risk he took aimed more at influencing the UN than the warring factions.[96] The Serbs responded to the first strike by shelling all of the safe areas except Zepa with especially appalling results in Tuzla, where 70 civilians were killed and more than a hundred others were wounded.[97] After the second strike, the Serbs rounded up UN peacekeepers throughout Bosnia, taking more than 300 hostages and using many as human shields against further attacks.[98]

The Pale air strikes lanced the Bosnia boil, and although there was an awful mess to be cleaned up, the procedure helped to cure the underlying problems inhibiting the use of airpower in Bosnia.[99] The first problem the UN had to deal with was getting its hostages back, but the hostage crisis itself proved useful to UNPROFOR and to those who wished to intervene more forcefully against the Bosnian Serbs. Whereas Smith's predecessor had reportedly discouraged the use of the term *hostage* to describe UN peacekeepers taken by the Bosnian Serbs after the air strikes at Gorazde and again after the SEAD strikes in November of 1994,[100] General Smith did nothing to downplay the fact that the Serbs held hundreds of his men hostage against further NATO air strikes.[101] The UN hostages were seen around the world for what they were, including those hostages who were chained to potential targets as human shields. These images could only strengthen the case for people who viewed the Bosnian Serbs as the "bad guys." The hostage crisis exposed, in dramatic fashion, the dilemma UNPROFOR faced when trying to take enforcement action. It demonstrated the futility of simultaneously conducting peacekeeping and enforcement action in Bosnia, and it forced the international community to confront the choice between the two.

As Gow has argued, after the Pale air strikes, General Smith was able to strengthen his forces and begin to reduce the ready supply of UN hostages.[102] In the aftermath of the Pale air strikes, the British and French governments were unusually quick to reinforce UNPROFOR with a 12,000-strong multinational Rapid Reaction Force (RRF) to Bosnia.[103] The Dutch also contributed 180 soldiers to the force.[104] Honig and Both have inferred from the speed of the offer to send the RRF that the decision to reinforce UNPROFOR had been made before the Pale air strikes.[105] Gow has suggested it was Rupert Smith's idea to reinforce UNPROFOR and that British political authorities were supporting him, rather than Smith being the mere executor of policy.[106] Later Admiral Smith judged that if Rupert Smith had not received the RRF, then Gen Smith probably would not have agreed to the Deliberate Force air strikes a few months later.[107] The Pale air strikes and subsequent hostage taking also contributed to the collapse of the UN's heavy weapons control regime, greatly reducing the number of UN soldiers deployed in vulnerable positions around Sarajevo.[108] Over the next three months, General Smith continued to redeploy his forces to more defensible sites.[109] By dramatically demonstrating UNPROFOR's untenable position, Rupert Smith was able to reinforce and redeploy UNPROFOR, thus removing the main obstacle to NATO air strikes.[110]

During the hostage crisis General Janvier repeatedly restrained General Smith from using force in Bosnia and, with Akashi, Janvier wanted to keep UNPROFOR from becoming a tool for enforcement action. On the evening of 26 May, Janvier returned from New York, where he had been to brief the Security Council.[111] The next afternoon, at Rupert Smith's urging, French forces in Sarajevo recaptured an observation post at Vrbanja Bridge from BSA soldiers who had taken it earlier in the day.[112] Fighting at the bridge cost the French two dead and 14 wounded; the Bosnian Serbs suffered four dead and an unknown number of lesser casualties.[113] The Vrbanja Bridge episode also netted the UN four Bosnian Serb "POWs," putting the world body in an awkward position.[114] As Honig and Both have shown, two days after the Vrbanja Bridge incident, Janvier issued a policy directive to General Smith stating: "The execution of the mandate is secondary to the security of UN personnel. The intention being to avoid loss of life defending positions for their own sake and unnecessary vulnerability to hostage-taking."[115] On 2 June, General Janvier blocked a request from General Smith to open a road into Sarajevo, noting, "We must definitely avoid any action which may degenerate into confrontation, further escalation of tension, and [thus] the potential use of air power."[116] A week later, Janvier, Akashi, and Rupert Smith met in the Croatian coastal town of Split to discuss the RRF that was being assembled to support UNPROFOR in Bosnia.[117] During their meeting, Smith argued that he did not want the RRF unless he could use it for fighting.[118] According to Smith, "the Serbs want to conclude this year and will take every risk to accomplish this," and Serb designs "will lead to a further squeezing of Sarajevo or an attack on the eastern enclaves, creating a crisis that short of air strikes we will have difficulty responding to."[119] Janvier and Akashi disagreed, doubting Smith's analysis of Serb intentions and explaining the need to return to traditional peacekeeping.[120] When the meeting ended, Akashi informed the press that the arrival of the RRF would not alter UNPROFOR's peacekeeping mission.[121] Later that day, Boutros-Ghali wrote a letter to the Security Council confirming that the RRF "would operate under the existing UN rules of engagement."[122] Clearly, Rupert Smith did not enjoy support from Zagreb or New York in his effort to clear the way for stronger action in Bosnia.

F-16 Downing and Hostage Deals

Hostage-taking was, as Gow has argued, the Bosnian Serbs' primary tool for countering Western coercion.[123] With General Smith working successfully to remove this option, the Serbs needed to find a new way to exploit international political divisions and to stymie American intervention. In retrospect, the downing of an American aircraft over Bosnia may have been an attempt by the Bosnian Serbs to net a US pilot to help forestall more forceful intervention by the international community.

Following the Pale air strikes, the Bosnian Serbs declared all agreements with the UN void and, as with earlier NATO air attacks, the Bosnian Serbs also threatened to shoot down NATO aircraft.[124] A few days later, on 2 June 1995, a Bosnian Serb SA-6 surface-to-air missile system shot down US Air Force Capt Scott O'Grady, who was flying an F-16 over Bosnia on a no-fly zone patrol.[125] The Serbs were thought to have intentionally targeted a US aircraft.[126] In what was later recognized as a "trap," the Serbs had moved a mobile SA-6 from the known SAM sites to a position 40 kilometers south of Banja Luka airfield and were flying military jets from Udbina near the border with Bosnia.[127] As Admiral Smith recalled,

> When Scott O'Grady got shot down, we were . . . trying to shoot down [a Serb] airplane as he came slipping across the border [from Croatia to Bosnia]. We were hoping he'd come across the border, but they were flying these feints. You know in retrospect it looks like what they did is just set us up, and I should have been smarter—I mean I should have seen that. . . . They were setting up a trap. But as you go down that path, it doesn't look that way.[128]

NATO commanders had gradually relaxed the requirements put in place at the end of 1994 for all flights over Bosnia to be escorted by SEAD aircraft. The escorted packages of aircraft gradually gave way to unescorted flights relying on looser protection from specialized SEAD aircraft operating independently over Bosnia instead of being dedicated to protect specific missions.[129] Eventually, commanders in AFSOUTH allowed flights into Bosnia without any SEAD protection, so long as the aircraft remained outside of the range of known SAM sites.[130]

O'Grady's flight, call-sign BASHER 51, purposely avoided Serb SAM coverage.[131] The flight lead demonstrated a small measure of complacency by continuing to orbit over northwestern Bosnia after he was momentarily illuminated by an SA-6 tracking radar.[132] However, given the rules of engagement for Deny Flight and the prohibition against preemptively eliminating such threats, it was not uncommon for NATO airmen to continue their missions after being locked onto by SAM radar.[133] This was precisely the environment General Ryan and Admiral Smith had hoped to avoid when they moved to eliminate the SAM threat in late 1994, but British and French reluctance and the dual-key control over NATO airpower precluded such proactive steps.[134] When O'Grady was locked onto by the SA-6's radar, he blindly took evasive maneuvers, but within a few seconds, the second of two missiles Serb forces fired at him split his aircraft in two.[135] The BSA forces operating the SA-6 battery were able to take the shots, with little warning to O'Grady, by drawing on radar information from the wider integrated air defense network rather than using their own radar.[136] With hundreds of UN hostages—some being used as human shields—the Bosnian Serbs could be fairly certain that the downing of a US aircraft would not lead to any immediate retaliatory action.

O'Grady's downing complicated the release of the UN hostages taken after the Pale raids and indicated that the Bosnian Serbs may have been trying to capture an American pilot. On 2 June the Bosnian Serbs began releasing some of the 377 hostages taken following the raids on Pale, but they began taking additional peacekeepers hostage.[137] One hundred twenty-one hostages were freed that day, but 61 others were taken.[138] Though Milosevic was credited with helping to win the release of UNPROFOR troops, Gow has suggested that General Smith was confident that the Bosnian Serbs would release the hostages unharmed.[139] Whatever Smith's calculations, the downing of an American combat aircraft led to renewed pressure from the United States for air strikes against the Serb SAM sites.[140] Furthermore, any attempt to rescue O'Grady threatened to lead to an escalating use of force in Bosnia, especially if one of the rescue aircraft were shot down. General Joulwan recalled French anxieties over the F-16 downing,

> The French were very concerned that we would mount a rescue of O'Grady. In fact, I was having a dinner the night O'Grady was shot down. Willy Claes was coming to the dinner. . . . And we already had a

> very extensive search ongoing. And Willy came to dinner that night and said: "You know the French are concerned that any rescue attempt may interfere with their hostage negotiations." And I said: "Willy, this is a NATO pilot. We're going to find him. And I'm going to use everything at my disposal to find him."[141]

This exchange illustrated a central feature of hostage taking in Bosnia: matters were quickly taken out of military hands and worked at the political level. Though the French could not stop American generals in NATO from taking action, they could certainly give instructions to the French generals working for the UN in the former Yugoslavia.

Even before O'Grady's fate was known, General Mladic sought assurances against air strikes in exchange for the UN hostages.[142] Within two days of the downing, the UN reported that Mladic wanted to meet with General Janvier; Mladic was refusing to discuss the hostages until he was given guarantees his forces would not come under further air attacks.[143] When O'Grady was rescued on 8 June, the Bosnian Serbs still held more than 140 UN soldiers hostage.[144] Within a week of the rescue, leaders in Pale claimed Serbia's President Milosevic had secured international guarantees against further NATO air strikes.[145] Allegations of a secret deal with the French to block NATO air strikes arose soon after the last hostages were freed on 18 June,[146] and General Janvier's delay in authorizing close air support for Dutch peacekeepers when Srebrenica fell in July seemed to lend credence to the charge.[147] At the end of May, Janvier's predecessor, General de Lapresle, was dispatched by the French government to negotiate the release of the hostages, and he later confirmed that Mladic pressed him for guarantees against NATO air strikes.[148] But the former UN commander said he told Mladic that the Bosnian Serbs would have to discuss that with Janvier and Akashi.[149] General de Lapresle recalled that while he was trying to win back the French soldiers, "Janvier was simultaneously, of course, involved in the process of trying to obtain the release of these hostages, and so, I expect, were a lot of other guys— Churkin . . . and many others."[150] But the problem for the Bosnian Serbs, according to de Lapresle, was that they did not know who could reliably deliver on the promise they were seeking.[151] General Janvier has denied being involved in any negotiations over the hostages, which seems surprising.[152] However, as other researchers have argued, even if Janvier was involved in negotiating the release of the hostages, the principal deal-making over the French hostages was going on at a higher level, between Presidents Chirac and Milosevic.[153] Given the Bosnian Serb claims about international guarantees to President Milosevic, the most likely explanation is one suggested by David Rohde: "Milosevic, desperate to curry favor with the West and free the hostages, may have lied and told the Bosnian Serbs he received a verbal assurance when he did not."[154] Whether General Janvier played a role in helping to strike a deal for the release of the French hostages remains unknown. However, if Janvier gave Mladic any assurances against air strikes, he was probably acting under political instructions.

Apparently, the Bosnian Serbs also wanted to strike a deal with the United States over O'Grady. Immediately following the downing of O'Grady's F-16, the Serbs claimed to have captured him, only to state a few days later that they had not.[155] Then, on 7 June, one of Mladic's confidants, working through a humanitarian organization, managed to contact Col Chuck Wald, the American wing commander at Aviano Air Base in Italy.[156] The man claimed the Bosnian Serbs "were willing to release the pilot, unharmed, in exchange for a secret line of communication to the US."[157] A pilot from O'Grady's squadron was sent with Air Force special agents and Italian intelligence officers to meet Mladic's representative in the coastal town of Trieste, bordering Slovenia.[158] After negotiating through the night and into the morning, one of the agents received word by cellular phone that O'Grady had been rescued.[159] The Americans abruptly walked out on the Serb, leaving Italian authorities to do as they liked with him.[160] Possible explanations for the Bosnian Serb ruse are (1) they wanted the Americans to give up the search for O'Grady so that Mladic's men could find him, or (2) they suspected he was dead or lost and would not be found soon, thus giving them a chance to extract guarantees against further air strikes by exploiting US uncertainty over the fate of O'Grady.

The downing of O'Grady's jet indicated that the Bosnian Serbs may have been trying to capture an American pilot in order to neutralize the primary force behind NATO air strikes—the United States. Netting a US airman held several advantages over taking UN soldiers hostage. It was in the Bosnian Serbs' interest to keep the UN in Bosnia,[161] and taking its peacekeepers hostage could only dampen the enthusiasm of troop-contributing nations and the UN secretariat for continuing UNPROFOR's mission. By 1995, the BSA was war weary and outnumbered.[162] Its adversaries were growing stronger with outside help.[163] Belgrade was less able—and arguably less willing—to offer assistance to the Bosnian Serbs.[164] The best hope for the Serbs was to use the UN to try to hang on to their territorial gains, much as they had done in Croatia prior to losing Western Slavonia. If war were to come, UNPROFOR could be pushed aside where necessary, and it could be used to block NATO air strikes—either through UN self-deterrence and the dual key, or through more hostage taking. If the UN pulled out, the dual key and the potential hostages would be gone. By the spring of 1995, it looked as though UNPROFOR might be withdrawn from Bosnia, thus removing the dual key and the potential hostages. Moreover, the Clinton administration was under pressure from Congress to act unilaterally.[165] The Bosnian Serbs may have reasoned they needed a US pilot as a hostage to continue to neutralize the threat of air strikes.

There is not enough evidence to reach a definite conclusion about whether the shootdown of O'Grady was a premeditated attempt to capture an American airman or just an act of retribution for the Pale air strikes.[166] The bid to open a secret line of communication through the US Air Force wing at Aviano, however, suggests the Bosnian Serbs were trying to make a deal with the United States. Because the downing of an American jet held the potential to evoke more of the air strikes the Serbs were trying to avoid, retribution would seem to have been an insufficient motive for setting what appears to have been a baited trap. The Serbs were probably trying to capture an American pilot or drive a wedge between the United States and its allies by provoking the United States while shielding themselves behind UN hostages.

Kicking the Problem Back Upstairs

The F-16 downing forced political authorities in the United States and NATO to recognize the threat posed by the Bosnian Serb air defense system, and, in the process, it paved the way for the execution of air operations planned in AFSOUTH. Disagreement between the US, Britain, and France over the best strategy for Bosnia had been one of the principal weaknesses of international efforts to intervene in the former Yugoslavia.

These unresolved political disputes had been passed down to military proxies in AFSOUTH and UNPF, but the military efforts to work out a solution had failed. The shooting down of O'Grady helped to kick the problem back upstairs where it could get resolved. Because the shootdown failed to net a hostage, there was no US inhibition to counter the increased frustration American political authorities felt over the loss of the F-16.[167] General Ryan was ready with the Dead Eye plan and a plan for a wider air campaign—Deliberate Force. At the same time, Admiral Smith forced political authorities in NATO to confront the need to eliminate the Bosnian Serb air defense threat by refusing to send aircraft over Bosnia without heavy SEAD escorts. These restrictions made it impossible for NATO to enforce the no-fly zone or the heavy weapons exclusion zones, leading NATO to reassess its Deny Flight operations.

US Response to the F-16 Downing

O'Grady's downing added to the factors impelling the Clinton administration to take a leading role in the Balkans while simultaneously highlighting the risks American airmen faced because of the dual key. At a time when the 1996 presidential race was starting to heat up, the shooting down and subsequent rescue of O'Grady aroused American public interest in Bosnia more than any event before it.[168] Under domestic political pressure, the administration backed away from hints made by the president at the end of May that the United

States might send ground troops to help UN forces in Bosnia regroup and reestablish their credibility.[169] Though American public opinion militated against sending US ground forces to Bosnia, the administration had promised to provide 25,000 soldiers to assist in a NATO withdrawal of UNPROFOR. Leading administration officials believed breaking that promise might break the alliance.[170] Thus, from a US policy perspective, UNPROFOR had to be made to work, at least until a solution could be found for Bosnia. In the meantime, airpower was the only acceptable US military contribution to the equation. On 6 June, President Clinton's top national security advisors gathered at the first in a series of meetings that culminated in a new administration policy for the Balkans.[171]

The shooting down of O'Grady also demonstrated to US and other NATO political authorities the sophisticated nature of the Bosnian Serb integrated air defense system and the risks to their airmen over Bosnia, thus adding political support to military demands to neutralize the air defenses.[172] There had always been a risk to NATO aircrews over Bosnia, and it had increased significantly in late 1994 when the Serbs became more active at employing their radar-guided SAMs. However, the senior commanders in AFSOUTH had to contend with the distinct lack of appreciation for these risks. The downing of a state-of-the-art fighter with its American pilot changed the perception in the United States that airpower was a risk-free option; as General Ryan noted,

> We were using force in Bosnia on the air side, and putting people at risk on the air side, which for some strange reason isn't considered putting Americans at risk. It's only Americans at risk when you put them on the ground. The stark reality of that was [revealed] when O'Grady got shot down, and suddenly we have this hue and cry back in the United States.[173]

As the facts surrounding the downing emerged, it did not take long for politicians in the US to recognize the risks. Sen. John Warner, then second ranking Republican on the Senate Armed Services Committee, was the first to question Pentagon officials who had been sent to brief the committee on the downing of the F-16. He got straight to the point: "We are still subjecting our airmen to some measure of risk . . . thrust upon us by virtue of the UN decision as they balance the risk to the airmen against the risk to the ground forces."[174] The senator wanted to know, "Why do not the American commanders say: Well by God, we are not going to put our American airmen at risk?"[175] When the briefers explained that there were no risk-free military operations and that technically the NATO airmen were not combatants in Bosnia, Warner retorted: "You are not a combatant, but you are taking combatant consequences. . . . I just do not know how our commander in chief, the president, and others in authority can continue to submit these men in the aircraft to risks because of a policy decision by the United Nations."[176]

The downing of O'Grady's jet was a reveille for Washington, and America's newfound attention to Bosnia opened the floodgates for US resources to the CAOC.[177] It strengthened the case of those arguing for preemptive attacks against Bosnian Serb air defenses in the event of any air campaign against the BSA, and it helped ensure General Ryan would get the equipment he needed to prosecute air attacks against both the air defenses and the BSA.[178] As General Ryan recalled,

> O'Grady going down caused an uproar and a substantial increase in the help we were getting. It was very difficult to get funding for the CAOC . . . and after O'Grady went down, we got all kinds of help.[179]

CAOC Director, Maj Gen Hal Hornburg, was later asked if the UN hostage crisis was a contributing factor to the sudden US interest in Bosnia; his tongue-in-cheek response was "What hostage crisis? It was Scott O'Grady."[180] According to Hornburg:

> We had requirements identified long before Scott O'Grady got shot down, but everybody thinks that we only started wondering about where we were going to go in the CAOC on the 2d of June. That is not true. That is when *Washington* started caring.[181]

Generals Ryan and Hornburg invited a Pentagon team to evaluate the CAOC and to recommend any changes or additional equipment needed to modernize it.[182] The CAOC expanded significantly before the end of August with an influx of American personnel and computer hardware and software for managing an air campaign.[183]

In addition, General Ryan began to gain a reputation at the Pentagon for issuing short-term requests for limited, high-demand aircraft such as KC-10 tankers and electronic combat aircraft, and then holding onto them long past the time covered by his requests.[184] In another step in the process of preparing for air action in Bosnia, USAFE established a new command at Aviano Air Base in Italy on 1 July: the 7490th Wing (Provisional). According to USAFE historians, "The purpose of the action was to bring all aircraft supporting Deny Flight at the base under a single chain of command."[185] Col Chuck Wald, commander of the 31st Fighter Wing permanently based at Aviano, commanded the new organization.[186] The move enhanced America's ability to employ its airpower in the region, whether it intended to act unilaterally or in concert with its NATO allies.

Because General Ryan had ordered air campaign planning months earlier, he had something to offer US political authorities when the need to settle matters in Bosnia came to the fore in June 1995. The week of the Pale air strikes, a team of US Air Force officers from the "Checkmate" division at the Pentagon visited Italy to analyze Colonel Zoerb's plans for air operations in Bosnia[187]—hereafter referred to as the Deliberate Force plan.[188] Although General Ryan believed Deliberate Force would be needed, he and Admiral Smith were not ready to share the details of the plan with other NATO members.[189] As General Ryan later recalled,

> I briefed it to [General] Shali[kashvili] on the US side, and I briefed it to the national security advisor. So, on the US side they were fairly familiar with what we were doing, what we were planning. We did not take it around to [the other NATO] capitals.[190]

Deliberate Force aimed at an objective not all NATO capitals were willing to endorse: "[To] adversely alter BSA advantage to conduct military operations against the BiH [i.e., the Bosnian government army]."[191] The Deliberate Force plan also targeted the entire Bosnian Serb air defense system as well as their command and control facilities so it overlapped with the Dead Eye plan.[192] Throughout June General Ryan and his staff continued to refine both plans and the lists of associated targets that went with them.[193] General Hornburg invited Col Dave

Deptula to come to Vicenza to teach the CAOC staff what Deptula had learned through experience as one of the principal "Black Hole" planners for the air campaign in Desert Storm.[194] Though the date on which General Ryan briefed the plan for Deliberate Force to US political authorities is unclear, evidence suggests the briefing took place sometime in June or early July.[195] Broader allied participation in the planning and integration of the air plans with the RRF's ground scheme of action did not begin until late July when NATO was more united in its approach to Bosnia.[196] If General Ryan had delayed planning until the North Atlantic Council (NAC) specifically directed it, he would not have had a viable air campaign plan to offer US political authorities when they suddenly felt compelled to come up with a new policy on Bosnia.

NATO Response to the F-16 Downing

While General Ryan worked on the plans, Admiral Smith forced political authorities in NATO to confront the implications of the SAM threat; however, doing so strained his relations with some of his superiors. After the downing of O'Grady's F-16, NATO's Deny Flight mission took a clear back seat to the safety of forces in the region.[197] All practice air support to UNPROFOR stopped, and combat air patrols to enforce the no-fly zone were shifted south from Bosnian airspace to the skies above the Adriatic.[198] The UN abandoned the weapons control regime, and, without UN cooperation, NATO ceased to be able to enforce the exclusion zones around the safe areas.[199] Only essential missions were flown over Bosnia, and these required heavy SEAD escorts.[200] Despite RAF protests, Admiral Smith refused to permit British F-3 Tornado aircraft to fly over Bosnia because he deemed their electronic countermeasures equipment inadequate.[201] The Dutch ministry of defense recalled to Holland six of its 18 F-16s supporting Deny Flight.[202] Meanwhile, in a historic move, Germany's parliament voted to deploy 16 jets to the southern region, including eight Tornado aircraft specially equipped for dealing with surface-to-air threats.[203] Thus, with help from Admiral Smith, the downing of O'Grady's jet focused the attention of NATO's

European political authorities on the air defense threat in Bosnia.

Notwithstanding pressures from Brussels for more aggressive policing of the no-fly zone, Admiral Smith refused to put NATO aircrews at risk, forcing NATO to reevaluate the Deny Flight mission. With Deny Flight operations greatly curtailed, the Serbs began flying military jets from Banja Luka airfield in northern Bosnia—perhaps baiting NATO for another SAM trap.[204] Admiral Smith recalled General Joulwan's pressing for more intensive air patrols over Bosnia to enforce the no-fly zone, but Smith refused:

> They had SAM sites up there, and we knew we couldn't take them out, and I just said: "I'm not going to put our pilots in danger." I mean, I did that in Vietnam. I trolled around trying to get SAM sites to shoot at us so that we could knock them down—that's dumb. And these were not unsophisticated missiles. So I just told George: "We've got to change the way we're doing business." They had complete radar coverage. . . . They knew exactly what we were doing . . . I told my boss: "You told me not to do anything stupid, [well] . . . I'm not going to troll for missiles up there. I'm not going to do it. Period. They can fly airplanes out of Banja Luka all they want to.[205]

The AFSOUTH commander saw three options open to NATO: (1) let the Serbs fly; (2) destroy the Serb SAM threat and put patrols back over Bosnia; or (3) conduct an air strike against Banja Luka.[206] Despite NATO policy requiring its commanders to coordinate closely with their UN counterparts, Admiral Smith remembered being reprimanded for writing to General Janvier suggesting air strikes at Banja Luka: "What a firestorm that was . . . I had to go up to Brussels and spend a little time with the secretary-general while he told me that I was out of my box. So you're damned if you do, and damned if you don't."[207] The NATO Secretary-General, Willy Claes, probably wanted to avoid a rerun of the impotent raid on Udbina, which occurred in the first month of Claes's tenure at NATO. With backing from Mr. Akashi, General Janvier had predictably refused the request anyway, so NATO was down to two options: let the Serbs fly, or destroy the SAM threat.[208] But Janvier and Akashi were still trying to revive the UN's moribund peacekeeping mission and to reestablish ties with the Bosnian Serbs; they were not about to let NATO go after the

Bosnian Serb integrated air defense system.[209] With the UN unwilling to make use of NATO airpower, and NATO's own commander in the region refusing to put aircrews at increased risk to enforce the no-fly zone, NATO was forced to conduct a complete reassessment of Deny Flight operations.[210]

Admiral Smith believed his expertise and his responsibility as a commander obligated him to stand firm when it came to decisions over how to conduct air operations in Bosnia.[211] Furthermore, he was willing to accept the backlash that came from standing up to the people above him in both the US and NATO chains of command. The AFSOUTH commander later averred,

> I knew more about air strikes and air operations than anybody above me, and I figured if they didn't like what I was doing, then they could just remove me, and that was just fine with me. It's real easy to say that when you have absolutely no promotion potential, but I was prepared to be fired on a lot of issues. One of them was trolling in SAM sites.[212]

Admiral Smith recognized that General Janvier was the supported commander, and without the permission of his UN counterpart, Admiral Smith could not eliminate the SAM threat. As Smith saw it:

> Western militaries are obligated to follow the political guidance of their masters. They had very clear guidance. I had sort of fuzzy guidance. I was getting pushed to do more, do more, do more. And yet, I couldn't do it without the permission of the ground commander, so I was sort of caught between a rock and a hard place.[213]

Admiral Smith could have easily ordered a resumption of air operations over Bosnia that entailed greater risks to NATO aircrews, but instead, he stood his ground. As a result, the problems created by the SAM threat and the dual-key controls over the proper defense for aircrews were kicked back upstairs to the political level.

The viability of enforcing the no-fly zone was in question, and NATO political authorities in Brussels tasked their military staff to come up with options for the future continuance of the flight ban over Bosnia. The military committee responded by presenting six options ranging from doing nothing, that is, abandoning the no-fly zone, to attacks that would neutralize the Bosnian Serb air defenses.[214] Furthermore, the military authorities in Brussels supported Admiral Smith in his decision to control the risks to alliance aircrews by shifting the no-fly zone patrols to the airspace over the Adriatic.[215] Back in the United States, the undersecretary of defense for policy, in a briefing to the Senate Armed Services Committee, said of the NATO commanders: "If they at any point make a determination that they think the risk to American or other NATO flyers is unacceptable, we will fully back them in either standing down the operation or modifying it to a level that they find is acceptable."[216] Though some NATO officials were displeased about the disruption of the no-fly zone, apparently no one was willing to accept the responsibility for overruling Admiral Smith. Until the end of August when Operation Deliberate Force began, NATO air operations over Bosnia remained severely curtailed because of the SAM threat.[217] However, the downing of O'Grady's jet and Admiral Smith's restrictions moved NATO political authorities to accept more liberal ROE for SEAD, including preemptive attacks against early warning radar in the event future air strikes were needed to defend the safe areas.[218]

Conclusion

During the first half of 1995, theater-level commanders in the UN and NATO laid the groundwork for more effectively using airpower in Bosnia. However, the strongest advocates for enforcement were not at the top of the theater chains of command for either the UN or NATO. They were one level down, at the level of their principal subordinate commanders— Generals Rupert Smith and Mike Ryan. This represented no real shift in General Ryan's attitude, but it was a marked change for the UN command in Bosnia. Absent clear policy direction, the commanders at the top of each chain, General Janvier and Admiral Smith, refused to take greater risks to accomplish the enforcement elements of their respective missions. General Janvier consistently acted so as to minimize short-term risks to UN forces and to move the mission in Bosnia toward peacekeeping. He did this through policies restricting Gen Rupert Smith's initiative on the ground and by refusing to turn the UN key for air strikes, whether they were urged by NATO or by General Smith.

Likewise, Admiral Smith refused to accept greater risks without clearer political direction. However, unlike Janvier, Admiral Smith's mission was primarily one of enforcement, and his efforts to minimize the short-term risks to his forces pushed NATO toward forceful action. Admiral Smith's refusal to expose NATO aircrews to the SAM threat in Bosnia was an important factor in forcing political authorities in NATO to face squarely the dilemma posed by the dual-key controls over SEAD strikes. If the Bosnian Serbs were attempting to capture an American pilot, then the AFSOUTH commander's contribution may have been more important than previously recognized. However, Admiral Smith did not seem to have that specific possibility in mind. He was, instead, trying to balance force protection and mission accomplishment, and he refused to put NATO airmen at an increased risk just to keep up appearances in the no-fly zone. This eventually helped to kick the dual key problem back upstairs where it could get resolved. By his own account, Admiral Smith felt that his expertise and responsibility demand that he take a strong stand and accept the consequences of displeasing his superiors.

One level below the theater commanders, the principal subordinate commanders, Generals Rupert Smith and Mike Ryan, were stronger advocates of enforcement. To push enforcement, Mike Ryan and Rupert Smith were willing to take greater risks—especially General Smith—and in so doing they helped to shape events as they unfolded. General Ryan was consistent in pressing for enforcement action in the no-fly zone over Bosnia. His initiative to use American officers assigned to NATO for air campaign planning, rather than officers from the US Sixteenth Air Force, might have raised the ire of some NATO nations. Though he might have been told to stop, there was little serious risk associated with the planning. Conversely, sending no-fly zone patrols over northern Bosnia without SEAD escort right after the bombing of Pale was risky. This may have been intended to draw ineffective fire from older, long-range SA-2s and SA-3s operating from well-known fixed sites. NATO fighters could more easily defeat those older

SAM systems. General Ryan would then have had grounds to press the UN for SEAD strikes. There is, however, no evidence for or against that hypothesis. If O'Grady had been captured or killed, or if another airplane had been shot down, it is quite possible that Admiral Smith would have asked for a new air component commander. Though the shooting down of Captain O'Grady had a significant impact on the future use of airpower in Bosnia, it is difficult to credit that to General Ryan, since there is no evidence he intentionally exposed O'Grady to the threat. Indeed, it was Ryan's effort to make Deny Flight safe for his pilots *and* to make it succeed rather than letting the mission fail, that inadvertently led to the downing. General Ryan's main influence during this period, then, was to direct the air campaign planning that became an important element in the US government's policy for Bosnia.

Gen Rupert Smith did the most to clear the way for the effective use of force in Bosnia, including airpower. The UNPROFOR commander took a big risk in order to end the facade that the UN and NATO were okay just muddling through in Bosnia. The UN hostage crisis after the Pale air strikes proved what others had argued about the nonviable nature of UNPROFOR's bifurcated mandate for enforcement and peacekeeping. Though he raised the short-term risks to his forces by precipitating the hostage crisis, he undoubtedly lowered the longer-term risks of perpetuating UNPROFOR's untenable peacekeeping mission in a land where there was no peace. The UNPROFOR commander was also taking risks with his own career, for if the Bosnian Serbs had killed some hostages, General Smith very well might have been replaced. Janvier and Akashi would have been vindicated in arguing against the use of force and would have been in a stronger position to push for the UN's preferred option of peacekeeping without enforcement. General Smith did not succeed entirely in removing the Bosnian Serbs' primary countercoercive weapon: hostages. However, he prepared the ground so that he could succeed later. The Bosnian Serbs would get to play the hostage card one more time, at Srebrenica in early July. After that, the importance of General Ryan's air campaign planning would come into play. With the exception of General Janvier, the theater-level commanders in NATO and the UN were lead-ing actors in the move toward effective employment of air-power in Bosnia.

Notes

1. For evidence of General Smith's role in precipitating the hostage crisis in order to reinforce UNPROFOR and move the UN mission in Bosnia toward enforcement action, see James Gow, *Triumph of the Lack of Will: International Diplomacy and the Yugoslav War* (New York: Columbia University Press, 1997), 267–70; and Jan Willem Honig and Norbert Both, *Srebrenica: Record of a War Crime* (London: Penguin Books, 1996), 141–59.

2. Brig Gen Victor E. Renuart, USAF, interviewed by author, 28 May 1998, Spangdahlem, Germany, transcript of taped interview, author's per-sonal collection; and Brig Gen Charles F. Wald, USAF, chief of plans CAOC (June–November 1994), commander, 31st Fighter Wing, Aviano Air Base (AB), Italy (May 1995–June 1997), interviewed by author, 7 May 1997, Aviano AB, Italy, tape recording, author's personal collection.

3. Renuart interview; and Maj Gen Hal M. Hornburg, USAF, interviewed by Maj Tim Reagan and Dr. Wayne Thompson, 16 October 1995, Vicenza, Italy, transcript of tape recording, Balkans Air Campaign Study (BACS) Collection, Air Force Historical Research Agency (AFHRA), Maxwell Air Force Base (AFB), Alabama.

4. Renuart interview; and "B-H SEAD Campaign," NATO CAOC briefing of B-H Enemy Air Defenses, c. mid-December 1994, File B3d-3, BACS Collection.

5. Maj Gen Hal M. Hornburg, USAF, interviewed by author, 17 July 1998, tape recording of telephone interview, author's personal collection; Renuart interview; and Col Daniel R. Zoerb, USAF, director, Deny Flight Air Operations Center, Naples, Italy, January 1994–May 1996, interviewed by author, 27 May 1998, Spangdahlem AB, Germany, author's notes, author's personal collection.

6. Gen Michael E. Ryan, USAF, commander, Allied Air Forces Southern Europe and commander, US Sixteenth Air Force, September 1994–April 1996, interviewed by author, 6 June 1997, Ramstein AB, Germany, tran-script of taped interview, author's personal collection; Col Daniel R. Zoerb, interviewed by author, 30 April 1997, Spangdahlem AB, Germany, tran-script of tape recording, author's personal collection; Hornburg interview by Reagan and Thompson; Lt Col Lowell R. Boyd Jr., USAF, AFSOUTH staff offi-cer, February 1993–1996, interviewed by Lt Col Rob Owen, 6 December 1995, Naples, Italy, transcript of taped interview, BACS Collection; and Renuart. The targeting scheme for Colonel Zoerb's air campaign plan was married to a planning document called Deliberate Force some time around May or early June of 1995.

7. Col Daniel R. Zoerb, USAF, director, Deny Flight Air Operations Center, Naples, Italy, January 1994–May 1996, interviewed by author, 29

April 1997, Spangdahlem AB, Germany, transcript of tape recording, author's personal collection.

8. Ibid.; and Ryan interview.

9. Ryan interview; and Zoerb interview, 29 April 1997.

10. Ryan interview.

11. Ibid.; Zoerb interview, 29 April 1997; and Military Official Y.

12. Ryan interview.

13. Ibid.; Gen Michael E. Ryan, USAF, "NATO Air Operations in Bosnia-Herzegovina: 'Deliberate Force,'" 29 August–14 September 1995. Transcript of briefing to Air Power Conference, London, 13 September 1996; and Renuart interview.

14. Ibid.; and Zoerb interview, 29 April 1997.

15. Ryan, transcript of Air Power Conference; Ryan interview; and Hornburg interview by Reagan and Thompson.

16. Ryan interview.

17. Ibid.

18. Military Official Y; and Renuart interview.

19. Ryan, transcript of Air Power Conference; Ryan interview; and Zoerb interview, 29 April 1997.

20. Ryan, transcript of Air Power Conference; Wald interview; Renuart interview; Col Robert C. Owen, *Deliberate Force: A Case Study in Effective Air Campaigning* (Maxwell AFB, Ala.: Air University Press, January 2000), 55, 98, and 101–2.

21. Renuart interview; Hornburg interview by Reagan and Thompson; Owen, *Deliberate Force*, 101.

22. Renuart interview; Wald interview; and Owen, *Deliberate Force*, 101.

23. Gen Joseph W. Ashy, USAF, interviewed by Lt Col Robert Owen, 29 April 1996, Washington. Unclassified version of General Ashy's Oral History Interview, (66 pp.) redacted by the AFHRA, October 1997. Office of History, Air Force Space Command, Peterson AFB, Colo.

24. Lowell Boyd interview.

25. Gen George A. Joulwan, USA, supreme allied commander Europe, 22 October 1993–11 July 1997, interviewed by author, 11 February 1998; Lowell Boyd interview; and Senate, *Current Operations Abroad–Bosnia*, 12 January 1995, 11–13.

26. Joulwan interview, 11 February 1998; and MOD Official D.

27. Joulwan interview, 11 February 1998; Gen Vincent Lanata, chief of staff of the French air force, 1991–1994, interviewed by author, 8 September 1998, Paris, tape recording, author's personal collection; and MOD Official D; and Senate, *Current Operations Abroad–Bosnia*, 12 January 1995, 13.

28. Joulwan interview, 11 February 1998.

29. Lowell Boyd interview.

30. Honig and Both, 158–59 n. 4.

31. Zoerb interview, 29 April 1997; and Renuart interview.

32. This statement refers to the reinforcement of UNPROFOR with the Rapid Reaction Force after the Pale air strike and the expansion and imple-

mentation of plans for a SEAD campaign and a wider air campaign after the O'Grady shootdown and the Srebrenica crisis respectively.

33. Before leaving Bosnia, Rose's promotion to four-star general had already been announced. Some observers viewed the promotion as a reward from the British government for a job well done. See Joel Brand, "Rose Considered Showing Airstrike Plans to Serbs," *Times* (London), 16 April 1995, 12; and Jane M. O. Sharp, *Honest Broker or Perfidious Albion: British Policy in Former Yugoslavia* (London: Institute for Public Policy Research, 1997), 46.

34. Nine British soldiers under General Smith's command were killed by "friendly fire" from American A-10 aircraft. See Rick Atkinson, *Crusade: The Untold Story of the Persian Gulf War* (New York: Houghton Mifflin, 1998), 464; and House of Commons, Defence Committee, Fifth Report, *Implementation of Lessons Learned from Operation Granby* [Granby was the British name for Desert Storm], session 1993–1994, 25 May 1994, 23. Prior to the Gulf War, General Smith had also been briefed about the planned air campaign by Gen Buster Glosson, USAF, who directed air operations and ran the "Black Hole" planning group. MOD Official G.

35. Robert Fox, "Gulf Commander Named to Take Over from Rose," *Daily Telegraph* (London), 10 December 1994, 17.

36. As noted earlier, General Rose's primary avenue of influence was through the British army, specifically through General Wilsey at Wilton.

37. Lt Gen Bernard Janvier, interviewed by author, 12 January 1998, Paris, author's notes, author's personal collection.

38. Janvier interview.

39. "Three Separate Operations Created on 31 March," *UN Chronicles* 32, no. 2 (June 1995): 23–24.

40. Ibid., 23.

41. Gow, 270–71 n. 9.

42. UN, Report of the Secretary-General Pursuant to Resolution 959 (1994)(S/1994/1389, 1 December 1994).

43. Ibid., par. 42.

44. Ibid., pars. 57 and 58.

45. UN, Report of the Secretary-General on the Work of the Organization. "Supplement to an Agenda for Peace: Position Paper of the Secretary-General on the Occasion of the Fiftieth Anniversary of the United Nations" (A/50/60, S/1995/1, 3 January 1995), pars. 77–79.

46. Ibid., par. 79.

47. Janvier interview; and Honig and Both, 152–53.

48. Honig and Both, 153.

49. UN, Report of the Secretary-General Pursuant to Resolution 987 (1995) (S/1995/444, 30 May 1995), pars. 72 and 78–82 (hereafter cited as S/1995/444).

50. UN, Letter from the Secretary-General to the President of the Security Council, 28 January 1994 (S/1994/94, 28 January 1994).

51. "Supplement to an Agenda for Peace," pars. 35 and 36; and S/1995/444, par. 62. The foregoing discussion should not be taken as a criticism of the UN secretariat. As others have noted, the Security Council members, especially the permanent members, failed to resolve their political differences and bequeathed an impossible task to the UN secretariat and to UNPROFOR (i.e., implementing Resolution 836 to the satisfaction of the Security Council members who could not agree on it themselves). See for instance, Dick A. Leurdijk, *The United Nations and NATO in Former Yugoslavia, 1991–1996: Limits to Diplomacy and Force* (The Hague: The Netherlands Atlantic Commission, 1996), 35–37; Richard Caplan, *Post-Mortem on UNPROFOR*, London Defence Studies, no. 33 (London: Brassey's for the Centre for Defence Studies, 1996), 7–9; Honig and Both, 5–6 and 152–53; and Gow, 136–37.

52. Adm Leighton W. Smith, USN, interviewed by author, 10 February 1998, Arlington, Va., transcript of tape recording, author's personal collection.

53. Ibid.

54. "Three Separate Operations Created on 31 March," *UN Chronicle* 32, no. 2 (June 1995): 25–27.

55. Ibid.; and *Facts On File Yearbook 1995* (USA: Facts On File, Inc., 1995), 36.

56. The United Nations, *The Blue Helmets: A Review of United Nations Peace-keeping*, 3d ed. (New York: United Nations Reproduction Section, 1996), 556; *Facts On File 1995*, 221; and Honig and Both, 143.

57. This was the first shelling of Gorazde since NATO established an exclusion zone around the safe area on 23 April 1994. Gorazde was shelled again on 11 April 1995. For more on the deteriorating conditions at Gorazde, see Royal Welch Fusiliers (RWF), 1st Battalion, *White Dragon: The Royal Welch Fusiliers in Bosnia* (Wrexham, UK: RWF Regimental Headquarters, 1995), 44–45 and 110.

58. *Facts On File 1995*, 221.

59. Ibid., 288.

60. *Blue Helmets*, 549–50; *Facts On File 1995*, 362–63.

61. *Facts On File 1995*, 325.

62. Ibid., 362; and Honig and Both, 150–51.

63. Senate, *Impact of the Unilateral United States Lifting of the Arms Embargo*, 23 June 1994, 20–21.

64. Ibid., 20.

65. Ibid., 20–22.

66. Ibid., 81.

67. Fox, 17.

68. Lowell Boyd interview; and Joulwan interview, 11 February 1998. Also see Hans-Christian Hagman, "UN-NATO Operational Co-operation in Peacekeeping 1992–1995" (PhD diss., King's College, University of London, 1997), 264 n. 130.

69. Lowell Boyd interview.

70. Joulwan interview, 11 February 1998. Also see Senate, *Current Operations Abroad–Bosnia*, 12 January 1995, 11–13.

71. "UN Stages Bosnia Pullout Drill," *Times* (London), 20 February 1995, 12; Leurdijk, 66; and *Facts On File 1995*, 131.

72. Shortly before taking up his post in Bosnia, General Smith was again in Washington, apparently meeting with members of the US JCS. Senate, *Current Operations Abroad–Bosnia*, 12 January 1995, 21.

73. For a fuller discussion of General Smith and the events leading up to the Pale air strikes in May 1995, see Honig and Both, 141–59; and Gow, 265–70.

74. Gow, 267–68.

75. Honig and Both, 141–42.

76. Ibid., 141–57.

77. Gow, 267–68.

78. Honig and Both, 150; and *Facts On File 1995*, 362.

79. Honig and Both, 151.

80. Ibid., 151–52.

81. Ibid.

82. Ibid.

83. Ibid.

84. Ibid., 152; and Janvier interview.

85. Janvier interview; and S/1995/444, par. 9.

86. "Fighting Escalates, UN Role in Question," *UN Chronicles* 32, no. 3 (September 1995): 31.

87. Ibid.

88. S/1995/444, par. 11; and Janvier interview.

89. Ryan interview; and Renuart interview. Also see Honig and Both, 153–54.

90. Renuart interview; and Zoerb interview, 29 April 1997.

91. Ryan interview.

92. Janvier interview.

93. Ibid.

94. Ibid.

95. Gow, 267–68; and Honig and Both, 149.

96. Ryan interview; Ryan, transcript of Air Power Conference; and Zoerb interview, 29 April 1997.

97. "Fighting Escalates," 31; and Honig and Both, 154.

98. "Fighting Escalates," 31.

99. Gow, 268.

100. Military Official U; and UN Official A.

101. Indeed, as Gow, Honig and Both, and General Ryan have suggested, demonstrating the vulnerability of UNPROFOR was General Smith's intention.

102. Gow, 267–68; and Gow, "Coercive Cadences: The Yugoslav War of Dissolution," in *Strategic Coercion: Concepts and Cases*, ed. Lawrence Freedman (Oxford: Oxford University Press, 1998), 293.

103. Honig and Both, 155.

104. Ibid.

105. Ibid.

106. Gow, *Triumph*, 269–70. Also see Sharp, 51–52.

107. Admiral Smith interview.

108. *Blue Helmets*, 557.

109. Gow, "Coercive Cadences," 293; Gow, *Triumph*, 268; and Ryan transcript of Air Power Conference.

110. Ryan, transcript of Air Power Conference; Gow, *Triumph*, 267–68; Gow, "Coercive Cadences," 293; and Honig and Both, 153–54.

111. Janvier interview.

112. *Blue Helmets*, 557; "Fighting Escalates," 31; and Janvier interview. David Rohde claimed it was Smith who urged the French commander in Sarajevo to take the action. David Rohde, *A Safe Area, Srebrenica: Europe's Worst Massacre Since the Second World War* (London: Pocket Books, 1997), 27.

113. Janvier interview; and *Blue Helmets*, 557.

114. Janvier interview.

115. General Janvier, UNPROFOR directive 2/95, 29 May 1995, cited in Honig and Both, 156.

116. Honig and Both, 156.

117. For an abridged account of the meeting based on an internal UN document, see Rohde, 419–22.

118. Ibid., 420–21.

119. Ibid., 420.

120. Ibid., 420–22.

121. Ibid. On the proposed mission of the RRF, see Leurdijk, 71.

122. S/1995/470, 9 June 1995, cited in Leurdijk, 71.

123. Gow, "Coercive Cadences," 290; and *Triumph*, 267–69.

124. Michael Lindemann, Bruce Clark, and Laura Silber, "West and Russia in Bosnia Pact," *Financial Times* (London), 30 May 1995, 1; Scott O'Grady with Jeff Coplon, *Return With Honor* (London: Doubleday, 1995), 13; and Tim Ripley, "NATO Strikes Back," *World Airpower Journal* 22 (autumn/winter 1995): 25.

125. O'Grady and Coplon, 10–20.

126. Senate, *Briefing on the F-16 Shootdown in Bosnia and Current Operations: Hearings before the Committee on Armed Services*, 104th Cong., 1st Sess., 13 July 1995, 52 (hereafter cited as Senate, *Briefing on Shootdown*).

127. Admiral Smith interview; Senate, *Briefing on Shootdown*, 2 and 34; Brig Gen David A. Sawyer, USAF, deputy director, Combined Air Operations Center, Vicenza, Italy, interviewed by Maj Tim Reagan and Dr. Wayne Thompson, 11 October 1995, Vicenza, Italy, transcript of tape recording, BACS Collection; and Barbara Starr, "Deny Flight Shootdown May Put USAF on the Offensive," *Jane's Defence Weekly*, 24 June 1995, 24.

128. Admiral Smith interview.

129. Sawyer interview; and Zoerb interview, 27 May 1998.

130. Sawyer interview.

131. O'Grady and Coplon, 24; and Senate, *Briefing on Shootdown*, 33.

132. Wald interview; and Maj Michael O. Beale, *Bombs over Bosnia: The Role of Airpower in Bosnia-Herzegovina* (Maxwell AFB, Ala.: Air University Press, 1997), 33.

133. Senate, *Briefing on Shootdown*, 54; O'Grady and Coplon, 25; and Wald interview.

134. Ryan interview; Admiral Smith interview; Wald interview; and Military Official U.

135. Senate, *Briefing on Shootdown*, 36; and O'Grady and Coplon, 28.

136. Senate, *Briefing on Shootdown*, 36, 45, and 52.

137. Bruce Clark and Laura Silber, "Bosnian Serbs Release 120 UN Hostages: US Jet Downed as West Looks to Reconsider Military Role in Former Yugoslavia," *Financial Times* (London), 3 June 1995, 1.

138. Ibid.; and *Facts On File 1995*, 405.

139. Gow, *Triumph*, 267. Excerpts from the logbook of the UK's battalion commander in Gorazde could be interpreted as an indication that Gow is correct. Royal Welch Fusiliers, 50. According to a news report by Jurek Martin, US secretary of defense Perry defended the Pale air strikes, noting "the risks to UN personnel had been taken account of in advance" [Martin's words, not Perry's]. Jurek Martin, "Clinton Pledge on Role of Troops in Bosnia," *Financial Times* (London), 1 June 1995, 2.

140. Bruce Clark, Laura Silber, and Jurek Martin, "US Jet Shot Down over Serb-held Part of Bosnia," *Financial Times* (London), 3 June 1995, 1; George Parker and Bruce Clark, "Serbs Free 108 UN Hostages," *Financial Times* (London), 7 June 1995, 1; Barry James, "U.S. and Allies Set on Collision Course Over Bosnia Policy," *International Herald Tribune*, 1 July 1995, 5; and Starr, 24.

141. Gen George A. Joulwan, USA, supreme allied commander, Europe, 22 October 1993–11 July 1997, interviewed by author, 11 February 1998, Washington, D.C., transcript of tape recording, author's personal collection. General Joulwan went on to point out that he and Admiral Smith made just as intense an effort to find the two French pilots who were shot down later, on 30 August 1995, the first day of Operation Deliberate Force.

142. George Parker and Bruce Clark, "Hurd Warns over Bosnia Mission," *Financial Times* (London), 5 June 1995, 1.

143. Ibid.

144. Parker and Clark, "Serbs Free 108," 1.

145. Laura Silber, "Serbs Claim Deal With West over Release of Hostages," *Financial Times* (London), 14 June 1995, 24.

146. Laura Silber, Harriet Martin, and Bruce Clark, "Diplomatic Effort Stepped Up in Bosnia," *Financial Times* (London), 20 June 1995, 2; James, 5; and Royal United Services Institute (RUSI), *International Security Review 1996* (London: RUSI, 1996), 63.

147. For a well-reasoned analysis of Janvier's role that concludes his delays were probably not the result of an explicit deal, see Rohde, 359–73.

148. Gen Bertrand de Lapresle, UNPROFOR force commander, 15 March 1994–28 February 1995, interviewed by author, 13 January 1998, Paris, transcript of tape recording, author's personal collection.

149. Ibid.

150. Ibid.

151. Ibid.

152. Janvier interview.

153. Jane Sharp, citing a report based on a 19 June cable from Akashi to Annan, says the guarantee was made over the course of three phone calls between the two presidents on 3, 9, and 11 June 1995. Citing different sources, David Rohde offers corroborating evidence of the Chirac-Milosevic phone calls about the hostages. Sharp, 53; and Rohde, 359–64.

154. Rohde, 364.

155. *Facts On File 1995*, 405.

156. Maj Paul C. Strickland, USAF, "Trouble In Trieste," *Daedalus Flyer*, winter 1996, 9.

157. Ibid.

158. Ibid., 9–10. The pilot, Maj Paul Strickland, was sent to help determine whether or not the Bosnian Serbs in fact had O'Grady.

159. Ibid.

160. Ibid., 12.

161. Senate, *Situation in Bosnia: Hearings before the Committee on Armed Services*, 103d Cong., 2d Sess., 1 December 1994, 18.

162. Gen Charles G. Boyd, USAF, "Making Peace with the Guilty," *Foreign Affairs* 74, no. 5 (September/October 1995): 30–31; and Military Official Y.

163. General Boyd, 30–31; and Military Official Y.

164. General Boyd, 30–31.

165. Bob Woodward, *The Choice: How Clinton Won* (New York: Simon & Schuster, 1996), 263–65.

166. A Pentagon official briefing the Senate Armed Services Committee said the Department of Defense study of the shootdown concluded it was an act of retaliation for the Pale air strikes. Senate, *Briefing on Shootdown, 52.*

167. Senate, *Briefing on Shootdown*, 44 and 52.

168. Public opinion polls showed that American public interest in Bosnia was never very high. Typically the number of survey respondents who followed the war in Bosnia "very closely" hovered around the 10 to 15 percent level. American interest peaked at the time of Capt Scott O'Grady's shootdown and rescue, with 24 percent of Americans—about double the average—claiming to follow events in Bosnia "very closely." The Pew Research Center for the People & the Press, "Support for Independent Candidate in '96 Up Again," transcript of media survey, 24 August 1995. Despite the low numbers of Americans claiming to follow the war closely, a Harris poll conducted in June of 1995 found that more than 85 percent of Americans had "seen, heard, or read" something "about the recent fighting in Bosnia and the former Yugoslavia." Louis Harris and Associates, "Public Opinion Survey, Study no. 951103," June 1995.

169. Jurek Martin, "Protests Force Clinton to Retreat on Troops," *Financial Times* (London), 5 June 1995, 2; and *Facts On File 1995*, 406.

170. Woodward, 255–57; and Richard Holbrooke, *To End A War* (New York: Random House, 1998), 65–67.

171. Thomas W. Lippman and Ann Devroy, "Clinton's Policy Evolution: June Decision Led to Diplomatic Gamble," *Washington Post*, 11 September 1995, A16; and Woodward, 254–55. Note: Woodward's version confirms the timing of the increased policy attention but credits the UN hostage crisis as the catalyst for it.

172. Lord (Field Marshal) Richard Vincent, chairman of NATO's Military Committee, interviewed by author, 22 September 1998, London, author's notes, author's personal collection; Senate, *Briefing on Shootdown*, 36–37, 42–43, and 51–54; and Michael Evans, "Serb Radar Link-up Poses Challenge to NATO Pilots," *Times* (London), 29 June 1995, 15.

173. Ryan interview.

174. Senate, *Briefing on Shootdown*, 42.

175. Ibid.

176. Ibid., 43.

177. Ryan interview; and Hornburg interview by Reagan and Thompson.

178. Maj Jim Riggins, USAF, chief, Force Application, HQ USAF/XOOC (CHECKMATE), "Five at ATAF Combined Air Operations Center: History, Organization, and Function, From April 1993," Draft Edition 2, December 1995 (Vicenza, Italy: History Office, NATO CAOC), 9; Ryan interview; Hornburg interview by Reagan and Thompson; Sawyer interview; and Renuart interview.

179. Ryan interview.

180. Hornburg interview by Reagan and Thompson.

181. Ibid.

182. Col Robert Owen, USAF, "The Balkans Air Campaign Study: Part 1," *Airpower Journal* 11, no. 2 (summer 1997): 21.

183. Ibid.; Owen, *Deliberate Force*, 55–56, 97, and 482; and Riggins, 9–11 and 41.

184. Brig Gen Walter E. Buchanan, USAF, chief, Joint Operations Division, US EUCOM/CENTCOM Branch, J-3, Joint Chiefs of Staff, interviewed by author, 26 May 1998, Kalkar, Germany, tape recording, author's personal collection; and Wald interview.

185. Dr. Thomas S. Snyder and Dr. Daniel F. Harrington, USAFE Office of History, *USAFE Historical Highlights, 1942–1997: Fifty-fifth Anniversary Edition* (Ramstein AB, Germany: Headquarters USAFE, 1997), 182.

186. "USAF Fact Sheet: 4190th Provisional Wing." On 1 January 1996, the 7490th Provisional Wing became the 4190th Provisional Wing.

187. Owen, *Deliberate Force*, 55, 98, and 127 n. 13; and Zoerb interview, 27 May 1998.

188. Deliberate Force was originally the name of a planning document that was used in conjunction with a targeting scheme built by Colonel Zoerb. The targeting scheme had previously been simply called "Air Operations in

Bosnia-Herzegovina." For the remainder of this study, Colonel Zoerb's targeting scheme is referred to as the Deliberate Force plan, but it was not an official NATO plan akin to OPLAN 40101, "Deny Flight." To the author's knowledge, there was never an official US plan called Deliberate Force either. According to the Balkans Air Campaign Study, Colonel Zoerb's planning "existed in the form of briefing slides and memos only, and was the immediate precursor to DELIBERATE FORCE." Owen, *Deliberate Force*, 98–102.

189. Ryan interview; and Admiral Smith interview.

190. Ryan interview.

191. Air Campaign Targeting Briefing, AIRSOUTH, Naples, Italy, 2 June 1995, cited in Owen, *Deliberate Force*, 285.

192. Zoerb interview, 30 April 1997.

193. Owen, *Deliberate Force*, 103–5, 285–88.

194. Hornburg interview by Reagan and Thompson; and Owen, *Deliberate Force*, 98.

195. The concept of operations for what later became Deliberate Force had been briefed to General Joulwan during the winter of 1994–1995. However, the plan itself was still being refined when O'Grady was shot down. Since Deliberate Force seems to have been the basis of General Shalikashvili's proposal when he met in London with the British and French chiefs of defense staff on 16 July, the author concludes that General Ryan most likely briefed the plan to the US national security advisor in June, or early July at the latest.

196. Col David V. Nicholls, Royal Marines, "Bosnia: UN and NATO," *RUSI Journal* 141, no. 1 (February 1996): 34; and idem, interviewed by author, 9 January 1998, Exmouth, England, tape recording, author's personal collection.

197. Senate, *Briefing on Shootdown*, 37–38.

198. Ibid.; Hagman, 156–57; Beale, 33–34; and Steve Watkins, "Does Deny Flight Still Work?" *Air Force Times*, 24 July 1995, 3.

199. *Blue Helmets*, 557.

200. Senate, *Briefing on Shootdown*, 48–49; Hagman, 156–57; Watkins; and Tim Ripley, "Silence of the SAMS," *Aircraft Illustrated* 28, no. 1 (November 1995): 38.

201. Air Chief Marshal Sir William Wratten, RAF, commander RAF Strike Command, September 1994–July 1997, telephone interview by author, 18 May 1998, London, author's notes, author's personal collection.

202. Stacy Sullivan, Michael Evans, and Eve-Ann Prentice, "NATO Scales Down 'No-Fly' Operation Despite Serb Threat," *Times* (London), 21 June 1995, 13.

203. Rick Atkinson, "Germans Vote to Send Planes and Troops," *International Herald Tribune*, 1 July 1995, 1.

204. Admiral Smith interview; and Tim Butcher, "NATO Request for Bosnia Air Strike," *Daily Telegraph* (London), 22 June 1995, 11.

205. Admiral Smith interview.

206. Ibid.

207. Ibid.

208. Janvier interview; Admiral Smith interview; and Butcher, "NATO Request," 11.

209. Rohde, 419–21 n. 8; Honig and Both, 155–57; Senate, *Briefing on Shootdown*, 42–43; Admiral Smith interview; and Janvier interview.

210. MCM-KAA-050-95, "Operation Deny Flight — Viability of No-Fly Zone Enforcement," 13 July 1995, File B4-2, BACS Collection; and Evans, "Serb Radar Link-up," 15.

211. Admiral Smith interview.

212. Ibid.

213. Ibid.; and de Lapresle interview, 13 January 1998.

214. MCM-KAA-050-95.

215. Ibid.

216. Walter B. Slocombe, undersecretary of defense for policy, cited in Senate, *Briefing on Shootdown*, 44.

217. Senate, *Briefing on Shootdown*, 37; Watkins; Mate Granic, Croatian minister of foreign affairs, TLS (photocopy), to Yasushi Akashi, Zagreb, 6 August 1995, BACS collection (The letter complains about Serb jets taking off from Banja Luka to bomb a factory in Croatia); and Boutros Boutros-Ghali, TLS (photocopy), to Willy Claes, Brussels, 15 August 1995, BACS Collection (The letter turns down NATO requests to take preemptive action against portions of the Serb integrated air defense network in Croatia).

218. Senate, *Briefing on Shootdown*, 58–59.

Chapter 8

Srebrenica and the Decisions
to Use Airpower: July–August 1995

*The problem is not only that the boundaries between policy,
strategy, and tactics are rarely clear but that civilian leaders may insist on the right to control operations because of
their political implications.*

—Richard K. Betts
*Soldiers, Statesmen
and Cold War Crises*

The fall of Srebrenica in July 1995 had a major impact on
Western governments' policies toward Bosnia. In addition to
the Pale hostage crisis and the downing of O'Grady's F-16, the
loss of the safe area and reports of atrocities afterwards led the
UN and NATO to endorse US proposals to use airpower in
Bosnia. Srebrenica also reinforced Western concerns of UN
impotence and the problems inherent in the dual-key controls
over NATO airpower. However, as the first section of this chapter argues, the notion that airpower could have defended
Srebrenica was unrealistic, and the blame heaped upon
General Janvier for delaying the use of airpower was more
indicative of the hazards of command than of any mistake on
his part.

After the fall of Srebrenica, the United States faced a dilemma
in pushing to use airpower more forcefully in Bosnia. Acting unilaterally would have been easier but potentially devastating to
NATO, the UN, and many bilateral foreign relationships; however, acting within the existing UN-NATO framework promised to
emasculate or even paralyze attempts to use airpower. The second part of this chapter shows how theater military commanders remained caught up in the political struggles over using airpower in Bosnia. American commanders in NATO and the
UNPROFOR commander, General Smith, willingly pushed at the
boundaries constraining airpower while General Janvier had to

245

be put under political pressure before he veered from traditional UN reluctance to endorse air strikes.

Srebrenica: 6–11 July 1995

The difficulties encountered by the UN and NATO in trying to use airpower effectively at Srebrenica typified many problems with Deny Flight. First, there was a mismatch between the capabilities of airpower and the expectations for airpower on the part of some of the people involved in the decisions over whether and how to use it. Second, concern for the safety of UN soldiers led national political authorities to get directly involved in decisions about using airpower. Third, there was confusion over close air support (CAS) and air strikes; and fourth, negotiations on other important issues helped to paralyze the UN chain of command. Fifth, the Serbs were able to monitor NATO air operations and apparently timed their ground activities so as to avoid air attacks. Lastly, the recriminations after the fall of Srebrenica highlighted the accountability inherent in command, even when a commander lacks the means and authority to fulfill his responsibilities.[1]

When the Bosnian Serb assault against Srebrenica began in the dark, early hours of 6 July, it followed a familiar pattern of Serb ethnic cleansing.[2] The apparent random and sporadic nature of the initial assault made it difficult for the battalion of 450 Dutch peacekeepers and the remaining Muslim defenders to predict the scale of the operation and its ultimate purpose.[3] Though it would be several days before the Dutch commander in Srebrenica, Lt Col Ton Karremans, concluded that the Serbs were determined to take the entire safe area, he phoned the UNPROFOR chief of staff in Sarajevo, Dutch Brig Gen Cees Nicolais, to discuss the option of calling in NATO airpower.[4] With the attackers' objectives still unclear and existing UN policy against any action that might lead to an escalation of violence, the two Dutch officers elected to forego a request for air support.[5]

At first the UN was self-deterred from calling on airpower, both by its policy of avoiding the use of airpower to prevent retaliation and by its concerns about disrupting talks that were going on between Carl Bildt and Serbian president

SUNDAY	MONDAY	TUESDAY	WEDNESDAY	THURSDAY	FRIDAY	SATURDAY
JULY 2	3	4	5	6 BSA assault begins at 0315 hrs; Dutch officers decide against air request	7	8
9 Peace-keepers ordered into blocking positions, 2200 hrs BSA warned	10 First CAS request to reach Zagreb 1930 hrs; Conditions set for next day's approval	11 UN authorizes CAS 1210 hrs CAS at 1430 Dutch MOD calls halt	12	13	14	15

Figure 2. Six-Day Outline of Attack on Srebrenica. The shaded area shows the days Srebrenica was under attack.

Milosevic over Serb recognition of Bosnia.[6] By Saturday evening, 8 July, the Bosnian Serbs had taken their first Dutch soldiers as prisoners, and, by the next afternoon, they held 20 peacekeepers hostage.[7] On 9 July, American demands within NATO for air strikes against the Bosnian Serbs were overridden by the Dutch because, as Honig and Both have revealed, the Dutch considered air strikes "dangerous" and "counterproductive."[8]

The Fall of Srebrenica: July 1995

Repeated Serb assaults on Srebrenica led the Dutch peacekeepers to finally ask for air support on the morning of 10 July, but the request was turned down within the UN chain of command.[9] Despite the UN's reluctance to call on NATO, a swarm of combat aircraft gathered over the Adriatic.[10] When another Serb attack developed that evening, the peacekeepers in Srebrenica issued a second request for air support, and the UN battalion submitted a list of approximately 40 targets around Srebrenica.[11] This time the request made it quickly to

General Janvier, but by the time he consulted his staff, Mr. Akashi, the Bosnian Serbs, the Dutch government, and NATO, it was after 9:00 P.M., the fighting had died down, and air support no longer seemed like a useful option.[12] Janvier asked that a strong NATO air force be available for the next morning, but he stipulated it would be used only for CAS and only if the BSA used heavy weapons in their attack.[13] Somehow the message was misconstrued or misinterpreted, so that the commander of the besieged peacekeepers expected massive air strikes against the BSA forces surrounding the enclave on the morning of 11 July.[14]

The next morning, NATO put up a package of approximately 60 aircraft, including a dozen attack jets for the forward air controllers in the enclave.[15] Below the orbiting air armada, General Ryan and Admiral Smith monitored the situation from a specially equipped command and control ship, the USS *Lassalle*.[16] At 10:00 A.M., with clear skies over Srebrenica, the Dutch requested air support, but the anticipated Serb attack had yet to materialize.[17] Although the request was forwarded to General Janvier and Mr. Akashi shortly before 11:00 A.M., the situation did not meet the criteria for air support specified by Janvier the night before.[18] By 11:00 A.M. the package had been holding in its orbit over the Adriatic for approximately four hours and had reached the limit of its endurance.[19] Soon after the package of NATO aircraft began returning to Italy, the final Serb ground assault on Srebrenica began.[20] The Bosnian Serbs had evidently been tipped off through their air defense network that the NATO planes were departing and would not be available to provide air support.[21] About an hour after the final assault began and while NATO aircraft were being serviced in preparation for an afternoon package, General Janvier signed a "Blue Sword" order authorizing CAS.[22]

The Serbs moved quickly to take the city, and as the enclave's Muslim defenders made for the hills in an effort to escape the hopeless situation, the Dutch peacekeepers found themselves surrounded, outgunned, and swamped by refugees.[23] Several peacekeepers had been taken hostage by the BSA in the first days of the assault, but from the outset, everyone in Srebrenica was a virtual hostage. At around 2:30 P.M., two

Dutch F-16s, guided by a Dutch forward air controller, executed attacks against two tanks just south of the town.[24] The next flight into the area was a pair of USAF F-16s, but the pilots failed to find their target—an artillery piece in a heavily wooded area.[25] Following the attacks on the tanks, the Serbs threatened to kill the peacekeepers they were holding hostage and to shell the civilians and soldiers in the enclave unless the air attacks ceased.[26] With another batch of fighters scheduled into the Srebrenica area, the news raced up the Dutch national chain of command; Defense Minister Voorhoeve phoned directly from The Hague to a Dutch officer at NATO's air operations center in Vicenza and ordered an immediate end to air operations.[27] Left out of the decision-making loop, the NATO commanders aboard the *Lassalle* were caught by surprise.[28] General Ryan insisted on going ahead with the attacks, but the forward air controller on the ground honored the demands of the Dutch government and ordered the NATO aircraft away.[29]

Within days, Srebrenica was "ethnically cleansed" of its Muslim population, and 23,000 more women and children became refugees of the war. Herded, with methodical Serb assistance, to the town of Potocari just north of Srebrenica, the women and children then moved westward, out of Bosnian Serb-held territory, to Kladanj.[30] Thousands of men went missing during the cleansing and were presumably killed.[31] When the Bosnian Serbs finished with Srebrenica, they moved on to the safe area of Zepa, 12 miles to the southeast.

Expectations and Blame

The fall of Srebrenica demonstrated the unrealistic expectations of airpower that some people held—participants and observers. On the night before Srebrenica fell, the Dutch battalion commander thought massive air strikes would force Mladic to back off, or make the BSA suffer grave consequences with "bombing everywhere."[32] David Rohde later claimed that "if NATO close air support had been used earlier, . . . the 7,079 missing might still be alive today."[33] Neither air strikes, nor close air support would have made that much difference at Srebrenica. Airpower alone could not defend the safe areas, as senior NATO and UN commanders had been warning since the spring of 1993.[34] First, the number of Bosnian Serb soldiers attacking Srebrenica was at most a few thousand, and their heavy weapons—hidden around the enclave—made difficult targets for air strikes.[35] Even when they were massed for an attack, the Bosnian Serb forces were hard to find and hit from the air, as the problems with CAS on 11 July demonstrated. Second, the BSA had an SA-6 surface-to-air missile battery in eastern Bosnia, so NATO aircrews could safely go to Srebrenica only with SEAD escort.[36] That translated into limited periods of air support by large packages of aircraft. Since the Bosnian Serbs were able to monitor NATO air operations, they could adjust the timing of their ground operations as necessary and take cover whenever NATO aircraft approached. Third, Dutch peacekeepers and citizens of Srebrenica were virtual hostages from the outset. By the afternoon of 9 July, hours before the first request for airpower reached UN leaders in Zagreb, the Bosnian Serbs held 20 Dutch soldiers whom they later threatened to kill when NATO started dropping bombs. In summary, there was not much for NATO to bomb, the conditions for bombing were poor, and the Serbs could and did turn off the bombing by threatening to make things worse. Though airpower could have been used sooner and perhaps more effectively at Srebrenica, it would have been most unlikely to stop the Bosnian Serbs from taking the enclave. Problems with airpower and the fall of Srebrenica lay not with the slowness of decisions or any failure in the execution of air support but in the unrealistic expectation that airpower could defend the enclave.

The attention and blame General Janvier has received since the fall of Srebrenica highlight the accountability that accompanies command. Honig and Both noted that Janvier was in a no-win situation, recognized it, and tried to raise the alarm.[37] So Janvier was not guilty of failing to see the danger at Srebrenica. But rather than credit Janvier with foresight, David Rohde concluded,

> Whether Janvier was cynical or misguided, he is more responsible than any other individual for the fall of Srebrenica. The restrictions on the use of airpower that he actively endorsed and his decision not to

approve close air support on Monday, July 10, had disastrous results.[38]

As Honig and Both have pointed out, "General Janvier, in particular, has unjustly been much maligned. He is often blamed for losing Srebrenica because he did not authorize massive air strikes."[39] Though they disagreed about whether to fault Janvier, neither Rohde nor Honig and Both made mention of any civilian policy maker singled out in the manner in which Janvier was. General Smith was away on leave during the fall of Srebrenica, so he largely escaped any blame.[40] General Janvier inherited the problems associated with Srebrenica. Like his predecessors, he lacked control over the forces under his command; he could neither remove the Dutch peacekeepers nor reinforce them. Nor could he order air strikes without higher UN approval, and, in this case, without Dutch national approval. An alternative evaluation of Janvier's role, opposed to the one offered by Rohde, is that Janvier believed he could not stop the fall of Srebrenica, and he saw no point in further endangering the Dutch peacekeepers or the people of Srebrenica by authorizing air attacks against the Bosnian Serbs. General Briquemont had previously quit as the UN commander in Bosnia rather than persist in a situation where he lacked the means and authority to fulfill the responsibilities for accomplishing his mission and protecting his forces.[41] And as Briquemont had noted, the clear accountability that goes with command explains to a large extent why generals and not policy makers have been called to The Hague to answer questions about war crimes. The focus on Janvier after Srebrenica has illustrated one of Briquemont's principal concerns during his tenure in Bosnia: Commanders are likely to be held accountable even when they are not given the tools to fulfill their responsibilities.

The London Conference and the Decisions to Use Airpower

Stung by the debacle at Srebrenica and their own inability to take effective action in the face of Serb audacity, Western governments decided to meet at a conference in London on 21

July to consider future options for Bosnia. From Srebrenica, Mladic's forces moved on to take the safe area of Zepa, which was smaller and less well defended than Srebrenica.[42] This would make Gorazde, with its battalion of British soldiers, the last of the safe areas in eastern Bosnia and the next likely target for ethnic cleansing by the Bosnian Serbs.[43] In advance of the London Conference, the uniformed chiefs of defense from the United States, the United Kingdom, and France met in the British capital to discuss military options for halting Mladic's forces.[44] At the meeting, General Shalikashvili reiterated US calls for air strikes and briefed a three-phased air campaign plan.[45] France's Adm Jacques Lanxade put forward several options for reinforcing Gorazde with some or all of the UN's new RRF.[46] The British did not have a plan of their own and tentatively backed the American option for air strikes with the stipulation that strikes take place only after British troops were mostly out of harm's way—British soldiers in Gorazde were scheduled to leave at the end of August.[47]

The London Conference was partially successful as a consensus-building exercise, and it demonstrated continuing attempts by the United States, Britain, and France to wield influence through their military commanders. When the conferees met in London, at least one of them—Field Marshal Sir Richard Vincent, chairman of NATO's Military Committee—could perceive no overall purpose for the gathering; however, he noted that there were numerous bilateral meetings going on behind the scenes.[48] At the end of the London Conference, Britain and the United States agreed, in general, to use airpower to prevent the fall of Gorazde.[49] France was skeptical of the plan, and the Russian delegate refused to sanction the option for a stronger use of NATO airpower.[50] Even the British-US agreement was an uneasy compromise. The British insisted on retaining the dual-key arrangement that gave the UN veto power over any air strikes proposed by the American-dominated NATO chain of command.[51] General Shalikashvili and US secretary of defense Perry reportedly urged eliminating the dual-key controls on airpower altogether.[52] Through their compromise in London, the British and Americans tentatively agreed to remove UN civilians from the air strike decision-making process by delegating the UN key to Gen Rupert Smith. This, however, bypassed the senior French officer, General Janvier.[53] On the NATO side, General Ryan would hold the key for air strikes. As General Ryan later recalled, "At first they wanted to push it down to Rupert and me, because they wanted to cut Janvier out of it. But then that didn't make any sense."[54] It did not make sense because France, the nation with the most soldiers on the ground in Bosnia, would not have had a role in decisions to use airpower.

Decision to Use Airpower to Protect Gorazde

In late July, decisions made in Brussels and New York modified the agreement reached between the US and Britain over the dual key and further demonstrated the influence of theater commanders in shaping the use of airpower in Bosnia.[55] On 25 July, the NAC met for almost 12 hours before finally authorizing more robust air strikes in response to any Bosnian Serb attacks on Gorazde.[56] Significantly, General Joulwan urged NATO political authorities to consider wider zones of action rather than limiting air operations to the vicinity of Gorazde, and NATO Secretary-General Willy Claes included the suggestion in a letter to his UN counterpart outlining NATO plans for air strikes.[57] The next day, Boutros-Ghali wrote back to Claes agreeing that the new NATO initiative for air strikes could be authorized within the bounds of existing UN Security Council resolutions and that he had "instructed United Nations military commanders in the former Yugoslavia to commence preparations for defining . . . the 'zones of action' referred to in your letter."[58] Boutros-Ghali also acknowledged that "the question of Option 3 remains to be decided, both within the North Atlantic Council and in the United Nations Security Council."[59] Significantly, the UN secretary-general agreed to delegate the UN's key for NATO airpower to the military commanders beneath Mr. Akashi.[60] However, instead of delegating it to General Smith, authority to request NATO air strikes was passed to General Janvier.[61] Janvier would then have to coordinate air strikes with Adm Leighton Smith rather than with General Ryan.[62] For CAS, Janvier was authorized to further delegate the UN key to General Smith.[63] Finally,

Boutros-Ghali told the NATO secretary-general he had issued instructions to Mr. Akashi "to take all measures necessary to protect the United Nations personnel in the theatre and to reduce their vulnerability to retaliation and hostage taking."[64] By stymieing the attempt to push control over air strikes down to Generals Smith and Ryan, the UN secretary-general and the NAC signaled the lingering reluctance at the political level to fully endorse NATO air strikes. However, there was a definite shift away from NATO's being a supporter of UNPROFOR toward the Alliance's becoming more of an independent actor in Bosnia.

Events on the ground in Bosnia during late July led NATO ambassadors to expand their threats to use airpower to stop Serb military advances. On the first day of the London Conference, the remaining Dutch peacekeepers taken hostage at Srebrenica were freed, thus removing one of the factors inhibiting NATO air attacks.[65] Four days later, on 25 July, General Smith negotiated with General Mladic for the evacuation of Zepa's 17,000 Muslims, leaving just four of the original six safe areas remaining.[66] Rather than attacking Gorazde as anticipated, the Bosnian Serbs joined the Croatian Serbs and rebel Muslim forces to launch a three-pronged assault on Bihac.[67] The Bosnian government forces around Bihac were no match for the three factions arrayed against them, and as the prospects of losing another safe area loomed, NATO considered extending the threat of air strikes to protect all four of the remaining safe areas.[68] Of all the Bosnian enclaves, Bihac was the most difficult to support with airpower; the lines between the warring factions were less clearly drawn there than at the other safe areas, and the peacekeepers in Bihac had no forward air controllers.[69] Moreover, Bihac lay near the Bosnian Serb air defense stronghold in northwestern Bosnia.[70] On 27 July NATO concerns for Bihac eased somewhat as thousands of Croatian troops joined the fighting against the Serbs.[71] The Croatian assault quickly cut Serb lines of communications south of Bihac and relieved the pressure on the beleaguered government forces in the enclave.[72]

Decision to Use Airpower in Defense of Other "Safe Areas"

Not to be outflanked, NATO announced a decision on 1 August to extend the threat of air strikes against any faction threatening any of the remaining safe areas.[73] The NAC decision authorized NATO military authorities to conduct graduated air operations up to Option 2—a reference to the "Operational Options for Air Strikes," developed two years earlier.[74] In a statement to the press, Secretary-General Claes claimed that: "These decisions are intended to protect the safe areas and not to help any party fight against the other."[75] Allied officers at the CAOC, not just Americans, built target lists, so that by early August there were individual "plans" for Sarajevo, Tuzla, Bihac, and Gorazde.[76] However, senior airmen in AFSOUTH believed it was impossible to defend the safe areas with airpower alone.[77] At the suggestion of using airpower to defend the safe areas, General Ryan later exclaimed,

> Not defend the "safe areas"! I FOUGHT that language—that language was going around, and I said: "There's no way we can defend those 'safe areas.' You cannot defend the 'safe areas' with air . . . you can't defend the 'safe areas' without a competent ground force."[78]

In General Ryan's view the best way to relieve the threat to the safe areas was to compel the Bosnian Serbs to stop attacking them by using airpower to attrit Bosnian Serb military capabilities.[79] While this approach may have been the best way to use airpower to stop attacks on the safe areas, it could not help but upset the balance of military power among the warring factions.[80] Throughout August, planners at the CAOC and in Naples continued to refine plans for the safe areas, the Dead Eye plan, and plans for a wider air campaign.[81]

NATO ministers helped to open the door for General Ryan's air campaign plan by agreeing to "authorize operations 'to support the defense of the Safe Areas within a wider zone of action' (ZOA) than had previously been considered."[82] By authorizing wider ZOAs, NATO ministers freed their military commanders from restrictions limiting air strikes to only those targets in the vicinity of a particular safe area. This, in turn, helped to push NATO thinking on airpower toward General

Ryan's plan for a wider air campaign. After General Joulwan proposed the ZOAs, planners in AFSOUTH were tasked to help define them. One NATO officer suggested dividing all of Bosnia into two zones, using a line taken from a map used for planning Dead Eye operations.[83] The line had originally been drawn on the map as a "do not cross line" for separating aircraft that would be simultaneously attacking the northwest and southeast segments of the Bosnian Serb air defense system.[84] It had been nothing more than a tactical expedient for avoiding midair collisions. When the UNPROFOR commander, Gen Rupert Smith, saw the proposed zones, he suggested modifying them by making the area around Tuzla part of both zones; thus the Posavina corridor—a key route for Serb access to western Bosnia—was in both zones (see fig. 3).[85]

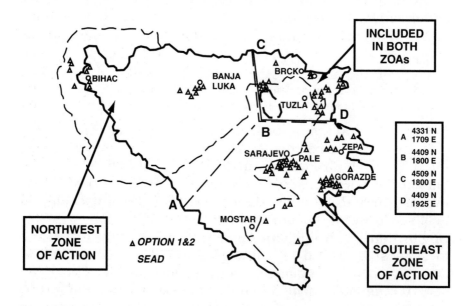

Figure 3. Zones of Action and Target Distribution for Operation Deliberate Force. The southeastern zone included all targets south and east of the line defined by points A-B-C. The northwestern zone included targets north and west of the line defined by points A-B-D. Areas within the wedge near Tuzla, defined by line C-B-D, were part of both zones.

Source: General Ryan, briefing to Air Power Conference, slide no. 8.

No matter where a triggering event might occur, NATO would be able to strike targets in the area where the zones overlapped.[86] Smith's modifications also meant that a provocation in Tuzla could trigger air strikes in the zone of the commanders' choosing. General Joulwan, who was intent on being able to limit the maneuverability of Mladic's forces, approved the zones.[87] However, General Janvier initially balked at the larger zones, telling Admiral Smith he had been contemplating zones 25 to 30 kilometers around the safe areas—slightly larger than the heavy weapons exclusion zones at Sarajevo and Gorazde.[88]

Though the military commanders in AFSOUTH wanted political guidance and needed political approval for their actions, they also controlled access to their plans so as to maintain operational security and their own autonomy. Commenting on briefings of Deliberate Force given in the summer of 1995, Admiral Smith recalled, "We wanted very much to not let the Military Committee and the NAC get into the details of those targets."[89] General Ryan was given a broad mission statement by the NAC, which had the "aim of deterring attacks on safe areas and responding, if necessary, through the timely and effective use of airpower . . . until attacks on or threats to the safe areas have ceased."[90] This broad guidance suited General Joulwan, who believed NAC involvement in operational decisions would be politically divisive, hurting both alliance cohesion and military effectiveness.[91] Though Admiral Smith did not want any "help" in operational matters, he would have preferred to have political authorities in the UN and NATO come to an agreement on a common approach for the operation rather than leaving it to him and General Janvier to sort out matters.[92] General Ryan appreciated and would soon make good use of the latitude given him by the NAC mission statement. At an airpower conference on the anniversary of Operation Deliberate Force, Ryan observed,

> The biggest lesson I think we learned is that if we have a chance on the military side to be influential in writing the mission statement, we'd better have our best people standing there doing it, because that's what you're going to get graded on.[93]

The NATO commanders were not without political oversight, though. On 3 August, in Italy, General Ryan and Admiral Smith briefed NATO Secretary-General Claes and General Joulwan on the Dead Eye plan, the Deliberate Force plan, and the target sets for the individual safe area defense plans.[94] For his part, Secretary-General Claes attempted to reassure the commanders about the depth of political backing for a robust air campaign.[95] While the commanders wanted operational autonomy, it appears they also wanted, or needed, some form of political blessing from Brussels.

Changing Landscape and US Political Leadership

Croatian "ethnic cleansing" of Serbs from UN protected areas marked the further decline of UN influence in the former Yugoslavia and set the stage for American leadership within NATO. On 4 August, the Croatian army launched an offensive to retake the Serb-controlled Krajina region of Croatia. It did not help UN-NATO relations, when, on the first day of the Croatian offensive, US aircraft providing air presence to Canadian peacekeepers in Croatia fired two antiradiation missiles in self-defense against a Krajina Serb SAM site near Knin.[96] To make matters worse, a Croatian air force MiG aircraft attacked a UN observation post, killing a Danish peacekeeper; yet, NATO was not empowered to conduct counterair operations against Croatia.[97] In four days, the fighting was mostly over, and Croatian forces sent 150,000 Serb refugees fleeing into Serbia and Bosnia.[98] The operation highlighted the UN's impotence. Even worse, from a UN standpoint, the Croatian move appeared to have US support, or at least acquiescence.[99]

Neither the BSA nor the Yugoslav army rendered assistance to their Krajina kinsmen, fueling speculation that Presidents Tudjman and Milosevic had made an agreement to let Zagreb take control of the Serb-occupied lands within Croatia.[100] In Bosnia, Karadzic was publicly critical of Milosevic, and the Bosnian Serb leader reportedly attempted to dismiss his army commander, General Mladic. Mladic had supposedly been meeting with Milosevic in Belgrade just prior to the Croatian assault.[101] On the first day of the Croatian offensive, Karadzic ordered Mladic to step down. The general refused, and two days later 18 Bosnian Serb generals signaled their support for Mladic.[102] As one news reporter put it: "Mr. Radovan Karadzic, leader of the Bosnian Serbs, has lost control of his armed forces, whose commanders now clearly take their orders from Belgrade."[103] For NATO planners, knowing whether this family squabble amongst the Serbs was genuine or merely affected was important; if General Mladic really was more responsive to Milosevic than to Karadzic, then a NATO strategy based on coercing the Bosnian Serbs would have to focus on Belgrade, not just Pale. After the late July NATO decision for a graduated air campaign, a trio of NATO generals—one British, one American, and one French—was dispatched to Belgrade to give General Mladic a final warning, but Mladic was unimpressed by the threat of NATO bombing.[104]

In August of 1995, the Clinton administration committed itself to taking the lead in the West's approach to Bosnia. With the political risks attending this new assertiveness, the US wanted as much control as possible over the various components in its strategy for the Balkans. By 1 August, US national security advisor Anthony Lake had worked out a new US strategy for Bosnia.[105] A week later, after several meetings with President Clinton and his top national security advisors, Mr. Lake traveled to the capitals of the other Contact Group[106] countries—France, Germany, Russia, and Britain—to present the administration's latest plan for a comprehensive settlement in the former Yugoslavia.[107] In contrast to earlier administration efforts to win allied acceptance for its policies, one reporter noted, "this time Lake was given permission to present the US plan as something Clinton was determined to pursue with or without the allies' support."[108] In another account, President Clinton acknowledged that by taking the lead on Bosnia: "I'm risking my presidency."[109] On 11 August as Congress left Washington for its summer recess, President Clinton vetoed a bill lifting the arms embargo on the Muslims—temporarily making it easier for the Europeans to follow America's lead in the Balkans.[110] Meanwhile, Assistant Secretary of State Richard Holbrooke visited leaders in former Yugoslavia to push the administration's new plan.[111] Though the details of the plan remained secret, Bosnian foreign minister Muhamed Sacirbey revealed to the press that "the Bosnian government will play a role in compelling the Serbs to accept the plan, and our military is an integral part of this process."[112] Such candidness about a secret plan was indicative of the limits of US influence over Bosnian Croat and government Federation forces. On 17 August in a note about Croatian military forces passed from Robert Frasure, the head US negotiator for the Balkans, to Richard Holbrooke, Frasure wrote: "Dick: We 'hired' these guys to be our junkyard dogs because we were desperate. We need to try to 'control' them. But this is no time to get squeamish about things."[113] When Frasure was killed in a road accident on Mount Igman two days later, Holbrooke took over as the lead US negotiator and quickly moved to sideline the Contact Group, while still preserving it, so that it could later "endorse and legitimize any agreement" he might achieve.[114] With the high political stakes the US administration was facing, it needed as much control as possible over the disparate components of its Balkan strategy.

The extent of US control over NATO airpower remains unclear. Senior US officials were aware of General Ryan's Deliberate Force plan, and robust air strikes had long been a part of the administration's policy toward Bosnia.[115] However, Richard Holbrooke, a long-time supporter of bombing the Bosnian Serbs, has claimed that there was no connection between the US diplomatic initiative and NATO bombing:

> Almost everyone came to believe that the bombing had been part of a master plan. But in fact in none of our discussions prior to our [late-August diplomatic] mission had we considered bombing as part of a negotiating strategy.[116]

A different account, supposedly based on interviews with Anthony Lake, apparently contradicted Holbrooke's assertion:

> The Europeans loved the diplomatic effort with Clinton putting the reputation of the United States on the line, but they hated the idea of bombing. But Lake insisted that the two were bound together and that the president had already decided on US policy.[117]

Holbrooke was doubtful of European support for an air campaign, and, in all likelihood, he had no choice but to depend on America's theater commanders working within the alliance to do as much as they could to support the administration's strategy.[118]

AFSOUTH and UNPF Subject to Close Coordination

Though NATO—with the United States in the fore—was moving toward more forceful action in Bosnia, General Janvier was slow to accept plans for NATO bombing. After the 25 July and 1 August NAC decisions, NATO's military commanders were left to work out the details for implementing the decisions with their counterparts in UNPF and UNPROFOR, and it took nearly two weeks before a basic procedural agreement was reached.[119] During that time, General Janvier made his case against using NATO airpower, but was overruled by political authorities within the UN.[120] On 10 August, General Janvier and Admiral Smith signed a memorandum of understanding (MOU), which formalized and added some of the necessary details to the military arrangements for implementing the NATO decisions.[121] For instance, Willy Claes had announced, "There is a strong feeling among Allies that such [bombing] operations, once they are launched, will not lightly be discontinued."[122] In working out the new dual-key arrangements, this meant once bombing commenced, it would not stop until the commanders agreed that the conditions precipitating the bombing had been alleviated.[123] A dual-key decision by General Janvier and Admiral Smith would be needed to *stop* bombing, as well as to start it; according to the MOU, Janvier would not stop it on his own. The commanders also adopted the triggers for air strikes set by NATO: (1) by "any concentration of forces and/or heavy weapons, and the conduct of other military preparations which, in the common judgment of the NATO and UN military commanders, presents a direct threat to the safe areas;" or (2) by "direct attacks (e.g., ground, shelling, or aircraft) on the safe areas."[124] To the NATO military commanders, it seemed that these conditions for triggering bombing operations already existed at the time the decision was made establishing the triggers.[125] All it would take was some event to precipitate a recommendation from the commanders to commence air strikes.

General Janvier also agreed to NATO control over air strikes for suppressing Bosnian Serb air defenses, but he remained suspicious of SEAD operations. Admiral Smith and General Ryan insisted that once a dual-key decision was made to initiate air attacks, then the NATO commanders would be free to execute all or part of the Dead Eye plan without requesting further approval from General Janvier. As Admiral Smith recalled: "When we put together the MOU, we included that in writing—that the turning of the key would authorize me to strike, at will, those targets which I thought were necessary to neutralize the integrated air defense sites."[126] It was a matter of force protection, and Janvier understood it and agreed to it in principle.[127] However, he was wary that Ryan and Admiral Smith might use Dead Eye to conduct air strikes unrelated to the Bosnian Serb air defenses in circumvention of the target approval procedures governing Deliberate Force; therefore, Janvier insisted he be kept informed of all Dead Eye operations.[128]

On 14 August, General Ryan presented a detailed briefing on his concept of operations for Deliberate Force to General Janvier and Admiral Smith.[129] The meeting also served as a joint targeting board, whereby the commanders vetted potential targets to ensure they were valid military targets that could be linked to desired military and political objectives. In this case the objective was to make the BSA stop attacking or threatening a safe area.[130] As General Ryan's chief planner, Colonel Zoerb, later noted, this objective was easy to state but it did not do much to define the shape the air operations would eventually take.[131] The military objective of Deliberate Force was to destroy the things that gave the BSA superiority over their adversaries.[132] This meant attacking BSA command and control facilities as well as certain supply and infrastructure targets that Mladic needed in order to maneuver his more capable, but less numerous, forces.[133] Of approximately 150 potential targets General Ryan put before the board, just under 90 were approved as viable Option 1 and 2 candidates for NATO air strikes.[134] While General Janvier agreed these were valid air strike targets, he was very careful to ensure he was not giving his advanced approval for hitting the entire list of targets should he decide to turn the UN key in the days ahead.[135] By this point, General Janvier had come to accept the two wider zones of action, each covering over half of Bosnia. The target sets for the safe area defense plans covering Sarajevo and Gorazde contained many of the same targets, so with the wider ZOAs approved, planners at the CAOC combined the two into one overall plan called Operation Vulcan.[136] The targets approved by Janvier on 14 August also belonged to the Vulcan target set and served as the initial menu of targets for Operation Deliberate Force two weeks later.[137]

Additional procedural arrangements between UNPROFOR and AIRSOUTH were ironed out on Thursday, 17 August, when General Ryan, General Smith, and Maj Gen David Pennefather, who headed the operations staff of the RRF, met to discuss a draft Air-Land Coordination Document.[138] With no doctrine to guide them, the UN and NATO commanders invented the air-land document to coordinate and deconflict, among other things, targets and use of the airspace over Bosnia.[139] If air operations commenced, Generals Ryan and Smith would nominate targets to Admiral Smith and General Janvier, who would decide whether to approve the attacks.[140] In agreeing on procedures for nominating targets, General Ryan proposed that General Smith pick all CAS targets and that the two commanders share responsibility for nominating interdiction targets near the RRF.[141] General Ryan would be responsible for picking air strike targets farther afield and for deciding which air defense targets to strike.[142] This division of responsibilities reflected the needs of the commanders to ensure force protection and mission accomplishment. For General Smith to be able to use airpower to protect his forces, he needed control over CAS. Likewise, Ryan needed to have a free hand in selecting air defense targets. Since part of General Smith's mission was to forestall a BSA attack on Sarajevo, he needed to be able to nominate the close-in interdiction targets.[143] For Ryan, interdiction targets were important to limiting BSA mobility and attriting its military capability.

Conclusion

In the judgment of the UN and NATO theater commanders, it was not possible to defend the safe areas with airpower alone. The fall of Srebrenica might have served to make that point had airpower been used earlier and with greater commitment. However, as political factors aligned behind US leadership for a more robust use of airpower, heralding its limitations would not have served the interests of America, the US commanders in NATO, or, arguably, the Alliance. As Western impatience with the UN's approach in Bosnia opened the door for forceful air operations, NATO theater-level commanders and Gen Rupert Smith actively pushed back the boundaries constraining the use of airpower.

This set the stage so that when airpower was called for, it could be used in a way the commanders believed was most effective. Moreover, senior airmen insisted upon preapproval for a SEAD campaign in the event of NATO air operations. By building a plan around real tactical limitations, and setting it as a precondition for air strikes, the NATO commanders ensured General Janvier would not falter in decisions to authorize SEAD during Deliberate Force. Amongst the theater-level commanders, General Janvier harbored the greatest misgivings about the utility of a NATO bombing campaign, and he resisted the shift from UN to NATO primacy. Ultimately, however, Janvier took his political orders and went along with the NATO plans, even though he remained uneasy about a policy that publicly implied the continuation of the UN's primacy and its impartial role in Bosnia but in reality was headed in a more belligerent direction. However, Janvier's mission was waning, and his forces were growing increasingly less vulnerable even as the importance of NATO's mission and the likelihood that NATO airmen would be put in harm's way were growing.

Notes

1. As the footnotes show, the next six paragraphs are mainly a distillation of research done by others, especially Honig and Both, but with a focus on NATO airpower. The author would be remiss not to acknowledge a debt to them at the outset.

2. Jan Willem Honig and Norbert Both, *Srebrenica: Record of a War Crime* (London: Penguin Books, 1996), 4.

3. Ibid., 4–7; and David Rohde, *A Safe Area, Srebrenica: Europe's Worst Massacre Since the Second World* War (London: Pocket Books, 1997), 23.

4. Honig and Both, 4–17.

5. Ibid., 8.

6. Ibid.; and Rohde, 23 and 81–82. Bildt replaced Lord David Owen as the EU cochairman to the Geneva peace conference when Owen resigned in June of 1995.

7. Honig and Both, 10; and Rohde, 41 and 79.

8. Honig and Both, 13.

9. Ibid., 16.

10. Rohde, 99.

11. Honig and Both, 18.

12. Ibid., 19–20; and Rohde, 118–24.

13. Honig and Both, 20; and Rohde, 133.

14. Honig and Both, 21–22; and Rohde, 132–33.

15. Honig and Both, 22; and Adm Leighton W. Smith, USN, "NATO Close Air Support-Srebrenica-11 July 95," transcript of news conference, Naples, Italy, 12 July 1995, http://www.afsouth.nato.int/archives/archives.htm.

16. Gen Michael E. Ryan, USAF, commander, Allied Air Forces Southern Europe and commander US Sixteenth Air Force, September 1994–April 1996, interviewed by author, 6 June 1997, Ramstein Air Base (AB), Germany, transcript of taped interview, author's personal collection; and Admiral Smith transcript.

17. Honig and Both, 23.

18. Ibid., 20; and Rohde, 133.

19. Honig and Both, 22; and Rohde, 144.

20. Honig and Both, 23–25.

21. Ibid. The ability of the Bosnian Serbs to monitor NATO flying activities closely, and the networking of the Serbian air defense system and that of the Bosnian Serbs, was well known at the time. See Senate, *Briefing on the F-16 Shootdown in Bosnia and Current Operations: Hearings before the Committee on Armed Services*, 104th Cong., 1st Sess., 1995, 36, 45, and 51–52; and Tim Ripley, "Silence of the SAMS," *Aircraft Illustrated* 28, no. 1 (November 1995): 36–37.

22. Honig and Both, 24. A "Blue Sword" order was used for CAS—not air strikes.

23. Ibid., 23–24.

24. Ibid., 25; and Admiral Smith transcript.

25. Honig and Both, 25; and Rohde, 162.

26. Honig and Both, 25; and Rohde, 162.

27. Honig and Both, 25–26; Joris Voorhoeve, "Protecting the Peacekeepers on the Day Srebrenica Fell," *Washington Post,* 20 November 1995, A20. Note: In the *Washington Post* article, Voorhoeve says: "I called UN headquarters in Zagreb at 4 P.M. and asked to call off a new round of air support." Other sources indicate that Honig and Both's version is accurate; so that even if Voorhoeve phoned Zagreb at 4:00 P.M., he apparently phoned the CAOC first.

28. Ryan interview.

29. Ibid.

30. Honig and Both, 19, and 45–66.

31. Rohde, 343–49. Rohde uses the Red Cross figure of 7,079.

32. Honig and Both, 21.

33. Rohde, 354.

34. For examples, see comments by General Briquemont in chap. 4, first paragraph of section entitled "Airpower and coercion at Mount Igman: August 1993"; by General de Lapresle in chap. 5, section entitled "Turning Point: Gorazde, April 1994"; and by Generals Ryan and Rupert Smith, chap. 7, section entitled "The Beginning of the End." Also see comments by General Ryan from April 1993 in, Elaine Sciolino, "U.S. Military Split on Using Air Power against the Serbs," *New York Times*, 29 April 1993, A1.

35. *Facts On File Yearbook 1995* (USA: Facts on File, Inc., 1995), 494; and Military Official Y.

36. Senate, *Briefing on Shootdown*, 33 and 45; and Honig and Both, 19. The SA-6 in eastern Bosnia was one of the first targets hit at the start of Operation Deliberate Force. On 30 August 1995, it was located near the town of Sokolac between Pale and Srebrenica.

37. Honig and Both, 151–53 and 182–83.

38. Rohde, 368.

39. Honig and Both, 182.

40. Rohde, 366.

41. See chap. 4, section entitled "Command without Control: September–December 1993."

42. *Facts On File 1995*, 513.

43. Ibid.

44. Bruce Clark, Bernard Gray, and Lionel Barber, "Doubts Grow Over UN Bosnia Role," *Financial Times* (London), 17 July 1995, 1; and MOD Officials F and J.

45. MOD Official J.

46. Bruce Clark, John Kampfner, and Anthony Robinson, "Split Over Bosnia Air Strike Threat: Meeting Fails to Back US Calls for Tough Action Against Serbs," *Financial Times* (London), 22 July 1995, 1; *Facts On File 1995*, 513; and MOD Officials F and J.

47. MOD Officials F and J.

48. Lord (Field Marshal) Richard Vincent, chairman of NATO's Military Committee, interviewed by author, 22 September 1998, London, author's notes, author's personal collection.

49. Clark, Kampfner, and Robinson.

50. Ibid.

51. Ibid.; Bernard Gray, "Clinton Fights Uphill Battle with Congress: The Bosnia Crisis - Europe and the US Struggle to Agree on What to Do Next," *Financial Times* (London), 20 July 1995, 2; and Anthony Robinson and Bernard Gray, "Taking of Hostages Will Not Deter Attacks, Serbs Warned," *Financial Times* (London), 22 July 1995, 2.

52. Gray; and Robinson and Gray.

53. Ryan interview; and Robinson and Gray.

54. Ryan interview.

55. Allied Forces Southern Europe (AFSOUTH), "Operation Deliberate Force," Fact Sheet, 5 October 1995, 2. Col Robert C. Owen's *Deliberate Force: A Case Study in Effective Air Campaigning* (Maxwell AFB, Ala.: Air University Press, 2000) covers the evolution of NATO and US target planning. However, different aspects of the planning are captured with varying degrees of fidelity in three chapters of the book. The following discussion draws from Col Owen's book and other sources. See Col Owen *Deliberate Force*, 54–57, 98–103, and 285–91.

56. Dick A. Leurdijk, *The United Nations and NATO in Former Yugoslavia, 1991–1996: Limits to Diplomacy and Force* (The Hague: The Netherlands Atlantic Commission, 1996), 76; and NATO, "Press statement on Gorazde by Secretary-General Willy Claes, following North Atlantic Council meeting on 25 July 1995."

57. Gen George A. Joulwan, USA, Supreme Allied Commander Europe, 22 October 1993–11 July 1997, interviewed by author, 11 February 1998, Washington, D.C., transcript of tape recording, author's personal collection; Col Daniel R. Zoerb, USAF, director, Deny Flight Air Operations Center, Naples, Italy, January 1994–May 1996, interviewed by author, 29 April 1997, Spangdahlem AB, Germany, transcript of tape recording, author's personal collection.

58. Boutros Boutros-Ghali, UN secretary-general, TLS (photocopy), to Willy Claes, NATO secretary-general, Brussels, 26 July 1995, BACS Collection, Air Force Historical Research Agency, Maxwell AFB, Alabama.

59. Ibid.

60. Ibid.

61. Ibid.

62. *Facts On File 1995*, 530.

63. Boutros-Ghali, TLS, to Willy Claes, 26 July 1995.

64. Ibid.

65. *Facts On File 1995*, 529.

66. Paul Adams and Laura Silber, "UN in Talks with Serbs as Zepa 'Safe Haven' Falls: International Tribunal Charges Karadzic and Mladic With War Crimes," *Financial Times* (London), 26 July 1995, 1; and *Facts On File 1995*, 529. On the day Smith and Mladic met, the Yugoslav War Crimes Tribunal announced charges against Mladic and Bosnian Serb President Radovan Karadzic for "genocide, war crimes, and crimes against humanity."

67. *Facts On File 1995*, 530 and 549; and Laura Silber and Anthony Robinson, "Fear of Wider Conflict as Croatians Attack Serbs: UN and NATO Finalise Procedure for Air Strikes," *Financial Times* (London), 29 July 1995, 20.

68. *Facts On File 1995*, 549.

69. NATO, "Press Statement on Gorazde;" and Col Daniel R. Zoerb, USAF, interviewed by author, 30 April 1997, Spangdahlem AB, Germany, transcript of tape recording, author's personal collection.

70. Senate, *Briefing on Shootdown*, 33.

71. *Facts On File 1995*, 549 and 565.

72. Silber and Robinson, 20; and Laura Silber, Judy Dempsey, and Anthony Robinson, " 'Underdog' Croatia Learns How to Bite: Zagreb Has Made Good Use of the Backing it Receives from the US, Germany, and Austria," *Financial Times* (London), 2 August 1995, 2.

73. NATO, "Press Statement on Other Safe Areas by the Secretary-General Following North Atlantic Council Meeting on 1 August 1995."

74. MCM-KAD-057-95, "NATO Air Operations to Stabilize Bosnia-Hercegovina Beyond Gorazde," Memorandum to the Secretary-General, North Atlantic Treaty Organization, 31 July 1995, cited in Owen, *Deliberate Force*, 105 and 128 n. 19; "Operational Options" is discussed in chap. 4, section entitled NATO Air-to-Ground Missions: June–August 1993."

75. Leurdijk, 76; and NATO, "Press Statement . . . 1 August 1995."

76. Owen, *Deliberate Force*, 105; and Col Steven Teske, USAF, interviewed by author, 6 May 1997, Aviano AB, Italy, tape recording, author's personal collection. As Colonel Owen's study pointed out, these "plans" for the individual safe areas were little more than target lists and overhead briefing slides. As of May 1997, the individual safe area plans were still being held in a historical file in a safe in the Guidance Apportionment and Targeting Cell at the CAOC in Vicenza.

77. Admiral Smith transcript; Ryan interview; and Zoerb, 29 April 1997.

78. Ryan interview. This was consistent with General Ryan's testimony to Congress in April 1993; see Elaine Sciolino, A1 and A6.

79. Ryan interview.

80. Col Robert C. Owen, USAF, "The Balkans Air Campaign Study: Part 2," *Airpower Journal* 11, no. 3 (autumn 1997): 14.

81. Owen, *Deliberate Force*, 105–110.

82. Allied Forces Southern Europe (AFSOUTH), "Operation Deliberate Force," Fact Sheet, 5 October 1995, 3. The NAC decision for the wider zones of action reflected acceptance of a memorandum from the Military Committee to the secretary-general supporting "the wider application [of] airpower in a wider context." MCM-KAD-057-95, "NATO Air Operations to Stabilize Bosnia-Hercegovina Beyond Gorazde," cited in Owen, *Deliberate Force*, 105 and 128 n. 19.

83. Owen, "Balkans: Part 2," 19.

84. Ibid.; and Zoerb, 30 April 1997.

85. Gen Michael E. Ryan, "NATO Air Operations in Bosnia-Herzegovina: 'Deliberate Force,' 29 August–14 September 1995," transcript of Air Power Conference, London, 13 September 1996; and Zoerb, 30 April 1997. Generals Smith and Ryan were meeting in Kiseljak on 29 July 1995 to begin the process of coordinating NATO air operations with ground operations by the RRF. They had their key planners with them, including Colonel Zoerb, USAF, and Col David Nicholls, Royal Marines. General Smith may have made his input for the wider zones at this meeting. Col David V. Nicholls, Royal Marines, "Bosnia: UN and NATO," *RUSI Journal* 141, no. 1 (February

1996): 34–35; and Col Daniel R. Zoerb, "Notes From Kiseljak Meeting," 29 July 1995, File B4-3, BACS Collection.

86. Ryan transcript of Air Power Conference.

87. Joulwan interview, 11 February 1998; Ryan transcript of Air Power Conference; and Zoerb interview, 29 April 1997.

88. Admiral Smith transcript; and Nicholls, 34–35.

89. Admiral Smith transcript.

90. Gen Michael E. Ryan, "NATO Air Operations in Bosnia-Herzegovina," slides from a briefing to Air Power Conference, London, 13 September 1996, slide no. 6.

91. Joulwan interview, 11 February 1998.

92. Admiral Smith transcript.

93. Ryan transcript of Air Power Conference.

94. AFSOUTH, "Operation Deliberate Force," Fact Sheet, 3; Owen, *Deliberate Force*, 481; Ryan interview; and Zoerb interview, 30 April 1997.

95. Zoerb interview, 30 April 1997.

96. Lt Gen Bernard Janvier, French army, commander of United Nations Protection Force, Zagreb, Croatia, March 1995–December 1995, interviewed by author, 12 January 1998, Paris, author's notes, author's personal collection; The United Nations, *The Blue Helmets: A Review of United Nations Peace-keeping*, 3d ed. (New York: United Nations Reproduction Section, 1996), 552; and Laura Silber and Anthony Robinson, "Croats Unleash Attack on Krajina," *Financial Times* (London), 5 August 1995, 1.

97. Silber and Robinson, "Croats Unleash;" UN Security Council Resolution 1009 (1995) (S/RES/1009, 10 August 1995); and *Facts On File 1995*, 565.

98. *Blue Helmets*, 552.

99. *Facts On File 1995*, 565–66.

100. Ibid.; "Turn of the Tide?" *The Economist*, 5 August 1995, 47; and Patrick Moore, "An End Game in Croatia and Bosnia?" *Transition*, 3 November 1995, 10.

101. *Facts On File 1995*, 566.

102. Ibid.; and "Croatia's Blitzkrieg," *The Economist*, 12 August 1995, 41.

103. Edward Mortimer, "Slicing Up the Bosnian Cake: Brute Force Is Triumphing over Diplomacy in the Balkans," *Financial Times* (London), 8 August 1995, 13.

104. The officers were Gen James Jamerson, USAF, Air Chief Marshal Sir William Wratten, RAF, and a French army major general serving in the operations directorate of the French joint staff. After the meeting, Air Chief Marshal Wratten reported to the British Secretary of State for Defence, Michael Portillo, that the message had been delivered and that Mladic showed no signs of taking it seriously. Air Chief Marshal Sir William Wratten, telephone interview by author, 18 May 1997, London, author's notes, author's personal collection. Also see Jane M. O. Sharp, *Honest Broker or Perfidious Albion: British Policy in Former Yugoslavia* (London:

Institute for Public Policy Research, 1997), 57; and Owen, *Deliberate Force*, 480 and 519 n. 46.

105. Thomas W. Lippman and Ann Devroy, "Clinton's Policy Evolution: June Decision Led to Diplomatic Gambles," *Washington Post*, 11 September 1995, A1 and A16.

106. The Contact Group was an outgrowth of the international peace conference in Geneva. Established in April 1994, the Contact Group came up with a "take it or leave it" plan, which the Bosnian Serbs rejected in July 1994. The group was hamstrung by pretty much the same disparate alignment of allegiances that prevented effective action from the UN Security Council. By 1995, the Contact Group had become just another forum for disagreement between Britain, France, Russia, Germany, and the US.

107. Lippman and Devroy, A16; Bob Woodward, *The Choice: How Clinton Won* (New York: Simon & Schuster, 1996), 267–68.

108. James Carney, "Finally, The Leader of NATO Leads," *Time*, 11 September 1995, 54. President Clinton's determination to go it alone if necessary is also discussed in Woodward, 267–68.

109. Woodward, 265.

110. *Facts On File 1995*, 590–91.

111. Richard Holbrooke, *To End a War* (New York: Random House, 1998), 3–4 and 74–75; *Facts On File 1995*, 590; and "US Peace Plan for Bosnia Attacked," *Financial Times*, 16 August 1995, 2.

112. Harriet Martin, Bruce Clark, and John Ridding, "Bosnia Hails Force Element in US Plan," *Financial Times* (London), 17 August 1995, 2.

113. Holbrooke, 73.

114. Ibid., 84.

115. Ibid., 102; Woodward; and Ryan interview.

116. Holbrooke, 104.

117. Woodward, 268.

118. Holbrooke, 103–4.

119. Admiral Smith transcript; and Ryan interview.

120. NATO Official D; Military Official Q; Admiral Smith transcript; and Zoerb interview, 29 April 1997.

121. Dr. Thomas S. Snyder and Dr. Daniel F. Harrington, USAFE Office of History, *USAFE Historical Highlights, 1942–1947: Fifty-fifth Anniversary Edition* (Ramstein AB, Germany: Headquarters USAFE, 1997), 184; AFSOUTH, "Operation Deliberate Force," Fact Sheet, 3; and Leurdijk, 78.

122. NATO, "Press Statement on Gorazde," 25 July 1995.

123. Zoerb interview, 30 April 1997; and Military Official Q.

124. Owen, *Deliberate Force*, 406–7; and AFSOUTH, "Operation Deliberate Force," Fact Sheet, 2–3.

125. Ryan interview; and Ryan transcript of Air Power Conference.

126. Admiral Smith transcript.

127. Janvier; and Military Official Q.

128. Janvier; and Military Official Q.

129. Owen, *Deliberate Force*, 57, 107–8, and 282.

130. Zoerb interview, 30 April 1997.

131. Ibid.

132. Ryan transcript of Air Power Conference.

133. Ibid.

134. Owen, *Deliberate Force,* 107–8 and 281–85.

135. Military Official Q.

136. Owen, *Deliberate Force,* 105; Zoerb interview, 29 April 1997.

137. Owen, *Deliberate Force,* 111 and 483; and Col Daniel R. Zoerb, director, Deny Flight Air Operations Center, Naples, Italy, January 1994–May 1996, "AU's Deliberate Force Report, Remarks on an Early Draft of the Balkans Air Campaign Study, 20 November 1996 for General Ryan."

138. AFSOUTH, "Operation Deliberate Force," Fact Sheet, 3; Ryan transcript of Air Power Conference; and Owen, *Deliberate Force,* 106.

139. Nicholls, 35; Ryan transcript of Air Power Conference; and Ryan interview.

140. Ryan transcript of Air Power Conference; Ryan interview; and Zoerb interview, 30 April 1997.

141. Owen, *Deliberate Force,* 106; Ryan transcript of Air Power Conference; and Ryan interview. See also Nicholls, 35.

142. Ryan transcript of Air Power Conference; and Ryan interview.

143. Rapid Reaction Force Operations Staff, "HQ 1 (UK) ARMD DIV RRFOS Brief," 17 November 1995, slide no. 18; and Nicholls, 35.

Chapter 9

Deliberate Force:
August–September 1995

"The General who values his good name," wrote Marmont, "must see to it that he has a completely free hand. Either he must not be interfered with, or he must be removed from his command." But he must have a sufficiently clear-cut plan of his own on which to base his firmness. Nothing tends more surely to provoke interference from above than a lack of assurance below.

—Charles de Gaulle
The Edge of the Sword

Well, everybody had an opinion, but nobody [else] had a plan. So, we were the only ones that had a plan; so we got to execute.

—Gen Michael Ryan
Interview by author
6 June 1997

Operation Deliberate Force highlighted the political-military dimension of the struggle by theater-level commanders to influence the use of airpower in Bosnia. The ascendancy of Richard Holbrooke in negotiations for a settlement of the wider Yugoslav conflict led him to seek some control over NATO airpower. In his attempt to influence the campaign, Holbrooke clashed with Admiral Smith, the commander responsible for NATO forces and the success of Deliberate Force. The first section of this chapter shows that Admiral Smith invoked his command responsibilities to maintain control over operations: first with General Janvier to win UN approval for proposed targets and later with Holbrooke during a pause in the bombing. The need to balance risks to one's forces and mission accomplishment is a serious responsibility borne by commanders, and because of their military expertise, commanders may be the best judges of risks. The second section of this chapter demonstrates how a commander may set limits on risks when attempting to accomplish a given mission.

Responsibility also gives commanders leverage for shaping operations, and that influence is fortified when it is combined with expertise and control over information. Because air strategy revolves around targeting decisions, a commander who controls information about targets has a good chance of preserving operational autonomy while influencing air campaign strategy. During Operation Deliberate Force, General Ryan and Admiral Smith maintained a close hold on information about the campaign to keep control of it and ensure its success. However, this tight military governing of air operations led to friction between NATO's theater-level commanders—especially Admiral Smith—and some US and European political authorities.

Defense of Sarajevo

As August drew to a close, Serb shelling of Gorazde and Sarajevo prompted Bosnian government calls for NATO action. The UN announced on 18 August that no new peacekeepers would replace British forces set to leave Gorazde at month's end—a move which the Bosnian government feared might signal the international community's abandonment of Gorazde's 60,000 Muslims.[1] Four days later, a Bosnian Serb shell fell on Sarajevo, killing six people and wounding nearly 40 others.[2] The government in Sarajevo demanded the Serbs be punished, but the UN refused to act because the Serb shelling was provoked by Bosnian army attacks on the Serb suburb of Vogosca.[3] A similar transaction near Gorazde also failed to elicit air strikes.[4] While the Bosnian government seemed intent on creating a cause for Western intervention, Bosnian Serb leaders reportedly gathered in Belgrade and consented to make Serbia's President Milosevic their lead negotiator on the six-member team that would represent breakaway Serbs at upcoming US-led peace talks.[5] Richard Holbrooke, speaking on a US television news show on 27 August, warned Serbs of Western intervention should the upcoming round of peace talks fail.[6] However, intervention was triggered before talks even began.

The Trigger

Shortly after 10:00 on Monday morning, 28 August 1995, Serb shells began falling again on Sarajevo. Over the next 10 minutes, five rounds hit the capital, with the fourth round landing in the crowded Markale market, killing at least 37 people and wounding more than 80.[7] The Bosnian government threatened to boycott the upcoming peace talks unless NATO and the UN carried out air strikes against the Serbs.[8] When Admiral Smith learned of the blast, he phoned Zagreb to inform the UN of his intent to turn the NATO key if, indeed, the Serbs were the guilty party.[9] General Janvier was attending his son's wedding in France when the blast occurred, thus Gen Rupert Smith held the UN key for NATO air strikes.[10] As UN investigators sought to discover the origins of the blast, the last of the British forces in Gorazde withdrew eastward into Serbia. They reached Serbia around 8:30 P.M. on 28 August, arriving safely in Belgrade early the next morning—a little less than 24 hours before the first bombs of Deliberate Force slammed into targets in southeastern Bosnia.[11] UN investigators proved to General Smith's satisfaction that the Serbs had shelled the market, and on the night of 28 August, he and Admiral Smith decided to order air strikes against the Serbs.[12] However, General Smith asked for a one-day delay before commencing the air campaign so that he could secure his forces.[13] In the final hours leading up to Operation Deliberate Force, French soldiers withdrew from two observation posts near Sarajevo, leaving no UN peacekeepers for the Bosnian Serbs to take hostage.[14]

When the market blast occurred, General Ryan was already at the CAOC for an exercise—turned execution—of the Vulcan plan.[15] By the next morning he was joined by a small team of planners led by Colonel Zoerb.[16] Admiral Smith sent a message through NATO's military headquarters in Mons, Belgium, recalling aircraft tasked to support Deny Flight.[17] Likewise, he ordered the US aircraft carrier *Theodore Roosevelt* to steam into the Adriatic within easy striking distance of targets in Bosnia.[18] On 29 August, CAOC leaders received official orders to go ahead with the air campaign, but they elected to proceed with a scaled-down schedule of sorties that day in order to mask preparations for the next day's attacks.[19]

The Targets

Aware of impending air strikes, General Janvier hastily returned to his compound in Zagreb, arriving Tuesday morning, 29 August. At 9:30 A.M., his staff updated him on the situation; at the end of the meeting Janvier announced that as of that moment he once again held the UN key.[20] Though he did not overrule General Smith's decision to turn the key, that evening Janvier demurred when it came time to approve the first batch of air strike targets.[21] Inexplicably, General Janvier had not been shown the proposed list of 13 targets until late in the afternoon.[22] With the first wave of attacks just a few hours away, Admiral Smith phoned for word of Janvier's approval. Janvier asked for more time to consider the targets, but the AFSOUTH commander pressed him for a decision. In doing so, Admiral Smith later claimed he told Janvier: "My pilots are showing up in the ready rooms, and they don't know which targets to go hit, so I've got to have your answer now because you're endangering the lives of my pilots and I won't put up with that."[23] Under pressure from Admiral Smith, General Janvier agreed to hit five of the 13 targets nominated by General Ryan.[24] It was the only time Admiral Smith said he could recall losing his temper in his dealings with General Janvier.[25] Smith later said he told Janvier: "This is crazy. I will start the bombing operations, but I must tell you that I'm going to write a letter up my chain of command telling them that you've abrogated your side of the agreement, and that this is a failed campaign at the very outset."[26] After quick consultations with his advisors in Zagreb, Janvier consented to authorize 10 of the 13 targets, but he refused to approve three targets that had the word *barracks* in their title.[27] Admiral Smith gave General Ryan the go-ahead to hit the 10 targets and told him to change the names of the three barracks to more accurately reflect the nature of the objects NATO wanted to bomb at those sites.[28]

Admiral Smith's frustration with General Janvier reflected the shift for AFSOUTH from being the supporting to the supported element of the UN-NATO team. For Deliberate Force bombing operations, Smith's forces were at risk, not Janvier's. Furthermore, Admiral Smith, not the UN commander, was responsible for mission accomplishment. In pressuring Janvier, Admiral Smith invoked these two principal command responsibilities—force protection and mission accomplishment. As the commander accountable for the forces at risk and the outcome of the operation, Admiral Smith expected and even demanded support from Janvier—much as previous UN commanders had demanded support from Admiral Smith.

General Janvier's reluctance to authorize strikes against targets labeled as barracks was emblematic of a lack of understanding about airpower and targets that persisted well after Deliberate Force.[29] The concept denoted by the term *target* had changed with the advent of precision-guided munitions (PGM), but the military vernacular had failed to keep up with this technological change. Poor bombing accuracies in the Second World War drove allied air forces to conduct area bombing—even when theory and doctrine called for precision bombing.[30] By Desert Storm, some NATO air forces had the capability to strike precisely at individual targets, such as buildings, communications towers, and aircraft shelters. A large number of such targets might be concentrated at one site, an airfield for example; yet target libraries continued to refer to these sites, or target complexes, as single targets.[31] Planners at an operational headquarters were apt to use the term *target* to denote the entire site, while a pilot flying a mission might use the word *target* to describe the individual object to hit at the site. With PGMs it became increasingly important to distinguish between the two types of targets, but there was no official terminology for doing so.[32] For those whose business it was to plan and execute air attacks, the term *aim point* or DMPI (desired mean point of impact—pronounced *dimp-ee*) was used to differentiate the individual target from the larger target complex. As an air campaign, Deliberate Force was unique in that the majority of bombs dropped were PGMs.[33] After the Pale air strikes and the many briefings General Janvier had received on NATO air plans, Admiral Smith incorrectly assumed the UN commander understood the distinction between larger target complexes and individual targets, or DMPIs, that were going to be bombed.[34]

In Bosnia, targets such as the Hadzici and Pale ammunition storage sites contained up to 20 bunkers or buildings, each a separate target with a specific aim point.[35] NATO planners analyzed each of these individual targets with its respective aim point in terms of the utility for hitting it and its potential for collateral damage.[36] Moreover, in Bosnia, several large target complexes were concentrated in certain areas. In the vicinity of Hadzici, there were at least three target sites: a military vehicle repair facility, a military equipment storage site, and an ammunition storage site.[37] The number of individual targets at these three target sites ranged from 10 to more than 60.[38] It was two days after Deliberate Force began that Admiral Smith finally realized General Janvier had not distinguished between larger target sites and individual DMPIs.[39] Furthermore, many targets or target complexes in Bosnia still bore their old Cold War labels that by 1995 no longer reflected the true nature of the sites.[40] A target labeled a barracks might no longer have served primarily for housing troops. Target sites actually containing barracks often held other buildings or objects that NATO wished to bomb. For example, the Sarajevo army barracks contained BSA air defense assets and military storage facilities.[41] As directed by Admiral Smith, AFSOUTH planners changed the names of the three barracks, later resubmitted them for General Janvier's approval, and NATO aircrews bombed them without hitting any buildings housing Mladic's soldiers.[42]

General Janvier's reluctance to approve air strike targets was not due solely to inadequate time for considering the target list or concerns about what NATO was going to bomb. Even after he was delegated the UN key, Janvier continued to discuss all bombing decisions with Mr. Akashi, and Akashi remained philosophically opposed to NATO bombing operations.[43] In addition, General Janvier remained uncomfortable participating in the charade of UN impartiality while NATO conducted a campaign aimed solely at the Bosnian Serbs.[44] Richard Holbrooke has claimed that direct pressure from Kofi Annan, who was then serving as UN undersecretary-general for peacekeeping, was necessary in order for Janvier and Akashi to give in to NATO demands for bombing on 29 August.[45] Describing the target approval process with Janvier after the first stormy experience, Admiral Smith later said: "It was pretty pro forma after that."[46] Overall, Janvier's reluctance to initiate Deliberate Force stemmed to some degree from his lack of expertise and confidence in airpower; but more importantly, Janvier's hesitation derived from his need for political direction—despite public pronouncements about his authority over decisions for air strikes.

The Execution

Once Admiral Smith and General Janvier approved the proposed targets, General Ryan was responsible for executing Deliberate Force. Speaking at a press conference on the second day of Deliberate Force, Admiral Smith said: "Once General Janvier and I decided it was time to execute air operations, we turned the air operations over to General Ryan and he is responsible for execution."[47] General Ryan's means of control over the air operation were many. Within physical, meteorological, and logistical constraints, Ryan could decide which of the approved targets to hit, the sequence for attacking, and how rapidly to strike.[48] He determined how far to go in attacking the Bosnian Serb air defense system before going after other BSA targets.[49] The theater air commander was also free to choose which aim points to strike within a given target complex, what time of day to attack, and which aircraft and ordnance to employ.[50] Finally, General Ryan determined what restrictions or special instructions to issue to aircrews who were attacking the targets.[51] The latitude given to Ryan by Admiral Smith and the broad mission statement from the NAC allowed General Ryan to use airpower in a manner he thought most effective.

From the outset of Deliberate Force, General Ryan's decisions reflected the way in which a commander must use individual expertise to balance force protection against mission accomplishment. Given time, General Ryan would have preferred to destroy the entire Bosnian Serb integrated air defense system (IADS) before hitting any other BSA targets.[52] However, he felt compelled, initially, to confine attacks against air defenses to southeastern Bosnia and to forego the heart of the IADS in the northwest.[53] Eliminating the entire IADS would have delayed attacks Ryan believed were needed to diminish Bosnian Serb military capability.[54] Despite tough talk from some Western political leaders after the London Conference, experience suggested permission to continue bombing might not last long. Therefore, General Ryan opted to begin strikes against BSA targets after just one wave of attacks aimed at degrading Serb air defenses in the southeast zone of action.[55] Added risk to NATO aircrews caused by a delay in fully prosecuting Dead Eye was small so long as aircraft stayed clear of northwestern Bosnia.[56] By putting off attacks against the northwestern component of the air defense system, Ryan applied his expertise to fulfill his principal responsibilities as a commander—achieving his assigned mission with the least unnecessary risks and costs to his forces.

Though air operations between 30 August and 14 September 1995 have become known as Operation Deliberate Force, they were not simply an execution of the Deliberate Force plan crafted by Col Doc Zoerb earlier that year.[57] Operation Deliberate Force, as it unfolded, embodied elements of three distinct sets of plans built during the nine months before the Sarajevo market blast. First, in late 1994, planners at the CAOC developed a plan called Dead Eye, which was designed solely for defeating Bosnian Serb air defenses. The second relevant plan took shape in early 1995 when General Ryan instructed his planners to develop a campaign plan for degrading the BSA's fighting potential. The plan built by Colonel Zoerb—referred to herein as the Deliberate Force plan—contained targets throughout Bosnia and was not linked to the defense of any particular safe area. Third, after Srebrenica and Zepa fell, Western leaders vowed to prevent loss of the remaining four safe areas, and planners at the CAOC created target lists for the defense of each remaining enclave. In August, the plans for defending Gorazde and Sarajevo were combined into one new plan called Vulcan, which Ryan went to the CAOC to exercise on the morning of 28 August.[58] When General Ryan executed Deliberate Force, the operation contained elements of all three sets of plans. Air strike targets were initially chosen from the Vulcan plan.[59] Air defense targets came from a portion of the Dead Eye plan.[60] The heart of the operation—the logic behind the prosecution of the campaign—derived from the Deliberate Force plan.[61]

Ryan's execution of Operation Deliberate Force supported an observation made a century earlier by Moltke the Elder:

> Only the layman sees in the course of a campaign a consistent execution of a preconceived and highly detailed original concept pursued consistently to the end. Certainly the commander in chief (*Feldherr*) will keep his great objective (*Zweck*) continuously in mind, undisturbed by the vicissitudes of events. But the path on which he hopes to reach it can never be firmly established in advance.[62]

Moltke's comment fits the case of Deliberate Force, because in prosecuting the campaign General Ryan was guided by his view of the objective more than by details of existing plans.[63] Ryan was bent on undermining the BSA's military advantage.[64] In his view that was the surest way to end the threat to safe areas and to get Mladic to comply with UN resolutions and NATO ultimatums.[65] Mladic would determine whether bombing would lead to a quick cease-fire or whether air strikes would continue until BSA fighting potential was drawn down to a level on a par with Bosnian government forces. The speed with which General Ryan prosecuted Deliberate Force targets demonstrated his desire to level the playing field as much as possible before Mladic gave in or international political will gave out.[66]

Collateral Damage and Other Priorities

By doing his utmost to limit collateral damage, General Ryan again faced the potential need to make a trade-off between force protection and mission accomplishment; though, as with the decision to delay prosecuting the northwest part of Dead Eye, added risks were minimal. Collateral damage concerns factor into targeting decisions whenever Western nations consider employing airpower.[67] In operations other than war, such as Deliberate Force, it is probably safe to say that avoiding collateral damage will usually rank just behind protection of friendly forces as a commander's top priorities. Although Deliberate Force seemed like combat, General Ryan was acutely aware NATO was not at war.[68] In total war, an air component commander's priorities are likely to be (1) mission accomplishment; (2) force protection; and (3) collateral damage—in that order. In operations other than war, the priorities are more likely to be (1) force protection; (2) collateral damage; and (3) mission accomplishment.[69] As Lt Col Ronald M. Reed, a contributor to the Balkans Air Campaign Study averred, this was definitely the case in Deliberate Force.[70] And, as the surface-to-air threat declined in Bosnia, General Ryan's concern for collateral damage motivated him to issue instructions that appeared to place collateral damage on a near equal footing with force protection.[71] Several BACS contributors described a policy during the last two days of Deliberate Force restricting tactics during bombing attacks so as to further reduce chances for collateral damage. These examples clearly highlight how a commander must apply expertise to make judicious trade-offs between force protection and mission accomplishment.[72]

Col Robert Owen, head of the US Air Force's Balkans Air Campaign Study, has shown that commanders in AFSOUTH were more sensitive to collateral damage than the American diplomats involved in Deliberate Force.[73] However, General Ryan and Admiral Smith believed European and UN political sensibilities mattered as much as American tolerance for unintended damage.[74] At a briefing to the US Air Force's Air War College a few weeks after the campaign, Admiral Smith highlighted this point when he explained that had General Ryan been less diligent in planning air strikes, or NATO aircrews less careful when executing them, then

> I believe that we would have lost the political and the public support to continue these operations. They would have ceased. And I do not think we would have people in Dayton today talking about peace. That's a firm conviction of mine, and believe me, I'm probably as good as anybody in terms of experience and knowledge to make that judgment, because I was there watching it day by day.[75]

One high-ranking NATO official later put it in more personal terms, describing General Ryan's painstaking efforts to avoid collateral damage as "very wise because, if something had gone wrong, he would have been on the next plane out."[76] Moreover, General Ryan personally accepted responsibility for collateral damage, later telling an audience in London,

> If you're the commander of an air operation [collateral damage is] your business, nobody else's business. . . . Don't let it get down to the individual aircrew or unit. If they screw it up, it's normally your screw-up, not theirs.[77]

The lack of tolerance for collateral damage amongst NATO's political authorities was consistent with the concept of proportionality from the laws of armed conflict.[78] According to official NATO statements, there was no military objective other than to defend the remaining safe areas.[79] UN political authorities reportedly directed the RRF to halt offensive operations after the second day of Deliberate Force, demonstrating the absence of official support within the UN for any positive military objective.[80] With no enemy, ostensibly, and no overt political backing for leveling the playing field, it would have been difficult for NATO commanders to make the case that any appreciable collateral damage was proportional to the overall objective of the operation.[81] By minimizing collateral damage, General Ryan and Admiral Smith were working within the confines of the laws of armed conflict and the narrow objective for bombing established by the UN.

AFSOUTH commanders' concerns for collateral damage were apparently driven mainly by their desire to maintain political cohesion within the alliance and with the UN.[82] From the outset of Deliberate Force, NATO officers in Naples conducted a precision-attack marketing pitch. As with press conferences during the Gulf War, AFSOUTH displayed cockpit videos of precision munitions slamming into military targets.[83] In addition to these public presentations, Admiral Smith presented General Janvier a photograph to impress upon the UN commander NATO's sensitivity toward collateral damage and the alliance's ability to limit it.[84]

Contained in the photo was a large building with a red cross ringed by other buildings. The picture, taken by French reconnaissance aircraft, clearly showed the outermost buildings flattened, inner buildings left standing as a buffer, and the large building bearing the red cross untouched.[85]

Minimizing the number of BSA soldiers killed by Deliberate Force air operations was also important for keeping the UN on board with NATO, and it was something General Ryan elected to make a priority based on the peace-support nature of his mission. General Ryan's chief planner, Colonel Zoerb, identified certain elite BSA troops as desirable targets, believing the best way to stop Mladic was to attack his most effective fighting forces.[86] Two years after the campaign, when asked about the myriad political constraints bounding the air operation, General Ryan added,

> There was one that was unsaid . . . no one ever told me to do this, but, limit carnage—limit loss of life. So, we didn't hit buildings that had apparent administrative functions. . . . So we limited by time of day, by function, by location, loss of life on the Bosnian Serb Army side.[87]

As his chief of staff noted, "Anytime there was doubt, we didn't bomb. . . . When we went after targets where there might be people around, we went at two o'clock in the morning in a clear attempt on Mike's part to minimize loss of life."[88] General Ryan's efforts not only helped to keep the UN from breaking ranks, they also apparently facilitated the peace negotiations later at Dayton. At the Dayton peace talks, one member of the Bosnian Serb negotiating team alleged large numbers of casualties and collateral damage in an apparent attempt to strengthen the Serb bargaining position, but President Milosevic dismissed the ruse, claiming "that there were only 25 fatalities in the whole air campaign."[89]

General Ryan had good political and practical reasons for limiting BSA casualties. Political consent for the campaign, especially from the UN, dictated that NATO bombing go only so far in attacking the Serbs.[90] Avoiding BSA casualties as much as possible kept NATO from crossing a fuzzy line between coercive diplomacy and war. The UN could not have openly endorsed a campaign against the BSA without a new Security Council resolution, and Russia would certainly have vetoed that. Without the UN's legitimizing acquiescence for the campaign, NATO would probably have called for an end to Deliberate Force, leaving the US to decide whether to stop or continue with an ad hoc coalition. Moreover, had General Ryan purposely targeted BSA troops in their barracks or in the field, he would have initiated a dynamic that would have been difficult to control. As one senior NATO staff officer put it, "Lord knows that once you kill somebody over there, it becomes a family . . . vendetta, or religious thing, or whatever; and it's hard to stop the cycle."[91] AFSOUTH commanders knew that if Deliberate Force succeeded and a peace agreement followed, then NATO forces would be put on the ground in Bosnia to implement the agreement—and they would be responsible for commanding that force. In all likelihood, the commanders did not want to poison the post-Deliberate Force environment by giving the Bosnian Serbs cause for revenge. Thus, political and practical reasons militated against targeting BSA soldiers.

The Bombing Pause

Negotiations for a comprehensive settlement in the former Yugoslavia were ostensibly separate from the air strikes, which were conducted for the much narrower purpose of alleviating the Bosnian Serb threat to safe areas. Although General Ryan and Richard Holbrooke maintained an arms-length relationship and denied any connection between the negotiations and Deliberate Force, the two processes became linked on the second day of the campaign.[92] At Milosevic's instigation, through Paris and the UN—and with Holbrooke's support through Washington—General Janvier was invited to meet with General Mladic to discuss a halt to the bombing.[93] Janvier asked for a 24-hour hold on air strikes, and Admiral Smith consented.[94] Late evening on 31 August, the CAOC staff was notified to withhold all attacks after 4:00 A.M. the following morning—about 50 hours after the campaign had started.

On 1 September, Generals Janvier and Mladic met in the border town of Zvornik,[95] and Janvier sought to gain Mladic's signature on a document pledging compliance with UN and NATO demands.[96] The initial 24-hour pause was overcome by events as the meeting between the two commanders stretched toward the 14-hour mark. At the end of the meeting, Mladic brought Janvier a letter promising a Bosnian Serb cease-fire and a withdrawal from the Sarajevo exclusion zone so long as NATO and Bosnian government forces fulfilled certain Serb conditions.[97] Janvier refused to sign Mladic's letter but left for

Zagreb confident the BSA commander would soon agree to Western demands.[98] Admiral Smith and a small entourage from Naples flew to Zagreb to meet Janvier at his compound on the airport at Camp Pleso.[99] Janvier convinced Admiral Smith he had made significant progress toward getting Mladic to agree to halt BSA attacks on safe areas and to withdraw heavy weapons from around Sarajevo.[100] Without seeking political approval, Smith agreed to Janvier's proposal to extend the pause to 96 hours in order to give Mladic time to comply.[101] General Ryan's chief of staff, who was at the meeting between Janvier and Smith, notified the AIRSOUTH commander that it looked as though Deliberate Force might be over, but General Ryan "just postured the forces, getting ready to go again."[102]

The reactions of Holbrooke and Willy Claes to news of the longer pause demonstrated the political-military tension coercive diplomacy can engender over who gets to control the use of force. Upon learning of the elongated pause, the two political officials began pressing Admiral Smith and General Janvier to resume bombing. Richard Holbrooke spoke to Admiral Smith by phone, pushing him to restart the campaign.[103] Smith rebuffed pressures from outside the chain of command[104] and, in Holbrooke's opinion, the admiral "was edging into an area of political judgments that should have been reserved for civilian leaders."[105] As Holbrooke noted, "Smith saw it differently: He told me that he was 'solely responsible' for the safety and well-being of his forces, and he would make his decision, under authority delegated to him by the NATO Council, based on his own judgment."[106] However, Admiral Smith could not easily dismiss General Joulwan's complaints.[107] Although Admiral Smith had been given the NATO key for bombing, General Joulwan believed once operations commenced, he and the secretary-general were responsible for ensuring proper execution.[108] Meanwhile, the NATO secretary-general phoned Zagreb and asked Mr. Akashi to put Janvier on the phone. Even though Janvier was not in the NATO chain of command, Claes raged at the UN general for agreeing to the longer pause.[109] Given that NATO's credibility was at stake and given the importance of Holbrooke's diplomacy, Holbrooke and Claes apparently could not tolerate leaving the bombing decisions entirely to the discretion of the theater commanders.

The matter was finally settled by an ultimatum from the NAC. On the evening of 2 September, NATO ambassadors met to take up the issue of resuming Deliberate Force. Secretary-General Claes, "ruling on his own authority," told the NAC ambassadors they were assembled to reaffirm an earlier commitment to back the military commanders in their decisions; they were not gathered to decide themselves whether to resume bombing.[110] The meeting lasted into Sunday morning, 3 September, and ended with an ultimatum threatening to resume air strikes if the Bosnian Serbs did not (1) remove all heavy weapons from the 20-kilometer exclusion zone around Sarajevo; (2) cease all attacks on the remaining four safe areas; and (3) lift the siege of Sarajevo by allowing unhindered access by road and air to the Bosnian capital.[111] According to the ultimatum, the military commanders were free to recommence bombing operations "at any moment."[112]

The extended pause brought Admiral Smith and Richard Holbrooke, the two officials responsible for the different aspects of Western policy toward Bosnia, into conflict over who would control NATO airpower. According to Holbrooke, Admiral Smith used the risk to his forces and the authority granted him by NATO as a shield to block Holbrooke's attempt to influence bombing decisions. Holbrooke was leading negotiations on behalf of the West and was responsible for the outcome of what seemed to be the last, best chance to get a peace deal not only in Bosnia but in all of the former Yugoslavia.[113] Though he had a hand in stopping the bombing, he was blocked by Admiral Smith and General Janvier from restarting it. Moreover, according to Holbrooke, Admiral Smith forbade General Ryan from having any contact with Holbrooke's team.[114] Holbrooke could not invoke civilian control over the military himself to restart the bombing, so he pressed his views through those in Washington and Brussels who could exert pressure on Admiral Smith through US and NATO chains of command.[115] From a negotiator's perspective, it would have been helpful to have the legitimacy of alliance support and military responsiveness without the complications associated with getting 16 nations to agree on a common position and without having to act through military commanders whose allegiances were to their forces and to diverse international political authorities. As Holbrooke later wrote: "A great deal of any good negotiation is improvisation within the framework of a general goal."[116] Improvisation would not be possible without some control over the "sticks" used in coercive diplomacy. From the standpoint of a military commander, it would have been desirable to get clear objectives and political cover for operations without interference or remote steering from outside the chain of command. In addition to potential conflicts between military objectives of an operation and the shifting aims inherent in improvised negotiations, people outside the chain of command are unlikely to be held accountable for problems resulting from their interference in operational matters. Thus, with coercive diplomacy, political-military tension over who gets to control the use of force is probably inevitable.

The NATO ultimatum authorized General Janvier and Admiral Smith to resume bombing at their discretion, but the two commanders elected to give Mladic time to comply with the ultimatum.[117] On the night of 4 September, poor weather over Bosnia hindered NATO's attempts to verify signs of BSA compliance.[118] The weather cleared the next morning, and UN and NATO commanders were soon convinced that the vast majority of Serb heavy weapons remained inside Sarajevo's exclusion zone; by mid-morning they decided to go ahead with more air strikes.[119] At 1:05 P.M. on 5 September, NATO airpower once again began paring away at the BSA's war-fighting potential.[120]

Leveling the Playing Field and Coercing the Serbs

As discussed in chapter 2, air strategy is mainly a matter of targeting decisions intended to lead to the accomplishment of some objective. By keeping a tight hold on information about targets and battle damage assessment (BDA), General Ryan and Admiral Smith controlled bombing strategy.

SUNDAY	MONDAY	TUESDAY	WEDNESDAY	THURSDAY	FRIDAY	SATURDAY
AUGUST 27	28 **Trigger**	29	30	31	SEPTEMBER 1 **Pause**	2 **Pause**
3 **Pause**	4 **Pause**	5 **Bombing resumed; 1305 CET**	6	7	8	9 **First Dead Eye N-W Attack**
10 **Cruise missile strike**	11	12	13	14 **Cease-fire**	15	16

Figure 4. Time Line of Operation Deliberate Force. (The shaded area shows days on which NATO conducted bombing operations. Although 1 September is not shaded, NATO did drop bombs that day before the pause went into effect at 4:00 A.M. Central European Time.)

In doing so, the two sought to minimize risks to their forces while maximizing their chances of achieving the objectives of Deliberate Force. In the process though, Admiral Smith further alienated himself from Richard Holbrooke and upset some NATO political authorities who believed bombing operations were going too far.

New Objectives

During the bombing pause, NATO clarified the official objective of Deliberate Force, giving General Ryan a better chance to level the playing field and allowing Richard Holbrooke more scope to use the campaign as part of his coercive diplomacy. As Admiral Smith later put it, "The goalposts got moved." The day prior to the pause, the AFSOUTH commander told the press, "Our operation has one objective. It was stated clearly by Secretary-General Claes at NATO and that objective is to reduce the threat to the Sarajevo safe area and to deter further attacks there or on any other safe area."[121] However, at his first press conference after the pause, Smith stated,

> Now there are three conditions and you know that they are
> - no attacks on safe areas,
> - begin immediately a withdrawal of all heavy weapons from the 20-kilometer exclusion zone and complete that withdrawal without any halts or delays, and

- complete freedom of movement for the UN forces and recognized humanitarian aid distribution assets, as well as free access to Sarajevo airport.[122]

CINCSOUTH stressed, "Those objectives remain, they are not negotiable."[123] This suggested these three conditions for ending Deliberate Force had existed from the beginning of the campaign, but no such terms had been publicly articulated prior to the NAC ultimatum issued on 3 September.[124] More revealingly, Admiral Smith concluded the press conference by saying,

> Let me just tell you that we have a pretty good idea of what we want to accomplish in these operations. And whether it's visible to us or not, at this point I think we're making progress towards achieving the level that we desired. So I'm satisfied that we know enough about existing targets to affect the military capability if we continue this process.[125]

These remarks suggested the objective of Deliberate Force was to achieve a certain level of destruction against the Bosnian Serb military; that is, to level the playing field between BSA and Federation forces. Admiral Smith later conceded that "we never said what our objective was publicly," and that the objective was, in fact, to draw down the BSA's military capability in order to put them on a more even level with their adversaries.[126]

As a result of Admiral Smith's press conference on 6 September, General Joulwan issued a "Media Policy for Operation Deliberate Force."[127] The new policy directed subordinate commanders to "above all, keep NATO political authorities properly informed."[128] Aimed at preventing the first news about operations from reaching NATO ambassadors via their televisions, the new policy required all NATO officers to get clearance from Brussels before making any statements.[129] Admiral Smith subsequently left it to one of his senior staff officers, Group Capt Trevor Murray, to conduct press conferences for the remainder of Deliberate Force.[130] General Joulwan later explained that "a very important part for the strategic commander is to acquire the political consensus to give the operational commander flexibility, and to insure you hold 16 nations together."[131] In General Joulwan's view, when the NATO nations got together in the council and forged a position, then that one position set the objectives for the military even though the common position was unlikely to completely satisfy each individual nation—including the United States.[132] Satisfied that NATO had established conditions for success in Bosnia, General Joulwan did not want his subordinates upsetting the fragile political consensus arranged in Brussels.[133]

Battle Damage Assessment and Target Selection

Commanders in AFSOUTH were tight-lipped about the results of the bombing as Deliberate Force progressed, and that helped them to preserve their autonomy.[134] At the outset of Deliberate Force, General Ryan saw to it that a message went out directing all agencies involved in the operation to refrain from issuing estimates of BDA.[135] As General Ryan later explained, previous air operations stretching back to Vietnam taught him that tight controls were necessary:

> So that we didn't have nations, or particular intelligence agencies briefing BDA that was not corroborated and coming up with conclusions from that. None of the nations knew what targets were approved. . . . If you don't know what the target set is, you can't measure how you're doing, because you don't know what your objective is. And therefore, none of the other agencies were empowered in any way to say . . . whether we were accomplishing what we thought we needed to accomplish.[136]

General Ryan tracked the BDA very closely and provided all of the information to Admiral Smith, who then decided what to release.[137] Even General Janvier complained that he had difficulty getting BDA and never did get all of the damage assessments.[138] By controlling the BDA closely, AFSOUTH commanders prevented people on the fringes of policy making and people in the press from grading their performance.[139] It also kept NATO political authorities from "helping" the commanders with operational decisions. Finally, tight controls on BDA kept the Serbs in the dark about NATO operations and intentions. Speaking about BDA, General Ryan said,

> We didn't let Washington control it, or any of the other nations' capitals control it, because you didn't want to have people second-guessing what you were doing. The people you wanted second-guessing what you were doing were the Serbs, not the capitals.[140]

Thus, maintaining operational autonomy was one of the principal purposes for the tight controls over BDA.

In addition to restricting the release of BDA information, General Ryan exercised personal control in selecting every air strike target during Deliberate Force, further enhancing his autonomy.[141] Mike Ryan and Rupert Smith nominated targets for approval by Admiral Smith and General Janvier. Once those targets or target complexes were approved, General Ryan decided what to hit. In explaining his extraordinary degree of control over targeting, General Ryan told a US Air Force team studying the campaign that he was motivated mainly by his concern for collateral damage, saying:

> You cannot delegate selection . . . There will be no time in the future when [the air commander] will have the option to say, I delegate that responsibility. The commander must be accountable for all actions taken by his forces.[142]

A year after the Deliberate Force campaign, General Ryan expanded on that point at an airpower conference in London, noting: "Your targeting is always going to be joint, it's always going to be political, and I guarantee it's going to be on CNN, so you'd better get it right."[143] As the commander who was clearly responsible and accountable for the campaign, Ryan demanded control. Close control of target selection and, more importantly, the secrecy surrounding the target lists meshed well with controls on BDA to help General Ryan ensure he maintained autonomy in executing the campaign. Through the chain of command, General Ryan kept the NATO secretary-general informed of the campaign and its progress.[144] As noted above, Ryan did not want people outside the chain of command second-guessing his decisions, and keeping a tight control over targeting supported his freedom to operate without interference.

By controlling access to information about targets and BDA, General Ryan made it extremely difficult for outsiders to critique his performance. Undoubtedly it also helped maintain alliance cohesion and UN cooperation, at least for the duration of the campaign. Keeping quiet about the objective of leveling the playing field prevented nations in the UN or NATO that might have opposed weakening the BSA from breaking ranks. Governments that were sympathetic to the Bosnian Serb side, but had lost patience with the leaders in Pale, could go along with the bombing while genuinely claiming (naively perhaps) not to support measures that favored the Federation forces. Thus, the secrecy with which commanders in AFSOUTH guarded their objective, the targets they were hitting, and the progress of the campaign served to enhance the commanders' operational autonomy, alliance solidarity, and UN acquiescence while the bombs were falling. As the Balkans Air Campaign Study noted, secrecy was also necessary for operational security, enhancing both force protection and mission accomplishment.[145] Finally, it gave commanders and their political masters flexibility in deciding how far to go in prosecuting the campaign, making it difficult for outsiders to challenge claims that the operation succeeded in achieving the planned objectives. From the perspective of commanders responsible for the outcome of the campaign, there was no immediate downside to controlling information about targeting, BDA, or the campaign objective.

SEAD, Option 2½, and Coercion

When NATO commanders finally got around to attacking the heart of the Bosnian Serb air defense system in northwestern Bosnia, the attacks served several different objectives, thus demonstrating the potential leverage that force protection gives commanders for influencing the use of airpower. Shortly after bombing resumed on 5 September, Admiral Smith and General Ryan sought to eliminate the heart of the BSA air defense network in northwestern Bosnia. Admiral Smith later stated he had received intelligence reports that the BSA had moved SAM batteries south from Banja Luka to positions from which they could threaten NATO aircraft traveling to and from their targets.[146] Individual missile batteries were difficult to track; however, the threat they posed to NATO aircraft could be greatly reduced by destroying about a dozen command, control, and communications facilities located in northwestern Bosnia.[147] In that way, missile batteries would be forced to work in an autonomous mode without the benefit of information provided by the larger integrated air defense system. Operating autonomously, missile batteries would need to use their own radar, giving allied aircrews more warning while simultaneously making SAM operators more susceptible to attack from NATO SEAD aircraft. By deciding to execute the remainder of the Dead Eye plan, Admiral Smith and General Ryan made Deliberate Force operations safer for NATO aircrews.[148]

The response from Brussels over a cruise missile attack during the execution of Dead Eye-northwest demonstrated the accountability thrust upon commanders, even for problems they had not caused. To reduce risks to allied airmen, Admiral Smith requested permission from Washington to use cruise missiles against air defenses, and President Clinton reportedly authorized the attacks on 7 September.[149] However, the missile attacks, scheduled for the night of 8–9 September, were delayed for approximately 36 hours by General Joulwan so he could give NATO political authorities advance notice.[150] The AFSOUTH commanders elected to go ahead with the first strikes into northwestern Bosnia early on 9 September, using stand-off munitions from NATO aircraft. Hurriedly put together and marred by technical glitches, the raid achieved disappointing results.[151] When cruise missile strikes finally did go ahead on 10 September, they caused an uproar in Brussels, particularly from the French who complained NATO military authorities had overstepped their bounds by using cruise missiles.[152] For the military planners in AFSOUTH, the cruise missile was just another weapon, and it had the advantage of accuracy without risk to the lives of NATO airmen.[153] The missile attack was coordinated through NATO headquarters, but notification to NAC ambassadors went out late Sunday afternoon, 10 September, and the attack was made that evening.[154] Although the delays in notification originated in Brussels,[155] and even though AFSOUTH had approval from NATO Headquarters and Washington before the strike, Admiral Smith was made to bear the brunt of the political criticism for the cruise missile attack.[156] This indicated there would be no political shielding from Brussels if military operations went awry.[157]

The political consternation over the cruise missile strikes probably had more to do with political sensitivities over how far NATO should go with its graduated air campaign than with the use of the missiles, per se. The French had lost a Mirage 2000 on the first day of Deliberate Force, and its two-man crew was still missing, so it would have been illogical for the French to be upset about sending American missiles instead of French airmen against the Serb air defenses. By 10 September when the missile attack was made, AFSOUTH commanders were running low on worthwhile Option 1 and 2 targets in southeastern Bosnia and wanted to ratchet up the pressure on the Serbs to get them to comply with the NATO ultimatum from the previous week.[158] Hitting Dead Eye targets in northwestern Bosnia not only gave commanders their long awaited opportunity to eliminate threats to NATO aircrews but also gave them more targets to bomb. General Janvier recognized the larger military significance of the Bosnian Serb command and control facilities and other targets on the Dead Eye list.[159] The Bosnian Serbs were facing a ground offensive from Federation forces in western Bosnia, and Janvier viewed some Dead Eye northwest strikes as equivalent to Option 2½ air strikes.[160] Admiral Smith recalled discussing the issue with Janvier when General Ryan proposed hitting a large target complex called the "Banja Luka SAM Repair Facility;" Smith later said he told Janvier,

> I could defend it as an Option 2 target because that's where the facilities are, and we know that damned well they've got some SAMs in there. Or, I can say it's a 2½, to 3, and take it off [the list for now] and let's try to get it later. I was frankly afraid, at this point, that if we overstepped at all, the NAC would say: Stop. Or the UN would say: Stop. The UN had already told the RRF to cease and desist. They said: "You're not an offensive force. Stop."[161]

Thus, the French reaction to the cruise missile strike was probably a signal of growing discomfort over the shape Deliberate Force was taking, rather than a sign of displeasure about the choice of weapons being used in the campaign.[162]

Having nearly run out of Option 1 and 2 targets, Admiral Smith refused to risk the lives of NATO airmen by sending them to revisit targets that had been destroyed on earlier attacks. However, the lack of targets created a problem for

Richard Holbrooke because NATO bombing was a useful tool for his negotiations with Milosevic.[163] As General Ryan recalled,

> Holbrooke did some coordination, in telephone calls with [Admiral] Snuffy [Smith], and with Joulwan, and through the State Department. But, his biggest thing was: "Keep it up." That was his advice. . . . Keep hitting them. Because it's giving me great leverage, particularly over in Serbia.[164]

But the AFSOUTH commanders needed something to bomb in order to continue the campaign.[165] Admiral Smith later professed he was willing to get fired over certain issues, and "one of them was going back after targets that didn't make any difference, and bombing holes in the ground."[166] By 12 September, there were few targets and DMPIs left to bomb, and poor weather continued to interfere with Deliberate Force operations. Though they could scrape together enough targets for about another two days' worth of bombing, the commanders in AFSOUTH believed they were reaching the point of diminishing returns with Option 1 and 2 targets.[167] Furthermore, the UN secretary-general appeared to be trying to find a way to end the bombing,[168] and on 12 September Russia introduced a draft resolution in the Security Council, calling for an end to Deliberate Force.[169] As Admiral Smith later recalled,

> When we started getting down to the bottom of that funnel, and we were running out of targets, I was encouraged by at least one individual up the chain of command to go back and hit targets a second time. And I said: "No. I've been down that road, too. And I ain't going to send these pilots in there hitting holes in the ground because we don't have the political stomach to ratchet up the price. And we're not going to do that."[170]

According to Richard Holbrooke, some people in Washington did not believe the NATO commanders were running out of targets.

> [US Secretary of State Warren] Christopher told me he doubted that the military had really exhausted all its authorized Option Two targets. But there was no way to question the military within its own area of responsibility—the military controlled the information and independent verification was virtually impossible.[171]

Holbrooke was forced to make an unplanned return to Belgrade on 13 September to try to get a cease-fire before NATO commanders ran out of targets.[172]

As Deliberate Force air operations were coming to a close, commanders in AFSOUTH turned up the psychological pressure on the Serbs, including President Milosevic. At a news conference in Naples on 12 September, a member of the AFSOUTH staff handed out fact sheets on the F-117 stealth aircraft to journalists as they entered the room.[173] When the NATO spokesman, RAF Group Capt Trevor Murray, began taking questions, reporters asked about the F-117, a topic that had not been featured in Murray's briefing.[174] Apparently taken by surprise, Group Capt Murray denied plans to bring F-117s into theater, much to the bemusement of the journalists who were left wondering why they had been given the fact sheets.[175] F-117s had originally been a serious consideration for attacks against Bosnian Serb air defenses, and support equipment and personnel for the stealthy planes were already in Italy.[176] By 12 September, F-117s were no longer needed for Bosnia, and the apparent press conference snafu was a calculated attempt to make Serbia's president wonder what might be coming next.[177] Around the same time, officials at AFSOUTH began admitting to the press that NATO was running out of Option 1 and 2 targets, and it was time to consider Option 3.[178] Admiral Smith and General Ryan believed these psychological pressures might intimidate not only General Mladic, but also Milosevic, who would have been concerned already over the influx of refugees poised to enter Serbia because of the Federation ground offensive in Bosnia.[179] Poor weather over Bosnia led NATO to cancel nearly half of its sorties on 13 September as Richard Holbrooke held a hastily arranged meeting with Milosevic in Belgrade.[180] Holbrooke later wrote that this was his "moment of maximum leverage" and NATO bombing his "best bargaining chip."[181] After several hours of talks, Milosevic produced President Karadzic and General Mladic, and that night the Serbs agreed to the terms of the 3 September NATO ultimatum.[182] The bombing was suspended for 72 hours to give the Serbs a chance to comply with the agreement they had signed. After another 72 hours to allow the BSA to complete its withdrawal of heavy weapons from around Sarajevo, Deliberate Force officially ended.

Aftermath: More of the Same

Though Deliberate Force helped end the war in Bosnia, it did nothing to resolve two of the principal tensions underlying the contest to control airpower during Deny Flight: (1) the political-military tension over who controls the use of force and (2) the soldier-airman controversy over the efficacy of airpower. As NATO planners made preparations for the peace implementation force (IFOR), they sought to "NAC proof" the aerial rules of engagement to make sure NATO airmen would not again be hobbled in using force for self-defense.[183] Meanwhile, to make sure Admiral Smith was responsive to political direction from Brussels, someone at NATO headquarters proposed sending to Naples a special representative of the NATO secretary-general.[184] This political overseer would operate much the same as Mr. Akashi had for the UN secretary-general.[185] Admiral Smith balked at the suggestion, later claiming,

> I got a call one time from Mons saying that the NAC was going to send a Secretary-General's Special Rep to whom I would be responsible. . . . And I said: "Well when you send him, send another CINC, because I'm going to be gone." They didn't send him.[186]

When Smith later came under fire for not using the authority granted to him in the Dayton accords to apprehend suspected war criminals, he claimed,

> I told [NATO political authorities] time and again: "You want me to go after the [war] criminals, fine. You give me the orders, get . . . out of the way, but understand there's a price. There are going to be a lot of people killed. Probably going to set this peace process back a long way. But you give me the order, we'll go get them. We may not be successful, but we'll give it a . . . good try." They didn't like that.[187]

Admiral Smith apparently believed that whatever authority was given to him under the Dayton agreement, he still needed specific political orders from Brussels before using alliance forces in dangerous circumstances. And once given those orders, he wanted the alliance's political authorities to stay out of the operational details. At his change of command and premature retirement in July 1996,[188] Admiral Smith cautioned his successor,

> The further away people are from the problems, the more apt they are to have a solution for them. And . . . those who shout loudest for this or that action, are the ones who bear absolutely no responsibility for the consequences of those actions.[189]

Political authorities are unlikely to be comfortable making the sort of explicit commitments Admiral Smith desired. As Richard Betts argued, diplomats and politicians value flexibility just as military officers value commitment to policy objectives.[190] Moreover, using force creates a dynamic all of its own, and there is little incentive for a politician to commit to supporting a course of action that might lead to unintended and undesired consequences. It is far safer, politically, to keep one's choices open and to keep an arms-length relationship with policy implementation when it has the potential to backfire. This calculus can lead to political pressure for action without guarantees of political support for a commander should things go wrong. The riskier the venture, the greater disincentive a political official would have for making himself accountable for the consequences. However, when an operation poses high risks, military commanders will want to make their political masters aware of potential dangers and will want assurances that a proposed course of action is really what is desired. Guarantees from special representatives, secretary-generals, and assistant secretaries of executive departments are unlikely to suffice. Their authority is derivative, and they may have agendas not fully supported by the elected political leaders at the top of the chain of command. Furthermore, because of the clear accountability that goes with a military chain of command, commanders cannot depend on these second- and third-tier officials for top cover. Though the need to use airpower diminished greatly with the end of Deliberate Force, the political-military tension over controlling the use of force in Bosnia continued.

Assessments of Deliberate Force have confirmed Richard Betts's conclusion that beliefs for and against airpower tend to become articles of faith and that people on both sides of the airpower debate often draw opposite conclusions from the same evidence.[191] General Cot saw the Deliberate Force air strikes as long-range air support, and he judged that the RRF was a more important factor in the campaign's success, at least around Sarajevo, especially because, unlike airpower, "it did not depend on the weather of the moment."[192] General Briquemont believed what really mattered in 1995 was the change in the balance of power on the ground against the Serbs.[193] Finally, General Rose did not give the air campaign much credit for bringing the war to an end, noting,

> The NATO air campaign in Bosnia in August and September 1995 formed part of a series of strategic actions taking place at that time. These included the use of artillery and mortar by the UN Rapid Reaction Force to neutralise [sic] the Bosnian Serb heavy weapons around Sarajevo, the Croat-Muslim Federation ground offensive in the west of Bosnia, and most important of all, the emergence of a political settlement acceptable to all sides. The NATO air campaign was no more than a useful signal to the Serbs that the peacekeeping option had been suspended and that the West was now prepared to use a greater level of enforcement than before.[194]

Such judgments were consistent with the thinking of these generals during their tenures in command with the UN—reflecting the traditional soldiers' views of airpower as a supporting arm for the land forces.

The views of NATO officers also changed little, and airmen placed greater weight than did nonairmen on airpower's contribution to ending the war. General Ashy viewed the campaign as a success, seeing it as an execution of the planning he had done as far back as 1993.[195] General Ryan averred, "There were lots of other things going on; there was a ground operation going on in the west, there was diplomatic effort. . . . There was a lot going on, but Air Power is a decisive force."[196] The Balkans Air Campaign Study team reached the same conclusion.[197] Presumably, being a decisive force means that it was a necessary but perhaps not a sufficient element amongst the factors leading the Bosnian Serbs to comply with the 3 September NATO ultimatum. General Ryan's chief planner, Colonel Zoerb, considered the NATO airpower contribution far more important than that of the RRF.[198] Admiral Smith, who had been less enthusiastic about using airpower than his air component commanders, believed there was "a confluence of events that occurred in the June, July, August, September time frame that all came together very, very nicely to make airpower look a lot better, perhaps, than airpower was."[199] The point here is not to decide which judgment on the air campaign best captures its significance in the confluence of events during the summer of 1995, but to note that the participants' views on airpower changed little as a result of the campaign and that airmen placed a higher value on the airpower contribution than did soldiers.

Conclusion

During Deliberate Force, the soldier-airman dimension of the struggle for control over NATO airpower was less significant than the political-military dimension. Once General Janvier approved the first list of targets at the start of the campaign, tension between Janvier and Admiral Smith diminished greatly. This reflected the alignment of expertise and command responsibility; airmen controlled airpower in pursuit of a mission for which they were responsible. As the responsible air commander, General Ryan was given the freedom to use his expertise to manage the campaign and the risks to his forces. Thanks largely to Rupert Smith, UN ground forces were able to defend themselves and had little need to call for air support.[200] Because General Smith was delegated UN control for CAS, and Ryan had agreed that Smith would nominate CAS targets, General Smith possessed virtually complete control over the CAS mission. Therefore, as the responsible ground commander, Smith controlled resources commensurate with his responsibilities. These arrangements worked well not because of any formal doctrine (there was none) but because they reflected the advantages, from a military perspective, of marrying expertise, responsibility, and autonomy.[201]

The political-military aspect of the contest to control NATO airpower was less harmonious. Because the bombing gave Holbrooke leverage in his negotiations, he wanted some control over airpower—more than Admiral Smith was willing to concede. Holbrooke's negotiations were part of a larger policy that Deliberate Force supported. Therefore, it was only natural for Holbrooke to want to control NATO airpower, especially in light of his limited ability to influence other elements supporting his coercive diplomacy, such as the Federation ground offensive. However, Admiral Smith's superior expertise in military matters and his responsibility for the lives of allied forces—not just US forces—led him to resist pressures coming from outside the chain of command. Expertise, control of information, and responsibility for NATO forces also worked for theater-level commanders as powerful tools for keeping control over Operation Deliberate Force. This strong military influence in such a highly politicized operation did not sit well with some of the political authorities concerned.

Notes

1. *Facts On File Yearbook 1995* (USA: Facts On File, Inc., 1996), 619.

2. Ibid.

3. Ibid., 629.

4. David Binder, "Bosnia's Bombers," *The Nation*, 2 October 1995, 337; and Joris Janssen Lok, "Deny Flight Turns to Affirmative Action," *Jane's Defence Weekly*, 9 September 1995, 57.

5. Kevin Fedarko, "Louder Than Words," *Time*, 11 September 1995, 57; and John Ridding, Harriet Martin, and Laura Silber, "Bosnian Threat to Quit Talks Unless NATO Punishes Serbs," *Financial Times* (London), 30 August 1995, 1.

6. Laura Silber and Bruce Clark, "US Warns Serbs as Bosnia Moves Resume," *Financial Times* (London), 28 August 1995, 2.

7. Rick Atkinson, "The Anatomy of NATO's Decision to Bomb Bosnia," *International Herald Tribune*, 17 November 1995, 2; Binder, 336–37; and Bruce W. Nelan, "The Balkans: More Talking, More Bombing," *Time*, 18 September 1995, 76.

8. Nelan, 76; and Harriet Martin, "UN Threatens Raids as Mortar Attack Kills 37 in Sarajevo," *Financial Times* (London), 29 August 1995, 1.

9. Maj Gen Michael C. Short, USAF, chief of staff, Allied Air Forces Southern Europe, July 1995–May 1996, Naples, interviewed by author, 2 May 1997, Ramstein Air Base (AB), Germany, tape recording, author's personal collection; Col Daniel R. Zoerb, USAF, director, Deny Flight Air Operations Center, Naples, Italy, January 1994–May 1996, interviewed by author, 25 May 1997; Col Steven Teske, USAF, CAOC director of plans, May–November 1995, interviewed by author, 6 May 1997, Aviano AB, Italy, tape recording, author's personal collection; and Atkinson, 2.

10. Military Official Q.

11. Royal Welch Fusiliers (RWF), 1st Battalion, *White Dragon: The Royal Welch Fusiliers in Bosnia* (Wrexham, UK: RWF Regimental Headquarters, 1995), 69–70.

12. Atkinson, 2; Col Robert C. Owen, *Deliberate Force: A Case Study in Effective Air Campaigning* (Maxwell Air Force Base (AFB), Ala.: Air University Press, 2000), 135; and Military Official Q.

13. Owen, 131.

14. Lt Gen Bernard Janvier, French army, commander of United Nations Protection Force, Zagreb, Croatia, March 1995–December 1995, interviewed by author, 12 January 1998, Paris, author's notes, author's personal collection; and Maj Michael O. Beale, *Bombs over Bosnia: The Role of Airpower in Bosnia-Herzegovina* (Maxwell AFB, Ala.: Air University Press), 36. A report citing a US admiral said that by the end of August the UN had reduced the number of peacekeepers in Bosnia from a peak of "22,000 to fewer than 3,600." Steve Komarow, "U.N. Pullback Gives NATO Jets Breathing Room," *USA Today,* 13 September 1995, 1. There were some Russian soldiers in a Bosnian Serb-held area near Sarajevo but, because of the traditional close relationship between the Serbs and Russians, they were not expected to be in any danger of being taken hostage. *Facts On File Yearbook 1995,* 630.

15. Col Robert C. Owen, USAF, "The Balkans Air Campaign Study: Part 2," *Airpower Journal* 11, no. 3 (autumn 1997): 7, (hereafter cited as Owen, "Balkans: Part 2").

16. Owen, *Deliberate Force,* 110.

17. Ibid., 131–32; Col Steve Teske, USAF, interviewed by Lt Col Christopher Campbell, et al., 14 February 1996, Ramstein AB, Germany, transcripts of taped interview, Balkans Air Campaign Study (BACS) Collection, Air Force Historical Research Agency, Maxwell AFB, Ala.; and Col Daniel R. Zoerb, interviewed by author, 29 April 1997, Spangdahlem AB, Germany, transcript of tape recording, author's personal collection.

18. United States Department of Defense (DOD), "DOD News Briefing," Pentagon, 29 August 1995 (1:30 P.M.), transcript of press conference, http://www.dtic.mil:80//defenselink/news.

19. Owen, *Deliberate Force,* 135; and Teske, 14 February 1996.

20. Military Official Q.

21. Adm Leighton W. Smith, USN, interviewed by author, 10 February 1998, Arlington, Virginia, transcript of tape recording, author's personal collection; Short interview; and Atkinson.

22. Janvier interview; and Smith interview.

23. Smith interview. Admiral Smith admitted he was exaggerating the urgency slightly because the first round of strikes were going after air defense targets and did not require Janvier's approval. However, the second batch of strikes, which Janvier did need to approve, was scheduled within two hours of the first.

24. Ibid.

25. Ibid.

26. Ibid.

27. Ibid.; Janvier interview; Military Official Q; and Owen, *Deliberate Force,* 410.

28. Smith interview; and Zoerb interview, 29 April 1997.

29. During and after Deliberate Force, some observers interpreted the repeated bombing of certain targets as wasted attacks against holes in the ground. See Allied Forces Southern Europe (AFSOUTH), "NATO Operation Deliberate Force," transcript of press briefing, Naples, 9 September 1995

(5:00 P.M.), http://www.afsouth.nato.int/archives/archives.htm; idem, 12 September 1995; and Jan Willem Honig and Norbert Both, Srebrenica: Record of a War Crime (London: Penguin Books, 1996), 186 n.11.

30. Col W. Hays Parks, " 'Precision' Bombing and 'Area' Bombing: Who Did Which, and When?" *Journal of Strategic Studies* 18, no. 1 (March 1995): 145–74.

31. Target Descriptions: Pale Ammo Depot South and Hadzici Ammo Storage Depot, File C2a(2), BACS Collection.

32. The *DOD Dictionary of Military Terms* contains four US definitions for the word *target* and five NATO definitions. The first definition offered for both United States and NATO usage is: "a geographical area, complex, or installation planned for capture or destruction by military forces." The dictionary does not include a listing for either *aim point* or *desired mean point of impact*, or *DMPI*, which air planners, targeteers, and aircrews use to denote specific targets within a larger target complex. Joint Chiefs of Staff, US Department of Defense, *Dictionary of Military Terms* (London: Greenhill Books, 1991), 388.

33. Owen, *Deliberate Force*, 199; and Gen Michael E. Ryan, USAF, commander Allied Air Forces Southern Europe and commander US Sixteenth Air Force, September 1994–April 1996, slides from a briefing to Air Power Conference, London, 13 September 1996, slide nos. 43 and 44. Of the total 1,026 bombs dropped, 738 were PGMs.

34. Adm Leighton W. Smith, commander in chief NATO Allied Forces Southern Europe, briefing to the US Air Force Air War College, Maxwell AFB, Ala., 9 November 1995, videocassette of briefing, File MISC-19, folder H-4, BACS Collection.

35. Target Descriptions: Pale Ammo Depot South and Hadzici Ammo Storage Depot, File C2a(2), BACS Collection.

36. Owen, *Deliberate Force*, 410–11; and Gen Joseph W. Ashy, USAF, interviewed by Lt Col Robert Owen, 29 April 1996, Washington, unclassified version of "General Ashy's Oral History Interview," (66 pp.) redacted by the Air Force Historical Research Agency, October 1997, Office of History, Air Force Space Command, Peterson AFB, Colo. MCM-KAD-084-93, "Operational Options for Airstrikes," from August of 1993 contained an explicit statement directing NATO commanders to try to minimize collateral damage.

37. Target Descriptions: Hadzici Ammo Storage Depot, Military Repair Depot, and Storage Facility, File C2a(2), BACS Collection.

38. Ibid.

39. Smith, briefing to Air War College.

40. Zoerb interview, 29 April 1997.

41. Target Description: Sarajevo Army Barracks and Ordnance Depot, File C2a(2), BACS Collection.

42. Smith, briefing Air War College; and Col Daniel R. Zoerb, USAF, interviewed by author, 30 April 1997, Spangdahlem AB, Germany, transcript of tape recording, author's personal collection.

43. Smith interview; and Military Official Q.

44. Janvier interview; and Military Official Q.

45. Richard Holbrooke, *To End A War* (New York: Random House, 1998), 99 and 103. According to Holbrooke: "Annan's gutsy performance in those twenty-four hours was to play a central role in Washington's strong support for him a year later as the successor to Boutros Boutros-Ghali as secretary-general of the United Nations. Indeed, in a sense, Annan won the job on that day."

46. Smith interview.

47. Adm Leighton W. Smith, USN, "NATO Air Strike Against Bosnia Serbs," transcript of news conference, 31 August 1995 (10:00 A.M.) http://www.afsouth.nato.int/archives/archives.htm.

48. Owen, "Balkans: Part 2," 9.

49. Ryan interview; and Zoerb interview, 29 April 1997.

50. Owen, "Balkans: Part 2," 9; Lt Gen Hal M. Hornburg, USAF, deputy commander Sixteenth Air Force and CAOC director, November 1994–September 1996, interviewed by Maj Tim Reagan and Dr. Wayne Thompson, 16 October 1995, Vicenza, Italy, transcript of tape recording, BACS Collection; Zoerb interview, 30 April 1997; and Short interview.

51. Owen, "Balkans: Part 2," 9; and Owen, *Deliberate Force*, 159–60 and 410–11.

52. Gen Michael E. Ryan, USAF, "NATO Air Operations in Bosnia-Herzegovina: Deliberate Force, 29 August–14 September 1995," transcript of briefing to Air Power Conference, London, 13 September 1996; and Zoerb interview, 29 April 1997.

53. Ryan, transcript of briefing to Air Power Conference; and Zoerb interview, 29 April 1997.

54. Ryan, transcript of briefing to Air Power Conference; and Zoerb interview, 29 April 1997.

55. Owen, *Deliberate Force*, 111 and 136–37.

56. The French Mirage 2000 shot down on the first day of Deliberate Force was hit by a shoulder-fired, infrared-guided SAM near Sarajevo. Attacking the Bosnian Serb IADS could do little to neutralize such threats, and the best defense against them was to stay above their reach.

57. See chap. 7 of this publication.

58. Owen, "Balkans: Part 2," 7.

59. Owen, *Deliberate Force*, 111 and 136.

60. Zoerb interview, 29 April 1997; and Owen, *Deliberate Force*, 111 and 136.

61. Ryan interview; and Zoerb interview, 30 April 1998.

62. Daniel J. Hughes, ed., *Moltke on the Art of War* (Novato, Calif.: Presidio Press, 1993), 45.

63. To differentiate between the types of targets that were bombed, I will refer to targets hit in order to degrade the BSA's war-fighting potential as "Deliberate Force targets," using that term interchangeably with "air strike targets." The other category of targets hit during Operation Deliberate Force will be referred to as "Dead Eye targets," a term I will alternate with "air defense targets" or "IADS targets."

64. Ryan interview.

65. Ibid.; and Ryan, transcript of Air Power Conference.

66. General Ryan and a handful of other CAOC leaders and US planners hardly slept from the outset of Deliberate Force until the pause two days later. Owen, "Balkans: Part 2," 10; Owen, *Deliberate Force*, 113, 364, and 487; Teske interview by author; and Ryan interview.

67. See, for example, United States Department of Defense, Conduct of the Persian Gulf War: Final Report to Congress (n.p.: Government Printing Office, April 1992), appendix O, "The Role of the Law of War," esp. 611–17; and Royal United Services Institute (RUSI), *The Democratic Management of Defence*, Whitehall Paper 16 (London: RUSI, 1992), 48–52.

68. Ryan interview; and Ryan, transcript of Air Power Conference.

69. The reason why the priorities ought to align this way follows the same logic as in the discussion of ROE, weakness errors, and escalation errors covered in chap. 2, section entitled "Rules of Engagement: Circumstances for Force."

70. Owen, *Deliberate Force*, 383 and 416–21. Admiral Smith made this point repeatedly in his press conferences during Deliberate Force and in his briefing to the Air War College.

71. Owen, *Deliberate Force*, 150 and 411–12.

72. Ibid.

73. Owen, "Balkans: Part 2," 17–18.

74. Smith, briefing to Air War College; and Ryan, transcript of Air Power Conference.

75. Smith, briefing to Air War College.

76. NATO Official C.

77. Ryan, transcript of Air Power Conference.

78. As discussed in chap. 6. For a discussion of collateral damage, proportionality, and future implications regarding PGMs, see Owen, *Deliberate Force*, 410–12 and 416–21.

79. NATO, Press Release (95) 73, 30 August 1995; and Smith, transcript of news conference, 31 August 1995.

80. Smith interview; Owen, "Balkans: Part 2," 14. A key planner and Chief G2/G3 on the RRF Operations Staff (RRFOS), Col D. V. Nicholls, made no mention in his article for *RUSI Journal* of UN orders to halt offensive operations. However, RUSI's annual *International Security Review* for 1996 reported the RRF fired 1,000 shells before the pause on 1 September, and an RRFOS briefing showed 1,381 total rounds fired when the campaign ended on 14 September. Col David V. Nicholls, Royal Marines, "Bosnia: UN and NATO," *RUSI Journal* 141, no. 1 (February 1996): 35–36; Royal United Services Institute, *International Security Review 1996* (London: RUSI, 1996), 69; Rapid Reaction Force Operations Staff, "HQ 1 (UK) ARMD DIV RRFOS Brief, 17 November 95," slide no. 25.

81. For a discussion of collateral damage, proportionality, and future implications regarding PGMs, see Owen, *Deliberate Force*, chap. 14 by Lt Col Ronald M. Reed.

82. Smith, briefing to Air War College.

83. Smith, "NATO Air Strikes," press conference, 31 August 1995; Rick Atkinson, "NATO Tailors Bombing Information," *Washington Post*, 16 September 1995, A20; and William Matthews, "Accuracy is Phenomenal," *Air Force Times*, 2 October 1995, 10.

84. Smith, briefing to Air War College.

85. When the author interviewed General Janvier in 1998 and asked about the photo, the general had his military aid fetch the framed photograph from his office.

86. Zoerb interview, 29 April 1997.

87. Ryan interview.

88. Short interview.

89. Amb. Christopher Hill, US State Department, interviewed by Lt Col Robert Owen, 27 February 1996, transcript of tape recording, File H-1, BACS Collection. Also see Beale, 37. Note: The figure of 25 killed is not to be taken as an official or reliable estimate of the number of casualties from Deliberate Force.

90. Janvier interview.

91. Lt Gen Patrick K. Gamble, USAF, assistant chief of staff, Operations and Logistics, SHAPE, interviewed by author, 2 July 1998, Washington, tape recording, author's personal collection.

92. The connections between the two appear to have been indirect, with Holbrooke working through the State Department or NATO Headquarters, only once calling Admiral Smith directly.

93. Janvier interview; Holbrooke, 107–14; and Atkinson, "Anatomy of NATO's Decision."

94. AFSOUTH, "Operation Deliberate Force" Fact Sheet, 5 October 1995, 4.

95. Janvier interview; *Facts On File Yearbook 1995*, 645.

96. Military Official Q.

97. Ibid.

98. Short interview; Rick Atkinson, "Put to the Test, NATO Shows Its Mettle," *International Herald Tribune*, 20 November 1995, 2; and Military Official Q.

99. Smith interview; Short interview; and Military Official Q.

100. Ibid.

101. Smith interview; and Military Official Q.

102. Short interview; and Atkinson, "Put to the Test."

103. Joulwan interview, 11 February 1998; Smith interview; and Holbrooke, 118.

104. Smith interview; Holbrooke, 118.

105. Holbrooke, 118.

106. Ibid.

107. Smith interview; Joulwan interview, 11 February 1998; and Holbrooke, 118–19.

108. Joulwan interview, 11 February 1998. In my interview with General Joulwan, he said he cited the terms of reference set up by the first SACEUR,

General Eisenhower, to support his case for taking the role as chief executor for Operation Deliberate Force.

109. Janvier interview; and Atkinson, "Put to the Test."

110. Holbrooke, 120; NATO Officials C and D.

111. DOD News Briefing, Pentagon, 5 September 1995.

112. NATO, "Statement by the Secretary-General Following Council Meeting-2 September 1995," Press Release, 3 September 1995.

113. Holbrooke, 119.

114. Ibid., 145 and 362.

115. Holbrooke, 118–20.

116. Ibid., 111.

117. NATO, "Statement Following Council Meeting," 3 September 1995.

118. Admiral Smith, "NATO Recommences Air Strikes Against Bosnian Serbs," transcript of press conference, 6 September 1995.

119. Smith, "NATO Recommences;" and Military Official Q.

120. Smith, "NATO Recommences;" and John Thornhill, John Ridding, and Bruce Clark, "Hardline Serbs Solve West's Dilemma," *Financial Times* (London), 6 September 1995, 2.

121. Admiral Smith, "NATO Air Strike Against Bosnian Serbs," transcript of news conference, Naples, 31 August 1995.

122. Smith, "NATO Recommences."

123. Ibid.

124. Smith interview.

125. Ibid.

126. Ibid.

127. Joulwan interview, 11 February 1998; and Atkinson, "NATO Tailors."

128. Gen George Joulwan, cited in Atkinson, "NATO Tailors."

129. Joulwan interview, 11 February 1998; and Atkinson, "NATO Tailors."

130. Admiral Smith next appeared at a press conference on 15 September, a day after suspending Deliberate Force bombing operations. Group Captain Murray ran the meetings with the media on 9, 11, and 12 September. Group Captain Murray's press conferences were all held at 5:00 P.M. Central European Time (CET), in keeping with General Joulwan's guidance. See transcripts of AFSOUTH press conferences 6, 9, 11, 12, and 15 September 1995; and Atkinson, "NATO Tailors."

131. Joulwan interview, 11 February 1998.

132. Ibid.

133. Ibid.

134. For a discussion of the other reasons for controlling BDA during Deliberate Force, see the chapter by Maj Mark McLaughlin entitled, "Combat Assessment: A Commander's Responsibility," in Owen, *Deliberate Force.*

135. Ryan interview. See also Owen, *Deliberate Force*, 183–84; and Owen, "Balkans: Part 2," 13.

136. Ryan interview.

137. Ibid.; and Smith interview.

138. Janvier interview.

139. Owen, "Balkans: Part 2," 13; and Owen, *Deliberate Force*, 360.

140. Ryan interview.

141. Owen, "Balkans: Part 2," 9.

142. Gen Michael E. Ryan, USAF, interviewed by Balkans Air Campaign Study team, 7 February 1996, Maxwell AFB, Ala., cited in Owen, *Deliberate Force*, 57–58.

143. Ryan, transcript of Air Power Conference.

144. Joulwan interview, 11 February 1998; Smith interview; and Ryan interview.

145. Owen, *Deliberate Force*, 185.

146. Smith, briefing to Air War College.

147. 7490 Composite Wing (P), memorandum for CAOC, 7 September 1995, File C2a(2), BACS Collection.

148. Smith, briefing to Air War College.

149. Smith interview; and Bradley Graham, "U.S. Fires Cruise Missiles at Bosnia Serb Sites," *Washington Post*, 11 September 1995, A18.

150. Joulwan interview, 11 February 1998; Smith interview; and NATO Official D.

151. Lt Col Joseph Wood, USAF, commander 492d Fighter Squadron, F-15Es, interviewed by author, 5 March 1997, London, transcript of tape recording, author's personal collection.

152. Owen, "Balkans: Part 2," 12; Smith interview; NATO Official D; and Tim Ripley, *Operation Deliberate Force* (Lancaster, UK: Centre for Defence and International Security Studies, University of Lancaster, 1999).

153. Smith interview; and Zoerb interview, 29 April 1998.

154. Joulwan interview, 11 February 1998; and NATO Official D.

155. Joulwan interview, 11 February 1998; Smith interview; Gamble interview; and NATO Official D.

156. Smith interview.

157. NATO Official D.

158. Short interview; Ryan interview; and Smith interview.

159. Janvier interview; and Military Official Q.

160. Janvier interview.

161. Smith interview.

162. The nature of Deliberate Force and the coincidental Federation ground offensive have made it difficult to determine whether the connection between the two campaigns was preplanned or opportunistic. Research for this study has not uncovered any evidence to contradict official claims that it was not preplanned, but that is hardly surprising or definitive.

163. Holbrooke, 145–51.

164. Ryan interview.

165. The officer running the BDA cell for General Ryan was RAF Wing Comdr Andy Bachelor. He told BACS researchers that during the campaign there was no intentional bombing of targets that had already been

destroyed. Due to the shortage of targets with a higher payoff, some partially destroyed targets were reattacked late in the campaign. Wing Comdr Andy Bachelor, RAF, head of Battle Damage Assessment Cell during Operation Deliberate Force, interviewed by Maj John C. Orndorff, USAF, 14 February 1996, Ramstein AB, Germany, tape recording, BACS Collection. Ratios for bombs dropped compared to targets, or DMPIs, attacked supported Bachelor's assertion: 2.8 PGMs and 6.6 general-purpose bombs per DMPI. PGMs are usually dropped in pairs, and general-purpose bombs (i.e., non-PGMs) are usually dropped in multiples of two, with six per pass being common. General Ryan, transcript of Air Power Conference. Also see Richard P. Hallion, "Precision Guided Munitions," *Air Power History* 43, no. 3 (fall 1996): 13.

166. Smith interview.

167. Ibid.; Ryan, transcript of Air Power Conference; and Ryan interview.

168. Laura Silber and Bruce Clark, "UN in Split with NATO on Bosnia Bombing Campaign," *Financial Times* (London), 13 September 1995, 22.

169. Facts On File 1995, 662.

170. Smith interview.

171. Holbrooke, 146.

172. Ibid.

173. Military Official X.

174. AFSOUTH, transcript of press briefing, Naples, 12 September 1995.

175. Military Official X.

176. General Ryan requested six F-117s on 8 September. They were approved by the US secretary of defense on 9 September. Personnel and equipment needed to support F-117 operations were deployed to Italy, but on 11 September the Italian government turned down the American request to bring the planes into Italy. Owen, *Deliberate Force*, 243–45; and Ryan, transcript of Air Power Conference.

177. Ryan interview; and Smith interview.

178. Daniel Williams and Rick Atkinson, "Limits on Targets Hamper NATO, U.N. Officers Say," *Washington Post*, 13 September 1995, A1 and A14; Eric Schmitt, "NATO Commanders Face Grim Choices," *New York Times*, 14 September 1995, 1; Bruce Clark, "Bombing Raids Damage Diplomatic Bridges," *Financial Times* (London), 14 September 1995, 2.

179. Smith interview; and Ryan interview.

180. AFSOUTH, "Operation Deliberate Force," Fact Sheet, 7; and Holbrooke, 146–48.

181. Holbrooke, 151.

182. Ibid., 148–52.

183. Private discussion with US Air Force officer responsible for IFOR planning.

184. Smith interview; and Zoerb interview, 27 May 1998.

185. Joulwan interview, 11 February 1998; Smith interview; and Zoerb interview, 27 May 1998.

186. Smith interview.

187. Ibid.

188. Admiral Smith received his fourth star in conjunction with his assignment as commander in chief Allied Forces Southern Europe. When he retired two years later, he still had not reached the 35-year mandatory retirement point.

189. Remarks of Admiral Smith in, AFSOUTH, "AFSOUTH Change of Command," transcripts from change of command ceremony, 31 July 1996. Admiral Smith was later given an honorary knighthood by Britain, which some observers viewed as a gesture of appreciation for Smith's resistance to using force more often in Bosnia.

190. Richard K. Betts, *Soldiers, Statesmen, and Cold War Crises* (Cambridge, Mass.: Harvard University Press, 1977; reprint with new preface and epilogue, New York: Columbia University Press, 1991), 36 and 76.

191. Betts, 203.

192. Gen Jean Cot, French army, "Dayton ou la Porte Etroite: Genese et Avenir d'un Désastre," in *Dernière Guerre Balkanique?* 2d ed., ed. Jean Cot (France: Editions L'Harmattan, 1996), 123.

193. Lt Gen Francis Briquemont, *Do Something, General!: Chronique de Bosnie-Herzégovine 12 juillet 1993–24 janvier 1994* (Bruxelles: Éditions Labor, 1997), 133.

194. Gen Sir Michael Rose, British army, retired, *Fighting for Peace: Bosnia 1994* (London: The Harvill Press, 1998), 238. General Rose erroneously claimed that "nearly 100 cruise missiles" were fired during Deliberate Force. The actual number of cruise missiles fired was 13—all on 10 September.

195. Ashy interview by Owen. The targets struck during Operation Deliberate Force had their roots in the planning begun under General Ashy. Like Deliberate Force, General Ashy's plans would have degraded the BSA's military capability. However, research done for this study suggests the logic behind Deliberate Force was based on studies of the BSA undertaken during General Ryan's tenure. The center of gravity analysis, determination of an end state, and heavy reliance on PGMs were the product of planning conducted under General Ryan. Moreover, Dead Eye was also produced during General Ryan's time in Naples.

196. Ryan, transcript of Air Power Conference.

197. Owen, "Balkans: Part 2," 24.

198. Zoerb interview, 27 May 1998.

199. Smith interview.

200. Ten CAS missions were executed the first day of Deliberate Force, all against preplanned heavy weapons sites. As the CAOC plans director, Col Steve Teske, describes these missions, they were really battlefield air interdiction with forward air controllers, rather than what would normally be considered close air support. Despite the large number of CAS sorties flown just in case they might be needed, few expended ordnance because the BSA did not attack UN forces. One exception to this occurred around Tuzla on 10 September.

201. On the absence of doctrine, see Owen, "Balkans: Part 1," 11–12; and Col Maris McCrabb's "US and NATO Doctrine for Campaign Planning," chap. 3 in Owen, *Deliberate Force.*

Chapter 10

Conclusions: Military Influence on Airpower in Bosnia

When the external threat is low, policy decisions appear less consequential and so policy costs are lower—what does it matter if civilian interference has disastrous side effects when there is no Soviet menace to capitalize on the error?

—Peter D. Feaver
"Crisis as Shirking: An Agency
Theory Explanation of the Souring
of Civil-Military Relations"

Theater-level commanders in the UN and NATO served as more than mere executors of policy, and, in so doing, they significantly influenced the use of airpower in Bosnia between the summers of 1993 and 1995. Of the various reasons commanders chose to play the roles that they did, their expertise and responsibilities as commanders were important factors. However, expertise and responsibility for mission accomplishment and force protection often reinforced other forces motivating theater-level commanders, such as national political pressures and UN and NATO organizational preferences. If one examines the actions of commanders across the entire period of Deny Flight, certain patterns emerge indicating the role of expertise and command responsibility. During Deny Flight, theater-level commanders demonstrated an appreciation for their responsibility for and to people under their command, not just responsibility upward to the state or to multinational political authorities. Unlike tactical determinism, which rests on limitations in the capabilities of military means (i.e., What feasibly can be done?), responsibility sets limits based on what ought to be done and who will be held accountable (i.e., Is it worth it?). Without clear, authoritative guidance about objectives, theater-level commanders in NATO and the UN turned to their own internal compasses for direction in decisions

313

about how much risk to take in order to use airpower in Bosnia. Commanders also demonstrated that responsibility for people's lives served as more than just a basis for decisions; it also worked as a tool for gaining autonomy and influence in operational matters.

How UN Commanders Influenced Airpower

The UN's theater-level commanders significantly influenced the use of airpower in Bosnia. They all wanted close air support, and, with the exception of Gen Rupert Smith, all opposed air strikes. Generals Briquemont and Cot were the first (and last) UN commanders to attempt to reconcile the ambiguities inherent in the safe areas policy. Both left their tours of duty early because of clashes with civilian political authorities over acquiring and controlling the means for fulfilling command responsibilities of mission accomplishment and force protection. Unlike Briquemont and Cot, who sought clearer political direction for their mission, General Rose offered his own interpretation via his campaign plan. By winning approval in the UK and the UN for a campaign plan focused on the humanitarian and peacekeeping elements of UNPROFOR's mandate, General Rose reduced UNPROFOR's needs for NATO airpower. Later, General Rose not only shaped the terms of the Sarajevo ultimatum to mirror the impartiality needed for peacekeeping, he also used UN forces to help Bosnian Serbs meet the ultimatum deadline. In addition, he controlled information about the degree of Bosnian Serb compliance with the ultimatum and later lapses in Serb compliance with the exclusion zone around Sarajevo in order to head off NATO air strikes. At Gorazde, General Rose held tight control over NATO airpower, and he attempted to conduct limited air strikes in the guise of close air support for his special forces. However, after Gorazde, he used the dual key to delay air strikes so he could issue warnings to the Bosnian Serbs and control targeting decisions for air strikes. General Rose was a central figure in influencing NATO's first-ever uses of airpower for bombing operations, and the course he chose minimized the need to make trade-offs between the lives of his soldiers and his interpretation of UNPROFOR's mission.

General Rose's immediate superior in the UN chain of command, General de Lapresle, initially played a less direct role in influencing the use of NATO airpower. De Lapresle helped solidify the UN's stance against the use of airpower to enforce the safe areas policy. He did this by educating Mr. Akashi in the ways of using airpower and by adding military legitimacy to the UN Secretariat's position that UNPROFOR's job was to deter through its presence and that it could not be expected to act more forcefully without the necessary ground forces for doing so. Later in 1994, General de Lapresle took a more direct role in shaping the employment of airpower by using the dual key to limit NATO air strikes at Udbina and to block SEAD operations after the first air defense suppression missions on 23 November 1994. De Lapresle's successor, General Janvier, was equally opposed to robust air action and tried to restrain his more activist subordinate, Gen Rupert Smith. Though influential in advising against air strikes in early May of 1995 and in delaying close air support at Srebrenica, Janvier was ultimately outmaneuvered by other theater-level commanders and overruled by political authorities. Rather than dumping the enforcement elements of UNPROFOR's mandate, as Janvier and the UN Secretariat preferred, General Smith cleared the way for forceful action, including NATO air strikes. He did so by precipitating a hostage crisis. He also helped commanders in NATO broaden the allowable zone for air strikes by proposing that the area around Tuzla be contained in both zones of action for Deliberate Force.

Generals Briquemont, Cot, de Lapresle, and Janvier used fairly conventional means to try to influence the use of airpower in Bosnia. Except for Briquemont's public criticism of air strikes in August 1993 and Cot's complaints to the press about not having approval authority for close air support missions, these commanders generally worked within the UN chain of command or their own national chains of command. The other UN commanders, Michael Rose and Rupert Smith, took unusual measures to influence the use of airpower: Rose, by issuing warnings to the Serbs; Smith, by causing the hostage crisis. Even when working within the UN chain of command, certain commanders took active roles in shaping

315

policy. General Rose demonstrated the enduring truth in Betts's finding: "Advocates of an existing plan have an advantage over opponents who do not have one of their own."[1] By introducing his own campaign plan, Rose moved the UN mission away from enforcement. UN Security Council ambassadors such as Madeleine Albright, who favored a more forceful approach in Bosnia, had no military advocate in the UN to counter General Rose's plan. Likewise, General de Lapresle's endorsement of the interpretation of UNPROFOR's mission put forward by Mr. Akashi effectively altered UN policy, and divisions within the Security Council prevented it from overruling UNPROFOR's interpretation. Even after the UN agreed to go along with NATO demands for multiple targets, General de Lapresle remained master of the decision-making process for air strikes.

Why UN Commanders Influenced Airpower

Answering the question of why commanders chose to influence the use of airpower in the ways they did is more complex than seeing how they exercised their influence. As shown throughout this study, the factors impelling theater-level commanders to try to win control over airpower were often mutually reinforcing rather than in tension with one another. The UN Secretariat's organizational bias for peacekeeping meshed well with the British government's reluctance to see NATO conduct air strikes. British army doctrine for peacekeeping added to the list of reasons that might explain why, for instance, General Rose resisted applying all but minimal doses of airpower in Bosnia. French political pressures were also consistent with British and UN desires to avoid the sort of robust air attacks that American commanders in NATO believed were needed to coerce the Serbs. Although army commanders were skeptical about using airpower while air force generals advocated its use, the unusual alignment of commanders (i.e., European US soldiers commanding UN forces and US airmen commanding in NATO) makes it difficult to test the theoretical proposition that army and air force officers took their respective positions because of their service affiliations. The challenge, then, is to determine when, how, and to what degree expertise and command responsibility motivated commanders. UN commanders provided plenty of testimonial evidence that their actions were guided by their concerns for the safety of their forces and the need to sustain the UN mission in Bosnia. While that is a strong indicator in and of itself, it cannot be counted as sufficient evidence.[2] To better gauge their motivations, it is necessary to look at their actions, especially when expertise and responsibility pushed commanders in directions that cannot be explained well by other factors.

General Briquemont warrants special attention because national political pressures were not a strong factor for him. Furthermore, political instigation from the EC directed Briquemont toward more aggressive measures, which he resisted. Briquemont took command shortly after creation of the safe areas when UN leaders still expected to get the 7,600 reinforcements promised under the light option. Moreover, he was not of the UN peacekeeping culture, and he was not imbued with doctrinal ideas about peacekeeping. His failure to see the coercive value in the threat of NATO air strikes was consistent with a soldier's view of airpower. Interestingly, Briquemont sought more infantry from the Danish ministry of defense instead of tanks the Danes were planning to send to Bosnia. This suggests that aside from differences between soldiers and airmen, soldiers from different army branches prefer different weapon systems according to the soldiers' backgrounds. General Briquemont threatened to quit over air strikes, but not because they were inconsistent with UNSCR 836; he accepted that the ambiguities in the resolution allowed for such action. He threatened to quit because he considered himself *the* commander in Bosnia, and he demanded control over operations in his area of responsibility—especially when they might put his forces at risk. When General Briquemont ultimately did quit, it was because he was pushed to take greater risks and responsibilities by unaccountable officials without being given the resources to fulfill additional tasks being thrust upon him. Thus, for General Briquemont, expertise as a soldier and the responsibility inherent in command weighed heavily in his decisions and actions.

317

General Cot left Bosnia because he clashed with the civilian hierarchy in the UN over control of close air support. The frustrations that precipitated his departure came at a time when fighting in Bosnia was escalating and UN forces were increasingly endangered. He was already on his way out when the Sarajevo ultimatum nearly led to NATO air strikes, and his responsibilities were lightened by the open accountability of elected political leaders (especially President Mitterrand) for the pending strikes. However, three weeks later, when French soldiers came under fire at Bihac, he demanded air support and threatened to make Mr. Akashi bear the blame for the consequences of inaction. Thus, Cot's behavior also indicated the importance of responsibility and accountability for human lives as a factor motivating his behavior.

General Rose's repeated attempts to employ Special Forces in Bosnia, first at Gorazde, later as part of Operation Antelope, and again at Bihac, indicated the influence of his past and his expertise as a former commander of Special Forces. Rose had cause to be embittered toward the Bosnian government after its forces apparently created the situation leading to the death of the Special Forces soldier Rose had sent to Gorazde. Given the risk he took with his Special Forces in sending them to Gorazde to help protect the safe areas and the urgency with which he pleaded to Mr. Akashi for CAS, it seems reasonable to argue that Rose was motivated by his sense of responsibility to his forces to block later uses of airpower, to select meaningless targets, and to issue warnings to the Serbs. These actions lowered the risks to his forces and increased his chances of succeeding in the UN's humanitarian mission but not in its mission to protect the safe areas. However, General Rose's case is complicated because, presumably, the British government would have put extra pressure on Rose to be less aggressive after a British soldier was killed in Gorazde and a British Sea Harrier was shot down the next day. Furthermore, the British government sent hundreds of peacekeepers to Gorazde in the spring of 1994, giving leaders in London strong reasons for wanting to avoid confrontation with the Serbs. Thus, national political pressures, doctrinal beliefs, expertise, and responsibility all pointed in the same direction, and all played a role in shaping Rose's influence on the use of air-power.

General de Lapresle did not share General Rose's expertise in peacekeeping and seems to have been driven away from trying to protect safe areas by the inadequacy of the means at his disposal for executing tasks relating to safe areas. Furthermore, de Lapresle, an armored officer, felt the need for forces that could fill the gap between light infantry and NATO fighter aircraft—unlike General Briquemont, who wanted more ground forces, but not tanks. Again, evidence suggests theater-level commanders were most comfortable employing and advocating the need for forces with which they were most familiar. That rule seemed to apply not just between services (e.g., soldiers and airmen) but also to officers from different backgrounds or branches within the same type of service.

Except for Rupert Smith, European army officers who served as theater-level commanders with the UN exhibited the sort of risk-averse behavior ascribed to the Vietnam generation of professional military officers in the United States. General Briquemont, during the Mount Igman crisis, and General Rose, during the assault on Gorazde, took risks with their forces. However, the generals resisted political pressures to do more when risks outweighed the value of taking tougher action later in their tours. The same could be said of General de Lapresle; he authorized General Rose's plan to send Special Forces to Gorazde, but after that he became reluctant about using airpower to uphold the UN safe areas policy. Generals Rose, de Lapresle, and later, Janvier helped steer the UN mission away from enforcement of the UN's safe areas policy, which held the greatest potential to endanger lives of UN forces. What set General Smith apart from other UN theater-level commanders was not a predilection for taking unnecessary risks with his troops. What set him apart was his view of a worthwhile objective for taking short-term risks in order to lower costs to his forces over the long term. Only when UN commanders had a clear, attainable, positive objective for using force were they willing to take risks with their forces. Thus, responsibility for people's lives inherent in command was a factor motivating senior UN commanders to resist political pressures to "do something" until that something was defined and weighed against the risks of attempting to do it. While the Vietnam War undoubtedly sensitized a generation of American officers to the imperative of avoiding risks in the absence of worthwhile and achievable objectives, their risk aversion was not a uniquely American phenomenon. Nor was it confined to one generation. Risk aversion is a natural product of the special expertise and responsibility of professional military officers, and theater-level commanders are likely to possess an uncommonly high degree of both expertise and responsibility.

How NATO Commanders Influenced Airpower

American commanders in NATO also influenced the use of airpower beyond being mere executors of policy. General Joulwan helped define heavy weapons to include elements of the BSA that were only indirectly related to the siege of Sarajevo, and his inputs were incorporated in the terms of the Gorazde ultimatum as well. He called for zones of action that helped move NATO political thinking beyond the offending weapons surrounding each individual safe area, thus opening the door for General Ryan's air campaign. Finally, General Joulwan pushed his subordinate commanders, especially Admiral Smith, to resume bombing during the pause in Deliberate Force and to avoid saying anything to the press about broader implications of the campaign that might disturb alliance cohesion.

General Ashy's early planning and his apparent success in winning General Briquemont's approval for NATO's target list helped move NATO toward the sort of robust air action favored by the US government. In addition, Ashy's efforts with Admiral Boorda to limit details of target information presented to NATO ambassadors, while convincing them that AFSOUTH commanders had done everything necessary to limit collateral damage, was intended to prevent micromanagement from Brussels. General Chambers's main contribution was to set up an efficient system for enforcing the no-fly zone and for providing close air support to the UN. There was nothing unusual about how he did this, but his expertise was evident in the successful working of each system. In addition, his efforts to make Deny Flight bombing operations overtly multi-national boosted the apparent legitimacy of the operation.

General Ryan demonstrated the value of having a plan ready in advance of political orders for such planning. He and Admiral Smith greatly increased the impact of Deliberate Force by making Dead Eye an automatic component of NATO air operations. Admiral Smith's earlier refusal to patrol the no-fly zone more aggressively without first suppressing Bosnian Serb air defenses was a helpful precursor for Dead Eye opera-tions, heightening political awareness within NATO of the threat to allied airmen. Together General Ryan and Admiral Smith controlled information about targets, BDA, and the mil-itary objective of Deliberate Force to maintain operational autonomy during the campaign. Efforts by NATO theater-level commanders to influence the use of airpower were fairly con-ventional and confined to the NATO chain of command, and they all moved NATO toward a forceful air campaign.[3]

Why NATO Commanders Influenced Airpower

The factors motivating NATO commanders tended to be mutually reinforcing. Thus, explaining why they chose to influence airpower as they did raises the same difficulties encountered in trying to explain the actions of UN command-ers. For the most part, the capabilities and limitations of air-power, the commanders' expertise, the imperative for protect-ing their forces, and US political pressure all worked together to push commanders toward robust air operations. However, Admiral Smith demonstrated a willingness to upset some US and NATO superiors in order to meet his responsibility for the people under his command. Admiral Smith's behavior under-scored the dilemma a commander might face in trying to ful-fill responsibilities up and down the chain of command.

At the risk of stating the obvious, negative objectives cannot substitute for positive objectives when a commander weighs the responsibility for forces against the objectives for using force. Yet, for much of 1994 the absence of an overriding pos-itive objective for using force meant that negative objectives defined how and when airpower was used in Bosnia. This was true at Gorazde in April, for the air strikes around Sarajevo in August and September, and for the attack against Udbina in November. In each case, there was a positive objective for air operations, but it was not sufficiently important to overcome the negative objectives, or objections, for using airpower. By the end of 1994, Admiral Smith had seen enough to know that NATO was not politically united behind a positive objective for its air operations. After that he twice restricted no-fly zone activities over Bosnia to avoid unnecessary risks to NATO airmen: first at the end of November 1994 and again after the downing of O'Grady. As Deliberate Force wound down, Smith again resisted air operations that might have needlessly put NATO airmen in harm's way when he refused to stretch out the bombing campaign to hit previously destroyed targets.

Smith's actions suggest that when a commander must decide how much risk to take with forces, there is need for a positive objective (one not overshadowed by negative aims). Without a positive objective, commanders cannot judge whether they are taking excessive risk. A policy of getting tough or being more forceful is unlikely to suffice. Overall, expertise and command responsibility were strong motivators shaping the actions of NATO theater-level commanders in their attempts to influence the use of airpower over Bosnia— even if the importance of responsibility was most clearly discernible on the rare occasions when it ran counter to other factors motivating commanders.

Objectives, Authority, and Responsibility

The absence of a palpable threat to national interests robbed those who chose to intervene in Bosnia's war of a rationale for accepting costs and risks. As leading nations— principally the US, the UK, and France—tried to resolve their differences, they did so in a cost-intolerant environment. Theater-level commanders who served in the UN and NATO were enlisted in the battle to hold down costs (a negative objective) aside from whatever positive objectives they were supposed to pursue. In addition to pressures from home, political and military leaders from nations contributing troops to UNPROFOR constantly reminded UN commanders in

Zagreb that the contributing countries were unwilling to see their soldiers put at risk. These external political pressures to guard the lives of forces entrusted to UN commanders reinforced the internal pressures or responsibilities borne by commanders to balance mission accomplishment against force protection. The need to contemplate trade-offs between mission and lives emerged for NATO commanders when the surface-to-air threat increased dramatically during the second half of 1994.

The sum of external and internal pressures for minimizing costs to friendly forces repeatedly worked to convince UN and NATO theater-level commanders to avoid the dangerous middle ground between peacekeeping and enforcement actions. The measure of a "good" commander is probably best demonstrated by how well that commander balances responsibility for accomplishing a mission with the responsibility to avoid unnecessary costs to the lives of people in the command. In Bosnia, theater-level commanders sought to affect the shape of their missions, their forces, and their rules of engagement in a way that would avoid trade-offs between their missions and their people's lives. When trade-offs had to be made, commanders often shouldered the responsibility. They had to decide how much risk to accept. They were usually the ones held accountable, or they expected to be held to account. When objectives for a military operation were unclear, or patently beyond the capabilities of the available forces, then it became impossible for commanders to strike a balance between mission and men. Under such circumstances, theater-level commanders leaned toward force protection. They tolerated, however unhappily, restrictions that kept them from accomplishing their missions, provided those restrictions did not also unnecessarily jeopardize the lives of their people. After briefly flirting with efforts to combine consent-based peacekeeping and enforcement actions in early 1994, theater-level commanders eschewed the middle ground and accepted the incompatibility of the two approaches.

As with tactical determinism, the responsibility for the lives of people under one's command can serve as a tool for shaping policy. Commanders in Bosnia used force protection as a powerful device for persuading their counterparts in the military-to-military dialogue over using airpower, as was evident at Udbina. Both sets of commanders in UNPROFOR and in AFSOUTH could—and to some extent did—take advantage of their expertise and the threat to their forces to further their respective missions. The argument was one-sided with UNPROFOR holding the floor until the summer of 1994 when the Serb SAM threat began to mount. After that, NATO commanders were able to take a firmer stand in dictating how airpower would be used. An example of the leverage commanders gain by the need to protect their forces occurred during Deliberate Force. AFSOUTH commanders expanded and prolonged bombing in Bosnia by prosecuting attacks against Dead Eye targets in the northwestern part of the country. General Janvier (and almost certainly the French government) saw this as a circumvention of controls on the NATO bombing campaign. Ironically, policy makers in Washington suspected AFSOUTH commanders were not doing enough to keep the bombing campaign going. Despite suspicions and grumbling on both sides—against and for continuation of the bombing—AFSOUTH commanders were not overruled. Thus, the commanders' prerogative to ensure force protection undoubtedly strengthened their demands for control over operational matters and allowed them to shape the use of airpower over Bosnia.

Political controls on military commanders can at best transfer, but not eliminate, the responsibility that goes with command. Some observers have advocated that NATO adopt the UN practice of assigning a special representative of the secretary-general to work alongside theater commanders.[4] This might be desirable for political leaders who wish to exercise tighter control over their theater commanders. The special representative could detect and curb unwanted independence on the part of commanders, while also providing a single point of contact for political inputs to commanders. However, the experience from Deny Flight indicates that to be effective a special representative would need real decision-making authority and, more importantly, would have to have accountability within the chain of command. Without authority, the special representative would likely hinder timely decision making. Without accountability, the special representative would probably find commanders unwilling to recognize the representative's authority to make decisions affecting the safety of friendly forces.

Perhaps the most important lesson of Deny Flight is the need for political and military leaders to explicitly recognize and agree upon the political objectives for using force and their shared responsibility for determining the acceptable costs for doing so. The dictate to *Do Something, General!* is no substitute for a clear objective. However, it may well be indicative of the guidance military commanders are likely to get as fewer and fewer elected officials in Western states have any personal experience serving in the military. The challenge for theater commanders will be to marry the means available to the desired political objectives and to do so within the bounds of acceptable costs. In Western democracies where the military is subordinate to civilian control, presidents and prime ministers sit atop the military chains of command. Therefore, political leaders at the highest level cannot entirely escape the responsibilities and accountability that go with commanding military operations. They are forced to share the concerns of theater commanders, who must strike a proper balance between force protection and mission accomplishment. Political leaders can best help to strike the right balance by establishing a positive objective for which force is to be used and a sense for the acceptable level of costs, including friendly losses, collateral damage, time, and material costs. However, these are variables that cannot be spelled out in precise terms, and they are likely to change over time. Therefore, theater commanders may not be able to wait for an objective to be assigned; they may have to become partners in establishing objectives and willingly embrace the responsibility for the consequences of their plans. The theater-level commander who can gauge the political currents and come up with a plan to connect the means available to the desired ends while staying within the bounds of acceptable costs will be well positioned to win political support. Thus, theater-level commanders will need to anticipate, plan, and expect to be held accountable if they wish to maintain operational autonomy and avoid orders to just "do something." If political leaders want action from commanders, they should recognize the limits to which military commanders can resolve unsettled political issues and understand that commanders will want clear positive objectives and explicit authority to act so that they can best balance the responsibilities for mission success and the lives of friendly forces. Striking the right balance will continue to be in the interest of both political authorities and their theater commanders, and it will continue to motivate commanders as they seek to influence the use of airpower in future interventions. While political leaders have the right to be wrong in ordering military operations, it will be in their interest and in the national interest that they get things right whenever military forces are put in harm's way, because disastrous side effects, so blithely dismissed in the opening epigraph, are just that—disastrous.

Notes

1. Richard K. Betts, *Soldiers, Statesmen, and Cold War Crises* (Cambridge, Mass.: Harvard University Press, 1977; reprint with new preface and epilogue, New York: Columbia University Press, 1991), 153.

2. Robert Jervis, *Perceptions and Misperceptions in International Politics* (Princeton, N.J.: Princeton University Press, 1976), 382–87. In Jervis's discussion of cognitive dissonance, he explains that decision makers become committed to their decisions, and they will seek justifications for their actions or decisions after the fact, which might not reveal their true reasoning at the time of the decision.

3. This conclusion would be challenged if later evidence revealed the commanders were intentionally baiting the Bosnian Serb SAM operators, and knowingly exposing NATO aircrews to added risks to create a cause for eliminating the SAMs.

4. This was a consideration as NATO readied to deploy IFOR in latter 1995. Also see Michael C. Williams, *Civil-Military Relations and Peacekeeping*, Adelphi Paper 321 (London: International Institute for Strategic Studies, 1998), 17 and 30.

Select Bibliography

UN Documents. The endnotes used the UN system of referencing UN documents. They are listed here chronologically, under "United Nations."

BACS Collection. The Balkans Air Campaign Study was commissioned by Air University and headed by Col Robert C. Owen, USAF. In addition to producing its own study, the team of researchers was chartered to collect documentary information on the background, planning, and execution of Operation Deliberate Force. The archival material from that study is held at the US Air Force Historical Research Agency at Maxwell Air Force Base (AFB) in Montgomery, Alabama. In this bibliography, the shortened form "BACS Collection" is used to refer to that archival material, in lieu of "Balkans Air Campaign Study Collection, Air Force Historical Research Agency, Maxwell AFB, Alabama."

Military Rank. For published works, or contemporaneous documents, the rank cited is that held by an individual at the time the cited item was produced. Interviews reflect the rank at the time of the interview; however, the position(s) listed are those held during the period of interest. For instance, the entry for Lt Gen Régnault includes posts he held as a brigadier general and as a major general.

Multiple works by same author. For news articles, books, and so forth, the order is alphabetical. For Congressional reports it is chronological. For transcripts of news conferences or press releases, the order is chronological.

. . . .

7490 Composite Wing (P). Memorandum for CAOC, 7 September 1995. File C2a(2), BACS Collection.

Adams, Paul, and Laura Silber. "UN in Talks with Serbs as Zepa Safe Haven Falls: International Tribunal Charges Karadzic and Mladic With War Crimes." *Financial Times* (London), 26 July 1995.

Air Force Manual (AFM) 1-1. *Basic Aerospace Doctrine of the United States Air Force.* Vol. 1, March 1992.

Air Force Manual (AFM) 1-1. *Basic Aerospace Doctrine of the United States Air Force.* Vol. 2, March 1992.

Akashi, Yasushi. "The Limits of UN Diplomacy and the Future of Conflict Mediation." *Survival* 37, no. 4 (winter 1995–1996): 83–98.

———, Zagreb. TLS (photocopy), to Dr. Radovan Karadzic, Pale, 10 December 1994. BACS Collection.

Alexander, Martin. "The French Experience 1919–1962: French Military Doctrine and British Observations, from World War One to the Algerian War." In *The Origins of Contemporary Doctrine.* Edited by John Gooch. Occasional Number 30. Camberley, England: Strategic and Combat Studies Institute, 1997.

Alger, John I. *The Quest For Victory: The History of the Principles of War.* Foreword by Gen Fredrick J. Kroesen. London: Greenwood Press, 1982.

Allied Forces Southern Europe (AFSOUTH). "AFSOUTH Change of Command." Transcripts from Change of Command Ceremony, 31 July 1996, Naples, Italy. http://www.afsouth.nato.int/archives/archives.htm.

———. "NATO Airstrike at Pale Ammunitions Dump." AFSOUTH Press Release 95–12, 25 May 1995. http://www.afsouth.nato.int/archives/archives.htm.

———. "NATO Operation Deliberate Force." Transcript of press briefing, Naples, 1 September 1995 (11:00 A.M.). http://www.afsouth.nato.int/archives/archives.htm.

———. "NATO Operation Deliberate Force." Transcript of press briefing, Naples, 9 September 1995 (5:00 P.M.). http://www.afsouth.nato.int/archives/archives.htm.

———. Transcript of press briefing, Naples, 11 September 1995 (5:00 P.M.). http://www.afsouth.nato.int/archives/archives.htm.

———. Transcript of press briefing, Naples, 12 September 1995 (5:00 P.M.). http://www.afsouth.nato.int/archives/archives.htm.

———. "Operation Deliberate Force." Fact Sheet, 5 October 1995.

———. "Operation Deny Flight." Fact Sheet, 5 October 1995.

Allison, Graham T. *Essence of Decision: Explaining the Cuban Missile Crisis.* N.p.: HarperCollins, 1971.

Almond, Mark. "A Faraway Country." In *With No Peace to Keep: United Nations Peacekeeping and the War in the Former Yugoslavia.* Edited by Ben Cohen and George Stamkoski. London: Grainpress, 1995.

Almond, Peter. "US Angry over Bosnia Arms Delivery Claim." *Daily Telegraph* (London), 4 March 1995.

Anderson, Jon R. "Rivalries on U.S. Side Emerged in Airstrikes." *Air Force Times,* 9 October 1995, 6.

Andrews, Lt Col William F., USAF. *Airpower Against an Army: Challenge and Response in CENTAF's Duel with the Republican Guard.* CADRE Paper. Maxwell AFB, Ala.: Air University Press, 1998.

Annex E: "Rules of Engagement (ROE)," to CINCSOUTH OPLAN 40101, Change 2, 13 August 1993. File B3e, NPL–21, BACS Collection.

AP 3000, 2d ed. *Royal Air Force (UK) Air Power Doctrine,* 1993.

Apple, R.W., Jr. "NATO Again Plans Possible Air Raids on Serbs in Bosnia." *New York Times,* 12 January 1994.

Army (UK). *Army Doctrine Publication.* Vol. 2: *Command.* March 1995.

Army Field Manual (AFM) (UK). *Wider Peacekeeping.* London: HMSO, 1995.

Arno Press. *Air War—Vietnam.* Introduction by Drew Middleton. New York: Arno Press, 1978.

Ashy, Gen Joseph W., USAF. Interviewed by Lt Col Rob Owen, 29 April 1996, Washington, D.C. Unclassified version of General Ashy's Oral History Interview, (66 pp.) redacted by the Air Force Historical Research Agency, October 1997. Office of History, Air Force Space Command, Peterson AFB, Colo.

———, commander, Allied Air Forces Southern Europe (AIR-SOUTH), December 1992–September 1994, and commander, US Sixteenth Air Force, February–September 1994. Interviewed by author, 3 July 1998, Fairfax, Va. Author's notes. Author's personal collection.

Aspin, Les. "The Use and Usefulness of Military Forces in the Post–Cold War, Post–Soviet World." Address. Jewish Institute for National Security Affairs, Washington, D.C., 21 September 1992. In Richard N. Haass, *Intervention: The Use of American Military Force in the Post Cold War World.* Washington, D.C.: The Brookings Institution for the Carnegie Endowment for International Peace, 1994.

Aspin, Les, and William Dickinson, representatives of the US Congress. *Defense for a New Era: Lessons of the Persian Gulf War.* Washington, D.C.: Brassey's, 1992.

"At Least: Slow the Slaughter." *New York Times,* 4 October 1992.

Atkeson, Maj Gen Edward B., USA, retired. "When Duty Demands: Resigning In Protest." *Army* 42, no. 12 (December 1992).

Atkins, Ralph. "Parliament and Politics: PM Fails to Calm Fears of Bosnia Action." *Financial Times* (London), 29 April 1993.

Atkinson, Rick. "Air Assault Set Stage for Broader Role." *Washington Post,* 15 November 1995.

———. "The Anatomy of NATO's Decision to Bomb Bosnia." *International Herald Tribune,* 17 November 1995.

———. *Crusade: The Untold Story of the Persian Gulf War.* New York: Houghton Mifflin, 1993.

———. "In Almost Losing Its Resolve, NATO Alliance Found Itself." *Washington Post,* 16 November 1995.

———. "Germans Vote to Send Planes and Troops." *International Herald Tribune,* 1 July 1995.

———. "NATO's Gunboat Diplomacy Not Assured of Smooth Sailing." *Washington Post,* 14 September 1995.

—. "NATO Tailors Bombing Information." *Washington Post*, 16 September 1995.

—. "Put to the Test, NATO Shows Its Mettle." *International Herald Tribune*, 20 November 1995.

Avant, Deborah D. "Are the Reluctant Warriors Out of Control? Why the US Military is Averse to Responding to Post-Cold War Low-Level Threats." *Security Studies* 6, no. 2 (winter 1996/1997).

—. "Conflicting Indicators of Crisis in American Relations." *Armed Forces and Society* 24, no. 3 (spring 1998).

Bacevich, Andrew J. "Absent History: A Comment on Dauber, Desch, and Feaver." *Armed Forces and Society* 24, no. 3 (spring 1998).

—. "Civilian Control: A Useful Fiction?" *Joint Forces Quarterly*, no. 6 (autumn/winter 1994–1995).

—. "New Rules: Modern War and Military Professionalism." *Parameters* 20, no. 4 (December 1990).

Bachelor, Wing Comdr Andy, Royal Air Force (RAF), head of Battle Damage Assessment Cell during Operation Deliberate Force. Interviewed by Maj John C. Orndorff, USAF, 14 February 1996, Ramstein AB, Germany. Tape recording. BACS Collection.

Bahnsen, John C., and Robert W. Cone. "Defining the American Warrior Leader." *Parameters* 20, no. 4 (December 1990).

Baker, James A., III, with Thomas M. DeFrank. *The Politics of Diplomacy: Revolution, War and Peace, 1989–1992.* New York: G. P. Putnam's Sons, 1995.

Baker, James H. "Policy Challenges of UN Peace Operations." *Parameters* 24, no. 1 (spring 1994).

Barber, Tony, and David Osborne. "France Accuses the US of Arming the Muslims." *Independent* (London), 1 July 1995.

Barlow, Maj Jason B., USAF. *Strategic Paralysis: An Airpower Theory for the Present.* Maxwell AFB, Ala.: Air University Press, 1994.

Bash, Maj Brooks L., USAF. *The Role of United States Air Power in Peacekeeping.* Maxwell AFB, Ala.: Air University Press, 1994.

———. "Airpower and Peacekeeping." *Airpower Journal* 9, no. 1 (spring 1995).

Baylis, John. "The Evolution of British Defense Policy, 1945–86." In *The Defence Equation: British Military Systems Policy Planning and Performance Since 1945.* Edited by Martin Edmonds. London: Brassey's, 1986.

Beale, Maj Michael O., USAF. *Bombs over Bosnia: The Role of Airpower in Bosnia-Herzegovina.* Maxwell AFB, Ala.: Air University Press, 1997.

Bertram, Christoph. "Multilateral Diplomacy and Conflict Resolution." *Survival* 37, no. 4 (winter 1995–1996).

Bethlehem, Daniel, and Marc Weller, eds. *The "Yugoslav" Crisis in International Law, General Issues Part I.* Cambridge International Documents Series, vol. 5. Cambridge: Cambridge University Press, 1997.

Betts, Richard K. *Soldiers, Statesmen, and Cold War Crises.* 1977. Reprint, with new preface and epilogue. New York: Columbia University Press, 1991.

Binder, David. "Bosnia's Bombers." *The Nation,* 2 October 1995.

Binyon, Michael. "Outburst Puts the Spotlight On Troops' Dilemma." *Times* (London), 29 April 1993.

Blackett, Comdr J., Royal Navy. "Superior Orders—The Military Dilemma." *RUSI Journal* 139, no. 1 (February 1994).

Blechman, Barry M. "The Intervention Dilemma." *The Washington Quarterly* 18, no. 3 (summer 1995).

Boorda, Adm J. M., USN. "Loyal Partner – NATO's Forces in Support of the United Nations." *NATO's Sixteen Nations* 39, no. 1 (1994).

Borger, Julian. "Bosnians Are Being Covertly Armed." *Guardian* (London), 25 February 1995.

Bosnia–Herzegovina Command (FWD), Sarajevo. TLS (photocopy), to chief of staff, HQ UNPROFOR, Zagreb, 1 January 1995. BACS Collection.

"Bosnia's Real Lesson." *The Economist,* 9 September 1995.

"Bosnia Update." *New York Times,* 23 April 1993.

Bourne, Christopher M. "Unintended Consequences of Goldwater–Nichols: The Effects On Civilian Control of the Military." In *Essays On Strategy XIV.* Edited by Mary A. Sommerville. Washington, D.C.: National Defense University Press, 1997.

Boutros-Ghali, Boutros, United Nations secretary-general. TLS (photocopy) to NATO secretary-general Willy Claes, Brussels, 26 July 1995. BACS Collection.

———. TLS (photocopy) to Willy Claes, NATO secretary-general, Brussels, 15 August 1995. BACS Collection.

Boyd, Gen Charles G., USAF, retired. "Making Peace with the Guilty." *Foreign Affairs* 74, no. 5 (September/October 1995).

———. Deputy commander in chief US European Command, October 1992–August 1995. Interviewed by author, 12 February 1998, Washington, D.C. Transcript of taped interview. Author's personal collection.

Boyd, Lt Col Lowell R., Jr., USAF, AFSOUTH staff officer, February 1993–1996. Interviewed by Lt Col Rob Owen, 6 December 1995, Naples, Italy. Transcript of taped interview. BACS Collection.

Bradford, Zeb B., Jr., and James R. Murphy. "A New Look at the Military Profession." In *American Defense Policy.* 6th ed. Edited by Schuyler Foerster and Edward N. Wright. Baltimore, Md.: Johns Hopkins University Press, 1990.

Bradley, Omar N., and Clay Blair. *A General's Life.* New York: Simon and Schuster, 1983.

Brady, Christopher, and Sam Daws. "UN Operations: The Political–Military Interface." *International Peacekeeping* 1, no. 1 (spring 1994).

Brand, Joel. "Rose Considered Showing Airstrike Plans to Serbs." *Times* (London), 16 January 1995.

Brand, Joel, and Michael Evans. "UN Troops Set To Defend Srebrenica from Serbs." *Times* (London), 22 April 1993.

Bremner, Charles. "Leaders Lose the Appetite for Action." *Times* (London), 20 April 1993.

Brett, Gordon, member of the Bosnia Task Force, NATO International Staff. Interviewed by author, 25 May 1998, Brussels. Tape recording. Author's personal collection.

Briquemont, Lt Gen Francis. *Do Something, General!: Chronique de Bosnie–Herzégovine 12 juillet 1993–24 janvier 1994*. Bruxelles: Éditions Labor, 1997.

———, Belgian army, commander of UNPROFOR's Bosnia–Herzegovina Command, July 1993–January 1994. Interviewed by author, 11 August 1998, Brussels. Transcript of tape recording. Author's personal collection.

British Broadcasting Corporation, The, and The Discovery Channel. "Episode 1: The Cracks Appear." In *Yugoslavia: Death of a Nation*. Produced by Brian Lapping Associates. Discovery Communications. 50 min., 1996. Videocassette.

———. "Episode 2: Descent Into War." In *Yugoslavia: Death of a Nation*. Produced by Brian Lapping Associates. Discovery Communications. 50 min., 1996. Videocassette.

———. "Episode 3: The Collapse of Unity." In *Yugoslavia: Death of a Nation*. Produced by Brian Lapping Associates. Discovery Communications. 50 min., 1996. Videocassette.

———. "Episode 4: The Gates of Hell." In *Yugoslavia: Death of a Nation*. Produced by Brian Lapping Associates. Discovery Communications. 50 min., 1996. Videocassette.

———. "Episode 5: No Escape." In *Yugoslavia: Death of a Nation*. Produced by Brian Lapping Associates. Discovery Communications. 50 min., 1996. Videocassette.

———. "Episode 6: Pax Americana." In *Yugoslavia: Death of a Nation*. Produced by Brian Lapping Associates. Discovery Communications. 50 min., 1996. Videocassette.

Broadbent, Sir Ewen. *The Military and Government: From Macmillan to Heseltine*. Foreword by Harold Macmillan. London: Macmillan Press, 1988.

Brodie, Bernard. *Strategy in the Missile Age*. Princeton, N.J.: Princeton University Press, 1959.

———. *War and Politics*. New York: Macmillan, 1973.

Broughton, Col Jack, USAF, retired. *Going Downtown: The War Against Hanoi and Washington*. New York: Orion Books, 1988.

———. *Thud Ridge*. New York: Bantam Books, 1969.

Brown, Douglas P., et al. *Operation Deny Flight Assessment: Final Report*. Alexandria, Va.: Science Applications International Corporation, 1994. DNA–TR–94–63–N.

Brungess, Lt Col James R., USAF. *Setting the Context: Suppression of Enemy Air Defenses and Joint War Fighting in an Uncertain World*. Maxwell AFB, Ala.: Air University Press, 1994.

Buchanan, Brig Gen Walter E., USAF, chief, Joint Operations Division, US EUCOM/CENTCOM Branch, J–3, Joint Chiefs of Staff, June 1994–September 1995. Interviewed by author, 26 May 1998, Kalkar, Germany. Tape recording. Author's personal collection.

Bucknam, Maj Mark A., USAF. "Lethal Airpower and Intervention." Master's thesis, School of Advanced Airpower Studies, Air University, Maxwell AFB, Ala., 1996. http://tuvok.au.af.mil/au/saas/studrsch/ class.htm.

———. "Talking Paper on Shoot Down of Galebs over Bosnia," 29 April 1994. Briefing notes. Author's personal collection.

Burk, James. "The Logic of Crisis and Civil-Military Relations Theory: A Comment on Desch, Feaver, and Dauber." *Armed Forces and Society* 24, no. 3 (spring 1998).

Burns, John F. "Muslim Defenders Disarmed, U.N. Says." *New York Times*, 22 April 1993.

———. "Standoff for Muslim Enclave in Bosnia." *New York Times*, 23 April 1993.

———. "U.N. Says Enclave Is Saved; Bosnians Call It Surrender." *New York Times*, 19 April 1993.

Burridge, Brian. *Defence and Democracy: The Control of the Military*. London Defence Studies no. 44. London: Brassey's for the Centre for Defence Studies, 1998.

Burridge, Air Commodore Brian, RAF. Interviewed by author, 3 February 1998, RAF, Bracknell, England. Author's notes. Author's personal collection.

Butcher, Tim. "NATO Request for Bosnia Air Strike." *Daily Telegraph* (London), 22 June 1995.

Calic, Marie-Janine. "German Perspectives." In *International Perspectives on the Yugoslav Conflict*. Edited by Alex Danchev and Thomas Halverson. London: Macmillan, 1996.

Campbell, Kenneth J. "Once Burned, Twice Cautious: Explaining the Weinberger–Powell Doctrine." *Armed Forces and Society* 24, no. 3 (spring 1998).

Caplan, Richard. *Post–Mortem on UNPROFOR*. London Defence Studies no. 33. London: Brassey's for the Centre for Defence Studies, 1996.

Carney, James. "Finally, The Leader of NATO Leads." *Time,* 11 September 1995, 54.

"Cautious Welcome, But End to War May Be Far Off." *Financial Times* (London), 9 September 1997.

Cerami, Joseph R. "Presidential Decision Making and Vietnam: Lessons for Strategists." *Parameters* 26, no. 4 (winter 1996–1997).

Chambers, Lt Gen James E., USAF, director of NATO's Combined Air Operations Center (CAOC), Vicenza, Italy. "Outstanding Air Support of UNPROFOR." Message to participating NATO units, 13 March 1994. BACS Collection.

——. Interviewed by author, 10 February 1998, Fairfax, Va. Author's notes. Author's personal collection.

Cheshire, Air Chief Marshal Sir John, RAF, assistant chief of Staff Policy, Supreme Headquarters Allied Powers Europe, Mons, Belgium, 1992–1994; UK military representative to the NATO Military Committee, 1995. Interviewed by author, 1 June 1998, RAF High Wycombe, England. Tape recording. Author's personal collection.

Chilton, Patricia. "French Policy on Peacekeeping." In *Brassey's Defence Yearbook, 1995.* Edited by The Centre for Defence Studies, King's College London. London: Brassey's, 1995.

Christman, Lt Gen Daniel W., USA, US military representative to the NATO Military Committee, September 1993–October 1994; assistant to the chairman of the Joint Chiefs of Staff, October 1994–June 1996. Interviewed by author, 18 July 1997, West Point, N.Y. Tape recording. Author's personal collection.

Chuter, David. *Humanity's Soldier: France and International Security, 1919–2001.* Oxford: Berghahn Books, 1996.

Ciechanski, Jerzy. "Enforcement Measures under Chapter VII of the UN Charter: UN Practice after the Cold War." In *The UN Peace and Force.* Edited by Michael Pugh. London: Frank Cass, 1997.

Cimbala, Stephen J. "United States." In *The Political Role of the Military.* Edited by Constantine P. Danopoulos and Cynthia Watson. London: Greenwood Press, 1996.

CJCSI 3121.01. *Standing Rules of Engagement for U.S. Forces.* Washington, D.C.: Office of the Chairman of the Joint Chiefs of Staff, 1 October 1994.

Clark, Arthur L. *Bosnia: What Every American Should Know.* New York: Berkley Books, 1996.

Clark, Bruce. "Bombing Raids Damage Diplomatic Bridges." *Financial Times* (London), 14 September 1995.

———. "NATO and Russia Enter Cold Peace." *Financial Times* (London), 12 September 1995.

———. "NATO Strikes in Bosnia." *Financial Times* (London), 31 August 1995.

———. "UN Mission in Bosnia to End Soon, Says US: NATO Fires Cruise Missiles at Serbs." *Financial Times* (London), 11 September 1995.

———. "West Shows Frustration with Serbs." *Financial Times* (London), 26 May 1995.

Clark, Bruce, David Buchan, and Harriet Martin. "West Sets Tough Military Goals in Bosnia." *Financial Times* (London), 5 June 1995.

Clark, Bruce, and Bernard Gray. "Poor Prospects for a Formula: The Chances of Finding a Solution in Bosnia Remain Bleak for the UN." *Financial Times* (London), 3 June 1995.

———. "United Front Splinters: NATO Powers Are Putting National Interests First in Bosnia." *Financial Times* (London), 30 May 1995.

Clark, Bruce, Bernard Gray, and Lionel Barber. "Doubts Grow Over UN Bosnia Role." *Financial Times* (London), 17 July 1995.

Clark, Bruce, John Kampfner, and Anthony Robinson. "Split over Bosnia Air Strike Threat: Meeting Fails to Back US Calls for Tough Action against Serbs." *Financial Times* (London), 22 July 1995.

Clark, Bruce, and Harriet Martin. "NATO Poised to Resume Raids Despite Cease-fire by Serbs." *Financial Times* (London), 5 September 1995.

Clark, Bruce, and Laura Silber. "Bosnian Serbs Release 120 UN Hostages: US Jet Downed as West Looks to Reconsider Military Role in Former Yugoslavia." *Financial Times* (London), 3 June 1995.

Clark, Bruce, Laura Silber, and Harriet Martin. "US Jet Shot Down over Serb-held Part of Bosnia." *Financial Times* (London), 3 June 1995.

Clark, Col Dan, USAF, Zagreb. TLS (photocopy) to Brigadier General Sawyer, USAF, Vicenza, Italy, 12 January 1995. BACS Collection.

Clarke, Michael. "Air Power and Force in Peace Support Operations." In *The Dynamics of Air Power*. Edited by Group Capt Andrew Lambert and Arthur C. Williamson. Bracknell, UK: HMSO, 1996.

———. "Foreign Policy Implementation: Problems and Approaches." *British Journal of International Studies* 5 (1979).

———. "The Lessons of Bosnia for the British Military." In *Brassey's Defence Yearbook, 1995*. Edited by The Centre for Defence Studies, King's College London. London: Brassey's, 1995.

———. "Threats and Challenges in the UK's Security Environment." In *Perspectives on Air Power: Air Power in Its Wider Context*. Edited by Stuart Peach. London: The Stationery Office, 1998.

Clausewitz, Carl. *On War*. Ed. and trans. by Michael Howard and Peter Paret. Princeton, N.J.: Princeton University Press, 1976.

"Clinton Considers Sending Troops to Help in Bosnia: Lord Owen to Step Down as Peace Envoy." *Financial Times* (London), 1 June 1995.

Clodfelter, Mark. *The Limits of Air Power: the American Bombing of North Vietnam*. New York: Free Press; Collier Macmillan, 1989.

Cohen, Ben, and George Stamkoski, eds. *With No Peace to Keep: United Nations Peacekeeping and the War in the Former Yugoslavia*. London: Grainpress, 1995.

Cohen, Eliot A. "Constraints on America's Conduct of Small Wars." *International Security* 9, no. 2 (fall 1984).

———. "The Mystique of U.S. Air Power." *Foreign Affairs* 73, no. 1 (January/February 1994).

Cohen, Eliot A., and John Gooch. *Military Misfortune: The Anatomy of Failure in War*. New York: Free Press, 1990, Vintage Books, 1991.

Collins, Lt Col Joseph J., USA. "Desert Storm and the Lessons of Learning." *Parameters* 22, no. 3 (autumn 1992).

Conversino, Maj Mark J., USAF. "Sawdust Superpower: Perceptions of U.S. Casualty Tolerance In the Post-Gulf War Era." *Strategic Review* 25, no. 1 (winter 1997).

"Correspondence." *Strategic Review* 22, no. 3 (summer 1994).

Corsini, Col Roberto, Italian air force. "The Balkan War: What Role for Airpower?" *Airpower Journal* 9, no. 4 (winter 1995).

Corum, James S. "Airpower and Peace Enforcement." *Airpower Journal* 10, no. 4 (winter 1996).

Cot, Gen Jean, French army. "Dayton ou la Porte Etroite: Genese et Avenir d'un Désastre." In *Dernière Guerre Balkanique?* 2d ed. Edited by Jean Cot. France: Editions L'Harmattan, 1996.

———. "L'Europe et l'Otan." *Défense Nationale* 53, no. 4 (October 1997).

———. "Ex–Yugoslavie: une paix bâclée." *Défense Nationale* 53, no. 3 (*July*1997).

———. "Les Leçons de l'ex–Yugoslavie." *Défense* no. 67 (March 1995).

———, ed. *Dernière Guerre Balkanique?: Ex–Yugoslavie: Témoignages, analyses, perspectives.* 2e ed. Paris: Editions L'Harmattan, 1996.

———. UNPROFOR force commander, July 1993–March 1994. Interviewed by author, 30 September 1998, Paris. Transcript and translation of tape recording. Author's personal collection.

Covault, Craig. "Air Power Alters Bosnia Equation." *Aviation Week and Space Technology,* 4 September 1995.

———. "NATO Air Strikes Target Serbian Infrastructure." *Aviation Week and Space Technology,* 11 September 1995.

———. "NATO Flights Accelerate for Sarajevo Recon." *Aviation Week and Space Technology,* 21 February 1994.

———. "NATO Hits Missile Sites; Large Force Bombs Air Base." *Aviation Week and Space Technology,* 28 November 1994.

———. "Precision Missiles Bolster NATO Strikes." *Aviation Week and Space Technology,* 18 September 1995.

"Croatia's Blitzkrieg." *The Economist,* 12 August 1995.

Crowe, Adm William J., Jr., U.S. Ambassador to the United Kingdom (June 1994 – September 1997). Interview by author, 4 August 1997, London. Tape recording. Author's personal collection.

Crowe, Adm William J., Jr., USN, with David Chanoff. *The Line of Fire: From Washington to the Gulf, the Politics and*

Battles of the New Military. New York: Simon and Schuster, 1993.

Cruickshanks, Air Commodore Colin, RAF, NATO liaison officer to UNPROFOR Headquarters, Zagreb, Croatia, November 1993–May 1994. Interviewed by author, 20 October 1997, RAF Boscomb Down, England. Author's notes. Author's personal collection.

Danchev, Alex, and Thomas Halverson, eds. *International Perspectives on the Yugoslav Conflict.* London: Macmillan, 1996.

Dandeker, Christopher. "National Security and Democracy: The United Kingdom Experience." *Armed Forces and Society* 20, no. 3 (spring 1994).

———. "New Times for the Military: Some Sociological Remarks on the Changing Role and Structure of the Armed Forces of the Advanced Societies." *The British Journal of Sociology* 45, no. 4 (December 1994).

Daniel, Donald C. F., and Bradd C. Hayes. "Securing Observance of UN Mandates through the Employment of Military Force." In *The UN Peace and Force.* Edited by Michael Pugh. London: Frank Cass, 1997.

Danopoulos, Constantine P., and Cynthia Watson, eds. *The Political Role of the Military.* London: Greenwood Press, 1996.

Dauber, Cori. "The Practice of Argument: Reading the Condition of Civil-Military Relations." *Armed Forces and Society* 24, no. 3 (spring 1998).

Davidson, Michael W. "Senior Officers and Vietnam Policymaking." *Parameters* 16, no. 1 (spring 1986).

Dean, Lt Col David J., USAF. *Airpower in Small Wars: The British Air Control Experience.* Maxwell AFB, Ala.: Center for Aerospace Doctrine, Research, and Education, 1985.

Dempsey, Judy. "Bosnian PM Lauds 'Raids for Peace': Bosnian PM Urged to Show Restraint." *Financial Times* (London), 1 September 1995.

Denaro, Brig A.G., British army. "Warrior or Worrier: Is the British Army Producing the Right Man to Command its

Troops on Operations?" *RUSI Journal* 140, no. 3 (June 1995).

Deptula, Col David A., USAF. *Firing for Effect: Change in the Nature of Warfare*. Defense Airpower Series. Arlington, Va.: Aerospace Education Foundation, 1995.

DeRemer, Maj Lee E., USAF. "ROE: Leadership Between a Rock and a Hard Place." *Air Power Journal* 10, no. 3 (fall 1996).

Desch, Michael C. "A Historian's Fallacies: A Reply to Bacevich." *Armed Forces and Society* 24, no. 4 (summer 1998).

———. "Soldiers, States, and Structures: The End of the Cold War and Weakening U.S. Civilian Control." *Armed Forces and Society* 24, no. 3 (spring 1998).

Devroy, Ann, and Bradley Graham. "NATO Suspends Bombing in Bosnia." *Washington Post,* 15 September 1995.

Dillon, G. M., ed. *Defence Policy Making: A Comparative Analysis*. King's Lynn, England: Leicester University Press, 1988.

"Discussions between the United Nations and NATO," 27 October 1994. File B4–2, BACS Collection.

Dixon, Norman. *On the Psychology of Military Incompetence*. London: Pimlico, 1976.

Dobbs, Michael. "White House Seeks to Defuse Russian, Italian Concerns on Bosnia." *Washington Post,* 13 September 1995.

Donegan, Comdr Kevin M., USN, aide and later Flag Lieutenant to Admiral Smith; NATO liaison officer to UNPROFOR during Operation Deliberate Force. Interviewed by author, 29 April 1998, London (Donegan was embarked aboard the USS *Stennis*). Printout from E–mail. Author's personal collection.

Doughty, Robert. *The Seeds of Disaster: The Development of French Army Doctrine, 1919–1939*. Ithaca, N.Y.: Cornell University Press, 1984.

Douhet, Giulio. *The Command of the Air.* Translated by Dino Ferrari. 1942. Reprint, Washington: Office of Air Force History, 1983.

Dowden, Richard. "NATO Angers UN in Bosnia Arms Mystery." *Independent* (London), 27 February 1995.

Downes, C. J. "To Be or Not To Be a Profession: The Military Case." *Defense Analysis* 1, no. 3 (1985).

Drake, Maj Ricky James, USAF. *The Rules for Defeat: The Impact of Aerial Rules of Engagement on USAF Operations in North Vietnam, 1965–1968.* Maxwell AFB, Ala.: Air University Press, 1993.

Drew, Dennis M. "Air Power in Peripheral Conflict." In *The War in the Air 1914–1994.* Edited by Alan Stephens. Fairbairn, Australia: Air Power Studies Centre, 1994.

Dunalp, Col Charles J., USAF. "Melancholy Reunion: A Report from the Future on the Collapse of Civil-Military Relations in the United States." *Airpower Journal* 10, no. 4 (winter 1996–1997).

———. "The Origins of the American Military Coup of 2012." *Parameters* 22, no. 4 (winter 1992–1993).

Eade, Gen George J. "Reflections on Air Power in the Vietnam War." *Air University Review* 25, no. 1 (November–December 1973).

"Early NATO Lesson: Smooth Political Links." *Aviation Week and Space Technology,* 18 September 1995.

Edemskii, Andrei. "Russian Perspective." In *International Perspectives on the Yugoslav Conflict.* Edited by Alex Danchev and Thomas Halverson. London: Macmillan, 1996.

Edmonds, Martin. *Armed Services and Society.* King's Lynn, England: Leicester University Press, 1988.

———. "Central Organizations of Defence in Great Britain." In *Central Organizations of Defense.* Edited by Martin Edmonds. Boulder, Colo.: Westview Press, 1985.

———, ed. *Central Organizations of Defense.* Boulder, Colo.: Westview Press, 1985.

———, ed. *The Defence Equation: British Military Systems Policy Planning and Performance Since 1945*. London: Brassey's, 1986.

"End-of-year Cease-fire Signed, Further Negotiations Urged." *UN Chronicle* 32, no. 1 (March 1995).

Ethell, Jeffrey, and Alfred Price. *Air War South Atlantic*. London: Sidgwick and Jackson, 1983.

Evans, M. G. D. "The Challenge of Integrating Civilians and the Military in Peace Support Operations." In *Meeting the Challenges of International Peacekeeping Operations: Assessing the Contribution of Technology*. Edited by Alex Gliksman. Proceedings from a conference held in Livermore, California, 9–10 September 1996. Livermore, Calif.: Center for Global Security Research, June 1998.

Evans, Martin. "The French Army and the Algerian War: Crisis of Identity." In *War and Society in Twentieth-Century France*. Edited by Michael Scriven and Peter Wagstaff. Oxford: Berg Publishers, 1991.

Evans, Michael. "RAF Prepares for NATO Bombing Raids on Serbs." *Times* (London), 28 April 1993.

———. "Serb Radar Link-up Poses Challenge to NATO Pilots." *Times* (London), 29 June 1995.

———. "Srebrenica Shield May Force Change in Bosnia Policy." *Times* (London), 23 April 1993.

———. "UK Officer Speaks Up for NATO's Top Brass." *Times* (London), 29 April 1993.

———. "West Weighs Risks and Rewards of Air Strikes." *Times* (London), 29 April 1993.

Facts On File Yearbook 1992. USA: Facts On File, Inc., 1993.

Facts On File Yearbook 1993. USA: Facts On File, Inc., 1994.

Facts On File Yearbook 1994. USA: Facts On File, Inc., 1995.

Facts On File Yearbook 1995. USA: Facts On File, Inc., 1996.

Fadok, Maj David S., USAF. *John Boyd and John Warden: Air Power's Quest for Strategic Paralysis*. Maxwell AFB, Ala.: Air University Press, 1995.

Feaver, Peter D. "Civil-Military Conflict and the Use of Force." In *U.S. Civil-Military Relations: In Crisis or Transition?* Edited by Don M. Snider and Miranda A. Carlton-Carew. Washington, D.C.: Center for Strategic and International Studies, 1995.

———. "The Civil-Military Problematique: Huntington, Janowitz, and the Question of Civilian Control." *Armed Forces and Society* 23, no. 2 (winter 1996).

———. "Crisis as Shirking: An Agency Theory Explanation of the Souring of American Civil-Military Relations." *Armed Forces and Society* 24, no. 3 (spring 1998).

———. "Modeling Civil-Military Relations: A Reply to Burk and Bacevich." *Armed Forces and Society* 24, no. 4 (summer 1998).

———. "An Agency Theory Explanation of American Civil-Military Relations during the Cold War." Paper prepared for the 1997 Annual Meeting of the Inter-University Seminar on Armed Forces and Society. Baltimore, Maryland, 24–26 October 1997.

Fedarko, Kevin. "Louder than Words." *Time*, 11 September 1995.

Fenske, John. "France." In *Defence Policy Making: A Comparative Analysis*. Edited by G. M. Dillon. King's Lynn, England: Leicester University Press, 1988.

"Fighting Escalates, UN Role in Question." *UN Chronicle* 32, no. 3 (September 1995).

Finer, S. E. *The Man on Horseback*. London: Pall Mall Press, 1962; Rev. ed., Peregrine Books, 1976.

"Flashpoints." *Jane's Defense Weekly*, 8 July 1995.

Fletcher, Martin. "Clinton Wrestles over the Next Step Amid Warnings of Vietnam." *Times* (London), 29 April 1993.

Flintham, Victor. *Air Wars and Aircraft: A Detailed Record of Air Combat, 1945 to the Present*. New York: Facts On File, 1990.

Flounders, Sara. *Bosnia Tragedy: The Unknown Role of the U.S. Government and Pentagon*. New York: World View Forum, 1995.

Foerster, Schuyler, and Edward N. Wright, eds. *American Defense Policy*. 6th ed. Baltimore, Md.: Johns Hopkins University Press, 1990.

Forget, Gen Michel, French air force. *Puissance Aérienne et Stratégies*. France: Addim, 1996.

Fox, Robert. "Bosnian Muslims Armed by Secret Flights." *Daily Telegraph* (London), 28 February 1995.

———. "Gulf Commander Named to Take Over from Rose." *Daily Telegraph* (London), 10 December 1994.

———. "Rehearsal Rules Out NATO Cover for Bosnia Retreat." *Daily Telegraph* (London), 20 February 1995.

Franzen, Lt Henning, Norwegian army, UNPROFOR peacekeeper, October 1993–May 1994. Interviewed by author, 18 February 1997, London. Transcript of taped interview. Author's personal collection.

Freedman, Lawrence. "The Future of Air Power." *Hawk Journal* (The Independent Journal of the Royal Air Force Staff College), 1993.

———. "Why the West Failed." *Foreign Policy* 97 (winter 1994–1995).

———, ed. *Military Intervention in European Conflicts*. Oxford: Blackwell Publishers, 1994.

———, ed. *Strategic Coercion*. Oxford: Oxford University Press, 1998.

Fulghum, David A. "U.S. Crews Strike Serb Positions." *Aviation Week and Space Technology*, 18 April 1994.

Fuller, J. F. C. *Generalship: Its Diseases and Their Cure: A Study of the Personal Factor in Command*. Harrisburg, Pa.: Military Service Publishing Co., 1936.

Gacek, Christopher M. *The Logic of Force: The Dilemma of Limited War in American Foreign Policy*. New York: Columbia University Press, 1994.

Gal, Reuven. "Commitment and Obedience in the Military: An Israeli Case Study." *Armed Forces and Society* 11, no. 4 (summer 1985).

Galbraith, John Kenneth. "How to Control the Military." *Harper's Magazine,* June 1969.

Gallego–Serra, Fermin. "Heavy Allied Air Activities Maintained over Bosnia." *Armed Forces Journal International* 30, no. 12 (July 1993).

Galvin, Gen John, USA, retired, Supreme Allied Commander Europe, 1987–1992. Interviewed by author, 14 July 1997. Transcript of taped telephone interview (Wilmington, Del., to General Galvin at Tufts University, Mass.). Author's personal collection.

Gamble, Lt Gen Patrick K., USAF, assistant chief of staff, Operations and Logistics, Supreme Headquarters Allied Powers Europe, Mons, Belgium, November 1994–August 1996. Interviewed by author, 2 July 1998, Washington, D.C. Tape recording. Author's personal collection.

Ganyard, Maj Stephen T., USMC. "Where Air Power Fails." US Naval Institute *Proceedings* 121, no. 1 (January 1995).

Garden, Timothy. "The Royal Air Force: Air Power and High Technology." In *The Defence Equation: British Military Systems Policy Planning and Performance Since 1945.* Edited by Martin Edmonds. London: Brassey's, 1986.

Garrison, John H. "The Political Dimension of Military Professionalism." In *American Defense Policy.* Edited by Peter L. Hays; Brenda J. Vallence; and Alan R. Van Tassel. 7th ed. Baltimore, Md.: Johns Hopkins University Press, 1997.

Gates, David. "Air Power and Aspects of Civil-Military Relations." In *Perspectives on Air Power: Air Power in Its Wider Context.* Edited by Stuart Peach. London: The Stationery Office, 1998.

———. "Air Power and the Theory and Practice of Coercion." *Defense Analysis* 13, no. 3 (1997).

Gaulle, Charles de. *The Edge of the Sword.* Translated by Gerard Hopkins. Originally published in France as *Le Fil de l'Epée,* 1932. London: Faber and Faber, 1960.

George, Alexander L. "Crisis Management: The Interaction of Political and Military Considerations." *Survival* 26, no. 5 (September/October 1984).

George, Alexander L., and William E. Simmons, eds. *The Limits of Coercive Diplomacy*. Boulder, Colo.: Westview Press, 1994.

———. "A Gift to the Serbs: NATO Commanders Should Leave Politics to Politicians." *Times* (London), 29 April 1993.

Goldfein, Maj David, USAF, aide-de-camp to Gen Michael Ryan, July 1995–July 1997. Interviewed by author, 1 May 1997, Ramstein Air Base, Germany. Tape recording. Author's personal collection.

Gombert, David C. "The United States and Yugoslavia's Wars." In *The World and Yugoslav's Wars*. Edited by Richard H. Ullman. New York: The Council on Foreign Relations, 1996.

Gordon, Michael R. "12 in State Dept. Ask Military Move against Serbs." *New York Times*, 23 April 1993.

———. "NATO General Is Reticent about Air Strikes in Bosnia." *New York Times*, 21 April 1993.

———. "Powell Delivers a Resounding No on Using Limited Force in Bosnia." *New York Times*, 28 September 1992.

Gordon, Michael R., and Gen Bernard E. Trainor. *The Generals' War: The Inside Story of the Conflict in the Gulf*. New York: Little, Brown and Company, 1995.

Gordon, Philip H. *A Certain Idea of France: French Security Policy and the Gaullist Legacy*. Princeton, N.J.: Princeton University Press, 1993.

Goulding, Marrack. "The Use of Force by the United Nations." *International Peacekeeping* 3, no. 1 (spring 1996).

Gow, James. "After the Flood: Literature on the Context Causes and Course of the Yugoslav War—Reflections and Refractions." *The Slavonic and East European Review* 75, no. 3 (July 1997).

———. "British Perspectives." In *International Perspectives on the Yugoslav Conflict*, eds. Alex Danchev and Thomas Halverson. London: Macmillan, 1996.

————. "Coercive Cadences: The Yugoslav War of Dissolution." In *Strategic Coercion: Concepts and Cases.* Edited by Lawrence Freedman. Oxford: Oxford University Press, 1998.

————. "The Future of Peacekeeping in the Yugoslav Region." In *Brassey's Defence Yearbook 1993.* Edited by the Centre for Defence Studies, King's College London. London: Brassey's, 1994.

————. *Legitimacy and the Military: The Yugoslav Crisis.* London: Printer Publishers, 1992.

————. "Settling Bosnia: The Balance of Forces." *Jane's Intelligence Review* 6, no. 4 (April 1994).

————. *Triumph of the Lack of Will: International Diplomacy and the Yugoslav War.* New York: Columbia University Press, 1997.

————. *Yugoslav Endgames: Civil Strife and Inter-state Conflict.* London Defence Studies no. 5. London: Brassey's for the Centre for Defence Studies, June 1991.

Gow, James, and Lawrence Freedman. "Intervention in a Fragmenting State: The Case of Yugoslavia." In *To Loose the Bands of Wickedness: International Intervention in Defence of Human Rights.* Edited by Nigel S. Rodley. London: Brassey's, 1992.

Gow, James, and Hans-Christian Hagman. "What Future for UNPROFOR?" *Jane's Intelligence Review* 7, no. 4 (April 1995).

Gow, James, and James D. D. Smith. *Peace-making, Peace-keeping: European Security and the Yugoslav Wars.* London Defence Studies no. 11. London: Brassey's for the Centre for Defence Studies, May 1992.

Graham, Bradley. "U.S. Fires Cruise Missiles at Bosnia Serb Sites." *Washington Post,* 11 September 1995.

Graham, George. "Aspin Orders Military Support to the Adriatic." *Financial Times* (London), 16 July 1992.

Granic, Mate, Croatian minister of foreign affairs. TLS (photocopy), to Yasushi Akashi, Zagreb, 6 August 1995. BACS Collection.

Gray, Bernard. "Clinton Fights Uphill Battle with Congress: The Bosnia Crisis—Europe and the US Struggle to Agree on What to Do Next." *Financial Times* (London), 20 July 1995.

Gray, Bernard; Laura Silber; and Harriet Martin. "US Senate Votes to End Arms Embargo on Bosnia." *Financial Times* (London), 27 July 1995.

Green, L. C. *The Contemporary Law of Armed Conflict.* Manchester, England: Manchester University Press, 1993.

Greenwood, David. "The United Kingdom." In *The Defense Policies of Nations: A Comparative Study.* Edited by Douglas J. Murray and Paul R. Viotti. 3d ed. Baltimore, Md.: Johns Hopkins University Press, 1994.

Grunawalt, Prof. Richard J. "The JCS Standing Rules of Engagement: A Judge Advocate's Primer." *The Air Force Law Review* 42 (1997).

Guerrero, Tech Sgt Phillip L., and Maj Martha Smythe, Arizona Air National Guard. "Resolute in Deny Flight." *National Guard* 48, no. 12 (December 1994).

Guillot, Philippe. "France, Peacekeeping, and Humanitarian Intervention." *International Peacekeeping* 1, no. 1 (spring 1994).

Haass, Richard N. *Intervention: The Use of American Military Force in the Post Cold War World.* Washington, D.C.: The Brookings Institution for the Carnegie Endowment for International Peace, 1994.

———. "Military Intervention: A Taxonomy of Challenges and Responses." In *The United States and the Use of Force in the Post-Cold War Era.* Queenstown, Md.: The Aspen Institute, 1995.

Haave, Maj Chris, USAF, staff officer assigned French portfolio, USNATO. Interviewed by author, 4 June 1997, Spangdahlem AB, Germany. Tape recording. Author's personal collection.

Hackett, Gen Sir John. *The Profession of Arms.* London: Sidgwick and Jackson, 1983.

Hagman, Hans–Christian. "UN-NATO Operational Co-operation in Peacekeeping 1992–1995." PhD diss., King's College, University of London, 1997.

Hallion, Richard P. "Precision Guided Munitions." *Air Power History* 43, no. 3 (fall 1996).

———. *Storm Over Iraq: Air Power in the Gulf War.* Washington, D.C.: Smithsonian Institute Press, 1992.

———, ed. *Air Power Confronts an Unstable World.* London: Brassey's, 1997.

Halperin, Morton H. *Bureaucratic Politics and Foreign Policy.* Washington, D.C.: The Brookings Institution, 1974.

———. "The President and the Military." *Foreign Affairs* 50, no. 2 (January 1972).

Halverson, Thomas. "American Perspective." In *International Perspectives on the Yugoslav Conflict.* Edited by Alex Danchev and Thomas Halverson. London: Macmillan, 1996.

Hamilton, Cong. Lee H., chairman of the House Committee on Foreign Affairs. "Air Strikes? Not Yet." *New York Times,* 24 April 1993.

Hammond, Paul Y. "On Taking Peacekeeping Seriously." In *To Sheathe the Sword.* Edited by John P. Lovell and David E. Albright. London: Greenwood Press, 1997.

Hanford, Capt Thomas O., USAF, weapons officer 31st Fighter Wing; flight lead for O'Grady rescue. Interviewed by author, 2 May 1997, Ramstein Air Base, Germany. Tape recording. Author's personal collection.

Harding, Marshal of the Royal Air Force Sir Peter, RAF, UK, chief of defense staff, December 1992–March 1994. Interviewed by author, 19 May 1998, Camberley, England. Tape recording. Author's personal collection.

Harmon, Christopher C. "Illustrations of Learning in Counterinsurgency." *Comparative Strategy* 11, no. 1 (January–March 1992).

Harries-Jenkins, Gwyn. "The Concept of Military Professionalism." *Defense Analysis* 6, no. 2 (1990).

Harris Public Opinion Survey. Study No. 951103. New York: Louis Harris and Associates, June 1995. http://www.irss.unc.edu/data archive.

Hart, Stephen. "Montgomery, Morale, Casualty Conservation, and Colossal Cracks: 21st Army Group's Operational Technique in North–West Europe, 1944–45." *The Journal of Strategic Studies* 19, no. 4 (December 1996).

Hastings, Max. *The Korean War.* New York: Simon and Schuster, 1987.

Hayden, Maj Gen Michael V., USAF, director of Intelligence, U.S. European Command (May 1993–October 1995). Interviewed by author, January–February 1998. Printouts of E-mails between London and Seoul, South Korea. Author's personal collection.

Hayes, Bradd C. *Naval Rules of Engagement: Management Tools for Crisis.* Santa Monica, Calif.: RAND Corporation, 1989. N–2963–CC.

Hays, Col Guy, French air force, French air attaché in London. Interviewed by author, 22 April 1998, London. Author's notes. Author's personal collection.

Hays, Peter L.; Brenda J. Vallence; and Alan R. Van Tassel, eds. *American Defense Policy.* 7th ed. Baltimore, Md.: Johns Hopkins University Press, 1997.

Healy, Melissa. "US General Asks West to Do More in Balkans." *Los Angeles Times* (Wash. ed.), 12 January 1993.

Henry, John B., II. "February 1968." *Foreign Policy,* no. 4 (fall 1971).

Herbst, Col Chet, USAF, staff officer, USNATO. Interviewed by author, 28 April 1997, Brussels. Author's notes and tape recording. Author's personal collection.

Higgins, Rosalyn. "The New United Nations and Former Yugoslavia." *International Affairs* 69, no. 3 (1993).

Hill, Amb. Christopher. Interviewed by Lt Col Robert Owen and Maj Mark McLaughlin, 27 February 1996. Transcript of taped interview. File H–1, BACS Collection.

Hillen, John F., III. "UN Collective Security: Chapter Six and a Half." *Parameters* 24, no. 1 (spring 1994).

Hitchins, Diddy R. M., and William A. Jacobs. "United Kingdom." In *The Political Role of the Military*. Edited by Constantine P. Danopoulos and Cynthia Watson. London: Greenwood Press, 1996.

Hoffman, Bruce. *British Airpower in Peripheral Conflict, 1919–1976*. A Project AIR FORCE report prepared for the United States Air Force. Santa Monica, Calif.: RAND Corporation, October 1989. R–3749–AF.

Hoffman, F. G. *Decisive Force: The New American Way of War*. Westport, Conn.: Praeger, 1996.

Hoffman, Stanley. "The Politics and Ethics of Military Intervention." *Survival* 37, no. 4 (winter 1995–1996).

Holbrooke, Richard. *To End A War*. New York: Random House, 1998.

———. US assistant secretary of state. Interviewed by Maj Mark McLaughlin and Dr. Karl Mueller, 24 May 1996, New York. Transcript of taped interview. File H–1, BACS Collection.

Honig, Jan Willem, and Norbert Both. *Srebrenica: Record of a War Crime*. London: Penguin Books, 1996.

Hood, Ronald Chalmers, III. "Bitter Victory: French Military Effectiveness during the Second World War." In *Military Effectiveness*. Vol. 3, *The Second World War*. Edited by Allan R. Millet and Williamson Murray. London: Allen and Unwin, 1988.

Hoopes, Townsend. *The Limits of Intervention*. New York: David McKay Company, 1969.

Hornburg, Lt Gen Hal M., USAF, deputy commander, Sixteenth Air Force and CAOC director, November 1994–September 1996. Interviewed by author, 17 July 1998, tape recording of telephone interview, London to Shaw AFB, S. C. Author's personal collection.

———. Interviewed by Maj Tim Reagan and Dr. Wayne Thompson, 16 October 1995, Vicenza, Italy. Transcript of tape recording. BACS Collection.

Horne, Alistair. *The French Army and Politics, 1870–1970.* London: Macmillan, 1984.

———. *A Savage War of Peace: Algeria 1954–1962.* 1977. Reprint, New York: Papermac, 1996.

Horner, Gen Charles A., USAF. "New Era Warfare." In *The War in the Air 1914–1994.* Edited by Alan Stephens. Fairbairn, Australia: Air Power Studies Center, 1994.

Howard, Michael. "Leadership in the British Army in the Second World War: Some Personal Observations." In *Leadership and Command: The Anglo–American Military Experience Since 1861.* Edited by G. D. Sheffield. London: Brassey's, 1997.

———. "The Concept of Air Power: An Historical Perspective." *Air Power History* 42, no. 4 (winter 1995).

Howorth, Jolyon. "The Debate in France Over Military Intervention in Europe." In *Military Intervention in European Conflicts.* Edited by Lawrence Freedman. London: Blackwell Publishers, 1994.

———. "The Defence Consensus and French Political Culture." In *War and Society in Twentieth–Century France.* Edited by Michael Scriven and Peter Wagstaff. Oxford: Berg Publishers, 1991.

Huffman, Kenneth, director, Defense Operations Division USNATO. Interviewed by author, 25 May 1998, Brussels. Tape recording. Author's personal collection.

Humphries, Lt Col John G., USAF. "Operations Law and the Rules of Engagement in Operations Desert Shield and Desert Storm." *Airpower Journal* 6, no. 3 (fall 1992).

Hunt, Maj Peter C., USAF. *Coalition Warfare: Considerations for the Air Component Commander.* Maxwell AFB, Ala.: Air University Press, 1998.

Hunter, Robert, American Ambassador to NATO. Interviewed by author, 18 November 1997, NATO Headquarters, Brussels. Author's notes. Author's personal collection.

———. Interviewed by Lt Col Robert Owen, USAF. 23 July 1996, Brussels. Transcript of tape recording. File H–1, BACS Collection.

Huntington, Samuel P. *The Soldier and the State: The Theory and Practice of Civil-Military Relations.* Cambridge, Mass.: Harvard University Press, 1957.

Hughes, Daniel J., ed. *Moltke on the Art of War.* Novato, Calif.: Presidio Press, 1993.

Hust, Maj Gerald R., USAF. *Taking Down Telecommunications.* Maxwell AFB, Ala.: Air University Press, 1994.

Ifill, Gwen. "Clinton Considers Bosnia Air Strikes; Sees Allied Accord." *New York Times,* 24 April 1993.

Iklé, Fred Charles. *Every War Must End.* Rev. ed. New York: Columbia University Press, 1991.

Inge, Field Marshal Sir Peter, British army. "The Capability-Based Army." *RUSI Journal* 139, no. 3 (June 1994).

———. "The Roles and Challenges of the British Armed Forces." *RUSI Journal* 141, no. 2 (February 1996).

Inge, Lord (Field Marshal) Peter. Interviewed by author, 19 October 1998, London. Author's notes. Author's personal collection.

Jackson, Bill, and Dwin Bramall. *The Chiefs: The Story of the United Kingdom Chiefs of Staff.* London: Brassey's, 1992.

"The Jags Are Back." *Air Forces Monthly,* October 1995.

James, Barry. "U.S. and Allies Set on Collision Course over Bosnia Policy." *International Herald Tribune,* 1 July 1995.

"The Jane's Interview: Adm Leighton W. Smith, USN." *Jane's Defence Weekly,* 28 January 1995.

Janis, Irving L. *Air War and Emotional Stress: Psychological Studies of Bombing and Civilian Defense.* 1951. Reprint, Westport, Conn.: Greenwood Press, 1971.

Janowitz, Morris. *The Professional Soldier: A Social and Political Portrait.* 1960. Reprint, with new prologue and preface, Glencoe, Ill.: Free Press, 1971.

Janvier, Lt Gen Bernard, French army, commander of United Nations Protection Force (UNPF), Zagreb, Croatia, March 1995–December 1995. Interviewed by author, 12 January 1998, Paris. Author's notes. Author's personal collection.

Jehl, Douglas. "In NATO Talks, Bosnia Sets Off a Sharp Debate." *New York Times,* 11 January 1994.

Jervis, Robert. *Perceptions and Misperceptions in International Politics.* Princeton, N.J.: Princeton University Press, 1976.

Joersz, Maj Gen Eldon W., USAF. Message. To CINCSOUTH (Adm Leighton W. Smith, USN) and COMAIRSOUTH (Gen Michael E. Ryan, USAF), 25 November 1994. File B4–2, BACS Collection.

Johnsen, William T., and Thomas-Durell Young. "France's Evolving Policy Toward NATO." *Strategic Review* 23, no. 3 (summer 1995).

Johnson, Douglas, and Steven Metz. "Civil-Military Relations in the United States: The State of the Debate." *Washington Quarterly* 18, no. 1 (1994).

Joint Chiefs of Staff. *US Department of Defense Dictionary of Military Terms.* With an introduction by David C. Isby. London: Greenhill Books, 1991.

Joint Pub 1. *Joint Warfare of the US Armed Forces.* Washington, D.C.: Government Printing Office, 1991.

Joint Pub 3–0. *Doctrine for Joint Operations.* Washington, D.C.: Government Printing Office, 1993.

Joint Warfare Publication (JWP) 0–01. *British Defence Doctrine.* London: Ministry of Defence, 1996.

Joulwan, Gen George A., USA. "Foundation Stone—Interview With SACEUR." *NATO's Sixteen Nations* 39, no. 3/4 (1994).

———. "The New NATO." *RUSI Journal* 140, no. 2 (April 1995).

———. Supreme Allied Commander Europe, 22 October 1993–11 July 1997. Interviewed by author, 11 February 1998, Washington, D.C. Transcript of tape recording. Author's personal collection.

———. Interviewed by author, 2 July 1998, Washington, D.C. Author's notes. Author's personal collection.

Judah, Tim. "Defiant Serbs Open Front In Bihac as Sanctions Intensify." *Times* (London), 28 April 1993.

Judah, Tim, and Philip Webster. "France Threatens to Pull Troops Out of Bosnia." *Times* (London), 29 April 1993.

Judd, Alan. "One of the Good Guys." *Sunday Times* (London), 15 November 1998.

Kaplan, Robert D. *Balkan Ghosts: A Journey through History.* New York: St. Martin's Press, 1993.

Kehoe, Lt Gen Nicholas B., USAF, assistant chief of staff, Operations and Logistics, Supreme Headquarters Allied Powers Europe, Mons, Belgium, July 1992–October 1994. Interviewed by author, 18 November 1997, Brussels. Transcript of tape recording. Author's personal collection.

Kemp, Kenneth W., and Charles Hudlin. "Civil Supremacy over the Military: Its Nature and Limits." *Armed Forces and Society* 19, no. 1 (fall 1992).

Kent, Sarah A. "Writing the Yugoslav Wars: English-Language Books on Bosnia (1992–1996) and the Challenges of Analyzing Contemporary History." *American Historical Review,* October 1997.

Kinnard, Douglas. "Civil-Military Relations: The President and the General." *Parameters* 15, no. 2 (summer 1985).

Kissinger, Henry. *Diplomacy.* New York: Simon and Schuster, 1994.

Kiszely, John. "The British Army and Approaches to Warfare Since 1945." *The Journal of Strategic Studies* 19, no. 4 (December 1996).

Kitson, Frank. *Low Intensity Operations: Subversion, Insurgency, and Peacekeeping.* Boston: Faber and Faber, 1971.

Kohn, Richard H. "Out of Control: The Crisis in Civil-Military Relations." *The National Interest,* no. 35 (spring 1994).

Komarow, Steve. "U.N. Pullback Gives NATO Jets Breathing Room." *USA Today,* 13 September 1995.

Kramers, Diederik. "Dutch Peacekeepers under Fire in the Aftermath of Srebrenica." *Transition* 1, no. 20 (3 November 1995).

Kramlinger, Maj George D., USAF. "Sustained Coercive Air Presence (SCAP): Provide Comfort, Deny Flight and the

Future of Airpower in Peace Enforcement." Master's thesis, School of Advanced Airpower Studies, Air University, Maxwell AFB, Ala., 1996. http://tuvok.au.af.mil/au/saas/studrsch/class.htm.

Lambert, Group Capt Andrew, and Arthur C. Williamson, eds. *The Dynamics of Air Power.* RAF Staff College, Bracknell, UK: HMSO, 1996.

Lanata, Gen Vincent, French air force. "L'armée aérienne, cent ans après son apparition: De la troisième à la quatrième dimension." *ENA Mensuel,* no. 266 (November 1996).

Lanata, Gen Vincent, French air force, chief of staff of the French air force, 1991–1994. Interviewed by author, 8 September 1998, Paris. Tape recording. Author's personal collection.

Lancaster, John. "NATO's Neutrality May Be Early Casualty." *Washington Post,* 11 April 1994.

———. TLS (photocopy), to Adm Leighton Smith, Naples, 7 December 1994. File B1a, BACS Collection.

Lapresle, Gen Bertrand de, UNPROFOR force commander, 15 March 1994–28 February 1995. Interviewed by author, 13 January 1998, Paris. Transcript of tape recording. Author's personal collection.

———. Interviewed by author, 8 September 1998, Paris. Transcript of tape recording. Author's personal collection.

Lellouche, Pierre. "France in Search of Security." *Foreign Affairs* 72, no. 2 (spring 1993).

Lepick, Olivier. "French Perspective." In *International Perspectives on the Yugoslav Conflict.* Edited by Alex Danchev and Thomas Halverson. London: Macmillan, 1996.

Leurdijk, Dick A. *The United Nations and NATO in Former Yugoslavia, 1991–1996: Limits to Diplomacy and Force.* The Hague: The Netherlands Atlantic Commission, 1996.

Leurs, Michael. "Joint Doctrine: New Pubs, Old Controversies." *Joint Forces Quarterly,* no. 5 (summer 1994).

Lewis, Anthony. "Crisis of Credibility." *New York Times,* 7 January 1994.

Lewy, Guenter. "Some Political-Military Lessons of the Vietnam War." *Parameters* 14, no. 1 (spring 1984).

Lindemann, Michael, and Bruce Clark. "Germany to Deploy Forces in Bosnia." *Financial Times* (London), 27 June 1995.

Lindemann, Michael; Bruce Clark; and Laura Silber. "West and Russia in Bosnia Pact: Ministers Stress Need for Political Solution—UN Forces to Be Boosted." *Financial Times* (London), 30 May 1995.

Lippman, Thomas W., and Ann Devroy. "Clinton's Policy Evolution: June Decision Led to Diplomatic Gambles." *Washington Post*, 11 September 1995.

Littlejohns, Michael. "Bosnia on the Brink: UN Weighs New Measures." *Financial Times* (London), 7 May 1993.

Littlejohns, Michael, and Harriet Martin. "UN Chief Warns on Finances for Peacekeeping." *Financial Times* (London), 23 June 1995.

Llinares, Rick. "On the Prowl." *Air Combat*, August/September 1995.

———. "Seahawks On the Prowl." *Air Force Monthly*, June 1995.

Lok, Joris Janssen. "Deny Flight Turns to Affirmative Action." *Jane's Defence Weekly*, 9 September 1995.

Lorell, Mark A. *Airpower in Peripheral Conflict: The French Experience in Africa.* A Project AIR FORCE report prepared for the United States Air Force. Santa Monica, Calif.: RAND Corporation, January 1989. R–3660–AF.

Lovell, John P., and David E. Albright, eds. *To Sheathe the Sword.* Forewords by Fred Woerner and Vincent Davis. London: Greenwood Press, 1997.

Lovell, John P., and David E. Albright. "Merging Theory and Practice." In *To Sheathe the Sword.* Edited by John P. Lovell and David E. Albright. London: Greenwood Press, 1997.

Lovell, John P., and Arthur Cyr. "America's Security Commitments: Coming to Terms with Entanglement." In *To Sheathe the Sword.* Edited by John P. Lovell and David E. Albright. London: Greenwood Press, 1997.

Lushbaugh, Col Robert, USAF, retired, chief of operations for Provide Promise and Deny Flight, CAOC, Vicenza, February–June 1993. Interviewed by author, 9 July 1998, Langley AFB, Va. Author's notes. Author's personal collection.

Luttwak, Edward N. "Toward Post-Heroic Warfare." *Foreign Affairs* 74, no. 3 (May/June 1995).

———. "From Vietnam To Desert Fox: Civil-Military Relations in Modern Democracies." *Survival* 41, no. 1 (spring 1999).

———. "Washington's Biggest Scandal." *Commentary*, May 1994.

MacKenzie, Maj Gen Lewis, Canadian army. *Peacekeeper: The Road to Sarajevo.* 1993. Reprint, New York: HarperCollins, 1994.

Malcolm, Noel. *Bosnia: A Short History.* New York: New York University Press, 1994.

Mandeles, Mark; Thomas C. Hone; and Sanford S. Terry. *Managing Command and Control in the Persian Gulf War.* London: Praeger, 1996.

Mandeville, Anne. "The British Army in Northern Ireland, 1969–85: New Professionalism." In *The Defence Equation: British Military Systems Policy Planning and Performance Since 1945.* Edited by Martin Edmonds. London: Brassey's, 1986.

March, James G., and Roger Weissinger-Baylon. *Ambiguity and Command: Organizational Perspectives on Military Decision Making.* N.p.: Pitman Publishing, 1986.

Marichy, Jean–Pierre. "Central Organizations of Defense in France." In *Central Organizations of Defense.* Edited by Martin Edmonds. Boulder, Colo.: Westview Press, 1985.

Marks, Edward. "The Vietnam Generation of Professional American Military Officers." *Conflict* 5, no. 1 (1983).

Martin, Harriet. "UN Threatens Raids as Mortar Attack Kills 37 in Sarajevo." *Financial Times* (London), 29 August 1995.

Martin, Harriet, and Bruce Clark. "US Twin Strategy on Bosnia Prompts Peace Talks." *Financial Times* (London), 2 September 1995.

Martin, Harriet; Bruce Clark; and John Ridding. "Bosnia Hails Force Element in US Plan." *Financial Times* (London), 17 August 1995.

Martin, Harriet; Chrysta Freeland; and Bruce Clark. "NATO Gives Serbs Deadline to Move Heavy Weapons." *Financial Times* (London), 4 September 1995.

Martin, Harriet; John Ridding; and Bruce Clark. "NATO May Widen Aims of Anti–Serb Bombing Sorties." *Financial Times* (London), 1 September 1995.

Martin, Harriet; Laura Silber; and Bruce Clark. "US Peace Call After Bosnia Attack." *Financial Times* (London), 31 August 1995.

Martin, Jurek. "Clinton Looks for Peace Opening." *Financial Times* (London), 9 August 1995.

———. "Clinton Pledge on Role of Troops in Bosnia." *Financial Times* (London), 1 June 1995.

———. "Protests Force Clinton to Retreat on Troops." *Financial Times* (London), 5 June 1995.

Martin, Jurek, and David White. "Clinton Ponders Options on Bosnia." *Financial Times* (London), 29 April 1993.

Martin, Michel Louis. "France." In *The Political Role of the Military*. Edited by Constantine P. Danopoulos and Cynthia Watson. London: Greenwood Press, 1996.

———. *Warriors to Managers: The French Military Establishment Since 1945*. Chapel Hill, N.C.: University of North Carolina Press, 1981.

"Maryland's 175th FG Pilots Go Hot and Destroy Serb Target." *National Guard* 49, no. 3 (March 1995).

Mason, Air Vice Marshal Tony, RAF. *Air Power: A Centennial Appraisal*. London: Brassey's, 1994.

———. "Air Power in the Peace Support Environment." In *The Dynamics of Air Power*. Edited by Group Captain Andrew

Lambert and Arthur C. Williamson. Bracknell, England: HMSO, 1996.

———. "Operations in Search of a Title: Air Power in Operations Other Than War." In *Air Power Confronts an Unstable World*. Edited by Dick Hallion. London: Brassey's, 1997.

Matthews, Lloyd J., and Dale E. Brown, eds. *The Parameters of Military Ethics*. London: Pergamon-Brassey's, 1989.

Matthews, William. "Accuracy is Phenomenal." *Air Force Times*, 2 October 1995.

MCM–KAA–050–95, "Operation Deny Flight—Viability of No-Fly Zone Enforcement." Memorandum for the Secretary-General, North Atlantic Treaty Organization, 13 July 1995. File B4–2, BACS Collection.

MCM–KAD–084–93, "Operational Options for Air Strikes." Memorandum for the Secretary-General, North Atlantic Treaty Organization. NAC Decision Statement, 8 August 1993. File B1c–2, BACS Collection.

MCM–KAE–090–94, "Operation Deny Flight ROE," 22 November 1994. File D2 a–c, BACS Collection.

McMaster, H.R. *Dereliction of Duty: Lyndon Johnson, Robert McNamara, The Joint Chiefs of Staff, and the Lies that Led to Vietnam*. New York: HarperCollins, 1997.

McNamara, Lt Col Stephen, USAF. *Air Power's Gordian Knot: Centralized versus Organic Control*. Maxwell AFB, Ala.: Air University Press, 1994.

McPeak, Gen Merrill A., USAF. "Transition Challenges: Memorandum for the President–Elect," 21 December 1992. In *Selected Works: 1990–1994*. Maxwell AFB, Ala.: Air University Press, 1995.

McPherson, Karen A. "The American Military in Fiction Since 1945." *Armed Forces and Society* 9, no. 4 (summer 1983).

McQueen, Alastair. "Why I Am Quitting, by General Rose." *Sunday Telegraph* (London), 12 January 1997.

Meilinger, Col Phillip S., USAF. "Air Targeting Strategies: An Overview." In *Air Power Confronts an Unstable World*. Edited by Dick Hallion. London: Brassey's, 1997.

———. *Ten Propositions Regarding Air Power*. Washington, D.C.: Office of Air Force History, 1995.

———, ed. *The Paths of Heaven: The Evolution of Airpower Theory*. Maxwell AFB, Ala.: Air University Press, 1997.

Melvin, Col R. A. M. S., British army, Engineering Battalion commander in Bosnia, Sector Southwest, 1995. Interviewed by author, 15 December 1998, RAF Bracknell, England. Author's notes. Author's personal collection.

Menanteau, Gen Pierre, French air force, retired. "French Air Force in Bosnia." *Asian Defence Journal,* no. 9 (September 1994).

Messervy-Whiting, Brigadier Graham, British army, military assistant to Lord Owen, November 1992–August 1993. *Peace Conference on Former Yugoslavia: The Politico-Military Interface*. London Defence Studies 21. London: Brassey's for the Centre for Defence Studies, 1994.

Metz, Lt Col Bernhard, French air force, Mirage 2000 squadron commander. Interviewed by author, 30 January 1998, RAF Bracknell, England. Author's notes. Author's personal collection.

Metz, David R. *Land-Based Air Power in Third World Crises*. Maxwell AFB, Ala.: Air University Press, 1986.

Miller, David. "NATO Command and Information Systems." *International Defense Review* 27, no. 6 (1994).

Mills, Eleanor. "A Stiff Upper Lip and a Pair of Twinkling Eyes." *Sunday Times* (London), 1 November 1998.

Momyer, Gen William W., USAF, retired. *Airpower in Three Wars (WWII, Korea, Vietnam)*. Washington, D.C.: US Air Force Office of History, 1978.

Moody, Peter R., Jr. "Clausewitz and the Fading Dialectic of War." *World Politics* 31, no. 3 (April 1979).

Moore, Patrick. "An End Game in Croatia and Bosnia?" *Transition,* 3 November 1995.

————. "January in Bosnia: Bizarre Diplomacy." *Transition*, 15 March 1995.

Moran, Lord. *The Anatomy of Courage: The Classic Study of the Soldier's Struggle Against Fear.* 1945. Reprint, Garden City, N.Y.: Avery, 1987.

Morgan, Robert. "Hurd Warns of Dangers in Air Strikes Against Serbs." *Times* (London), 20 April 1993.

Morillon, Gen Philippe, French army. *Croire et Oser: Chronique de Sarajevo.* Paris: Bernard Grasset, 1993.

————. "UN Operations in Bosnia: Lessons and Realities." *RUSI Journal* 138, no. 6 (December 1993).

Mortimer, Edward. "Slicing Up the Bosnian Cake: Brute Force Is Triumphing over Diplomacy in the Balkans." *Financial Times* (London), 8 August 1995.

————. "Twin Track to Bosnia Peace: Air Attacks and Military Aid Are Complimentary, Not Alternatives." *Financial Times* (London), 12 May 1993.

Murray, Douglas J., and Paul R. Viotti, eds. *The Defense Policies of Nations: A Comparative Study.* 3d ed. Baltimore, Md.: Johns Hopkins University Press, 1994.

Murray, Group Capt Trevor, RAF, AFSOUTH chief of operations and plans and AFSOUTH spokesman. Interviewed by author, 17 April 1997, Uxbridge, England. Tape recording. Author's personal collection.

————. Interviewed by author, 10 October 1997, Uxbridge, England. Author's notes and tape recording. Author's personal collection.

Murray, Williamson. "Air War in the Gulf: The Limits of Air Power." *Strategic Review* 26, no. 4 (winter 1998).

Nambiar, Lt Gen Satish, Indian army. "A Commander's Perspective on the Role of the Developing States in Peace Operations." In *Meeting the Challenges of International Peacekeeping Operations: Assessing the Contribution of Technology.* Edited by Alex Gliksman. Proceedings from a conference held in Livermore, California, 9–10 September 1996. Livermore, Calif.: Center for Global Security Research, June 1998.

NAMILCOM. "Implementation of Council Decision on Subsequent Air Attacks Against an Identified Surface–to–Air Weapons System." Message. 230800 NOV 94. To SHAPE. File B4–2, BACS Collection.

NATO Airborne Early Warning Force. "Operation Deny Flight: A History." N.p.: February 1997. Unclassified, 17-page unit history. History Office, NATO CAOC, Vicenza, Italy.

NATO. "Decisions Taken at the Meeting of the North Atlantic Council on 9 August 1993." Press Release (93)52, 9 August 1993.

———. "Declaration of the Heads of State and Government Participating in the Meeting of the North Atlantic Council Held at NATO Headquarters, Brussels, on 10–11 January 1994." Press Communiqué M–1(94)3, 11 January 1994.

———. "Decisions Taken at the Meeting of the North Atlantic Council on 9th February 1994." Press Release (94)15, 9 February 1994.

———. "Decisions Taken at the Meeting of the North Atlantic Council on 22nd April 1994." Press Release (94)31, 22 April 1994.

———. Press Release (95)55, 27 May 1994.

———. "Decisions on the Protection of Safe Areas Taken at the Meeting of the North Atlantic Council on 22nd April 1994." Press Release (94)31, 22 April 1994.

———. "Decisions on the Protection of Safe Areas Taken at the Meeting of the North Atlantic Council on 22nd April 1994." Press Release (94)32, 22 April 1994.

———. "Decisions Taken at the Meeting of the North Atlantic Council on 9th August 1993." Press Release (93)52, 9 August 1994.

———. "NATO Aircraft Attack Bosnian-Serb Tank." Press Release (94)90, 22 September 1994.

———. "Press Statement Issued Jointly by UN and NATO." Press Release (94)103, 28 October 1994.

———. Press Release (94)111, 23 November 1994.

———. Press Release (94)112, 23 November 1994.

——. "NATO Airstrikes Again in Bosnia-Herzegovina." Press Release (95)53, 26 May 1995.

——. Secretary-General's Opening Remarks to the NAC, Noordwijk, 30 May 1995.

——. Press Communiqué M–DPC/NPG–1 (95)57, 8 June 1995.

——. "Meeting of the North Atlantic Council on 12 July 1995." Press Release (95)69, 12 July 1995.

——. "Press statement on Gorazde by Secretary-General Willy Claes, following North Atlantic Council meeting on 25 July 1995." In *NATO Review*, September 1995.

——. "Press statement on Other Safe Areas by the Secretary-General following North Atlantic Council meeting on 1 August 1995." In *NATO Review*, September 1995.

——. "Statement by the Secretary-General of NATO." NATO Press Release (95)73, 30 August 1995.

——. "Statement by the Secretary-General Following Council Meeting – 2 September 1995." NATO Press Release, 3 September 1995.

——. "Statement by the Secretary-General of NATO." NATO Press Release (95)79, 5 September 1995.

"NATO Uses Tomahawk on Serb Targets." *Jane's Defence Weekly*, 16 September 1995.

Nelan, Bruce W. "The Balkans: More Talking, More Bombing." *Time*, 18 September 1995.

New, Lt Col Terry L., USAF. "Where to Draw the Line between Air and Land Battle." *Air Power Journal* 10, no. 3 (fall 1996).

Nicholls, Col David V., Royal Marines. "Bosnia: UN and NATO." *RUSI Journal* 141, no. 1 (February 1996).

——. Interviewed by author, 9 January 1998, Exmouth, England. Tape recording. Author's personal collection.

Nixon, Richard. *No More Vietnams*. New York: Avon Books, 1985.

O'Grady, Capt Scott, USAF, with Jeff Coplon. *Return with Honor*. London: Doubleday, 1995.

"Operation Deliberate Force Factual Review." Draft ed., 14 November 1995, prepared by the CAOC. BACS Collection.

Operations Law Deployment Deskbook. Vol. 2. A textbook and reference book used by the Air Force Judge Advocate General School, Maxwell AFB, Ala.: International and Operations Law Division, Office of the Judge Advocate General, Department of the Air Force, 1996.

Osgood, Robert E. *Limited War Revisited.* Boulder, Colo.: Westview Press, 1979.

Owen, David. *Balkan Odyssey.* London: Victor Gollancz, 1995; Indigo, 1996.

———. *Balkan Odyssey.* Academic ed. CD ROM version 1.1. The Electric Company, 1995.

———, and Laura Silber, "Hurd Hints at Croatia Sanctions," *Financial Times* (London), 16 July 1993.

Owen, Col Robert C., USAF. "The Balkans Air Campaign Study: Part 1." *Airpower Journal* 11, no. 2 (summer 1997).

———. "The Balkans Air Campaign Study: Part 2." *Airpower Journal* 11, no. 3 (autumn 1997).

———. *Deliberate Force: A Case Study in Effective Air Campaigning.* Maxwell AFB, Ala.: Air University Press, January 2000.

Owens, Mackubin Thomas. "Civilian Control: A National Crisis?" *Joint Forces Quarterly,* no. 6 (autumn/winter 1994–1995).

———. "Lessons of the Gulf War." *Strategic Review* 20, no. 1 (winter 1992).

Paladini, Col Steven M., USAF, deputy assistant chief of staff for operations, AFSOUTH, Naples, February 1994–June 1996. Interviewed by author, 26 September 1997, RAF Lakenheath, England. Tape recording. Author's personal collection.

Palmer, Gen Bruce, Jr., USA. *The 25-Year War: America's Military Role in Vietnam.* N.p.: University Press of Kentucky, 1984; N.Y.: Simon and Schuster, 1985.

Pape, Robert A. *Bombing to Win: Air Power and Coercion in War.* Ithaca, N.Y.: Cornell University Press, 1996.

Parker, George, and Bruce Clark. "Hurd Warns over Bosnia Mission." *Financial Times* (London), 5 June 1995.

———. "Serbs Free 108 UN Hostages." *Financial Times* (London), 7 June 1995.

Parks, Col W. Hays, USMCR. "Air War and the Law of War." *The Air Force Law Review* (1990).

———. "Precision Bombing and Area Bombing: Who Did Which, and When?" *The Journal of Strategic Studies* 18, no. 1 (March 1995).

———. "Righting the Rules of Engagement." US Naval Institute *Proceedings* 115, no. 5 (May 1989).

Peach, Group Capt Stuart W., RAF. *Perspectives On Air Power: Air Power In Its Wider Context.* London: The Stationery Office, 1998.

———. "Air Power in Peace Support Operations: Coercion versus Coalition." Master's thesis, Downing College, University of Cambridge, 1997.

———. "Plans Director's Thoughts." Contemporaneous notes. n.d.

———. "Deny Flight: A Joint and Combined Operation." 2 May 1994.

Peck, Brig Gen William A., Jr., USAF, chief of plans for Deny Flight, CAOC, Vicenza, Italy, July 1993–June 1994, assistant director of operations, USAFE, July 1994–July 1995. Interviewed by author, 9 July 1998, Langley AFB, Va. Tape recording. Author's personal collection.

Perlmuter, Amos. "The Military and Politics in Modern Times: A Decade Later." *The Journal of Strategic Studies* 19, no. 1 (March 1986).

Peston, Robert, and Harriet Martin. "UK Poised to Double Troop Levels in Bosnia." *Financial Times* (London), 29 May 1995.

Petraeus, David H. "The American Military and the Lessons of Vietnam: A Study of Military Influence and the Use of Force in the Post-Vietnam Era." PhD diss., Princeton University, 1987.

———. "Military Influence and the Post-Vietnam Use of Force." *Armed Forces and Society* 15, no. 4 (summer 1989).

———. "Lessons of History and Lessons of Vietnam." *Parameters* 16, no. 3 (autumn 1986).

Petrea, Capt Howard, USN, CAOC planner, October 1993–March 1994; executive assistant to CINCSOUTH (Adm Leighton Smith), April 1994–June 1996. Interviewed by author, 12 February 1998, Crystal City, Va. Author's notes and tape recording. Author's personal collection.

Pew Research Center for the People and the Press, The. "Support for Independent Candidate in '96 Up Again." Transcript of media survey, 24 August 1995. http://www.people-press.org/augque.htm.

Posner, Theodore Robert. *Current French Security Policy: The Gaullist Legacy.* London: Greenwood Press, 1991.

Powell, Colin L. "The American Commitment to European Security." *Survival* 34, no. 2 (summer 1992).

———. "U.S. Forces: Challenges Ahead." *Foreign Affairs* 72, no. 5 (winter 1992/1993).

———. "Why Generals Get Nervous." *New York Times,* 8 October 1992.

Powell, Colin, with Joseph E. Persico. *My American Journey.* New York: Random House, 1995.

Powell, Colin, et al. "An Exchange on Civil-Military Relations." Four reactions to Richard H. Kohn's article in our spring 1994 issue, together with a response from the author. *The National Interest,* no. 36 (summer 1994).

Prentice, Eve-Ann. "Rose Letter Informs Serbs He Wants to Avoid Airstrikes." *Times* (London), 2 November 1994.

Previdi, Robert. *Civilian Control versus Military Rule.* New York: Hippocrene Books, 1988.

Pugh, Michael, ed. *The UN Peace and Force.* London: Frank Cass, 1997.

Quiggin, Capt Thomas, Canadian army, military information analyst, UNPF Headquarters, Zagreb, Croatia, February 1994–1997. Interviewed by author, 20 December 1998–7

February 1999, London. Printouts of E–mail. Author's personal collection.

Rapid Reaction Force Operations Staff. "HQ 1 (UK) ARMD DIV RRFOS Brief," 17 November 1995.

Ray, Vice Adm Norman W., USN, deputy chairman of NATO's Military Committee, July 1992–December 1995. Interviewed by author, 19 November 1997, Brussels. Transcript of tape recording. Author's personal collection.

"Record of Discussions: Meeting SRSG, FC and Staff to Review Fixed Targets, and the Implications of NATO Defence Ministers' Meeting—Seville—30 September 1994." (Includes additional points discussed by SRSG, FC, and HCA on 7 October 1994), c. 8 October 1994. File B4–2, BACS Collection.

Régnault, Lt Gen François, French air force, chief of Employment of Forces Division of the Joint Services Headquarters, October 1992–October 1993; chief of the Joint Operational Command Center, October 1993–September 1994; operations assistant of the Air Force Staff, September 1994–September 1995; assistant for Operations to the French Chief of the Joint Staff, 1 September 1995–1 June 1997. Interviewed by author, 9 September 1998, Paris. Tape recording. Author's personal collection.

Rehbein, Robert E. *Informing the Blue Helmets: The United States, UN Peacekeeping Operations, and the Role of Intelligence.* The Martello Papers Series. Kingston, Canada: Centre for International Relations, Queen's University, 1996.

Renuart, Brig Gen Victor E., USAF, chief of plans, NATO CAOC, Vicenza, Italy, November 1994–May 1995; assistant director of operations, Headquarters US Air Forces in Europe, June 1995–April 1996. Interviewed by author, 28 May 1998, Spangdahlem Air Base, Germany. Transcript of tape recording. Author's personal collection.

Richardson, Col Douglas J., USAF, chief of operations and chief of staff, NATO CAOC, Vicenza, Italy, July 1994–June 1996. Interviewed by author, 27 September 1997, RAF

Lakenheath, England. Tape recording. Author's personal collection.

———. Interviewed by Maj Mark Conversino, USAF, 16 January 1996, Vicenza, Italy. File H–1, BACS Collection.

Ricks, Thomas E. "The Widening Gap Between the Military and Society." *The Atlantic Monthly* 280, no. 1 (July 1997).

Riddell, Peter, and Martin Ivens. "Hurd Presses On for Quicker Response to Global Ills." *Times* (London), 21 April 1993.

Ridding, Alan. "France Presses U.S. for Stronger Stand on Bosnia." *New York Times,* 6 January 1994.

Ridding, John, and Bruce Clark. "Chirac Seeks Siege Relief for Sarajevo: Paris Broadens Aims." *Financial Times* (London), 1 September 1995.

Ridding, John; Harriet Martin; and Laura Silber. "Bosnian Leader Threatens to Quit Peace Talks." *Financial Times* (London), 30 August 1995.

———. "Bosnian Threat to Quit Talks Unless NATO Punishes Serbs." *Financial Times* (London), 30 August 1995.

Rifkind, Malcolm, UK secretary of state for defence. "Peacekeeping or Peacemaking?: Implications and Prospects," *RUSI Journal* 138, no. 2 (April 1993).

Riggins, Maj Jim, USAF, chief, Force Application, HQ USAF/XOOC (CHECKMATE), "Five ATAF Combined Air Operations Center: History, Organization, and Function, From April 1993." Draft ed., 2 December 1995. History Office, NATO CAOC, Vicenza, Italy.

Ripley, Tim. "A Deliberate Force on the Mountain." *International Defense Review* 28 (October 1995).

———. *Air War Bosnia: UN and NATO Airpower.* Osceola, Wisc.: Motorbooks International, 1996.

———. "Air Power Vindicated." *Flight International,* 1–7 November 1995.

———. "Blue Sword over Bosnia." *World Airpower Journal* 19 (winter 1994).

———. "Bosnia Mission Stretches Airborne Eyes and Ears." *International Defense Review* 27, no. 1 (1994).

———. "French Air Power in Bosnia," *Air Pictorial* 56, no. 8, August 1994.

———. "NATO Strikes Back." *World Airpower Journal* 22 (autumn/winter 1995).

———. "NATO's Air Command—Backing Up the Blue Helmets." *International Defense Review* 28, November 1995.

———. "Operation Deliberate Force." *World Airpower Journal* 24 (spring 1996).

———. *Operation Deliberate Force: The UN and NATO Campaign in Bosnia 1995.* Foreword by Nik Gowing. Lancaster, UK: Centre for Defence and International Security Studies, 1999.

———. "Operation Deny Flight." *World Airpower Journal* 16 (spring 1994).

———. "Reasons for Being." *Flight International,* 24–30 January 1996.

———. "Silence of the SAMs." *Aircraft Illustrated* 28, no. 1, November 1995.

Roach, Capt J. Ashley, USN. "Rules of Engagement." *Naval War College Review* 36, no. 1 (January–February 1983).

Roberts, Adam. "From San Francisco to Sarajevo: The UN and the Use of Force." *Survival* 37, no. 4 (winter 1995–1996).

Robinson, Anthony, and Bernard Gray. "Taking of Hostages Will Not Deter Attacks, Serbs Warned." *Financial Times* (London), 22 July 1995.

Rohde, David. *A Safe Area, Srebrenica: Europe's Worst Massacre Since the Second World War.* London: Pocket Books, 1997.

Romjue, John L. "The Evolution of American Army Doctrine." In *The Origins of Contemporary Doctrine.* Edited by John Gooch. *The Occasional,* no. 30. Camberley, England: Strategic and Combat Studies Institute, 1997.

Ronnfeldt, Carsten, and Per Erik Solli, eds. *Use of Air Power in Peace Operations.* NUPI Peacekeeping and Multinational Operations Report, no. 7. Oslo: Norwegian Institute of International Affairs, 1997.

Rose, Lt Gen Sir Michael, British army, Sarajevo. TLS (photo-copy), to Gen Ratko Mladic, Han Pijesak, with a copy to Dr. Karadzic, 18 September 1994. BACS Collection.

————. Sarajevo. Letter to the editor of the *Times* (London), 1 November 1994, published in *Times* (London), 2 November 1994.

————. Sarajevo. Letter to Gen Ratko Mladic, Han Pijesak, 30 September 1994, published in *Times* (London), 2 November 1994.

————. "Bosnia Herzegovina 1994—NATO Support for UN Wider Peacekeeping Operations." *NATO's Sixteen Nations* 39, no. 3/4 (1994).

————. "The Rubicon Crossed: Developments in Peacekeeping at the End of the Twentieth Century." The 1997 Kermit Roosevelt Lecture. London, May 1997.

————. "A Year In Bosnia: What Has Been Achieved." *RUSI Journal* 140, no. 3 (June 1995).

————. "A Year in Bosnia: What Was Achieved." *Studies in Conflict and Terrorism* 19, no. 3 (July–September 1996).

————, retired. "How Soon Could Our Army Lose a War?" *Daily Telegraph* (London), 16 December 1997.

————. "Among the Mad Dogs of War." *Sunday Times* (London), 15 November 1998.

————. *Fighting For Peace: Bosnia 1994*. London: The Harvill Press, 1998.

————. "Lies, Lies, Lies." *Sunday Times* (London), 8 November 1998.

————. "My Private War." *Sunday Times* (London), 1 November 1998.

————. Interviewed by makers of the television series *Yugoslavia: Death of a Nation*, c. 1995, transcript of filmed interview. "Death of Yugoslavia" Collection, Box 18, File 4 (R–Z), 1, Liddell Hart Archives, King's College, University of London.

————, retired. Commander, Bosnia–Herzegovina Command, January 1994–January 1995. Interviewed by author, 10

December 1997, London. Transcript of taped interview. Author's personal collection.

Rosen, Stephen Peter. "Vietnam and the American Theory of Limited War." *International Security* 7, no. 2 (fall 1982).

Rowe, Peter. "The British Soldier and the Law." In *The Defence Equation: British Military Systems Policy Planning and Performance Since 1945*. Edited by Martin Edmonds. London: Brassey's, 1986.

Royal United Services Institute. *The Democratic Management of Defence*. Whitehall Paper 16. London: RUSI, 1992.

———. *International Security Review 1995*. London: RUSI, 1995.

———. *International Security Review 1996*. London: RUSI, 1996.

Roxborough, Ian. "Clausewitz and the Sociology of War." *The British Journal of Sociology* 45, no. 4 (December 1994).

Royal Welch Fusiliers, 1st Battalion. *White Dragon: The Royal Welch Fusiliers in Bosnia*. Wrexham, UK: RWF Regimental Headquarters, 1995.

Rudd, Air Commodore Mike, RAF, NATO liaison officer to UNPF Headquarters, Zagreb, Croatia, February–December 1995. Interviewed by author, 15 September 1997, Easton-on-the-Hill, England. Transcript of tape recording. Author's personal collection.

Ruggie, John Gerard. "The UN and the Collective Use of Force: Whither and Whether?" In *The UN Peace and Force*. Edited by Michael Pugh. London: Frank Cass, 1997.

Rupert, James. "Croatia Claims Victory in Serb Breakaway Region." *Washington Post*, 8 August 1995.

Rupert, James, and Daniel Williams. "Serbs Say Hospital Hit by U.N. Shells; Russia Condemns Airstrikes." *Washington Post*, 10 September 1995.

Russett, Bruce. *Controlling the Sword: The Democratic Governance of National Security*. Cambridge, Mass.: Harvard University Press, 1990.

Rutledge, Brig Gen John W., USAF, executive officer to the deputy commander in chief, US European Command. Interviewed by author, 6 February 1998, RAF High Wycombe, England. Author's notes. Author's personal collection.

Ryan, Gen Michael E., USAF, commander Allied Air Forces Southern Europe (COMAIRSOUTH) and commander US Sixteenth Air Force, September 1994–April 1996. "NATO Air Operations in Bosnia-Herzegovina: Deliberate Force, 29 August–14 September 1995." Briefing. USAF School of Advanced Airpower Studies, Maxwell AFB, Ala., 7 February 1996. Author's personal notes.

———. "NATO Air Operations in Bosnia-Herzegovina: Deliberate Force, 29 August–14 September 1995." Transcript of briefing. Air Power Conference, London, 13 September 1996.

———. "NATO Air Operations in Bosnia-Herzegovina: Deliberate Force, 29 August–14 September 1995." Slides from briefing. Air Power Conference, London, 13 September 1996.

———. Interviewed by author, 6 June 1997, Ramstein AB, Germany. Transcript of taped interview. Author's personal collection.

Sabathe, Maj Gen Emile, French air force, French senior national representative to CAOC, Vicenza, Italy, 4 April–30 December 1993. Interviewed by author, 7 September 1998, Paris. Tape recording. Author's personal collection.

Sabin, Philip. "Air Power in Joint Warfare." In *Perspectives on Air Power: Air Power in Its Wider Context*, ed. Stuart Peach. London: The Stationery Office, 1998.

———. "The Counter-Air Contest." In *The Dynamics of Air Power*. Edited by Group Capt Andrew Lambert and Arthur C. Williamson. Bracknell, England: HMSO, 1996.

———. "The Counter-Air Mission in Peace Support Operations." In *The Dynamics of Air Power*. Edited by

Group Capt Andrew Lambert and Arthur C. Williamson. Bracknell, England: HMSO, 1996.

———. "Modern Air Power Theory—Some Neglected Issues." *Air Clues* 48, no. 9 (September 1994).

———. "Peace Support Operations—A Strategic Perspective." In *The Dynamics of Air Power.* Edited by Group Capt Andrew Lambert and Arthur C. Williamson. Bracknell, England: HMSO, 1996.

Sagan, Scott D. "Rules of Engagement." *Security Studies* 1, no. 1 (autumn 1991).

Sarkesian, Sam C. "Political Soldiers: Perspectives on Professionalism in the U.S. Military." *Midwest Journal of Political Science* 16, no. 2 (May 1972).

Sawyer, Brig Gen David A., USAF, deputy director, CAOC, Vicenza, Italy. Interviewed by Maj Tim Reagan and Dr. Wayne Thompson, 11 October 1995, Vicenza, Italy. Transcript of tape recording. BACS Collection.

Schmitt, Eric. "NATO Commanders Face Grim Choices." *New York Times,* 14 September 1995.

Schneider, Barry W., and Lawrence E. Grinter. *Battlefield of the Future: 21st Century Warfare Issues.* Air War College Studies in National Security, no. 3. Maxwell AFB, Ala.: Air University Press, 1995.

Schulte, Gregory L. "Former Yugoslavia and the New NATO." *Survival* 39, no. 1 (spring 1997).

———. Director, Bosnia Task Force, NATO International Staff. Interviewed by author, 28 April 1997, Brussels. Author's notes. Author's personal collection.

Sciolino, Elaine. "U.S. and France Resolve Dispute on NATO Talks." *New York Times,* 8 January 1994.

———. "U.S. Is Scrambling for a Strategy On Eve of Clinton European Trip." *New York Times,* 5 January 1994.

———. "U.S. Military Split on Using Air Power against the Serbs." *New York Times,* 29 April 1993.

Scriven, Michael, and Peter Wagstaff. *War and Society in 20th Century France.* Oxford: Berg Publishers, 1991.

Scruton, Roger. *A Dictionary of Political Thought.* 2d ed. London: Macmillan, 1982; Pan Books, 1996.

Seabury, Paul, and Angelo Codevilla. *War: Ends and Means.* New York: Basic Books, 1989.

"SEAD Role for F–16 Comes Closer." *Jane's Defence Weekly,* 20 August 1994.

Seidt, Hans–Ulrich. "Lessons Learnt from the Crisis in the Balkans." *European Security* 5, no. 1 (spring 1996).

Shalikashvili, Gen John, USA. Edited excerpts of SACEUR interview with Nick Doughty, Reuters TV and Wire News Service, 21 January 1993, SHAPE, Belgium. In *ACE OUTPUT.* Vol. 12, no. 1 (February 1993).

Shanahan, John N. T. "No-Fly Zone Operations: Tactical Success and Strategic Failure." In *Essays on Strategy XIV.* Edited by Mary A. Sommerville. Washington, D.C.: National Defense University Press, 1997.

Sharp, Jane M. O. *Bankrupt in the Balkans: British Policy in Bosnia.* London: Institute for Public Policy Research, 1993.

———. *Honest Broker or Perfidious Albion: British Policy in Former Yugoslavia.* London: Institute for Public Policy Research, 1997.

Sharp, Adm U.S. Grant, USN. *Strategy for Defeat: Vietnam in Retrospect.* With foreword by Hanson W. Baldwin. Novato, Calif.: Presidio Press, 1978.

Shea, Jamie, NATO spokesman. Interviewed by author, 28 April 1997, Brussels. Tape recording. Author's personal collection.

Sheffield, G. D., ed. *Leadership and Command: The Anglo-American Military Experience Since 1861.* London: Brassey's, 1997.

Short, Maj Gen Michael C., USAF, chief of staff, Allied Air Forces Southern Europe, July 1995–May 1996, Naples. Interviewed by author, 2 May 1997, Ramstein Air Base, Germany. Tape recording. Author's personal collection.

Shultz, Richard H., Jr., and Robert L. Pfaltzgraff Jr., eds. *The Future of Air Power in the Aftermath of the Gulf War.* Maxwell AFB, Ala.: Air University Press, 1992.

Silber, Laura. "Bosnia Factions Agree UN Control of Sarajevo." *Financial Times* (London), 17 August 1993.

———. "Serbs Claim Deal With West over Release of Hostages." *Financial Times* (London), 14 June 1995.

Silber, Laura, and Bruce Clark. "UN in Split with NATO on Bosnia Bombing Campaign." *Financial Times* (London), 13 September 1995.

Silber, Laura, and Bruce Clark. "US Warns Serbs as Bosnia Moves Resume." *Financial Times* (London), 28 August 1995.

Silber, Laura; Judy Dempsey; and Anthony Robinson. "Underdog Croatia Learns How To Bite: Zagreb Has Made Good Use of the Backing It Receives from the US, Germany, and Austria." *Financial Times* (London), 2 August 1995.

Silber, Laura, and Allan Little. *Yugoslavia: Death of a Nation.* N.p.: TV Books, Inc., 1996.

Silber, Laura, and Harriet Martin. "NATO Strikes Bosnia: Croats and Moslems in Mood for War." *Financial Times* (London), 31 August 1995.

Silber, Laura; Harriet Martin; and Bruce Clark. "Diplomatic Effort Stepped Up in Bosnia." *Financial Times* (London), 20 June 1995.

Silber, Laura, and Anthony Robinson. "Croats Unleash Attack on Krajina: Rebel Serb Capital Shelled as Zagreb Defies Calls for Restraint." *Financial Times* (London), 5 August 1995.

Silber, Laura, and Anthony Robinson. "US Envoy Hails Balkan Deal to Divide Bosnia." *Financial Times* (London), 9 September 1995.

Silber, Laura, and Anthony Robinson. "Fear of Wider Conflict as Croatians Attack Serbs: UN and NATO Finalize Procedure for Air Strikes." *Financial Times* (London), 29 July 1995.

Silber, Laura, and Gillian Tett. "Fighting Threatens Talks on Bosnia." *Financial Times* (London), 19 August 1993.

Silber, Laura, and Gillian Tett. "Karadzic Warns of War if NATO Air Strikes Go Ahead." *Financial Times* (London), 11 August 1993.

Silber, Laura, and Gillian Tett. "Serbs Agree to Pull Back Their Forces." *Financial Times* (London), 14 August 1993.

Silber, Laura; Gillian Tett; and George Graham. "Bosnian Peace Plan Under Fire." *Financial Times* (London), 25 August 1993.

Silber, Laura; Gillian Tett; and George Graham. "Sarajevo Accord Puts UN In Charge." *Financial Times* (London), 19 August 1993.

Silber, Laura, and David White. "Serb Forces Defy UN in New Attack." *Financial Times* (London), 28 April 1993.

Simmons, Dr. Dean; Dr. Phillip Gould; Dr. Verena Vomaslic; and Col Phillip Walsh, USMC, retired. "Air Operations over Bosnia." US Naval Institute *Proceedings* 123, no. 5 (May 1997).

Simpson, John. "We Are All Air Strikers Now." *The Spectator,* 9 September 1995.

Slater, Jerome. "Apolitical Warrior or Soldier-Statesman." *Armed Forces and Society* 4, no. 1 (November 1977).

Slim, Hugo. "The Stretcher and the Drum: Civil-Military Relations in Peace Support Operations." *International Peacekeeping* 3, no. 2 (summer 1996).

Smith, Lt Col Kevin W., USAF. *Cockpit Video: A Low Cost BDA Source.* Maxwell AFB, Ala.: Air University Press, 1993.

Smith, Adm Leighton W., USN, Naples. TLS (photocopy) to Gen Bertrand de Lapresle, Zagreb, 8 December 1994. File B1a, BACS Collection.

———. Transcript of News Conference. Naples, 11 April 1994. http://www.afsouth.nato.int/archives/archives.htm.

———. Transcript of News Conference. Naples, 5 August 1994 (9:00 A.M). http://www.afsouth.nato.int/archives/archives.htm.

———. Transcript of News Conference. Naples, 6 August 1994 (9:45 A.M.). http://www.afsouth.nato.int/archives/ archives.htm.

———. "NATO Air Strike Against Bosnian Serbs." Transcript of News Conference. Naples, 31 August 1995 (10:00 A.M.). http://www.afsouth.nato.int/archives/archives.htm.

———. "NATO Air Strike Against Udbina Airfield." Transcript of News Conference. Naples, 21 November 1994 (3:30 P.M.). http://www.afsouth.nato.int/archives/archives.htm.

———. "NATO Air Strike Against Udbina Airfield—Mission Assessment." Transcript of News Conference. Naples, 22 November 1994 (5:00 P.M.). http://www.afsouth.nato. int/archives/archives.htm.

———. "NATO Close Air Support – Srebrenica – 11 July 95." Transcript of News Conference. Naples, 12 July 1995. http://www.afsouth.nato.int/archives/archives.htm.

———. "NATO Recommences Air Strikes Against Bosnian Serbs." Transcript of press conference, Naples, 6 September 1995 (9:00 A.M.). http://www.afsouth.nato.int /archives/archives.htm.

———. Commander in Chief NATO Allied Forces Southern Europe. Briefing to the US Air Force Air War College. Maxwell AFB, Ala., 9 November 1995. Videocassette. File MISC–19, folder H–4, BACS Collection.

———. Interviewed by author, 10 February 1998, Arlington, Va. Transcript of tape recording. Author's personal collection.

Snow, Donald M., and Dennis M. Drew. *From Lexington to Desert Storm: War and Politics in the American Experience.* Armonk, N.Y.: M. E. Sharpe, Inc., 1994.

Snyder, Jack. "Civil-Military Relations and the Cult of the Offensive, 1914–1918." *International Security* 9, no. 1 (summer 1984).

Snyder, Dr. Thomas S., and Dr. Daniel F. Harrington, USAFE Office of History. *USAFE Historical Highlights, 1942–1997: Fifty-fifth Anniversary Edition.* Ramstein Air Base (AB), Germany: Headquarters USAFE, 1997.

Sobel, Richard. "U.S. and European Attitudes toward Intervention in the Former Yugoslavia: Mourir pour la Bosnie?" In *The World and Yugoslav's Wars*. Edited by Richard H. Ullman. New York: The Council on Foreign Relations, 1996.

Solli, Per Erik. "In Bosnia, Deterrence Failed and Coercion Worked." In *Use of Air Power in Peace Operations*. Edited by Carsten F. Ronnfeldt and Per Erik Solli. NUPI Peacekeeping and Multinational Operations Report no. 7. Oslo: Norwegian Institute of International Affairs, 1997.

———. *UN and NATO Air Power in the Former Yugoslavia*. NUPI Report no. 209. Oslo: Norwegian Institute of International Affairs, 1996.

Sorely, Lewis S. "Competence as Ethical Imperative: Issues of Professionalism." In *Military Ethics and Professionalism: A Collection of Essays*. Edited by James Brown and Michael J. Collins. Washington, D.C.: National Defense University Press, 1981.

Starr, Barbara. "Deny Flight Shootdown May Put USAF on the Offensive." *Jane's Defence Weekly*, 24 June 1995.

———. "Serbs Feel Force from NATO's CAS Missions." *Jane's Defence Weekly*, 16 April 1994.

Stein, David J. *The Development of NATO Tactical Air Doctrine, 1970–1985*. Santa Monica, Calif.: RAND, 1987. RAND R–3385–AF.

Stephens, Alan, ed. *The War in the Air 1914–1994*. Fairbairn, Australia: Air Power Studies Centre, 1994.

Stevenson, Charles A. "The Evolving Clinton Doctrine on the Use of Force." *Armed Forces and Society* 22, no. 4 (summer 1994).

Stewart, Col Bob. *Broken Lives: A Personal View of the Bosnian Conflict*. London: HarperCollins, 1993.

———. "Love In a Cold Place." *Sunday Times* (London), 12 October 1997.

———. "Massacre of the Innocents." *Sunday Times* (London), 12 October 1997.

Stoltenberg, Thorvald. "Introducing Peacekeeping to Europe." *International Peacekeeping* 2, no. 2 (summer 1995).

Strachan, Hew. *The Politics of the British Army.* Oxford: Clarendon Press, 1997.

Strickland, Maj Paul C., USAF. "Trouble in Trieste." *Daedalus Flyer* 36, no. 4 (winter 1996).

Sullivan, Stacy; Michael Evans; and Eve–Ann Prentice. "NATO Scales Down 'No-Fly' Operation Despite Serb Threat." *Times* (London), 21 June 1995.

Summers, Col Harry G., USA. *On Strategy: A Critical Analysis of the Vietnam War.* Novato, Calif.: Presidio Press, 1982.

Sweetman, Group Capt A. D., RAF. "Close Air Support Over Bosnia-Hercegovina." *RUSI Journal* 139, no. 4 (August 1994).

"Target Description: Hadzici Ammo Storage Depot." File C2a(2), BACS Collection.

"Target Description: Hadzici Military Repair Depot." File C2a(2), BACS Collection.

"Target Description: Hadzici Storage Facility." File C2a(2), BACS Collection.

"Target Description: Pale Ammo Depot South." File C2a(2), BACS Collection.

"Target Description: Sarajevo Army Barracks and Ordnance Depot." File C2a(2), BACS Collection.

Taylor, Telford. "Military Intervention in Civil Wars: Do Law and Morality Conflict?" In *The Parameters of Military Ethics.* Edited by Lloyd J. Matthews and Dale E. Brown. London: Pergamon-Brassey's, 1989.

Teske, Col Steven, USAF, CAOC director of plans, May–November 1995. Interviewed by Lt Col Christopher Campbell, Lt Col Brad Davis, and Maj Chris Orndorff, 14 February 1996, Ramstein AB, Germany. Transcript of taped interview. File H–1, BACS Collection.

————. Interviewed by author, 6 May 1997, Aviano AB, Italy. Tape recording. Author's personal collection.

Tharoor, Shashi. "Should UN Peacekeeping Go Back to Basics?" *Survival* 37, no. 4 (winter 1995–1996).

"The West's Two-track Mind." *The Economist,* 9 September 1995.

Thies, Wallace J. *When Governments Collide: Coercion and Diplomacy in the Vietnam Conflict, 1964–1968.* Los Angeles: University of California Press, 1980.

Thompson, Air Vice Marshal John H., RAF, NATO liaison officer to UNPROFOR Headquarters, Zagreb, Croatia, November 1994–February 1995. Interviewed by author, 7 November 1997, RAF Cranwell, England. Author's notes. Author's personal collection.

Thompson, Julian. "Command at Anzio and in the Falklands: A Personal View." In *Leadership and Command: The Anglo–American Military Experience Since 1861.* Edited by G. D. Sheffield. London: Brassey's, 1997.

Thompson, Wayne W. "Al Firdos: The Last Two Weeks of Strategic Bombing in Desert Storm." *Air Power History* 43, no. 2 (summer 1996).

Thompson, Wayne W., and Bernard Nalty. *Within Limits: The U.S. Air Force and the Korean War.* Washington, D.C.: Government Printing Office, 1996.

Thornberry, Cedric. "The Lessons of Yugoslavia." In *Brassey's Defence Yearbook 1994.* Edited by Centre for Defence Studies, King's College London. London: Brassey's, 1995.

Thornhill, John. "Debates on NATO's Role Sparks Fighting in Russian Parliament," *Financial Times* (London), 11 September 1995.

———. "Yeltsin Warns of New Cold War as NATO Hits at Serb Targets." *Financial Times* (London), 8 September 1995.

"Three Separate Operations Created on 31 March." *UN Chronicle* 32, no. 2 (June 1995).

Tiersky, Ronald. *The Mitterrand Legacy and the Future of French Security Policy.* McNair Paper No. 43. Washington, D.C.: National Defense University Press, 1995.

Tilford, Earl H., Jr. *Setup: What the Air Force Did in Vietnam and Why.* Maxwell AFB, Ala.: Air University Press, 1991.

Tirpak, John A. "The Chief Holds Course." *Air Force Magazine* 81, no. 1 (January 1998).

———. "Deliberate Force." *Air Force Magazine* 80, no. 10 (October 1997).

Toner, James H. *True Faith and Allegiance: The Burden of Military Ethics.* Lexington, Ky.: University Press of Kentucky, 1995.

Towle, Philip. "The British Debate About Intervention in European Conflicts." In *Military Intervention in European Conflicts.* Edited by Lawrence Freedman. London: Blackwell Publishers, 1994.

Towle, Philip Anthony. *Pilots and Rebels: The Use of Aircraft in Unconventional Warfare, 1918–1988.* London: Brassey's, 1989.

Trainor, Lt Gen Bernard E., USMC, retired. "Air Power in the Gulf War: Did it Really Succeed?" *Strategic Review* 22, no. 1 (winter 1994).

Trinquier, Roger. *Modern Warfare: A French View of Counterinsurgency.* Translated by Daniel Lee, with an introduction by Bernard B. Fall. London: Pall Mall Press, 1964.

Tubbs, Maj James O., USAF. *Beyond Gunboat Diplomacy: Forceful Applications of Airpower in Peace Enforcement Operations.* Maxwell AFB, Ala.: Air University Press, 1997.

Tucker, Robert W., and David C. Hendrickson. "America and Bosnia." *The National Interest,* no. 33 (fall 1993).

"Turn of the Tide?" *The Economist,* 5 August 1995.

Twining, David T. "Vietnam and the Six Criteria for the Use of Military Force." *Parameters* 15, no. 4 (winter 1985).

"U–2 Crashes in England." *Aviation Week and Space Technology,* 4 September 1995.

Ullman, Richard H. *The World and Yugoslavia's Wars.* New York: Council on Foreign Relations, 1996.

United Kingdom Parliament. House of Commons. Defence Committee. Fourth Report. *United Kingdom Peacekeeping and Intervention Forces.* Report together with the proceedings of the committee relating to the report. Session 1992–1993, 13 July 1993.

———. Fifth Report. *Implementation of Lessons Learned from Operation Granby.* Report together with the proceedings of the committee relating to the report. Session 1993–1994, 25 May 1994.

"UN General in Bosnia Quits." *New York Times,* 5 January 1994.

"UN Stages Bosnia Pullout Drill." *Times* (London), 20 February 1995.

United Nations, The. *The Blue Helmets: A Review of United Nations Peace-keeping.* 3d ed. New York: United Nations Reproduction Section, 1996.

———. Security Council Resolution 713 (1991) (S/RES/713, 25 September 1991).

———. Letter from the secretary-general to the president of the Security Council, 1 July 1992 (S/24222, 2 July 1992).

———. Further report of the secretary-general pursuant to Security Council Resolutions 757 (1992), 758 (1992), and 761 (1992) (S/24263, 10 July 1992).

———. Addendum to the further report of the secretary-general pursuant to Security Council Resolutions 757 (1992), 758 (1992), and 761 (1992) (S/24263/Add. 1, 10 July 1992).

———. Report of the secretary-general, 21 July 1992 (S/24333, 21 July 1992).

———. Report of the secretary-general pursuant to Security Council Resolution 762 (1992) (S/24353, 27 July 1992).

———. Security Council Resolution 770 (1992) (S/RES/770, 13 August 1992).

———. Report of the secretary-general, 10 September 1992 (S/24540, 10 September 1992).

———. Security Council Resolution 776 (1992) (S/RES/776, 14 September 1992).

———. Security Council Resolution 781 (1992) (S/RES/781, 9 October 1992).

———. Statement by the president of the Security Council, 30 October 1992 (S/24744, 30 October 1992).

———. Security Council Resolution 787 (1992) (S/RES/787, 16 November 1992).

———. Report of the secretary-general pursuant to Resolution 959 (1994), (S/1994/1389, 1 December 1994).

———. Statement by the president of the Security Council, 3 March 1993 (S/25361, 3 March 1993).

———. Statement by the president of the Security Council, 17 March 1993 (S/25426, 17 March 1993).

———. Letter from the secretary-general to the president of the Security Council, 19 March 1993 (S/25456, 22 March 1993).

———. Security Council Resolution 816 (1993) (S/RES/816, 31 March 1993).

———. Security Council Resolution 819 (1993) (S/RES/819, 16 April 1993).

———. Letter from the secretary-general to the president of the Security Council, 9 April 1993 (S/25567, 10 April 1993).

———. Letter from the president of the Security Council to the secretary-general, 10 April 1993 (S/25568, 10 April 1993).

———. Security Council Resolution 821 (1993) (S/RES/821, 28 April 1993).

———. Report of the secretary-general pursuant to Security Council Resolution 819 (1993) (S/25700, 30 April 1993) (Reissued).

———. Letter from the secretary-general to the president of the Security Council, 30 April 1993 (S/25705, 30 April 1993).

———. Statement by the president of the Security Council, 3 May 1993.

———. Security Council Provisional Verbatim Record, 6 May 1993 (S/PV.3208, 6 May 1993).

———. Security Council Resolution 824 (1993) (S/RES/824, 6 May 1993).

———. Statement by the president of the Security Council, 7 May 1993.

———. Statement by the president of the Security Council, 10 May 1993 (S/25746, 10 May 1993).

———. Statement by the president of the Security Council, 14 May 1993.

———. Security Council Resolution 827 (1993) (S/RES/827, 25 May 1993).

———. Statement by the president of the Security Council, 1 June 1993.

———. Security Council Provisional Verbatim Record, 4 June 1993 (S/PV.3228, 4 June 1993).

———. Security Council Resolution 836 (1993) (S/RES/836, 4 June 1993).

———. Report of the secretary-general pursuant to Security Council Resolution 836 (1993) (S/25939, 14 June 1993).

———. Addendum to the report of the secretary-general on the financing of UNPROFOR, 17 June 1993 (A/47n4 I /Add. 1, 17 June 1993).

———. Addendum to the report of the secretary-general pursuant to Security Council Resolution 836 (1993) (S/25939/Add. 1, 17 June 1993).

———. Security Council Provisional Verbatim Record, 18 June 1993 (S/PV.3241, 18 June 1993).

———. Security Council Resolution 844 (1993) (S/RES/844, 18 June 1993).

———. Further report of the secretary-general pursuant to Security Council Resolution 815 (1993) (S/25993, 24 June 1993).

———. Letter from the secretary-general to the president of the Security Council, 18 August 1993 (S/26335, 20 August 1993).

———. Letter from the president of the Security Council to the secretary-general, 20 August 1993 (S/26336, 20 August 1993).

———. Letter from the secretary-general to the president of the Security Council, 19 September 1993 (S/26468, 30 September 1993).

———. Security Council Provisional Verbatim Record, 4 October 1993 (S/PV.3286, 4 October 1993).

———. Security Council Resolution 871 (1993) (S/RES/871, 4 October 1993).

———. Report of the secretary-general submitted pursuant to paragraph 29 of General Assembly Resolution 48/88 (A/48/847, 7 January 1994).

———. Statement by the president of the Security Council, 7 January 1994 (S/PRST/1994/1, 7 January 1994).

———. Letter from the secretary-general to the president of the Security Council, 18 January 1994 (S/1994/50, 18 January 1994).

———. Letter from the secretary-general to the president of the Security Council, 28 January 1994 (S/1994/94, 28 January 1994).

———. Letter from the secretary-general to the president of the Security Council, 2 February 1994 (S/1994/121, 4 February 1994).

———. Letter from the president of the Security Council to the secretary-general, 4 February 1994 (S/1994/122, 4 February 1994).

———. Report of the secretary-general (S/1994/154, 10 February 1994).

———. Letter from the secretary-general to the president of the Security Council, 11 February 1994 (S/1994/159, 11 February 1994).

———. Letter from the secretary-general to the president of the Security Council, 15 February 1994 (S/1994/182, 16 February 1994).

———. Security Council Provisional Verbatim Record, 4 March 1994 (S/PV.3344, 4 March 1994).

———. Security Council Resolution 900 (1994) (S/RES/900, 4 March 1994).

———. Report of the secretary-general pursuant to Resolution 871 (1993) (S/1994/300, 16 March 1994).

———. Report of the secretary-general pursuant to Security Council Resolutions 844 (1993), 836 (1993), and 776 (1992) (S/1994/333, 24 March 1994).

———. Security Council Provisional Verbatim Record, 31 March 1994 (S/PV.3356, 31 March 1994).

———. Security Council Resolution 908 (1994) (S/RES/908, 31 March 1994).

———. Letter from the secretary-general to the president of the Security Council, 18 April 1994 (S/1994/466, 19 April 1994).

———. Letter from the secretary-general to the president of the Security Council, 22 April 1994 (S/1994/495, 22 April 1994).

———. Letter from the secretary-general to the president of the Security Council, 22 April 1994 (S/1994/498, 22 April 1994).

———. Letter from the president of the Security Council to the secretary-general, 29 April 1994 (S/1994/521, 29 April 1994).

———. Report of the secretary-general pursuant to Resolution 844 (1993) (S/1994/555, 9 May 1994).

———. Report of the secretary-general pursuant to Resolution 913 (1994) (S/1994/600, 19 May 1994).

———. Security Council Resolution 958 (1994) (S/RES/958, 19 November 1994).

———. Report of the secretary-general pursuant to Resolution 959 (1994) (S/1994/1389, 1 December 1994).

———. Report of the secretary-general on the work of the organization. "Supplement to an Agenda for Peace: Position Paper of the secretary-general on the Occasion of the Fiftieth Anniversary of the United Nations" (A/50/60, S/1995/1, 3 January 1995).

———. Report of the secretary-general pursuant to Resolution 987 (1995) (S/1995/444, 30 May 1995).

———. Security Council Resolution 998 (1995) (S/RES/998, 16 June 1995).

———. Security Council Resolution 1004 (1995) (S/RES/1004, 12 July 1995).

————. Security Council Resolution 1009 (1995) (S/RES/1009, 10 August 1995).

United States Department of Defense. *Conduct of the Persian Gulf War: Final Report to Congress.* [Washington, D.C.]: Government Printing Office, April 1992.

————. "Special DoD News Briefing," 11 April 1994 (3:00 P.M.), Washington. Transcript of press conference. http://www.dtic.mil:80//defenselink/news.

————. "DoD News Briefing." The Pentagon, 29 August 1995 (1:30 P.M.). Transcript of press conference. http://www.dtic.mil:80//defenselink/news.

————. "DoD News Briefing." The Pentagon, 5 September 1995 (1:30 P.M.). Transcript of press conference. http://www.dtic.mil:80//defenselink/news.

————. "DoD News Briefing." The Pentagon, 7 September 1995. Transcript of press conference. http://www.dtic.mil:80//defenselink/news.

————. "DoD News Briefing." The Pentagon, 12 September 1995 (12:00 P.M.). Transcript of press conference. http://www.dtic.mil:80//defenselink/news.

————. "DoD News Briefing." The Pentagon, 14 September 1995 (2:30 P.M.). Transcript of press conference. http://www.dtic.mil:80//defenselink/news.

Urban, Jan. "Sarajevo to NATO: Jetaime." *Transition* 1, no. 20 (9 November 1995).

Urban, Mark. *Big Boys' Rules: The SAS and the Secret Struggle Against the IRA.* London: Faber and Faber, 1992.

US House. *Unauthorized Bombing of Military Targets in North Vietnam: Hearings before the Armed Services Investigating Committee of the Committee on Armed Services.* 92d Cong., 2d Sess., 1972.

————. *Unauthorized Bombing of Military Targets in North Vietnam: Report of the Armed Services Investigating Committee of the Committee on Armed Services.* 92d Cong., 2d Sess., 1972.

————. *The Policy Implications of US Involvement in Bosnia: Hearings before the Committee on Armed Services.* 103d Cong., 1st Sess., 1993.

————. *Developments in Europe and the Former Yugoslavia: Hearings before the Subcommittee on Europe and the Middle East, Committee on Foreign Affairs.* 103d Cong., 1st Sess., 1993.

————. *The Crisis in the Former Yugoslavia and the U.S. Role: Hearings before the Committee on Foreign Affairs.* 103d Cong., 1st Sess., 1993.

"US Peace Plan for Bosnia Attacked." *Financial Times* (London), 16 August 1995.

US Senate. *Yugoslavia: The Question of Intervention: Hearings before the Subcommittee on European Affairs, Committee on Foreign Relations.* 102d Cong., 2d Sess., 1992.

————. *Ethnic Cleansing of Bosnia–Herzegovina: A Staff Report to the Committee on Foreign Relations.* 102d Cong., 2d Sess., 1992.

————. *Situation in Bosnia and Appropriate US and Western Responses: Hearings before the Committee on Armed Services.* 102d Cong., 2d Sess., 1992. S. Hrg. 102–840.

————. *American Policy in Bosnia: Hearings before the Committee on Foreign Relations.* 103d Cong., 1st Sess., 1993. S. Hrg. 103–33.

————. *To Stand Against Aggression: Milosevic, the Bosnian Republic, and the Conscience of the West: A Report to the Committee on Foreign Relations.* By Sen. Joseph R. Biden Jr. 103d Cong., 1st Sess., 1993. S. Prt. 103–33.

————. *Joint Chiefs of Staff Briefing on Current Military Operations in Somalia, Iraq, and Yugoslavia: Hearings before the Committee on Armed Services.* 103d Cong., 1st Sess., 1993. S. Hrg. 103–76.

————. Subcommittee of the Committee on Appropriations. *Department of Defense Appropriations for Fiscal Year 1994, Part 1.* 103d Cong., 1st Sess., 1993. S. Hrg. 103–53, pt. 1.

————. *Department of Defense Authorization for Appropriations for Fiscal Year 1994 and the Future Years Defense*

Program: Part 1: Military Posture, Unified Commands, Specified Commands, Service Chiefs, Budget Impact, Conversion and Reinvestment Program, Weapons Reduction and Arms Control: Hearings before the Committee on Armed Services. 103d Cong., 1st Sess., 1993. S. Hrg. 103–303, pt. 1.

———. *Briefing on Bosnia and Other Current Military Operations: Hearings before the Committee on Armed Services.* 103d Cong., 2d Sess., 1994. S. Hrg. 103–800.

———. *Impact of a Unilateral United States Lifting of the Arms Embargo on the Government of Bosnia–Herzegovina: Hearings before the Committee on Armed Services.* 103d Cong., 2d Sess., 1994. S. Hrg. 103–777.

———. *Situation in Bosnia: Hearings before the Committee on Armed Services.* 103d Cong., 2d Sess., 1994. S. Hrg. 103–1010.

———. *Current Operations Abroad—Bosnia, North Korea, and Somalia: Hearings before the Committee on Armed Services.* 104th Cong., 1st Sess., 1995. S. Hrg. 104–219.

———. *Condition of the Armed Forces and Future Trends: Hearings before the Committee on Armed Services.* 104th Cong., 1st Sess., 1995. S. Hrg. 104–231.

———. *Briefing on the F–16 Shootdown in Bosnia and Current Operations: Hearings before the Committee on Armed Services.* 104th Cong., 1st Sess., 1995. S. Hrg. 104–421.

———. *Situation in Bosnia: Hearings before the Committee on Armed Services.* 104th Cong., 1st Sess., 1995. S. Hrg. 104–587.

"USAF Fact Sheet: 4190th Provisional Wing." Aviano AB, Italy: 31st Fighter Wing Public Affairs Office, August 1996.

Van Creveld, Martin. *Command in War.* Cambridge, Mass.: Harvard University Press, 1985.

Vennesson, Pascal. "Institution and Airpower: The Making of the French Air Force." *Journal of Strategic Studies* 18, no. 1 (March 1995).

Vincent, Lord (Field Marshal) Richard, UK chief of Defence Staff, 1991–December 1992; chairman of NATO's Military

Committee, January 1993–1996. Interviewed by author, 22 September 1998, London. Author's notes. Author's personal collection.

Voorhoeve, Joris. "Protecting the Peacekeepers on the Day Srebrenica Fell." *Washington Post,* 20 November 1995.

Vuono, Gen Carl E., USA. "Desert Storm and the Future of Conventional Forces." *Foreign Affairs* 70, no. 2 (spring 1991).

Wald, Brig Gen Charles F., USAF, chief of plans, CAOC (June–November 1994); commander, 31st Fighter Wing, Aviano AB, Italy, (May 1995–June 1997). Interviewed by author, 7 May 1997, Aviano AB, Italy. Tape recording. Author's personal collection.

Walzer, Michael. *Just and Unjust Wars: A Moral Argument with Historical Illustrations.* 2d ed. N.p.: HarperCollins, 1992.

———. "Two Kinds of Military Responsibility." In *The Parameters of Military Ethics.* Edited by Lloyd J. Matthews and Dale E. Brown. London: Pergamon-Brassey's, 1989.

Warden, Col John A., III, USAF. *The Air Campaign: Planning for Combat.* Washington, D.C.: National Defense University Press, 1988; Pergamon-Brassey's, 1989.

———. "Airpower in the Gulf." *Daedalus Flyer,* spring 1996.

———. "The Enemy as a System." *Airpower Journal* 9, no. 2 (spring 1995).

Warnes, Alan. "The Battle for Bihac." *Air Force Monthly,* January 1995.

Watkins, Steve. "Does Deny Flight Still Work?" *Air Force Times,* 24 July 1995.

Waxman, Matthew C. "Coalitions and Limits on Coercive Diplomacy." *Strategic Review* 25, no. 1 (winter 1997).

Weigley, Russell F. "The American Military and the Principle of Civilian Control from McClellan to Powell." *Journal of Military History,* Special Issue 57 (October 1993).

———. *The American Way of War.* Bloomington, Ind.: Indiana University Press, 1973.

———. "The Political and Strategic Dimensions of Military Effectiveness." In *Military Effectiveness.* Vol. 3, *The Second World War.* Edited by Allan R. Millet and Williamson Murray. London: Allen and Unwin, 1988.

Weinberger, Caspar. *Fighting for Peace.* New York: Warner Books, 1990.

Wells, Mark K. *Courage and Air Warfare: The Allied Aircrew Experience in the Second World War.* London: Frank Cass, 1995.

Wesley, Michael. "Blue Berets or Blindfolds? Peacekeeping and the Hostage Effect." *International Peacekeeping* 2, no. 4 (winter 1995).

Weston, David. "The Army: Mother, Sister and Mistress: the British Regiment." In *The Defence Equation: British Military Systems Policy Planning and Performance Since 1945.* Edited by Martin Edmonds. London: Brassey's, 1986.

Wheeler, Capt Michael O., USAF. "Loyalty, Honor, and the Modern Military." *Air University Review* 24, no. 4 (May–June 1973).

White, David. "NATO Backs Vance-Owen." *Financial Times* (London), 26 May 1993.

———. "NATO Wavers on Bosnia." *Financial Times* (London), 27 May 1993.

———. "No Early End to Bloodshed: Proposals for Outside Military Intervention All Have Their Risks." *Financial Times* (London), 16 April 1993.

White House, The. "US Policy on Reform of Multilateral Peace Operations." Presidential Decision Directive 25, 5 May 1994.

———. *A National Security Strategy of Engagement and Enlargement.* Washington, D.C.: Government Printing Office, July 1994.

———. "Bosnia Rapid Reaction Force." Text of letter from President Clinton to Dole, Gingrich, 1 July 1995.

———. Statement by press secretary on Bosnia, 23 July 1995.

———. "Holbrooke Team's Return to Former Yugoslavia with New Members." Press statement by the press secretary, 23 August 1995.

———. Transcript of press briefing by Mike McCurry, 8 September 1995.

———. Statement by the president, 15 September 1995.

———. Radio address by President Clinton to the nation, 23 September 1995.

———. Transcript of press briefing by Mike McCurry, 25 September 1995.

———. Statement by the president, 26 September 1995.

Williams, Daniel. "Aid Flights Resume at Sarajevo Airport." *Washington Post,* 16 November 1995.

———. "Serbs Suffer Major Defeat In W. Bosnia." *Washington Post,* 14 September 1995.

Williams, Daniel, and Rick Atkinson. "Limits on Targets Hamper NATO, U.N. Officers Say." *Washington Post,* 13 September 1995.

Williams, Michael C. *Civil-Military Relations and Peacekeeping.* Adelphi Paper 321. London: International Institute for Strategic Studies, 1998.

Wilson, Gordon. "Arm in Arm after the Cold War?: The Uneasy NATO–UN Relationship." *International Peacekeeping* 2, no. 1 (spring 1995).

Winnefeld, James A., and Dana J. Johnson. *Joint Air Operations: Pursuit of Unity in Command and Control, 1942–1991.* Annapolis, Md.: Naval Institute Press, 1993.

Winton, Harold R. "An Ambivalent Partnership: US Army and Air Force Perspectives on Air-Ground Operations, 1973–1990." In *The Paths of Heaven: The Evolution of Airpower Theory.* Edited by Col Phillip S. Meilinger, USAF. Maxwell Air Force Base, Ala.: Air University Press, 1997.

Wolk, Herman S. "Antimilitarism in America." *Air University Review* 23, no. 4 (January–February 1974).

———. "Politicians, Generals, and Strategists." *Air University Review* 25, no. 2 (May–June 1972).

Wood, Lt Col Joseph, USAF, commander, 492d Fighter Squadron, F-15Es. Interviewed by author, 5 March 1997, London. Transcript of tape recording. Author's personal collection.

Wood, Pia Christina. "France and the Post–Cold War Order: The Case of Yugoslavia." *European Security* 3, no. 1 (spring 1994).

Woodward, Bob. *The Choice: How Clinton Won.* New York: Simon and Schuster, 1996.

Woodward, Susan L. *Balkan Tragedy: Chaos and Dissolution After the Cold War.* Washington, D.C.: The Brookings Institution, 1995.

Worden, Col Mike, USAF. *Rise of the Fighter Generals: The Problem of Air Force Leadership.* Maxwell AFB, Ala.: Air University Press, 1998.

"World News in Brief." *Financial Times* (London), 12 August 1993.

Wratten, Air Chief Marshal Sir William, RAF, commander, RAF Strike Command, September 1994–July 1997. Telephone interview by author, 18 May 1998, London. Author's notes. Author's personal collection.

Wrong, Dennis H. *Power: Its Forms, Bases, and Uses.* 1979. Reprint, New Brunswick, N.J.: Transaction Publishers, 1995.

Yost, David S. "France." In *The Defense Policies of Nations: A Comparative Study.* Edited by Douglas J. Murray and Paul R. Viotti. 3d ed. Baltimore, Md.: Johns Hopkins University Press, 1994.

———. "France and the Gulf War of 1990–1991: Political–Military Lessons Learned." *The Journal of Strategic Studies* 16, no. 3 (September 1993).

Zametica, John. *The Yugoslav Conflict: An Analysis of the Causes of the Yugoslav War, the Policies of the Republics and the Regional and International Implications of the Conflict.* Adelphi Paper 270. London: Brassey's for The International Institute for Strategic Studies, 1992.

Zandee, Dik, political advisor, NATO Headquarters. Interviewed by author, 28 April 1997, Brussels. Author's notes. Author's personal collection.

Zoerb, Col Daniel R., USAF, director, Deny Flight Air Operations Center, Naples, Italy, January 1994–May 1996. "AU's DELIBERATE FORCE Report." Remarks on an early draft of the Balkans Air Campaign Study, 20 November 1996, for General Ryan.

———. Interviewed by author, 29 April 1997, Spangdahlem AB, Germany. Transcript of tape recording. Author's personal collection.

———. Interviewed by author, 30 April 1997, Spangdahlem AB, Germany. Transcript of tape recording. Author's personal collection.

———. Interviewed by author, 25 August 1997, London. Tape recording of telephone interview. Author's personal collection.

———. Interviewed by author, 27 May 1998, Spangdahlem AB, Germany. Author's notes. Author's personal collection.

Index

404

185–86, 195, 198, 201, 217–18, 298, 306, 323

Russia, 74, 78, 238, 259, 270, 284, 296

Ryan, Gen John, 45, 175

Ryan, Lt Gen Michael, 5, 167, 175, 177, 181, 183–84, 186, 190–93, 203–6, 211–12, 214–15, 219, 223–27, 230–34, 248–49, 253–58, 260, 262–63, 273–76, 279–89, 291–97, 300–301, 320–21

SA-2, 180, 189, 198. *See also* surface-to-air missile

SA-3, 198. *See also* surface-to-air missile

SA-6, 180, 218–19, 250, 266. *See also* surface-to-air missile

Sabin, Prof. Phil., 54, 112, 179, 198, 200

Sacirbey, Muhamed, 260

safe area, 5, 23, 65, 86, 97, 100, 102, 134, 161, 174, 191, 236, 238, 245–46, 249, 252, 254–55, 258, 262–64, 268, 280, 289, 320. *See also* Bihac, Gorazde, Sarajevo, Srebrenica, Tuzla, Zepa

Sagan, Scott, 44, 55

SAM. *See* surface-to-air missile

sanctuaries, 53

sanctuary, 174

Sarajevo, 14, 22, 64–65, 71, 74, 81–84, 86, 90–91, 100, 102, 106, 110, 116, 120, 122–26, 128–29, 137, 139, 144, 146, 152–53, 157–60, 163, 166, 169, 173, 187, 192, 196, 200, 207–8, 210–11, 213–14, 216–17, 238, 246, 255, 257, 263, 274–75, 278, 280, 285–90, 297, 300, 302–5, 314, 318, 320, 322

SAS. *See* Special Air Service

Schulte, Greg, 22, 125, 151, 158, 195

Sea Harrier, 138, 145–46, 158, 318. *See also* Harrier

SEAD. *See* suppression of enemy air defenses

Secretary General's special representative. *See* Akashi, Yasushi

Security Council. *See* UN Security Council

self-defense, 45–46, 75–77, 97, 105, 108, 119, 160, 169, 171, 181, 184–88, 191, 209, 258, 298

Serb aircraft, 129, 174–75. *See also* Galeb

Serbian capital. *See* Belgrade

Seville, Spain, 170–71, 173, 195

Shalikashvili, Gen John, 67, 84, 111, 152, 242, 252

Sharp, 8, 22, 43, 54–55, 148–49, 200, 235, 238, 240, 269

Sharp, Adm U.S. Grant, 54

Sharp, Jane, 8, 148, 200, 240

Sheehan, Gen Jack, 136

shoot down, 63, 137, 165–66, 218. *See also* downing

Short, Maj Gen Mike, 302–3, 305, 307, 309

Smith, Adm Leighton, 6, 134–35, 138, 145–46, 161, 163–64, 172, 176–80, 183–85, 190–91, 193–201, 203, 209–10, 216, 218–19, 223, 226–32, 238–39, 242–43, 248, 257–58, 261–63, 265, 268–70, 273–79, 282–83, 285–301, 303, 306–8, 311, 320–22

Smith, Lt Gen Rupert, 7, 8, 18, 20, 124, 145, 164, 190–91, 203, 207–8, 211–17, 219, 228, 231–33, 235, 237, 245, 251, 253–54, 262–63, 268, 275–77, 279, 283, 286–87, 292–94, 297, 301, 315, 319

Sokolac, 266

Solli, Per Erik, 13, 23, 109, 153

Soubirou, Andre, 165–66, 194

Special Air Service (SAS), 155, 200

special forces, 118, 134, 137–38, 314, 318–19

Split, Croatia, 170

Srebrenica, 10, 12, 23, 65, 69, 99–100, 102, 106, 121, 124, 151, 161, 220, 232–33, 235, 238, 245–55, 257, 259, 261, 263–67, 269, 271, 280, 304, 315

stealth fighter. *See* F-117

Stewart, Col Bob, 23, 108

Stoltenberg, Thorvald, 22, 79–80, 89, 91–92, 98–101, 120

suppression of enemy air defenses (SEAD), 177, 180–82, 184–91, 201, 204, 215, 218, 223, 227, 230–33, 235, 250, 262, 264, 293–94, 315

Supreme Allied Commander Europe, (SACEUR), 21, 67, 84, 197, 234, 239, 267

surface-to-air missile, 4, 41, 45, 135–38, 173, 175, 180, 181–84, 186–88,